GAME ANALYTICS

Retention and Monetization in Free-to-Play Mobile Games

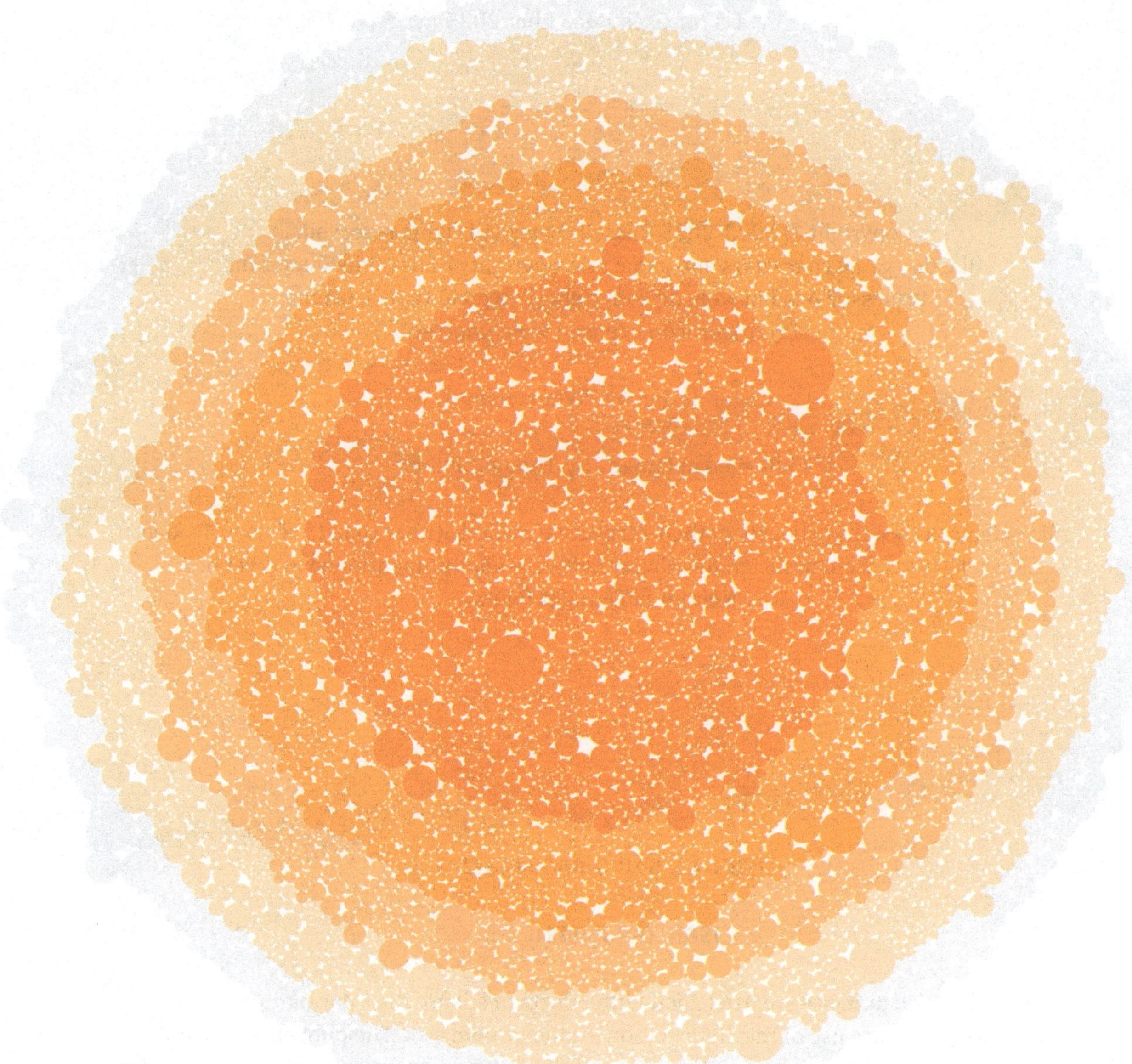

Russell Ovans

Game Analytics

Retention and Monetization in Free-to-Play Mobile Games

by Russell Ovans

v. 1.3 released December 2025

Cover design by Viviana Ramos.

Published in Canada by Thought Pilots.

ISBN-13: 978-0-9869418-2-5

ISBN: 0-9869418-2-5

Table of Contents

About the Author

Russell Ovans, Ph.D., is a computer scientist who has worked as both a software engineering professor and programmer for over 35 years. In 2007, he founded Backstage Technologies, a social game studio that pioneered the monetization of free-to-play games on Facebook. Best known for its *Family Feud* app, Backstage was acquired by RealNetworks in 2010, after which Russ returned to teaching college, worked as an executive-in-residence at a tech incubator, and opened a brewery. He returned to the games industry in 2018 to lead analytics, growth, and ad monetization at East Side Games (ESG), developers of hit mobile games such as *The Office: Somehow We Manage* and *Trailer Park Boys: Greasy Money*. During his tenure as Director of Analytics, ESG quadrupled revenue and went public. He lives in Vancouver.

Find Russ, his alter-ego Professor Arpdau, and the analytics tools he developed for this book at arpdau.com.

Acknowledgements

I wish to thank Jason Bailey for inviting me back to free-to-play games, and all my past and present colleagues at ESG; I only managed to avoid burning up on re-entry because of your kindness and exemplary industry knowledge. In particular, I am indebted to my data analyst colleagues who helped shape the ideas presented in this book: Justin Bondy, Francois Janin, Jes Simkin, and Zsanett Soreg. Special thanks to Tim Small for his feedback on an earlier draft, and to my editor, Bethany Williams.

Preface

When I started working at East Side Games (ESG) nobody handed me a book and said, "Read this – it contains everything you need to know to succeed as a data analyst in the free-to-play games industry." I wish they had, but there was no such book. After years of ad-hoc database queries, data wrangling, Tableau tutorials, Excel pivot tables, and failed A/B tests, I thought it was time to write the book I wish existed when I naively showed up for work that first day with a backpack full of books on machine learning and data science.

To those on the outside, the work of a mobile game data analyst may seem mysterious and important. In truth it is probably neither of those things – after all, it's just *games*. But I find it fascinating, and I hope you do, too. My goal in writing this book is to demystify some of the techniques used by data analysts in the process of delighting customers and making money from a product you give away for free. The focus on mobile games grounds the content in the details of a particular domain, but many of the ideas apply broadly to streaming, software-as-a-service, and other types of ad-supported, freemium, or subscription-based online products.

Who Are You?

You either already work in free-to-play games, or you really *want* to work in the games industry. And by "work" I don't just mean as a data analyst or data scientist. I mean in *any* capacity, for everyone can benefit from understanding their industry's basic metrics, how they are measured, what they mean, and how they are used. Still, a few assumptions about the non-data folks in the audience are necessary. First, you enjoy thinking quantitatively. You like numbers and have at least passing familiarity with a spreadsheet and how to use some basic formulas. If you have tangoed with an Excel pivot table, bravo! Second, you are open to evidence-based decision making. Ideally your educational background includes an introductory course in statistics, but regardless, the relevant concepts are reviewed. Third, while not required, I hope you have some prior experience with Structured Query Language (SQL) and relational databases. While the books contain a lot of SQL, it can be skipped over by readers more interested in the conceptual rather than the practical details. Besides, the datasets that result from the SQL are where the magic truly begins.

Who Am I?

I'm Russ, the Director of Analytics at ESG. I used to lead the growth team at ESG as well, where I developed a methodology to quickly make predictions about the effectiveness of our paid ad campaigns. I am a computer scientist and occasional professor, but mainly have worked as a software engineer since Rick Astley ruled the dance floor. In 2007 I accidentally founded one of the very first social game companies, Backstage Technologies, most famous for the *Family Feud* app on Facebook. I sold Backstage to RealNetworks in 2010, and immediately retired from the games industry. I came out of retirement in 2018 to support my brewery ownership habit, joining ESG to manage a team of analysts, despite the consensus amongst my colleagues that "Russ likes mentoring, but he hates managing." I do, however, love the data I get to play with, and spend most of my workday processing said data to answer ad-hoc questions from my colleagues about how our games are performing and how they can be improved.

ESG has been operating since 2011 and has developed numerous free-to-play mobile games including *Trailer Park Boys: Greasy Money* and *The Office: Somehow We Manage*. Many of our games are built in partnership with well-known intellectual properties (IPs) like *The [U.S.] Office*,[1] and most fall within the "idle" or "tycoon" genres. By working with huge IPs and their familiar characters, adding scripted story lines and plot points that unlock as you complete milestones and progress through the levels, we defined the **narrative idle** genre.

In addition to the games ESG develops internally, we also publish games created in partnership with external studios. These include *RuPaul's Drag Race Superstar* (Night Garden Studio) and *Star Trek: Lower Decks – The Badgey Directive* (Mighty Kingdom). As part of our publishing partnership, we provide analytics services to our partner studios, and manage their user acquisition through paid advertising.

Am I a *Data Analyst* or *Data Scientist?*

Data analysts and data scientists are people whose work centers on the processing of data for the purpose of generating **analytics**. Analytics – a singular and plural noun – is the information generated from the systematic analysis of data, whether the information comes from techniques based in statistics or the newer multidisciplinary field of data science (which includes

---

[1] All trademarks licensed to ESG, and other trademarks mentioned in this book, are property of their owners.

statistics plus a grab-bag of techniques borrowed from computer science and artificial intelligence such as data mining and machine learning).

There are four flavours of analytics, all of which are relevant to the games industry. In increasing order of complexity, they are: **descriptive** analytics, which include statistics and estimates of population parameters like average revenue per user; **diagnostic analytics**, which indicate why something happened like a drop in revenue; **predictive** analytics, which model the likelihood of unknown future events like customer churn or return on ad spend; and **prescriptive** analytics, which are used to recommend optimal actions like the amount of revenue to invest in marketing one game versus another.

There is a prevailing sense that the job title *data scientist* is more prestigious than *data analyst*. This assumption is based on the notion that data analytics is a subset of data science, and that a **data analyst** only works with "what we already know" about the data, writing SQL scripts to generate descriptive analytics, visualizations, and reports in support of business intelligence activities. Hypothesis (A/B) testing may be undertaken to improve products and practices, in which case the results are evaluated with predefined metrics. The data analyst relies on statistics as the foundation of their work.

Conversely, **data scientists** build models of data to discover new knowledge; i.e., "what we don't already know." They go beyond the traditional boundaries of statistics by incorporating tools like the programming language Python and its machine learning libraries to mine the data for new correlations, categorize customers in novel ways, and identify previously unknown patterns and trends. The data scientist relies on machine learning as the foundation of their work. Regardless of the tools utilized, data scientists are expected to derive more than just descriptive analytics.

At ESG, we use the job title *data analyst* even though much of our activities go beyond descriptive analytics. As a general rule, if your work attempts to model and predict individual player behaviour, that is data science. If your work makes predictions about cohorts (groups) of players based on statistical regression applied to historical data, that is analytics. The focus of this book is the latter, hence the title.

What to Expect: An Outline of this Book

In this book, we introduce the business of free-to-play games, and the data generated by the players. We learn to measure and visualize game metrics known as key performance indicators. Retaining and monetizing players is crucial to any successful game; thus, the focus of this book is on building predictive models of retention, monetization, and churn. This is the foundational material for any analyst at a game company. The complexity of the material increases as you level up through the first seven chapters.

After this foundation is in place, we cover how analytics are used to improve game retention and revenue, including a review of the relevant material from statistics in support of A/B testing. The treatment includes R scripts for bootstrapping and permutation testing, two modern approaches to hypothesis testing. The important topic of country-specific pricing is introduced. In addition to data analysts, this material should be of interest to product managers, game designers, and producers.

In the final chapter, we introduce the topic of growth: how game publishers measure the effectiveness of their paid ads and predict whether their ad spend will generate a positive return. This material should also interest user acquisition managers seeking to gain a better understanding of how analytics can help them avoid flying blind.

In terms of tools, the focus is squarely on querying with SQL, visualizing with Tableau, and a small amount of the programming language R. Sprinkled throughout are predictive analytics derived from regression analysis. But relax – everything we cover can be accomplished using only Tableau (or Excel, for that matter[2]). Where you take it from there is up to you!

Be sure to check out arpdau.com for some simple web-based tools I developed to help you out in your journey. Look for **Professor Arpdau** (right) in the text to alert you to particularly relevant tools to explore on the site.

This content started out as documentation for onboarding data analysts at ESG, but I hope has broader utility to people throughout the industry. The games sector can be secretive regarding its best practices, a disservice to not only the industry, but also its consumers and investors. In a small attempt at illumination, this book contains the details of how one successful game company uses analytics to measure and predict customer retention and lifetime value. Our approach may not be revolutionary, but we do know it works. Whenever we think we have discovered something cool or new, our suspicion quickly turns to "this is so obvious everyone must do it this way." But maybe not. Let's find out, shall we?

---

[2] "Relax – it's just a spreadsheet" is a wonderful quote from the back cover of *Data Smart*, Foreman (2014). See the Bibliography for further details.

The Business of Mobile Games:
LEVEL 1

If you are already familiar with how free-to-play mobile games are built, measured, published, and make money, you may want to skip this chapter. But if you are a complete newb, or don't know much about the role of analytics in games, this chapter covers the basics.

A **mobile game** is any kind of computer or video game that is played on a mobile device, such as a tablet or smartphone. ESG's games are available on both the Google Play and Apple App stores. These two **platforms** are where people find and download games for their respective mobile devices. We refer to these two platforms by the operating systems that run their devices; Android for Google, and iOS for Apple. There are other app stores out there, such as Amazon, Steam, and Samsung, but right now the mobile game landscape is dominated by Google and Apple.

Once upon a time, people paid money to download games (and ringtones!) to their mobile phone. The original *Angry Birds* cost something like $1.99 to download. Today, mobile games (and many mobile apps) are almost entirely free to download and play but offer in-app purchases to unlock premium content or power-ups.[1] This style of game is known as **free-to-play** (F2P) or **freemium** (a portmanteau of the words "free" and "premium").

Mobile games are built by a team of artists and programmers who work together at a game studio. A game is considered published when it goes live on a platform and first becomes available for download. A game is in **soft launch** when it is only available in a small set of countries (e.g., the Philippines and India) for the purpose of testing. There are often many phases to a soft-launch rollout. A game is said to be **world-wide (WW)** once testing is complete and the app is made available globally. The **publisher** – which may or may not be the same company as the studio who built the product – owns the game's listing in the App/Play store, receives all the revenue, and is responsible for marketing. ESG is both a game studio – building games

[1] Rovio – the makers of *Angry Birds* – recently published a version of the game that costs $0.99 to download but contains no ads nor in-app purchases.

in-house using Unity as our programming environment – and a game publisher. We publish our own games as well as those built by other studios in a partnership where we share some of the development costs, negotiate licensing deals with IP holders such as film and television studios, and market the game in exchange for a share of the profits. In either case, every game that ESG publishes adheres to the free-to-play paradigm.

If we are giving away our products for free, then how do we make money? Quite simply, we monetize our biggest resource: our players.

What is *Monetization?*

Monetization refers to the process of turning an asset into money. In the case of free-to-play games, players are typically monetized through the sale of **virtual currency** for real-world money. Virtual currencies go by names like credits, gems, tokens, etc., and are typically of two types: hard currency or soft currency. The former is rare and immune to the inflationary effects of leveling up, which means ascending through the levels of the game's design does not devalue the hard currency. In some games, you can only purchase the hard currency while the soft currency can only be earned through gameplay. For this reason, the hard currency is often referred to as **premium currency**. The game must be designed to maintain the scarcity and value of both currencies lest the game fall out of balance and the economy deteriorate to a point where players find the game too difficult or too easy to continue playing.

In addition to consumable virtual currencies, most free-to-play games have other **virtual goods** available for purchase. These include such things as rare characters and costumes for customizable avatars, subscriptions that unlock premium content or make the game ad-free, and monthly power-ups in player-vs-player games (also known as "battle passes"). For example, in ESG's *Trailer Park Boys: Greasy Money* (*TPB*), our players can buy three things with real money (see Figure 1.1):

1. virtual currency in the form of "hashcoins," the premium currency that can be used to buy soft currency ("liquor"), time skips, and loot boxes;
2. virtual goods in the form of time-limited sales or promotions ("promos") consisting of bundles of business cards, character cards, and premium or soft currency; or,
3. a weekly subscription that automatically generates premium currency the player collects through repeated gameplay.

Anything a player can purchase with real money in a mobile game must have a corresponding Shop-Keeping Unit (**SKU**) registered in the platform's dashboard. A SKU is identified by a unique product ID, such as "tpb.hashcoins.small," and a price ($4.99) in the default currency of your business. The purchase of a SKU by a player is known as an **in-app purchase** (IAP).

Figure 1.1 Two screenshots from the *TPB* virtual goods store. Players can buy a *Sh*tmobile* subscription (left), which generates 72 hashcoins per day for $6.49/week. By scrolling down, players can also buy bundles of hashcoins (right), the game's premium currency. Prices displayed are in Canadian dollars on iOS.

According to industry norms, only about 5% of free-to-play gamers will ever make an IAP. This bears repeating: if 1,000 people have downloaded your game, expect only 50 of them to ever make a purchase. And that is only if your game is super compelling and has implemented the correct game balance and economic levers to ensure players would even consider parting with real money.

Although most features of free-to-play games are generally attainable by putting in the necessary time and effort, exactly why people pay real money for virtual goods is a complex question of behavioural psychology. In ESG's idle games, the motivations to spend include impatience, competitiveness, and the compulsion to complete tasks and/or sets of items. Entertainment value aside, some critics believe IAPs are irrational, and addictive "pay to win" games are unethical. While interesting, these questions and issues are beyond the scope of this book.

IAPs are facilitated by the platforms, which collect the money from the player using the payment methods associated with the user's App Store or Google Play account. In exchange for providing this benevolent service, the platforms charge a fee of 30% of the after-tax proceeds. For example, if 60 hashcoins cost a player $4.99 on Android, Google keeps $1.50 as a fee. The $4.99 is called **gross IAP revenue**. Once a month the platforms remit to publishers their share of the proceeds – the **net IAP revenue.**

Besides IAPs, advertising is the other common monetization mechanism in freemium products. In ESG's games, players can choose to watch a non-skippable 30 second video ad in exchange for soft currency as a reward. These **rewarded video ads** are an important source of revenue for mobile game publishers, and an entire industry has surfaced around ad delivery, waterfall mediation, real-time bidding, reselling, and other components of a robust ad technology ecosystem led by the likes of ironSource and Applovin. This source of revenue is called ad monetization, or **ad mon** for short.

Another type of video ad is **interstitial**, which is a fancy word for "pops up out of nowhere and covers your entire screen but can be dismissed after only a few seconds." The word comes from *interstice*, which means a small, intervening space. These ads are placed in natural breaks during game play, like after completing a puzzle, milestone, or level.

Finally, some games contain an **offer wall**, where players engage with third-party advertisers to earn in-game currency.[2] The name comes from the presentation to the user (see Figure 1.2). A wall of incentivized offers implores the user to "Subscribe to SiriusXM and receive 359 hashcoins!" or "Complete a survey to earn up to 71 hashcoins." In those two examples, the respective third parties are Sirius XM and Tapjoy (a market survey company that also happens to supply the inventory for this offer wall). When a user completes an offer, the game publisher

---

[2] Jason Bailey – one of ESG's founders – has a storied history in this arena, having previously led SuperRewards, one of the first offer walls used by developers to monetize their Facebook apps. My company, Backstage, was the first SuperRewards customer when our game *Scratch and Win* integrated SuperRewards in December of 2007. As such, Jason likes to claim that I invented free-to-play social games.

is paid by the offer wall. Some of the offers are for competing games, where the reward occurs after the player has installed and completed a certain level or made an IAP.

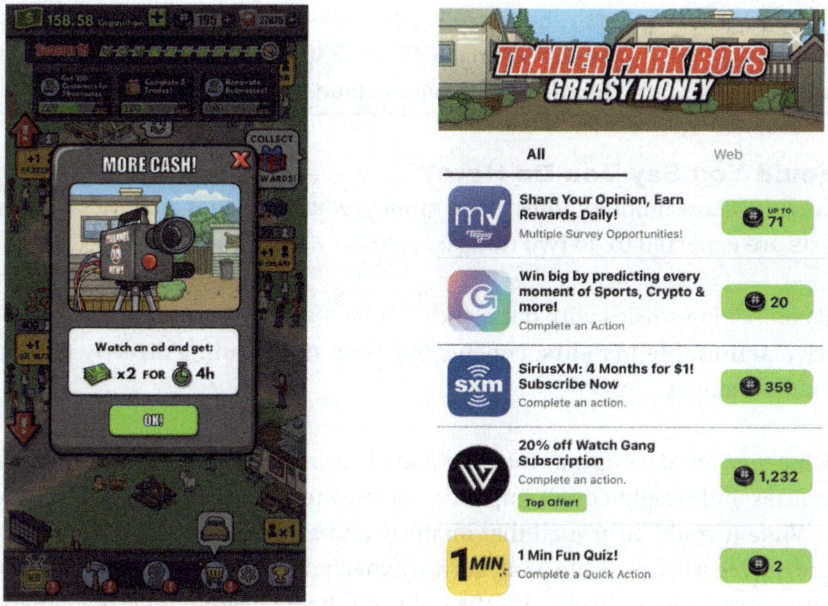

Figure 1.2. Two *TPB* screenshots displaying ad monetization placements. A player can choose to watch a 30 second rewarded video ad in exchange for a four-hour power-up (left), and/or complete a third-party offer (right) in exchange for hashcoins.

At ESG, most of our revenue comes from in-app purchases, with gross IAP contributing 75% to 80% of our total revenue. This revenue split is contrary to the public's assumptions about how free-to-play games make money, but is not unusual. Moreover, 85% of our IAP revenue comes from the time-limited weekend events, where players are motivated to spend real money to complete milestones and compete with other players to win rare virtual goods.

While only about 5% of users monetize through IAPs, players are much more willing to watch rewarded ads. About half of all players who install our games will watch at least one rewarded video ad. Engaged players watch an average of 15-20 per day, largely because they offer a clear in-game advantage. In contrast, only 10% of our players will peek at the offer wall, and only about 2% take the plunge and complete an offer. Despite being labeled "free," players typically prefer parting with real money rather than undertaking the effort required to complete most incentivized offers.

> Most game publishers use the same ad networks for both ad monetization and user acquisition. For example, ESG pays Google Ads to advertise its games while at the same time receiving revenue from Google for including their ad network (AdMob) in our ad mon mediation waterfall. When an ESG game is paid to show a rewarded video ad, we are the "publisher" and sit on the **supply side**, i.e., we supply the ad space. When ESG is buying ad space in a competitor's game, we are instead on the **demand side**; we demand (bid for) the ad space.

"What Would You Say You Do Here?"

Now that we know how mobile games make money, what role does analytics play in all of this? Data analysts are expected to do two things:

1. tell compelling stories with data; and,
2. derive **actionable insights**: conclusions from data leading directly to recommended product changes.

Pretty much every job description for a data analyst includes similar verbiage. That's great, but if my stories and insights don't improve our business's bottom line, I will quickly be unemployed. While it could be argued that analysts and analytics in mobile games are a necessity, they are indeed a luxury. Data analysts are expected to help the games retain their players and generate more revenue. Those are the only actionable insights that truly matter. How do we do that? First, by measuring game performance.

If you can't measure it, you can't improve it.
Peter Drucker

When in hospital with an illness, sensors are attached to a patient's body, enabling vital signs to be constantly measured by an expensive piece of medical equipment. Medical professionals consult the metrics (pulse, oxygen saturation, blood pressure, etc.) displayed on the machine's dashboard to help inform the decisions they make to improve patient health. This is an example of how data can tell a compelling story from which actionable insights are derived.

In the mobile games industry, the app is the patient, and the data analyst is the machine that goes "ping." Games don't measure themselves – they need help. To facilitate monitoring the health of a game, you need to collect data from the app as players engage with it on their devices. Data analysts are the measurement specialists who specify the data to collect and how to organize and store that information. They then query and calculate metrics from said data and build the dashboards to monitor and display the ongoing health of the game.

Armed with these measurements and dashboards, the data analyst identifies actionable insights that lead to product improvements in player satisfaction and game revenue. Some of the questions we are asked to answer include:

- Based on the current metrics, is this game going to be a success or should we cancel it?
- What features do our players use and what IAPs are they making?
- What first-time buyer pack[3] IAP is most likely to lead to a second IAP?
- Did that change to the game design improve our player engagement, or make it worse?
- Was that change we made to IAP pricing responsible for our recent increase in revenue or was that purely due to chance?
- How can we tell when a player is about to quit the game and uninstall the app?
- How much money is this game going to make next quarter?
- Are the advertising campaigns to acquire users we are running profitable, or are we lighting piles of cash on fire?
- If we stop spending money on acquiring players, what will our revenue be in six months?
- Where are the players dropping off during the tutorial?
- How much revenue will the players who installed the game seven days ago produce over the next 90 days?

To be a successful data analyst and answer these questions, two important skills are required. First, you must be able to write SQL queries that are correct and efficient. While larger workplaces may separate those who generate the dataset into a CSV file or spreadsheet from those who analyze it, most game studios combine those roles. Second, you must build dashboards with a data visualization tool like Tableau or Power BI (see Figure 1.3). The datasets extracted by your queries have a story to tell. Since a picture is worth a thousand words, a good story is succinctly told with a clear and usable dashboard. Your dashboards not only describe what has happened, but also predict what is likely to happen with regression models trained on historical data. These models relate a dependent variable (e.g., revenue) to an independent variable (e.g., time), then derive a formula to describe that relationship; e.g., revenue as a function of time.

The customers and consumers of your work are the game designers, producers, and product managers who operate the game once it is published – an activity referred to as **LiveOps**. You earn their trust by refining their questions about the data and delivering actionable insights

---

[3] A first-time buyer pack (or first-time buyer promo) is a SKU that can only be purchased once. It is usually low priced and steeply discounted over buying the same item(s) at regular price.

that help improve player satisfaction and generate revenue. You help them prove (or disprove) their great product improvement ideas.

Figure 1.3. Part of a typical dashboard built by a data analyst using Tableau. A curve (the dashed line) is fit to historical data using Tableau's built-in regression analysis. The curve's formula predicts how new groups of players are likely to behave.

But to accomplish any of these things, you first need data to query and visualize. Where does the data come from, and where does it go?

The Analytics Pipeline

A successful mobile game can generate a ton of data. Some might even call it Big Data. How your game generates and stores its data is referred to as an **analytics pipeline**. Some game publishers use a third-party service to collect and surface their game's data, but at ESG we built our own analytics pipeline called *Mentor*.

An analytics pipeline consists of three components:

1. **analytics events** initiated and sent deliberately by the game's software from the player's device;
2. a database or **data warehouse** to store these analytics events; and,
3. an **ingestion process** to receive and insert the analytics events into the data warehouse.

There is no right or wrong way to implement an analytics pipeline, but for illustrative purposes we will briefly discuss how ESG has implemented Mentor. Whether ESG has built the game in-house or is merely publishing a game built in partnership with an external studio, Mentor is the prescribed analytics pipeline. By convention, we refer to the publisher as the entity responsible for collecting and storing the analytics data.

Analytics Events

When you play a mobile game, the code that runs the app is not only busy entertaining you, but it's also capturing a myriad of details regarding how and when you play. This information is then sent over the internet – perhaps using some of your wireless data plan – to the publisher where it is processed, stored, and later analyzed. For example, whenever you open a game on your phone, an analytics event indicating you have started a new play session is sent to a server operated by the publisher, where it is ingested into their data warehouse. Watch a rewarded video ad or make a purchase? Those actions almost certainly result in more behind-the-scenes messaging. These analytics events contain discrete packets of information that facilitate the measurement of individual player behaviour, helping the publisher assess game health and meet business objectives. These are the sensors hooked up to the patient, and the process of transmitting the data is referred to as **telemetry**.

The typical core set of analytics events that every mobile game generates includes:

- *install*: when a new player is detected.
- *session_begin*: when a player loads, foregrounds, or otherwise returns to the game.
- *purchase*: when a player makes an IAP.
- *level_complete*: when a player successfully completes a level and ascends to the next.

- *ad_view*: when a player watches a rewarded video ad.
- *tutorial_complete*: when a user completes all of the steps or milestones associated with the first-time user experience (FTUE, and pronounced "fuh-two-ee").

Further specific events related to game play are highly dependent on the genre of the game; e.g., the idle mechanic captures information related to business or character upgrades and the generation of soft currency.

Analytics events include attributes regarding the reason for the event's generation. For example, which player generated the event, and when? All analytics pipelines employ a unique identifier, such as a `user_id`, to distinguish players. Events generated by the same player will use the same user identifier, allowing for tracking of user behaviour over time.

Analytics events don't just materialize out of thin air. They must be specified, then coded. To facilitate the collection of this data at ESG, our apps initiate the sending of analytics events by programming calls to a software development kit (SDK) developed by the data engineers in our game services team. The programmers who build every game we publish are presented with this SDK and an **analytics specification**, which is a document that defines the analytics events they should code and send with the SDK. This document also details what the events mean, and the attributes to include with each event. These specifications are owned by the analytics team, and its maintenance is part of the data analyst's job description.

By default, every Mentor analytics event sent by an ESG-published game includes the following attributes.

Attribute	Description	Data Type	Example Data
user_id	A unique identifier consistently used to (anonymously) identify a specific player	varchar(40)	1AE2279856
platform	The OS of the device	varchar(16)	ios android
version	The software version of the app that generated this event	varchar(16)	1.2.12
timestamp	The time (to the second) when the event was generated (or received)	UTC timestamp	2022-12-16 22:12:58
level	The game level the player was on when the event was generated	integer (1…n)	4

Attribute	Description	Data Type	Example Data
date[4]	The date when the event was generated/received	date	2022-12-16

Additional attributes specific to each type of analytics event are documented in the analytics spec. For example, in the case of a *purchase* event, additional attributes specify the IAP SKU, the currency used to buy the item, the price in the player's local currency, etc. An *ad_view* event includes the ad reward type (e.g., time-limited multiplier, soft currency bonus, welcome-back bonus, etc.), and whether the ad was watched to completion, or if the player bailed.

Here is an example from our analytics spec indicating the additional attributes and their meaning, data type, and example data for the *boss_fight* event, which is sent when a player completes each milestone in a boss fight at the end of a level.

`boss_fight: sent as the player progresses in a boss fight`

Attribute	Description	Data Type	Example Data
result	whether the player wins or loses the fight	varchar(16)	win, lose
timeRemaining	seconds remaining in boss fight	integer	17
tapPowerBase	base portion of player's current tap power in scientific notation	numeric(8,4)	1.235
tapPowerExp	exponent portion of player's current tap power in scientific notation	integer	2
reward	what type of loot box (*gacha* trunk) the player receives as a reward, or empty if no reward	varchar(64)	

The Data Warehouse

The analytics events generated by the people playing our games end up in a Redshift database hosted in the cloud by Amazon Web Services (AWS). SQL is the language to extract data from Redshift, the same language used to query relational database systems such as Oracle and MySQL.

[4] In hindsight, the names "timestamp" and "date" were a bad choice: those are both reserved words in SQL. Moreover, the date attribute is redundant with the timestamp. A better choice would have been a single attribute of type `timestamp` called `event_time`.

ESG has one (rather massive) Redshift cluster that hosts several database instances – one per game. Unlike some analytics stores that rely solely on one table with rows upon rows of key-value pairs to capture events, our Mentor schemas have separate tables for each type of analytics event. For example, there is a `session_begin` table, a `purchase` table, etc. The columns of each table match the attributes from the analytics specification; e.g., the `boss_fight` table consists of the following columns:

COLUMN_NAME	DATA_TYPE
user_id	varchar(40)
platform	varchar(16)
version	varchar(16)
timestamp	timestamp
date	date
level	integer
time_remaining	integer
reward	varchar(64)
result	varchar(16)
tap_power_base	numeric(8,4)
tap_power_exp	integer

Because Redshift is a data warehouse and *not* a relational database, primary key constraints are unenforced, and there is no referential integrity between tables. The data arrives with such velocity and volume (two of the five *V*s that define Big Data, the other three being value, variety, and veracity) there isn't the computing time available to enforce normalization constraints.

ESG's Mentor databases only contain data that each game's code explicitly sends as an analytics event. Mentor is not used by the games to store and maintain individual player state; e.g., what level is the player on, how much currency do they have, what cards do they have, what businesses have been unlocked, etc. Instead, each game has its own separate backend (a web application written in PHP that uses CouchDB or MySQL as its persistent storage) to maintain player state. Drawing from the client/server nomenclature, we use **client** to refer to a version of a game on the player's device, and **server** to refer to the backend web application that maintains player state. The ESG backend servers reside in a separate cluster hosted at AWS.

Because analytics events are generated when players complete levels, boss fights, and milestones, and when they unlock businesses and characters, it is theoretically possible to derive a player's current state by working forwards from their oldest to newest history of analytics events in Mentor. But given the amount of data this approach would need to traverse, this is grossly inefficient compared to the explicit state maintained by the game backend.

Event Ingestion

The payload (content) of an analytics event is formatted in the client as JavaScript Object Notation (JSON) and sent to an endpoint via an HTTP `POST` request. The process of web services listening for analytics events from player devices, parsing the JSON, and queuing the data for insertion into the data warehouse is known as **event ingestion**. At ESG, these endpoints are built and managed by a team of data engineers who also monitor the system to ensure uptime. The details of how this is accomplished is not typically the purview of the data analyst. Our work begins once the data is flowing and surfaced in the various tables that comprise the data warehouse.

Having said that, mobile game telemetry can be challenging. If a player is not connected to the internet, their events are saved to local storage on the device until such a time as connectivity is restored, which can be error-prone and unreliable. Events may go missing, arrive out of order, or be duplicated. Sometimes, due to bugs in the code or cheaters looking to gain an advantage by messing with the clock on their device, the timestamps are illogical and important attributes are missing. One of a data analyst's responsibilities is to tackle these challenges and to never assume the data is well-behaved. Fortunately, this is mostly possible through slight modifications to the SQL queries used to measure our games, as we are about to see in the next chapter.

With that intro to our industry out of the way, it is time to explore the landscape of data generated by free-to-play games.

Key Performance Indicators:
LEVEL 2

The overall health of a free-to-play game is based on a small set of industry-standard metrics. The metrics deemed fundamental to the business goals are called **key performance indicators** (KPIs). In this chapter, we define the core set of KPIs tracked at ESG, and present SQL used to calculate their values.

There are many ways to measure a game's performance, and different companies (or even people within the same company) have their own unique set of favourite KPIs compared to those described herein. The KPIs discussed in this chapter, while neither a complete list nor necessarily universally adopted across the industry, are a good start. If you already know your DAU *from your* ARPDAU, *think you're a SQL rockstar, and can tell the difference between a cohort and a calzone, you might find this review a little basic. But stay tuned – it's about to get a lot more technical.*

After defining the retention, monetization, and marketing categories of KPIs, we end this chapter with the **bathtub analogy**, an effective visualization of how the three categories work together.

KPI Categories

In games, KPIs are roughly categorized as specific to either **retention** (are we keeping our players?) or **monetization** (are our players generating revenue?). Retention and monetization are key to the business of mobile games. No matter how much you delight your players, you can't make payroll with five-star ratings as your only currency: your apps need to make money. If your game isn't keeping and converting players to payers, your corporate overlords will decide it is time to cancel the title and move on to a different and hopefully better game.

Marketing KPIs are the third category: can we grow our games by acquiring users profitably? In the crowded marketplace of mobile games, serious publishers are running paid advertising campaigns to drive downloads and build their player base. Players acquired in this manner are referred to as **paid users**, whereas those who somehow found the game in the App/Play store on their own are called **organic**.

A fourth category, which is beyond the scope of this book, are the **software quality** metrics related to game stability. A game is a computer program that runs on an operating system. If the game has bugs, it can crash or hang in a state known as ANR (app not responding). Analytics related to these two so-called "bad behaviours" are reported in the platform dashboards and are the responsibility of the producers to monitor and software engineers to address. The Google Play console provides a view into software quality in the *Android Vitals* section of the dashboard, which you can find under the *Quality* section of the navigation panel. Here is an example of an app in the "bad behavior" penalty box:

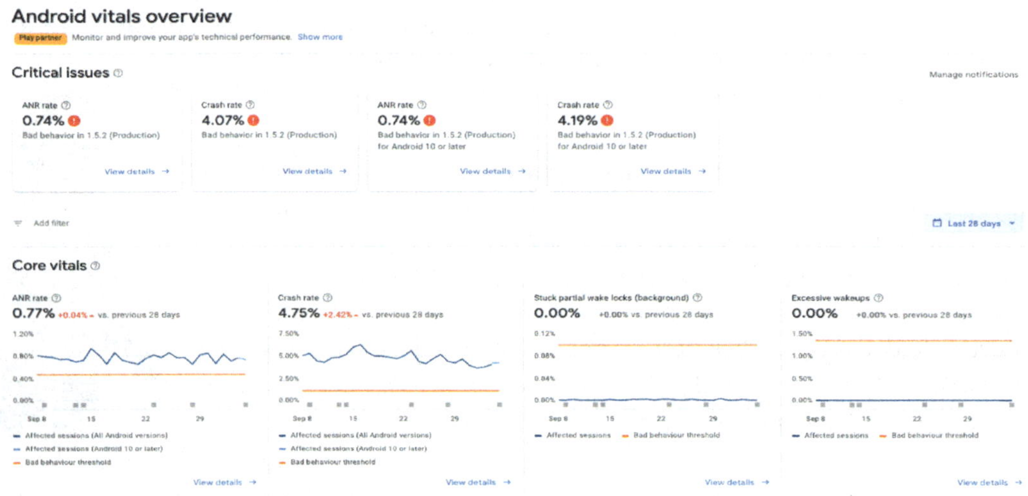

Apps that exhibit bad behaviour are never **featured**, which means they are not promoted by the platform or easily discovered by users when they visit, browse, and search the app store. Instead, bad-behaving apps are deliberately buried in the search results. Google wants Android users to have a good experience, and buggy software that crashes or hangs is not a good user experience. Therefore, it is vital that producers keep an eye on these vitals.

The *Quality* section of the Play console also contains an equally important metric called **star rating**, which is an average of every user-submitted rating of the game on a scale of 1 to 5, with 5 stars being the best. If an app's average user rating is below 4-stars, it will not be featured. A low star rating also creates friction for user acquisition: potential players visit the App/Play store listing but choose not to download the game because of negative reviews and poor ratings. Product managers can address this issue through tenacious customer support, responding to reviews, and placing a ratings prompt in the game at strategic moments where the user is likely to feel particularly good about their experience.

That's all we have to say about software quality and ratings. Our work begins with the assumption that the app is well-behaved, and any improvements to be made are at the product (rather than programming) level.

SQL: The Language of Data Analysts

As an analyst, you need to understand the definition of game KPIs and calculate them quickly and correctly with SQL. The dashboards you build and share depend on these calculations. In this chapter, we define an important set of game KPIs and provide sample SQL queries that illustrate how they are derived from the raw event data. However, this is not a SQL tutorial: we assume the reader interested in the particular details of how the queries are structured is already familiar with SQL, including joins, common table expressions (CTEs), aggregation, and window functions.

The SQL queries shown below are based on the tables and views in ESG's Redshift database. While the schema will differ in other organizations, the concepts introduced are hopefully universal. In other words, the datasets (the results of the query) are likely to contain similar metrics regardless of the underlying physical structure of how the data is generated, ingested, and stored.

Measure Twice, Cut Once

SQL is quite happy to give you an answer to anything you ask, provided the syntax is correct. It is essential that you test your results thoroughly before reporting back to the stakeholders with your confident answer to their ad-hoc questions. I can't stress this enough.

We find it is often useful to work top-down by first imagining a relation that has the columns you need to answer the question posed. Then we attack the problem by creating the subqueries or CTEs that you can build upon to derive the desired relation.

Regardless of your approach, always ask yourself, "does this number make sense given what I know about freemium games?" Even if you think it does, it is never a bad idea to verify your results by trying a different approach or asking another analyst on your team to independently calculate the metric.

Views as ETL

As mentioned in the previous chapter, mobile game telemetry can be messy, with missing, duplicated, or out of order data. To tidy up the mess, the analytics team at ESG constructed a collection of SQL views. A **view** is a virtual table defined by the results of a stored query. The following views implement our business rules, roll-up events, and filter out bogus data.

view	primary key	contents	underlying table
user_source	user_id	Attribution data. The origin and install date of every player	install session_begin
user_retention	user_id	Every user's retention history	session_begin
user_ltv	user_id	Every user's monetization history	purchase
purchases_view	transaction_id	Every valid IAP	purchase

The user_* views contain one (and only one) row for every unique player, past and present. The structure of each is described later in this chapter. In essence, these views are both an abstraction layer above the physical schema, providing a consistent query interface regardless of game-specific idiosyncrasies, and an alternative to building a separate **extract-transform-load** (ETL) system for data cleaning and normalization. However, while SQL is useful at scrubbing the data, the views can be computationally expensive depending on the size of the underlying table(s) queried. To increase efficiency at the expense of real-time updates, ESG employs materialized versions of these views. The SQL DDL script for the creation of each view is managed by the data analysts and kept under version control.

Cohorts

Data analysts tend not to think too much about individual players. Instead, descriptive statistics are drawn from a group of players called a cohort. A **cohort** is a set of players who have something in common. Normally, this is their install date, but additional attributes can be used to determine membership in a cohort. For example, a cohort might consist of all the organic Android players from the US who installed version 1.26.5 on July 3, 2022. Cohorts define the players used in the calculation of averages and other descriptive statistics that make up KPIs.

Cohorts are typically implemented in SQL with a `WHERE` clause that filters the set of users before an aggregation is applied. Keep in mind that more attributes will mean a smaller cohort, which can limit the statistical power of the analysis.

Time Series

A **time series** is made up of successive measurements, over consistent intervals, of the same variable. When charted or graphed, time is the independent variable and occupies the *x*-axis. Here is a simple example: active players by date.

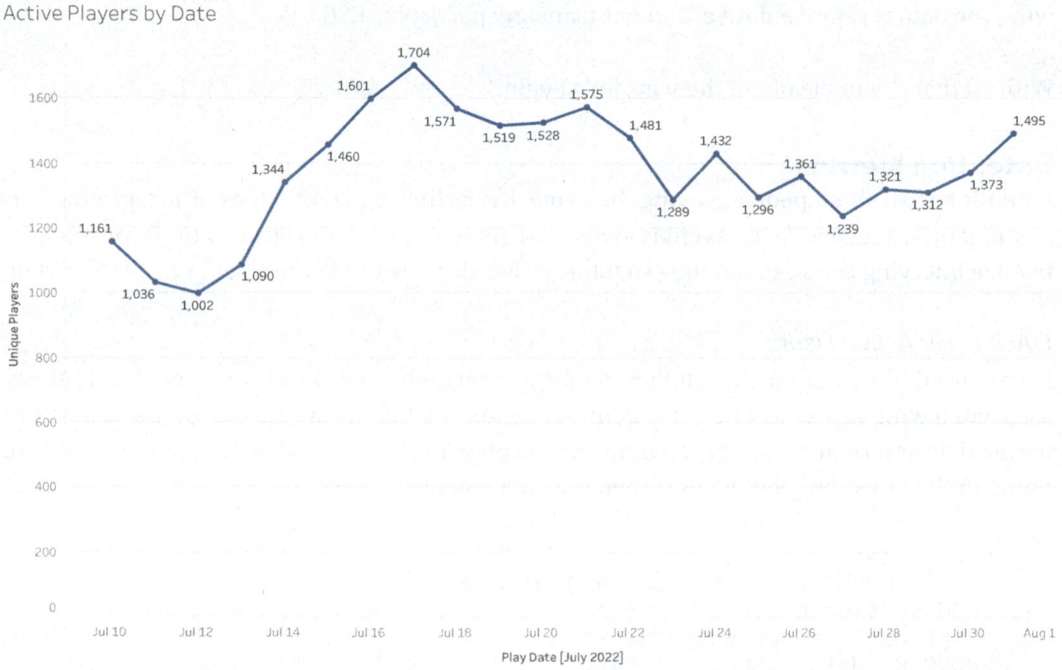

Almost all of the KPIs covered in this chapter are calculated daily and ultimately rendered as a time series. However, the *x*-axis can represent one of two very different types of dates:

1. a specific day when the game was *played* by a set of users; or,
2. a cohort *install* date that measures the evolving, future behaviour of only those users who installed the game on that date.

The graph above is a play-date time series. In practice, the difference between a **play date** vs. **cohort date** KPI is manifest in the table (or view) that is driving the query and its specific date field that aggregates are grouped by. For play dates, the query is driven by `session_begin`.

Once all the data for a calendar date has been ingested and the KPIs calculated, play-date KPIs never change. Conversely, for cohort metrics, queries use the install date in user_source. Cohort metrics are retroactive and continue to evolve and change as each day passes so long as any of the users in the cohort continue to play. We discuss this important distinction later as we introduce KPIs of each type.

In the case of time-series queries, we limit our result set to only the previous 30 days or a specific month of data. The result set itself is presented as a table immediately following the SQL, with one or more truncated rows indicated by an ellipse. Unless explicitly stated otherwise, the data is representative, and not from any particular ESG title.

With all that preamble out of the way, let's begin.

Retention Metrics

Retention is all about people playing the game. Every time a player opens or foregrounds one of our games, a *session_begin* event is generated. As such, most of the calculations for retention involve querying the session_begin table, either directly or via the user_retention view.

DAU: Daily Active Users

Pronounced "dow", this is the number of unique users who play on a given day. DAU is always associated with a specific date – it is *daily* active users after all – and is one of the easiest KPIs to calculate as it requires simply counting all the players (each identified by a unique user_id) found in the session_begin table, then grouping by play date:

```
SELECT date,
       COUNT(DISTINCT user_id) AS dau
FROM session_begin
WHERE date >= current_date - 30
GROUP BY date
```

date	dau
2022-07-04	53082
2022-07-03	52548
2022-07-02	52311
2022-07-01	53303
...	...

The DISTINCT modifier is necessary to avoid counting each session in each day, since it is very common for a person to play the same mobile game multiple times a day (see *Sessions* below).

There are also equivalent metrics for weekly (WAU) and monthly active users (MAU), sometimes also referred to as "weekly or monthly uniques." Only unique players are counted in these totals. In other words, you don't just sum the past seven days of DAU to get the WAU: you only count the unique users who played the game at any time over the past seven days. Here is MAU for the first two quarters of 2022:

```
SELECT DATE(DATE_TRUNC('month', date)) AS month,
       COUNT(DISTINCT user_id) AS mau
FROM session_begin
WHERE date BETWEEN '2022-01-01' AND '2022-06-30'
GROUP BY month
```

month	mau
2022-01-01	164313
2022-02-01	144987
2022-03-01	122447
2022-04-01	119082
2022-05-01	141905
2022-06-01	140118

Related **stickiness** metrics look at the ratio of DAU to WAU (or MAU), which indicate the percentage of players who stick around and play regularly. Creating an accurate daily time series for stickiness requires calculating the trailing seven or 30 days for WAU and MAU, respectively. Other implementations of stickiness look instead to the prior calendar week or calendar month when calculating the denominator. According to Carpenter (2018), the median weekly stickiness (DAU/WAU) ratio of the top grossing games on Google Play is 55%.

Installs

The platforms do not notify publishers (e.g., with a postback to a publisher-specified web service endpoint) when a person downloads one of their apps to a phone or tablet. Therefore, an *install* event happens not when a new player downloads the app to their device, but rather the first time the app is launched on this device. In particular, when the game's backend encounters a message from a mobile device it has never seen before.[1]

Install events are registered in the `install` table and include the usual attributes that are part of every analytics event: the unique `user_id` assigned to the new player; the `date` and `timestamp` of the event's generation; the `platform` of the mobile device; and, the `version` of

[1] This also means that if a player gets a new phone, we count them as a new install. One of the primary activities of ESG's customer service team is linking a new device to its previous player data. Otherwise, the player would need to start over and lose all their progress.

the app. We use the term **install** as a noun when referring to a new user. The number of lifetime players of a game is its total installs, but normally we track the number of installs per day (also known as **daily new users**):

```
SELECT date,
       COUNT(DISTINCT user_id) AS installs
FROM install
WHERE date BETWEEN '2022-07-01' AND '2022-07-31'
GROUP BY date
```

date	installs
2022-07-01	1653
2022-07-02	1380
2022-07-03	1289
2022-07-04	1963
...	...

If the platforms don't generate the *install* events, where do they originate? Our **mobile marketing partner** (MMP) generates an *install* event when their SDK embedded in our client is initialized for the first time with a device identifier they have never seen play this game before. These *attribution install* events include the player's country and information regarding the ad network, ad campaign, and specific ad creative the user last clicked/viewed (if any) before installing the game.

Using an MMP in a game is optional. Therefore, ESG's game backends also generate an *install* event when they can't find any pre-existing player data that matches the device identifier. The upshot is that for each new player, there are *two* records that appear in the `install` table: one from the game, and one from the MMP. The main purpose of the `user_source` view is to consolidate these two *install* events into a single representation of what we know about the origin of every player. Rather than query the `install` table directly, it is more expedient to query the view. The columns surfaced in `user_source` are:

```
describe user_source
```

COLUMN_NAME	DATA_TYPE	MEANING
user_id	varchar(40)	The unique ID assigned to this new player.
install_date	date	The install date for this player.
timestamp	timestamp	The install time.
type	varchar(16)	'Organic' or the name of the ad network responsible for the install.
source	varchar(256)	The ad campaign ID (or null if type is 'Organic').
subsource	varchar(64)	The ad creative ID (or null if user is 'Organic').

COLUMN_NAME	DATA_TYPE	MEANING
version	text	The software version of the client when the user first loaded the game.
platform	text	'ios' or 'android'
country	varchar(2)	The player's location indicated by a 2-character ISO country code like 'US', 'CA', 'IE', etc.

Not only does the `user_source` view consolidate the two types of *install* events, but it also handles cases of unordered (attribution before client install events) or missing data: it is not unusual for a `user_id` to have zero or only one record in the `install` table. To be included as a real install, a player must also generate at least one *session_begin* event. If a `user_id` only has an *attribution install* event, this is likely a mistake on the part of the MMP: their suppression list of devices that have already installed the game may be incomplete.

By taking care of this housekeeping, `user_source` provides an easy way to generate cohorts based on platform, paid vs. organic user type, country, and install date for every player in the game. Here is a query to find all users belonging to the cohort "all the Android, organic players from the US who installed version 1.26.5 on July 3, 2022."

```
SELECT user_id
FROM user_source
WHERE install_date = '2022-07-03'
  AND version = '1.26.5'
  AND platform = 'android'
  AND type = 'Organic'
  AND country = 'US'
```

Cohorts are essentially a `user_id` set defined by a `WHERE` clause that restricts the players involved in the calculation of a KPI. For example, DAU for this cohort only. Note the use of a common table expression (CTE) to first define `cohort` as a set of users.

```
WITH cohort AS
(
  SELECT user_id
  FROM  user_source
  WHERE install_date = '2022-07-03'
  AND   version = '1.26.5'
  AND   platform = 'android'
  AND   type = 'Organic'
  AND   country = 'US'
)
SELECT date,
       COUNT(DISTINCT user_id) AS dau
FROM cohort
```

```
  INNER JOIN session_begin USING (user_id)
GROUP BY date
```

date	dau
2022-07-03	128
2022-07-04	58
2022-07-05	42
2022-07-06	35
2022-07-07	30
...	...

Besides illustrating how a play-date KPI like DAU can also apply to a cohort, this query foreshadows the calculation of daily retention: the number of active users from the original install cohort of 128 players drops steadily with each passing day after install.

Sessions

How many times per day are players returning to the game? When a player first opens a game on their phone, a *session_begin* event is fired and stored in the `session_begin` table. But when does that session come to an end and a new session begin? An ongoing session ends when a user backgrounds the game and switches to a different app or puts the phone in their pocket long enough for the screen to lock. The next time the user returns to the game, a new *session_begin* event is fired.

A count of the number of distinct *session_begin* events per day per player is calculated as follows:

```
SELECT date, user_id, COUNT(DISTINCT timestamp) AS sessions
FROM session_begin
WHERE date >= current_date - 30
GROUP BY date, user_id
```

The use of `DISTINCT timestamp` ensures duplicates are not counted; compare with `COUNT(*)`, which counts duplicate events should any have managed to creep into the data.

We use a `WHERE` clause to limit the number of unique combinations of <date, user_id> that the query needs to find. Omitting one could cause performance issues for our Redshift server. With that in mind, let's see how many rows the query would return for *TPB* without a `WHERE` clause.

```
SELECT COUNT(*)
FROM (SELECT date,
             user_id,
             COUNT(DISTINCT timestamp) AS sessions
```

```
        FROM session_begin
        GROUP BY date,
                 user_id)
```

count(*)
202924417

Over 202M. Not quite Elon Musk's bank account balance,[2] but a very large and growing number, along with an even larger amount of data to pull through your home internet connection.

In addition to WHERE, judicious use of the LIMIT clause is highly recommended when you are querying tables with bazillions of rows.

Back to the task at hand: measuring sessions. The average number of sessions per DAU is really what we are looking to calculate, which is easily accomplished by turning that query into a subquery and wrapping it with an average aggregation:

```
SELECT date,
       AVG(sessions::FLOAT) AS avg_sessions
FROM (SELECT date,
             user_id,
             COUNT(DISTINCT timestamp) AS sessions
      FROM session_begin
      WHERE date >= CURRENT_DATE- 30
      GROUP BY date,
               user_id)
GROUP BY date
```

date	avg_sessions
2022-07-04	26.5511
2022-07-03	25.9705
2022-07-02	25.3286
2022-07-01	26.6028
...	...

The cast of sessions to a FLOAT is necessary to avoid integer truncation, a trick we will use often when calculating averages, rates, and proportions.

[2] I wrote this before he bought Twitter.

Retention by Day

Retention is the king of all KPIs, with ARPDAU (a monetization metric) its queen. You can only monetize the users you have, so if your game doesn't retain its players, you will struggle to generate revenue.

Retention is a cohort metric that is modified with a "days since install" index, which we denote with the variable *n*. You never talk about retention without specifying a particular day after a cohort's install date. The *n*th day after a user or cohort's install date is indicated by "D*n*." The install date is day zero (D0).

D*n* retention is the percentage[3] of a cohort that plays exactly *n* days after their install date: not the day before, not the day after. By definition, D0 retention is always 1.0 since the install date is equivalent to the date of a player's first *session_begin*. D1 retention (abbreviated as D1R) is the proportion of installs who played at any time in the calendar date immediately following their install date. Note that D1 is not defined as the first 24 hours after time of install; D1 starts at midnight on the day of install. Therefore, not all players have a D0 of the same length. If someone installs at one minute to midnight, their D0 is only 60 seconds long.

D*n* retention is reported for a standard set of days since install, typically for $n \in \{1, 7, 30, 90\}$. But in general, D*n*R can be measured for any day since install as

$$\text{D}n\text{R} = \frac{\text{DAU}_n}{\text{installs}}$$

where *installs* is the size of the cohort, and DAU_n is a count of the daily active users from the cohort who played on the nth day after their install date. Note that $\text{DAU}_0 \equiv installs$.

For a cohort to have a value for any D*n* retention metric their install date must be more than *n* days ago. For example, we can't calculate D7R for a cohort of installs until eight days after their install date, at which point we say the cohort and its users are "seven days **fully baked**." If a cohort is not fully baked with respect to a KPI, the value is null.

Here we calculate D1 retention for each daily install cohort in the month of July. Like all cohort metrics, aggregation is based on the install date from `user_source` (the installs) rather than play date from `session_begin` (the D1 players):

```
SELECT install_date,
```

[3] Or *proportion* if you prefer [0,1] over 0 – 100%. I use the terms interchangeably.

```
        COUNT(us.user_id) AS installs,
        COUNT(sb.user_id) AS d1_players,
        d1_players / installs::FLOAT AS d1r
FROM (SELECT install_date,
             user_id
      FROM user_source
      WHERE install_date BETWEEN '2022-07-01' AND '2022-07-31') us
  LEFT JOIN (SELECT DISTINCT date,
                    user_id
             FROM session_begin
             WHERE date BETWEEN '2022-07-02' AND '2022-08-01') sb
        ON us.user_id = sb.user_id AND date = install_date + 1
GROUP BY install_date
```

install_date	installs	d1_players	d1r
2022-07-01	754	230	0.305
2022-07-02	755	269	0.3563
2022-07-03	794	287	0.3615
2022-07-04	790	295	0.3734
2022-07-05	797	306	0.3839
2022-07-06	950	375	0.3947
2022-07-07	1034	401	0.3878
2022-07-08	1030	367	0.3563
2022-07-09	987	399	0.4043
...	...	...	...

The higher your retention, the better. For the idle genre, a good D1R is around 40%. For D7, we shoot for 20%. A game with long-tail retention has decent D30, D90, and even D180 retention. Seufert (2014) notes a recurring pattern with free-to-play games: D7R is typically half of D1R, D30R is half of D7R, D90R is half of D30R, and D180R is half of D90R. If your D7 retention is 20%, you can expect 10%, 5%, and 2.5% for D30R, D90R, and D180R, respectively. This pattern is a side-effect of the power function that best fits the retention profile of a game, a topic covered in depth in a subsequent chapter.

We've seen how to calculate daily retention, which constitutes a time series of proportions. But what is the *average* D1 retention? It is not uncommon to be asked of a game, "What is day one retention?" The implicit assumption is the inquirer wants some kind of average of the D1R values over a range of dates. For example, assume a game's D1R over the past two days was 0.4 and 0.3 from cohorts of size 500 and 1000, respectively. What was the average? There are two ways to approach this:

1. take the good old arithmetic mean, which is $(0.4 + 0.3)/2 = 0.35$; or,
2. calculate a **weighted average** by weighting each of the values by the number of installs in their cohort, which is $(0.4 * 500 + 0.3 * 1000)/(500 + 1000) = 0.33$.

These two approaches typically result in different answers when applied to the same range of dates. Of the two, the weighted average is superior: a data point based on 1,000 installs should carry more weight than one based on 500. With a simple arithmetic mean you run the risk of a skewed average due to daily measures that are based on small, unrepresentative samples.

Use Weighted Averages
If there is one important lesson to take away from this book it is this: taking the average of a set of averages is asking for trouble. This can particularly bite you in the butt if you make this mistake with visualization tools like Tableau. To avoid this trap, always use the raw data and recompute your averages.

However, when sample sizes are relatively similar and of generous size – such as the case of daily installs in *TPB* – calculating average D1R with a simple arithmetic mean is reasonable. For instance, consider D1R for the month of July 2022 for *TPB* using an average of the daily values versus a weighted average. For the arithmetic mean, we can simply employ the `AVG` aggregate over the `d1r` column from our previous query. As for the weighted mean, we can simply combine all of the raw data and forget about the specific `d1r` values:[4]

```
SELECT AVG(d1r) AS avg_d1R,
       SUM(d1_players)/SUM(installs)::FLOAT AS weighted
FROM (SELECT p.date,
             COUNT(p.user_id) AS installs,
             COUNT(r.user_id) AS d1_players,
             d1_players / installs::FLOAT AS d1r
      FROM (SELECT install_date AS date,
                   user_id
            FROM user_source
            WHERE date BETWEEN '2022-07-01' AND '2022-07-31') p
        LEFT JOIN (SELECT DISTINCT date,
                          user_id
                   FROM session_begin
              WHERE date BETWEEN '2022-07-02' AND '2022-08-01') r
               ON p.user_id = r.user_id AND r.date = p.date + 1
      GROUP BY p.date)
```

avg_d1r	weighted
0.3818	0.3838

[4] Alternatively, `SUM(d1r * installs)/SUM(installs)`, which is equivalent since `d1_players = d1r * installs`.

If we take the average of the 31 daily D1R values, we get 38.18%. But if we combine all of the installs into a single cohort and recompute D1R, the result is a little higher: 38.38%.

Retention is such an important concept that we created a view, called `user_retention`, that contains retention metrics for each player and simplifies the calculation of common retention metrics like D1R, D7R, etc.

```
describe user_retention
```

COLUMN_NAME	DATA_TYPE	MEANING
user_id	varchar(40)	unique identifier of user
install_date	date	the date user installed
platform	text	'ios' or 'android'
d1	integer {0, 1}	null if the user is not D1 fully baked, else 1 if a session on D1, otherwise 0
d7	integer {0, 1}	ditto, but for D7
d30	integer {0, 1}	ditto, but for D30
d90	integer {0, 1}	ditto, but for D90
d0_sessions	bigint	count of sessions played on D0
d1_sessions	bigint	the number of sessions played on D1
d3_sessions	bigint	the number of sessions played on D3
active	integer {0, 1}	1 if this user played any time within the past 14 days
played_yesterday	integer {0, 1}	1 if played yesterday
total_sessions	bigint	total lifetime sessions
last_played	date	date of last session
d7_level	integer	level attained by end of D7
max_level	integer	max level lifetime

The `d`*n* columns `d1`, `d7`, `d30`, and `d90` are binary, with a 1 if the player had a session on that day after install, otherwise 0. The fields are null if the user is not yet fully baked with respect to *n*. Summing that field and dividing by the count of users who share the same `install_date` is an easy way to generate retention KPIs:

```
SELECT install_date,
       SUM(d1) / COUNT(*)::FLOAT AS d1R,
       SUM(d7) / COUNT(*)::FLOAT AS d7R
FROM user_retention
WHERE install_date > CURRENT_DATE- 30
GROUP BY install_date
```

Or equivalently as:

```
SELECT install_date,
       AVG(d1::FLOAT) AS d1R,
       AVG(d7::FLOAT) AS d7R
FROM user_retention
WHERE install_date > CURRENT_DATE- 30
GROUP BY install_date ORDER BY install_date
```

install_date	d1r	d7r
...	...	...
2022-06-29	0.3401	0.1247
2022-06-30	0.3093	0.137
2022-07-01	0.3042	
2022-07-02	0.3577	
2022-07-03	0.3615	
2022-07-04	0.3739	
2022-07-05	0.3839	
2022-07-06	0.393	
2022-07-07		
2022-07-08		

Notice how nulls appear in the output (indicated by an empty table cell) when the install cohort is not yet fully baked. When executed on 2022-07-08, the query has not waited long enough to calculate a D7R for any date other than those installs from more than seven days ago: namely, June 30th and prior. Players who installed on July 1st have until midnight on July 8th to play on that day to be counted as part of the D7R numerator. Likewise, for D1R and the day before the query is executed. If we run this same query again any time on July 9th, we will get two additional values in the result set: D1R for July 7th, and D7R for July 1st.

Churn Rate

The opposite of retention, **churn** is when a user stops playing. However, there is no visible churn event: if a player uninstalls a game, publishers do not receive notification from the platforms. Therefore, we don't ever really know for sure when a player has quit. The best we can do is guess. At ESG, we consider a player churned if we haven't seen a *session_begin* event from them in two weeks. They may come back, but the probability is assumed to be low.

> What exactly is the probability a player returns if they haven't played in 14 days? This challenging question is addressed in the chapter devoted to churn.

At ESG, **churn rate** is measured as a percentage of DAU. On any day more than two weeks ago, we count the number of players who haven't played since, then divide by the total DAU on that date. Obviously the lower the churn percentage the better. For mature games, we look for a 5% daily churn rate (or lower). Here is a query to calculate churn rate by day:

```
WITH last_players AS
(
  SELECT last_played AS date,
         COUNT(*) AS churned
  FROM (SELECT user_id,
               MAX(date) AS last_played
        FROM session_begin
        GROUP BY user_id)
  GROUP BY last_played
)
SELECT date,
       churned / dau::FLOAT AS churn_rate
FROM last_players
  INNER JOIN (SELECT date,
                     COUNT(DISTINCT user_id) AS dau
              FROM session_begin
              GROUP BY date) d USING (date)
WHERE date BETWEEN CURRENT_DATE- 30 AND CURRENT_DATE- 15
ORDER BY date
```

Since we only consider a player churned if the last time they played was 15+ days ago, it is meaningless to calculate a churn rate for any dates within the past 14 days.

Alternatively, the `user_retention` view can simplify the calculation of the `last_players` CTE:

```
SELECT last_played AS date, COUNT(*) AS churned
FROM user_retention
GROUP BY last_played
```

However, both approaches calculate the last date played for *every* user who has ever played, past or present. For a game like *TPB*, with millions of rows in the `session_begin` table, this can take minutes to calculate. But if we only want the churn rate over the past 30 days, we only need to know who played during that time interval, and which of those 30 days was the last date each active user played. This is accomplished with the following modification to our CTE, which results in a significant optimization to the query:

```
SELECT date,
       COUNT(*) AS churned
FROM (SELECT user_id,
             MAX(date) AS date
      FROM session_begin
      WHERE date >= CURRENT_DATE - 30
      GROUP BY user_id)
GROUP BY date
```

Churn rate is unique in that it is a play-day metric that can retroactively change (decrease) over time as players thought to have churned suddenly reappear.

Regularity

A relative newcomer to the KPI scene, **regularity** attempts to quantify how addicted players are to a game; a regular user is one who plays every day. Regularity is defined as the percentage of DAU who are playing their seventh (or more) *consecutive* day. Generating this KPI is somewhat complex, but the solution appears obvious once presented. Try to solve it yourself first before reading further.

In our solution, we start by simplifying the problem with a CTE that defines a relation containing every date that a specific user was active over the past 40 days:

```
WITH players AS
(
  SELECT DISTINCT user_id,
         date
  FROM session_begin
  WHERE date >= CURRENT_DATE- 40
)
```

The choice of 40 days is arbitrary, but given we want to calculate regularity over the past 30 days, anything > 37 will suffice. To accomplish this, we need an additional column that indicates how many days out of the previous six each of these `players` were active. Why six? Well, we know they played on `date`, and if they had played six out of the previous six days, `date` must be the seventh. The relation should look like this, where a 0 indicates the user did not play any of the previous six days:

user_id	date	play_days
7371436	2022-06-25	0
8609300	2022-06-25	4
8077233	2022-06-25	4
8510215	2022-06-26	5
7954407	2022-06-26	5
...	...	...

For example, user `8609300` played on June 25, 2022, and played on four of the previous six calendar days – not necessarily in a row. The 25th is their fifth day playing out of seven. Pretty good, but not good enough to count as a regular player.

With a relation like that it is a simple matter to count all the rows `WHERE play_days = 6` and aggregate with a `GROUP BY date`. Moreover, `COUNT(DISTINCT user_id)` gives us the DAU.

But how do we generate that additional `play_days` column? The key is to join the `players` CTE with itself (i.e., a self-join), highlighted below. But since we are only interested in counting the users who have played six out of the last six days, we only need to look back over the prior six days and count the number of records that exist for each player. We count distinct dates, which we do in a CTE called `regs`:

```
regs AS
(
  SELECT a.user_id,
         a.date,
         COUNT(DISTINCT b.date) AS play_days
  FROM players a
    LEFT JOIN players b
           ON a.user_id = b.user_id
          AND b.date BETWEEN a.date - 6 AND a.date - 1
  GROUP BY a.user_id,
           a.date
)
SELECT date,
       COUNT(DISTINCT user_id) AS DAU,
       SUM(CASE WHEN play_days = 6 THEN 1 END) AS regulars,
       regulars / DAU::FLOAT AS regular_rate
FROM regs
WHERE date >= current_date - 30
GROUP BY date
```

date	dau	regulars	regular_rate
2022-07-01	53303	37690	0.7071
2022-07-02	52311	37253	0.7121
2022-07-03	52549	36993	0.704
2022-07-04	53103	36620	0.6896
2022-07-05	52148	36079	0.6919
2022-07-06	52085	35633	0.6841
2022-07-07	52543	35455	0.6748
...			

The result set above is actual data from *TPB*. Are you surprised at how high the percentage of DAU is who have played at least seven consecutive days? We sure were the first time we calculated it!

But wait, should we count new installs as part of the DAU? The current query penalizes games with a high number of installs relative to DAU. If the DAU contains players who installed within the past week, it is impossible for them to have played for seven consecutive days. We need to ignore those new installs. The fix is simple: since `players` on the left side of the join is driving the query, we simply filter out those whose install date is within seven days of the play date. The definition of the regs CTE becomes:

```
regs AS
(SELECT a.user_id,
        a.date,
        COUNT(DISTINCT b.date) AS play_days
FROM (SELECT p.user_id,
             p.date
       FROM players p
         INNER JOIN user_source s USING (user_id)
       WHERE p.date >= s.date + 6) a
  LEFT JOIN players b
         ON a.user_id = b.user_id
        AND b.date BETWEEN a.date - 6 AND a.date - 1
GROUP BY a.user_id,
         a.date)
```

Installs who are not seven-days fully baked are no longer counted as part of the DAU. Since this is the denominator in the regularity ratio, the percentage of regular players increases. But only slightly:

date	dau	regulars	regular_rate
2022-07-01	51447	37690	0.7326
2022-07-02	50557	37253	0.7369
2022-07-03	50772	36993	0.7286
2022-07-04	51313	36620	0.7137
2022-07-05	50425	36079	0.7155
2022-07-06	50175	35633	0.7102
2022-07-07	50458	35455	0.7027
...	...	...	...

Monetization Metrics

The metrics associated with how well a game is generating revenue are known as the monetization KPIs. The analytics events related to IAP are stored in the `purchase` table and surfaced via a view called `purchases_view`. Purchases are made by players all over the world in many different currencies; the `converted` column in `purchases_view` contains the gross IAP revenue converted to Canadian dollars (CAD) at the prevailing exchange rate on the date of purchase. Revenue related to ad monetization and offer walls is stored in the `altrev` table (named because this revenue is alternative to IAP), which contains data related to payments received from the various video ad networks[5] and offer walls implemented in ESG's games.

Revenue

How much money did we make today? The revenue a game generates per day is expressed as either gross IAP or net IAP, and may or may not include ad revenue. Here is a query for daily gross IAP revenue in ESG's *Bud Farm: Idle Tycoon (BFIT)*:

```
SELECT date, SUM(converted) AS gross_iap_revenue
FROM purchases_view
WHERE DATE BETWEEN '2022-07-01' AND '2022-07-31'
GROUP BY date
```

date	gross_iap_revenue
2022-07-01	34291.24
2022-07-02	25419.14
2022-07-03	22941.52
2022-07-04	16042.55
2022-07-05	21186.19
2022-07-06	42544.85
2022-07-07	48856.28
2022-07-08	39169.63
...	...

Revenue is usually the sum of monetization from a set of users, though it can also be for an individual player. In the case of daily revenue, the set of users are the DAU on that date.

Let's calculate the net IAP revenue plus ad monetization in *BFIT* for the entire month of July:

```
SELECT *,
       ROUND(net_iap + ad_mon,2) AS total_rev,
       100.0 *ad_mon / total_rev AS pct_ad_rev
FROM (SELECT DATE (DATE_TRUNC('month', date)) AS mm,
             ROUND(SUM(converted)*0.7,2) AS net_iap
      FROM purchases_view
      WHERE date BETWEEN '2022-07-01' AND '2022-07-31'
      GROUP BY mm) iap
  FULL OUTER JOIN (SELECT DATE (DATE_TRUNC('month', date)) AS mm,
                          SUM(converted) AS ad_mon
```

5 There are three ways to obtain this information: (1) using an API to request daily reports from the individual ad networks like Unity, Facebook, *et al* that make up your mediation waterfall; (2) using an API to request aggregate daily reports from your ad mediation partner like ironSource or Applovin; or (3) using an MMP like Singular that aggregates this data on your behalf and surfaces it via consolidated daily reports. Unlike *purchase* events, ad mon data is not updated in real-time.

```
     FROM altrev
    WHERE date BETWEEN '2022-07-01' AND '2022-07-31'
    GROUP BY mm) ads USING (mm)
```

mm	net_iap	ad_mon	total_rev	pct_ad_rev
2022-07-01	755978.43	370808.17	1126786.60	32.9084

BFIT made just over C$1.1M in total net revenue (after platform fees and including ad monetization) in July of 2022. Of that total revenue, ad monetization accounted for 33%. Note that with ad monetization (including offer walls), there is no distinction between gross and net revenue. Ad mon is always net of any fees the ad networks and mediation platform have held back for themselves. These fees are not transparent.

Total revenue can also apply to a cohort. As a cohort metric, revenue increases over time as more and more purchases are made by the users still active within the cohort. Here is gross IAP revenue by install date instead of play date for all users who installed in July of 2022:

```
SELECT install_date,
       SUM(revenue) AS revenue
FROM (SELECT user_id,
             install_date
      FROM user_source
      WHERE install_date BETWEEN '2022-07-01' AND '2022-07-31') s
  LEFT JOIN (SELECT user_id,
                    SUM(converted) AS revenue
             FROM purchases_view
             GROUP BY user_id) p USING (user_id)
GROUP BY instalL_date
```

install_date	revenue
2022-07-01	13753.63
2022-07-02	13872.25
2022-07-03	10811.61
2022-07-04	13527.84
2022-07-05	9470.70
2022-07-06	11937.44
...	...

Run the query again tomorrow and you may see some of the revenue totals increase.

Instead of current total revenue, it is common to track daily revenue for a cohort as a function of days since install. Let $revenue_n$ denote the daily revenue on the nth day after install for a cohort of players. For instance, the revenue for just the users who installed on July 1st, but on subsequent days after install:

```
SELECT install_date,
       date_diff('day', install_date, purchase_date) AS
days_since_install,
       SUM(revenue) AS revenue
FROM (SELECT user_id,
             install_date
      FROM user_source
      WHERE install_date = '2022-07-01') s
  LEFT JOIN (SELECT user_id,
                    date as purchase_date,
                    SUM(converted) AS revenue
             FROM purchases_view
             GROUP BY user_id,
                      date) p USING (user_id)
GROUP BY installL_date,
         days_since_install
```

install_date	days_since_install	revenue
2022-07-01	0	435.90
2022-07-01	1	202.43
2022-07-01	2	226.98
2022-07-01	3	278.51
2022-07-01	4	159.53
2022-07-01	5	189.88
2022-07-01	6	216.22
2022-07-01	7	252.79
2022-07-01	8	172.54
2022-07-01	9	2.66
2022-07-01	10	159.32
...	...	...

In the last row, $159.32 was the IAP revenue generated by that cohort on July 11th, which is 10 days after their install date. The sum of the `revenue` column is the total revenue ($13,753.63) calculated in the prior query.

LTV: Lifetime Value

Customer lifetime value (**LTV**) is the average total revenue derived from a user from the moment they install until they churn. At ESG, we define *value* as gross IAP only, but many game studios include ad mon in the calculation. LTV is a cohort metric where the cohort can be comprised of everything from all players to a single user. Regardless of the size of the cohort, LTV is always an average:

$$\text{LTV} = \frac{\text{total cohort revenue}}{\text{cohort size}}$$

Current LTV for all players is given by the following:

```
SELECT cohort_revenue / cohort_size::FLOAT AS ltv
FROM (SELECT COUNT(*) AS cohort_size
      FROM user_source) i
  CROSS JOIN (SELECT SUM(converted) AS cohort_revenue
              FROM purchases_view) p
```

ltv
12.357

LTV for the July 2022 install cohorts is a simple change to the prior query for cohort revenue:

```
SELECT install_date,
       count(*) AS cohort_size,
       SUM(revenue) AS cohort_revenue,
       cohort_revenue / cohort_size::FLOAT AS ltv
FROM (SELECT user_id,
             install_date
      FROM user_source
      WHERE install_date BETWEEN '2022-07-01' AND '2022-07-31') s
  LEFT JOIN (SELECT user_id,
                    SUM(converted) AS revenue
             FROM purchases_view
             GROUP BY user_id) p USING (user_id)
GROUP BY installL_date
```

install_date	cohort_size	cohort_revenue	ltv
2022-07-01	1023	13753.63	13.4444
2022-07-02	1050	13872.25	13.2117
2022-07-03	1060	10811.61	10.1996
2022-07-04	1105	13527.84	12.2424
2022-07-05	1303	9470.70	7.2684
2022-07-06	1164	11937.44	10.2555
...	...	...	...

The `ltv` column is the cohort's average gross IAP revenue per player to date. Run the query again tomorrow and it may go up slightly.

Since there is no specific churn signal, LTV is commonly bracketed by a specific day after install. For example, a player's LTV7 is the sum of that user's IAPs made within seven days of install. If a player installs on July 1, 2022, the LTV7 time window closes at midnight on July 8th. Unlike retention, any purchase on any day between D0 and D7 counts as part of LTV7.

Calculating total revenue and LTV*n* for a cohort of installs is such a common requirement, we designed the `user_ltv` view in support. The monetization equivalent of `user_retention`, the `user_ltv` view contains a single row for each user and captures summary statistics – all converted to a common currency – regarding that player's history of IAPs.

```
describe user_ltv
```

COLUMN_NAME	DATA_TYPE	MEANING
user_id	varchar(40)	unique player identifier
platform	text	'ios' or 'android'
install_date	date	player's install date
ltv_7	numeric(38,2)	sum of gross IAP up to and including 7 days after install, or null if not fully baked.
ltv_30	numeric(38,2	ditto, but for 30 days
ltv_90	numeric(38,2)	ditto, but for 90 days
ltv_180	numeric(38,2)	ditto, but for 180 days
last_7	numeric(38,2)	sum of IAP over prior 7 days
ltv	numeric(38,2)	sum of IAP to date
first_purchase_date	date	null if ~converted
last_purchase_date	date	null if ~converted
first_purchase_level	integer	the player's game level when the first purchase was made
last_purchase_level	integer	what level the player was on
last_purchase_amount	numeric	price of last IAP
first_purchase_item	text	SKU of first item purchased (else null)
num_purchases	bigint	{0..n}
converted	integer {0, 1}	ltv > 0 ? 1 : 0

To illustrate, this query was executed on July 22, 2022, and captures LTV7, 30, 90, and current lifetime value to date (`ltv`) for a random sample of 10 players who installed within the prior 120 days.

```
SELECT install_date,
       CURRENT_DATE - install_date AS days_old,
       ltv_7,
       ltv_30,
       ltv_90,
       ltv
FROM user_ltv
WHERE install_date > CURRENT_DATE - 120
ORDER BY RANDOM() LIMIT 10
```

install_date	days_old	ltv_7	ltv_30	ltv_90	ltv
2022-06-23	29	0.00			0.00
2022-05-16	67	0.00	0.00		0.00
2022-06-17	35	0.00	0.00		0.00
2022-05-13	70	15.27	34.36		77.70
2022-04-08	105	0.00	0.00	0.00	0.00

install_date	days_old	ltv_7	ltv_30	ltv_90	ltv
2022-04-03	110	0.00	0.00	0.00	0.00
2022-06-13	39	0.00	0.00		0.00
2022-07-19	3				0.00
2022-06-18	34	8.41	8.41		8.41
2022-07-15	7				4.99

If only 5% of your players convert, you can expect a lot of zeroes in this result set. Note the use of a calculated field `days_old` to reinforce this notion that only when a player is fully baked with respect to the *n* days since install will they have a non-null value for LTV_*n*. The exception to this rule is the `converted` and `ltv` attributes of the `user_ltv` view: they are never null, and initialized to 0 and $0.00, respectively for any new player. The user who installed on May 13th is an interesting example: they installed the game 70 days prior to when the query was executed, so we did not yet know where their `ltv_90` would land, but we knew it would be *at least* $77.70 as indicated by `ltv`.

Given the `user_ltv` view, an alternative query for lifetime average LTV is simply:

```
SELECT AVG(ltv)
FROM user_ltv
```

A `WHERE` clause can specify any cohort of interest. As a cohort metric, LTV*n* is the average revenue per cohort member by the nth day after install:

$$\mathrm{LTV}_n = \frac{\sum_{i=0}^{n} \mathrm{revenue}_i}{\mathrm{cohort\ size}}$$

Calculating LTV*n* for the July 2022 daily install cohorts is simplified by the `user_ltv` view:

```
SELECT install_date,
       AVG(ltv_7) AS ltv7,
       AVG(ltv_30) AS ltv30,
       AVG(ltv) AS ltv
FROM user_ltv
WHERE install_date BETWEEN '2022-07-01' AND '2022-07-31'
GROUP BY install_date
```

install_date	ltv7	ltv30	ltv
2022-07-01	1.18	3.30	13.43
2022-07-02	0.90	2.04	13.21
2022-07-03	1.18	2.45	10.19
2022-07-04	2.30	6.68	12.23
2022-07-05	1.10	1.70	7.26
...	...	...	...

ARPDAU: Average Revenue Per Daily Active User

Average revenue per daily active user (ARPDAU, pronounced "arp-dow") is massively important and a key predictor of game success. As the name suggests, it is calculated daily by play date, and is revenue divided by DAU:

$$\text{ARPDAU}_d = \frac{\text{revenue}_d}{\text{DAU}_d}$$

By convention, the subscript d is used in formulas to represent a calendar date, and the metrics obtained from users who play on that same date. Conversely, the subscript n is a natural number and represents statistics from cohort users on their n^{th} day after install. If instead we were looking to measure *cohort* ARPDAU, the formula and notation would be:

$$\text{ARPDAU}_n = \frac{\text{revenue}_n}{\text{DAU}_n}$$

Cohort ARPDAU is a topic covered in a later chapter. For now, we concentrate on ARPDAU as a function of all daily active users on a specific calendar date.

There are a few flavours of ARPDAU depending on how you calculate the numerator. At ESG, we use gross IAP revenue only, but some studios include ad revenue as well.

```
SELECT  date,
        revenue / user_count::FLOAT as arpdau
FROM
  (SELECT date, COUNT(DISTINCT user_id) as user_count
   FROM session_begin
   WHERE date BETWEEN CURRENT_DATE - 31 AND CURRENT_DATE - 1
   GROUP BY date)
LEFT JOIN
  (SELECT date, SUM(converted) as revenue
   FROM purchases_view
   WHERE date BETWEEN CURRENT_DATE - 31 AND CURRENT_DATE - 1
   GROUP BY date) USING(date)
```

date	arpdau
2022-07-01	0.9867
2022-07-02	0.7406
2022-07-03	0.6652
2022-07-04	0.4719
2022-07-05	0.6193
2022-07-06	1.2271
...	...

The higher the ARPDAU the better. If a game's revenue is dependent on LiveOps, ARPDAU oscillates with peaks driven by regularly scheduled time-limited events. New content releases may also create temporary bumps in ARPDAU.

ARPDAU is a special case of the more general metric **ARPU**. ARPDAU is a daily metric, while ARPU ("arr-poo") is average revenue per user calculated over any arbitrary period. Monthly ARPU is the total revenue earned in a month divided by the total number of unique players in that month, while daily ARPU is equivalent to ARPDAU.

Ad-ARPDAU (AARPDAU) only considers ad revenue in the numerator. For example, if your game had 10 daily active users and earned $2.00 from ads, the Ad-ARPDAU is $0.20. Unlike IAP revenue, Ad-ARPDAU is fairly constant, as we see here:

```
SELECT  date,
        revenue / user_count::FLOAT as ad_arpdau
FROM
  (SELECT date, COUNT(DISTINCT user_id) as user_count
   FROM session_begin
   WHERE date BETWEEN CURRENT_DATE - 31 AND CURRENT_DATE - 1
   GROUP BY date)
LEFT JOIN
  (SELECT date, sum(converted) as revenue
   FROM altrev
   WHERE date BETWEEN CURRENT_DATE - 31 AND CURRENT_DATE - 1
   GROUP BY date) USING(date)
```

date	ad arpdau
2022-06-21	0.2038
2022-06-22	0.1434
2022-06-23	0.1776
2022-06-24	0.2126
2022-06-25	0.2072
2022-06-26	0.1934
2022-06-27	0.1817
...	...

ARPPU: Average Revenue Per Paying User

A player who makes an IAP is said to have **converted** and become a **paying user**. Average revenue per *paying* user is a way to gauge how well your catalogue of SKUs and price-points are resonating with your most engaged players. Yes, it's pronounced "arr-pee-poo." ARPPU is similar to ARPDAU or ARPU, except the denominator is the number of users who made a purchase on that date or within that period, respectively. Because we are only interested in counting the unique purchasers, its calculation does not require a join:

```
SELECT date,
       SUM(converted)/ COUNT(DISTINCT user_id)::FLOAT AS arppu
FROM purchases_view
WHERE date BETWEEN CURRENT_DATE- 31 AND CURRENT_DATE- 1
GROUP BY date
```

date	arppu
2022-07-01	14.8062
2022-07-02	14.7357
2022-07-03	12.4614
2022-07-04	10.9505
2022-07-05	12.2181
2022-07-06	20.0683
2022-07-07	23.3762
...	...

PDAU: Paying Daily Active Users

PDAU (pronounced "pee-dow") is calculated by date and is the number of active users who have made at least one in-app purchase at any point on or before that date. Some definitions of PDAU exclude the current date, requiring a player to convert prior to the date for which the ratio is being computed. In this case, players who make their first IAP on that date are counted not as PDAU but as **first-time buyers**.

Note that PDAU only counts in-app purchasers, and not those who watch rewarded video ads or complete offers.

It turns out that computing past PDAU from a history of purchases is somewhat tricky. The complexity arises from the fact that you can't look at all-time purchasers to derive a list of paying users; you can only look up to and including the date for which you are calculating total PDAU. However, there is an elegant solution in the form of an `ON` clause to exclude future purchase dates from the `LEFT JOIN` condition.

```
SELECT s.date, COUNT(DISTINCT p.user_id) AS pdau
FROM session_begin s
  LEFT JOIN purchases_view p
      ON s.user_id = p.user_id AND p.date <= s.date
WHERE s.date >= CURRENT_DATE- 30
GROUP BY s.date
```

date	pdau
2022-07-07	21334
2022-07-06	21174
2022-07-05	21309
2022-07-04	21671
...	...

PDAU/DAU is the percentage of your daily active users who have made a purchase on that play date or any day prior. It doesn't have its own cute name, unless you think "pee-dow over dow" is dear. A good ratio is 30% or more. *TPB* has consistently hovered around 40% since mid-2020. Of course, it will take time at the launch of a new title to get the PDAU growing. Let's look at the first few days of data from the world-wide launch of *TPB* back on April 20, 2017. If we modify that query above, we can also include DAU and the ratio of PDAU/DAU.

```
SELECT s.date,
       COUNT(DISTINCT s.user_id) AS dau,
       COUNT(DISTINCT p.user_id) AS pdau,
       pdau / dau ::FLOAT AS pct
FROM session_begin s
  LEFT JOIN purchases_view p
       ON s.user_id = p.user_id AND p.date <= s.date
WHERE s.date BETWEEN '2017-04-20' AND '2017-05-31'
GROUP BY s.date
```

date	dau	pdau	pct
2017-04-20	167446	4994	0.0298
2017-04-21	290537	10180	0.035
2017-04-22	333507	14430	0.0433
2017-04-23	393596	18642	0.0474
...	...	...	...
2017-05-28	246788	35607	0.1443
2017-05-29	250378	36333	0.1451
2017-05-30	248229	36719	0.1479
2017-05-31	242836	36327	0.1496

Within 40 days of launch, the ratio of PDAU to DAU rose from 3% to 15%.

Conversion Rate

Conversion rate (often abbreviated as CVR) is the proportion of paying users to total users over a specific period. Conversion rate measures the percentage of your players who see enough value in the game to make an IAP.

Normally we are interested in daily conversion: the number of distinct players who made a purchase on that date divided by the total number of unique players on that day. The denominator is simply DAU; the numerator is easy:

```
SELECT date, COUNT(DISTINCT user_id) as converted_users
FROM purchases_view
GROUP BY date
```

We join that subquery with our subquery for DAU, and voila:

```
SELECT date,
       converted_users / dau::FLOAT AS cvr
FROM (SELECT date,
             COUNT(DISTINCT user_id) AS dau
      FROM session_begin
      GROUP BY date)
  LEFT JOIN (SELECT date,
                    COUNT(DISTINCT user_id) AS converted_users
             FROM purchases_view
             GROUP BY date) USING (date)
ORDER BY date DESC LIMIT 30
```

date	cvr
2022-07-31	0.041
2022-07-30	0.0415
2022-07-29	0.0428
2022-07-28	0.0412
2022-07-27	0.0471
2022-07-26	0.0357
...	...

A daily conversion rate of 4% is a good target. Note that we drove the query with DAU and used a left join to grab the purchasers. You can't have purchasers without DAU (i.e., you can't make a purchase if you don't play), so this ensures that any potential date with a 0% conversion rate is included in the output.

A game's lifetime conversion rate is simply the total number of converted users divided by the total number of installs. As hinted at previously, the norm for free-to-play games is 5%. What is it for *BFIT*? The following query indicates 5.24% is that game's current lifetime conversion rate:

```
SELECT installs,
       converted_users,
       converted_users / installs::FLOAT AS cvr
FROM (SELECT COUNT(DISTINCT user_id) AS installs
      FROM user_source),
     (SELECT COUNT(DISTINCT user_id) AS converted_users
      FROM purchases_view)
```

installs	converted_users	cvr
5592047	292879	0.0524

Note the use of the cross-product to join the two metrics without the use of a logical condition. We could have used a `LEFT JOIN` with a `WHERE 1=1` clause instead.

Day n Conversion

Conversion by day *n* after install is also something we look to measure: what percentage of new users have made at least one IAP within the first *n* days after they install? This metric is cohort-based, therefore measured retroactively for each install date. The denominator is the size of the cohort.

The `user_ltv` view simplifies computation of D3, D7, and lifetime conversion rate for a series of install cohorts. To calculate D3 conversion, we make use of the `first_purchase_date` (which is null if a player has never made a purchase). To calculate D7 conversion we count the number of players with `ltv_7 > 0` then divide by the size of the cohort. Finally for lifetime conversion of each cohort, the `converted` binary property (0 = never made a purchase, 1 = has made at least one purchase since install) is coerced to a `FLOAT` then averaged:

```
SELECT install_date,
       COUNT(*) AS cohort_size,
       SUM(CASE WHEN first_purchase_date-install_date <= 3 THEN 1
END) AS d3c,
       SUM(CASE WHEN ltv_7 > 0 THEN 1 END) AS d7c,
       SUM(converted) AS converts,
       d3c / cohort_size::FLOAT AS d3cvr,
       d7c / cohort_size::FLOAT AS d7cvr,
       AVG(converted::FLOAT) AS cvr
FROM user_ltv
WHERE install_date BETWEEN '2022-07-10' AND '2022-07-31'
GROUP BY install_date
```

install_date	cohort_size	d3c	d7c	converts	d3cvr	d7cvr	cvr
2022-07-10	1160	26	37	40	0.0224	0.0319	0.0345
2022-07-11	1036	18	23	27	0.0174	0.0222	0.0261
2022-07-12	1002	34	41	41	0.0339	0.0409	0.0409
2022-07-13	1090	25	31	32	0.0229	0.0284	0.0294
2022-07-14	1343	32	37	37	0.0238	0.0276	0.0276
2022-07-15	1459	31		39	0.0212		0.0267
2022-07-16	1601	29		35	0.0181		0.0219
2022-07-17	1704	51		55	0.0299		0.0323
2022-07-18	1571	35		35	0.0223		0.0223
2022-07-19	1519			36			0.0237
2022-07-20	1528			29			0.019
2022-07-21	1576			16			0.0102
2022-07-22	723			7			0.0097
...	...	...	...	...	...	...	...

D*n* conversion is typically calculated by install date – as we have done here – resulting in a time series of the various D*n* conversion rates by install date. Nulls appear if the cohort is not yet fully baked: we prefer to return no answer instead of an incomplete one in the case of (for example) D7 conversion rate if the cohort is less than seven days old.

It is important not to confuse cohort conversion with daily conversion. Over time, the lifetime conversion rate for an install cohort can continue to increase as more and more laggards take the plunge and convert, whereas daily conversion rate is fixed in time once that calendar date is over. This behaviour is observed in the prior result set, where the number of players who convert by D3 is less than or equal those who convert by D7, which is less than or equal those who have converted at any point up to when the query is run. If you run the query tomorrow, you may find more `converts` and a higher lifetime conversion rate (`cvr`) for some of the install cohorts.

D3 and D7 conversion are strong signals of game health. When a new version of a game is released, it is important to keep a careful eye on these metrics for signs that something might have broken with the FTUE or with the early-level promos.

Conditional Probabilities in SQL

We now take a slight detour to discuss something important before we carry on with the marketing metrics.

A typical ad-hoc request from a game's team is of the form "what is the LTV90 of users who play on D7?" or "what is the likelihood a player converts by D7 if they don't play on D1?" You might recognize the latter request as a conditional probability statement. Expressed using the fields of the `user_ltv` and `user_retention` views, we have:

$$P(\text{ltv\_7} > 0 \mid \text{d1} = 0)$$

We read this as "the probability LTV7 > 0 *given* no D1 session." We can solve for this using the formula for conditional probabilities; namely,

$$P(\text{ltv\_7} > 0 \mid \text{d1} = 0) = P(\text{ltv\_7} > 0 \cap \text{d1} = 0) \; / \; P(\text{d1} = 0)$$

Always remember that the probability of some outcome is simply the number of desired outcomes divided by all possible outcomes. The denominator, $P(\text{d1} = 0)$, is the number of players who do not play on D1 (desired outcomes) divided by the total number of installs (all possible outcomes).

$$\text{count}(\text{d1} = 0) \;/\; \text{count}(\text{installs})$$

The numerator, $P(\text{ltv\_7} > 0 \cap \text{d1} = 0)$, is the number of players who convert by D7 and did not play on D1 divided by the total number of installs.

$$\text{count}(\text{ltv\_7} > 0 \text{ AND d1} = 0) \;/\; \text{count}(\text{installs})$$

The *count(installs)* cancel, and we are left with the count of players who convert by D7 and did not play on D1 divided by the count of players who did not play on D1:

$$P(\text{ltv\_7} > 0 \mid \text{d1} = 0) \equiv \text{count}(\text{ltv\_7} > 0 \text{ AND d1} = 0) \;/\; \text{count}(\text{d1} = 0)$$

Here is the query to compute this probability for all players who installed in July of 2022. A *given* is just a cohort restricted by a `WHERE` clause that implements the pre-condition. In this case, the players who did not play on D1, which is easily facilitated with an inner join on the two views with the fields we require:

```
SELECT SUM(CASE WHEN ltv_7 > 0 THEN 1 ELSE 0 END) AS d7_converts,
       COUNT(*) AS notD1,
       d7_converts / notD1::FLOAT AS prob
FROM user_ltv l
  INNER JOIN user_retention r USING (user_id)
WHERE l.install_date BETWEEN '2022-07-01' AND '2022-07-31'
AND    r.d1 = 0
```

d7_converts	notD1	prob
92	23472	0.0039

Regarding the other ad-hoc request, an estimate of the LTV by day 90 for players who play on D7 is calculated from similar SQL:

```
SELECT AVG(ltv_90) AS ltv90
FROM user_ltv l
  INNER JOIN user_retention r USING (user_id)
WHERE l.install_date BETWEEN '2022-07-01' AND '2022-07-31'
AND    r.d7 = 1
```

The key takeaway here is that you don't need to resort to the laws of probability, Bayes theorem, sampling, or estimates of prior probabilities to answer questions of this ilk. One can simply use SQL to limit the cohort to those exhibiting the *given* attribute. In general, if asked for the $P(\textit{player does A} \mid \textit{player did B})$ this translates into SQL of the following form:

```
SELECT COUNT(player does A)/COUNT(*)::FLOAT AS P
FROM players that did B
```

Marketing Metrics

At a game studio or publishing company, the **growth team** is responsible for running paid advertising campaigns to acquire users. Spending money to advertise your mobile game is an investment. The money you spend to advertise your game on ad networks such as Google, Facebook, Unity, Applovin, etc. is called **ad spend.** Like most investments, there are associated risks. In this case, the risk is that the players acquired through paid advertising don't monetize at a rate sufficient to pay back that investment; i.e., you lose money. Or in the parlance of performance marketing speak, "the ad spend didn't back out." Conversely, the potential reward is that the players acquired through advertising generate revenue that far exceeds the cost to acquire them.

The **fundamental theorem of the freemium business model** is that – in the aggregate – the cost to acquire customers is less than their lifetime value. This is most certainly true if you spend nothing on user acquisition (UA): after all, organic installs are free. However, generating enough organic installs to make the venture worth the effort has become virtually impossible. You will need to buy installs. For your paid installs, how many days will it take to earn that ad spend back? Can your game sustain spending money on acquiring users, or does it not retain and monetize the players well enough to make that money back? These questions are the topic of a later chapter, but for now we introduce a few key concepts.

CPI: Cost Per Install

The cost per install (CPI) is what you spent (the cost) on average to acquire each paid user. CPI can apply to any period, and to any cohort (platform, ad network, etc.), but typically it is calculated at the individual ad campaign level. This requires the help of an MMP in identifying the ad campaign responsible for each paid install. Armed with that intel, we have:

$$\text{CPI} = \frac{\text{campaign ad spend}}{\text{installs attributable to that campaign}}$$

For example, if you spend \$1,000 on an Applovin ad campaign targeting Android users, and your MMP attributes 250 installs to that campaign, the CPI is \$1,000/250 = \$4.00.

It is typical to look at campaign CPI on a weekly basis. The cohort of players acquired during the week are bucketed and tracked over time to see how they monetize in hopes that someday soon their LTV exceeds their CPI.

There are two other flavours of CPI:

1. **blended CPI**= $(ad\ spend)/(paid\ installs + organics)$ is calculated at the game or platform level; and,
2. **effective CPI**, or eCPI, is the equivalent of blended CPI, but at the ad campaign level; i.e.,

$$\text{eCPI} = \frac{\text{campaign ad spend}}{\text{paid + organic installs attributable to that campaign}}$$

Let's calculate the CPI and blended CPI by platform in the month of July. Expenditure by ad campaign is reported by each ad network. At ESG, this data is stored in the `adspend` table, which is updated daily by an ETL process owned by the game services team. Platform ad spend by date is defined by:

```
WITH ads AS
(
  SELECT date,
         platform,
         SUM(converted) AS spend
  FROM adspend
  GROUP BY date,
           platform
),
```

Joining with the attribution data stored in `user_source` gives us `CPI` (paid installs only) and `blended` CPI (paid plus organic installs) by platform.

```
installs AS
(
  SELECT install_date AS date,
         platform,
         SUM(CASE WHEN type = 'Organic' THEN 1 END) AS organics,
         SUM(CASE WHEN type <> 'Organic' THEN 1 END) AS paid
  FROM user_source
  GROUP BY date,
           platform
)
SELECT date,
       platform,
       paid,
       organics,
       spend,
       spend / paid::FLOAT AS CPI,
       spend / (paid+organics)::FLOAT AS blended
FROM installs
  LEFT JOIN ads USING (date, platform)
WHERE date BETWEEN '2022-07-01' AND '2022-07-31'
ORDER BY date, platform
```

date	platform	paid	organics	spend	CPI	blended
2022-07-01	android	213	327	1608.85	7.5533	2.9794
2022-07-01	ios	58	156	315.76	5.4441	1.4755
2022-07-02	android	173	348	1606.69	9.2872	3.0839
2022-07-02	ios	72	162	417.75	5.8021	1.7853
2022-07-03	android	185	342	1654.81	8.9449	3.1401
2022-07-03	ios	73	194	499.97	6.8489	1.8725
2022-07-04	android	214	327	1668.18	7.7952	3.0835
2022-07-04	ios	82	167	478.98	5.8412	1.9236
2022-07-05	android	206	314	1628.37	7.9047	3.1315
2022-07-05	ios	75	202	479.15	6.3887	1.7298
...	...	...	...	...	...	...

This result set indicates how much, on average, it is costing to acquire installs.

ROI: Return on Investment

Free-to-play games are a viable business when LTV exceeds CPI, or equivalently when revenue (net of platform fees) exceeds ad spend. The return on investment (ROI) for ad spend is the profit it generates; i.e., total revenue from the users acquired minus the expenditure to acquire them. This is often normalized as a percentage by dividing the profit by the amount invested:

$$\text{ROI} = \frac{(\text{total revenue from acquired users} - \text{ad spend})}{\text{ad spend}}$$

This is similar to how an investment portfolio is measured. ROI can be positive (yah!) or negative (boo!). Let's say those 250 installs we bought from Applovin for $4.00 each ended up generating $1,500 in revenue before all 250 players churned. In that case, the ROI was $500, or 50%. However, if those 250 users only generated $850 in revenue, the ROI is -$150 or -15%.

ROAS: Return on Ad Spend

Rather than think in absolute terms such as CPI and LTV, the growth team prefers to think in relative terms; specifically, the proportion of ad spend that acquired users return as revenue. Return on ad spend (**ROAS**) is a percentage defined by the ratio of LTV to CPI.

$$\text{ROAS} = \text{LTV}/\text{CPI}$$

When ROAS is greater than 100%, the ROI is positive, and the ad spend has backed out.

Typically, ROAS is measured on a cohort basis at a specific day after install. For example, D7ROAS is the ratio of the total revenue by D7 from acquired players divided by the total ad spend to acquire those players. In general:

$$DnROAS = \frac{\text{revenue by } Dn}{\text{ad spend}}$$

Or equivalently:

$$DnROAS = LTVn/CPI$$

A related metric is the **days to break even**. If an ad campaign backed out, how many days did it take to become profitable? This is the day n when (net) LTVn = CPI. From that day on, every dollar earned from that cohort is profit. Ideally you want your ad spend to back out as quickly as possible. Industry norms are to aim for less than 180 days, but this is highly dependent on a company's cash flow and stomach for risk.

Ad campaigns are created and monitored by UA managers, who often have specific **ROAS targets** by day n in mind, where $n \in \{1, 3, 7, 30\}$, etc. For example, a D7ROAS target of 20% means the goal is for 20% of a campaign's cost to be recovered by D7; i.e., $\text{LTV7} \geq 0.2 * \text{CPI}$. If a campaign is hitting these targets, the UA manager is confident that it will break even by a specific day, say D90 or D180, regardless of whether the CPI is $1.00 or $20.00. How these ROAS targets are calculated and how they can reliably predict days to break even is covered in a later chapter devoted to ROAS. But for now, here is a sneak preview. Say we want our ad spend to back out within 90 days. Based on how our users have monetized over the past year, we know this:

```
SELECT AVG(ltv_7) AS ltv7,
       AVG(ltv_90) AS ltv90,
       ltv7 / ltv90 AS d7roas_target
FROM user_ltv
WHERE install_date BETWEEN CURRENT_DATE - 365 AND CURRENT_DATE -91
```

ltv7	ltv90	d7roas_target
1.32	5.68	0.2323

In this case, 0.2323 is the average proportion of total LTV90 accumulated by D7 for all 90D fully-baked installs over the past year. A suitable D7ROAS target is thus the ratio of historical average LTV7 to LTV90. If an ad campaign's D7ROAS is 23.23% or higher, chances are good that it will break even by D90, regardless of the absolute value of its CPI. Moreover, since $1/0.2323 = 4.30$, the expected value of LTV90 for any new install cohort is their observed LTV7 multiplied by 4.30. For example, if an install cohort's LTV7 is $2.00, their expected (predicted) LTV90 is $8.60.

The Bathtub Analogy

These retention, monetization, and marketing metrics do not exist in isolation; they are interrelated. To visualize the relationship, think of a game as a bathtub full of water: the water level is the DAU, the size of the drain is the churn rate, and the water temperature is ARPDAU. The water taps are controlled by the growth team. What you want is a tub of water that is as deep and warm as possible. This maximizes daily revenue since:

$$\text{revenue}_d = \text{DAU}_d * \text{ARPDAU}_d$$

Therefore, to grow a game's revenue you need to either increase DAU or increase ARPDAU. The challenge is to increase one without decreasing the other. To increase DAU, you need to open the taps to let more water into the tub while simultaneously plugging the drain.

The churn rate is the responsibility of the game teams, as they are responsible for improving retention by creating an addictive experience with plenty of new content to keep players coming back. They are also responsible for ARPDAU. To increase ARPDAU, they need to increase conversion, experiment with pricing, and find more effective strategies to monetize their players.

Conversely, the water taps are opened and closed by the growth team, who spend money to advertise the game. Some of their campaigns produce hot water (monetizing players) while others result in lukewarm water (players that watch ads but do not make IAPs) or cold water (players that do neither). Worse, some ad campaigns bring in a bunch of low-quality users who churn right away, effectively introducing a double whammy of badness by increasing the size of the drain while simultaneously lowering ARPDAU. This is why the growth team is always the first to be blamed when retention or ARPDAU dips.

Keep in mind that the growth team is only going to spend money on acquiring users if retention and ARPDAU are significant enough for the ad spend to return a profit. In other words, if the tub has a small drain and the water stays warm. Then and only then will the taps be turned on. However, even if the growth team turns the taps off and stops running any UA campaigns, a trickle of water continues to flow into the tub in the form of organic installs. Some of these organic installs are hot, and some are cold.

In the absence of paid UA, the daily organic installs will tend to settle on a consistent level, as will both the ad- and IAP-ARPDAU. But what happens to the DAU? If the growth team turns off the taps, the water level must surely begin to drop as players churn down the drain at a rate faster than the organic installs trickle in. Where does it settle?

It turns out that if the number of installs per day is roughly consistent, DAU will settle at $(daily\ installs)/(churn\ rate)$. Multiplying by average ARPDAU, daily revenue is:

$$\text{revenue}_d = \frac{\text{installs}_d}{\text{churn rate}} * \text{ARPDAU}$$

This handy formula provides a floor on the estimated revenue a game is expected to produce. For example, if you know your organic installs are about 500/day, the churn rate is 5%, and the total ARPDAU averages $0.50, your daily revenue should be 500/0.05 * $0.50 = $5,000. That works out to $1.825M annually. Not bad, eh?

For this reason, the mantra at ESG is that the game teams should only worry about two things: retention and ARPDAU. To control for the effects of poor UA campaigns, measure these KPIs using only organic, US traffic. Ignore top-line revenue, plug the drain, and keep the water warm. The growth team will do the rest.

The *DAU Predictor* service featured at arpdau.com employs a different technique – explained in Chapter 4 – to predict DAU and daily revenue. Professor Arpdau's method is more appropriate for determining expected DAU for a new game launch; i.e., when you know early retention signals, but not the churn rate.

In the next chapter, we move from raw data to dashboards – KPI visualizations in the form of reports, charts, and graphs that enable the stakeholders to keep an eye on the bathtub.

Dashboards:
LEVEL 3

We now introduce a typical workflow for a game data analyst by walking through the steps of taking requirements, building a SQL query to extract a dataset, creating a Tableau workbook to visualize the dataset, and publishing the dashboard online for others on the team to access. This chapter covers some of the best-practices for filters, breakdowns, and visualizations required in a game KPI dashboard.

Tableau is commonly used to build KPI dashboards. Analysts use the Tableau Desktop app to create **workbooks** that are then uploaded to their company's private Tableau Online account in the cloud. Once published, the workbook is accessible to team members with the appropriate license and access credentials. Finally, a refresh schedule is established with Tableau Online to ensure the data in the workbook is updated periodically.

This chapter is in no way a thorough Tableau tutorial. There are plenty of excellent resources for that, including the classroom courses offered by Tableau (and speaking from my own experience, these are highly recommended). My objective is simply twofold: first, to indicate some of the basic concepts I wish I knew when first playing with the software; and, second, to highlight some of the standards and best practices employed at ESG.

Step 1: Gather Requirements

The product manager (PM) on the game team comes to you and says "I like your bathtub analogy. Can you build a dashboard that includes those metrics?" PMs are responsible for the features that make up a game, whereas producers are responsible for how and when those features make it into the game. It makes sense that a PM would want to track installs, DAU, ARPDAU, and churn. We know from experience that PMs want the ability to filter or drill-down their visualizations by platform, country, user type (paid vs. organic), and client version, so we are sure to build those filters into any dashboard before asking for their feedback.

Step 2: Build the Query

A dataset is required to build a dashboard in Tableau, which can be a CSV file, spreadsheet, or a SQL query run against a direct connection to a database server. ESG employs direct connections to its Amazon Redshift instance. Therefore, we need a query that produces the result set needed to correctly build the dashboard. This iterative process is best conducted using a SQL desktop tool before deploying the query to Tableau. For this, I personally use SQL Workbench/J, but the kids these days all seem to be in love with something called DBeaver.

The bathtub analogy includes mostly daily player data as opposed to cohort metrics like retention and LTV. The exception to this is installs, which is a cohort metric. The basic metrics that make up the bathtub are:

```
<date, installs, dau, arpdau, churn>
```

We know from the previous chapter how to calculate all these metrics. However, to support the filters and breakdowns PMs like to use, we need to group these metrics by cohorts made up of the player's platform, country (also known as **geo**, short for geography), type, and software version running on their device. This dictates the following additional fields:

```
<date, platform, geo, user_type, version, installs,dau,arpdau,churn>
```

where:

- `platform` ∈{`'ios'`, `'android'`};
- `geo` ∈{`'US'`, `'CW'`, `'ROW'`} where `'CW'` are the major English-speaking commonwealth countries of Canada, Great Britain, Australia, and New Zealand, and `'ROW'` stands for the "rest of the world";
- `user_type` ∈ {`'Paid'`, `'Organic'`}; and,
- `version` is the software release number on the client active during the days covered by the query.

Instead of having one row per calendar day, we will have several. Some sample rows might look like this:

date	platform	geo	version	user_type	installs	dau	arpdau	churn
2022-07-02	android	ROW	1.26.5	Organic	111	2654	0.2955	0.0479
2022-07-02	android	ROW	1.26.5	Paid	37	3448	0.4566	0.0334
2022-07-02	android	US	1.26.3	Organic	19	1824	0.8795	0.0338
2022-07-02	android	US	1.26.3	Paid	1	1535	0.7	0.0274
2022-07-02	android	US	1.26.5	Organic	140	6009	0.8531	0.0294

date	platform	geo	version	user_type	installs	dau	arpdau	churn
2022-07-02	android	US	1.26.5	Paid	117	5013	1.093	0.0343
2022-07-02	ios	CW	1.26.3	Organic	1	535	0.9707	0.0262
2022-07-02	ios	CW	1.26.3	Paid	0	226	0.8711	0.0049
2022-07-02	ios	CW	1.26.5	Organic	45	4246	0.6359	0.0288
2022-07-02	ios	CW	1.26.5	Paid	0	1519	0.7469	0.0088
2022-07-02	ios	ROW	1.26.3	Organic	0	415	0.7694	0.0447
2022-07-02	ios	ROW	1.26.3	Paid	1	237	0.1992	0.0312
...	...	...	...	...	...	...	...	...

The values for `installs`, `dau`, `arpdau`, and `churn` are a function of the other attributes in each row.[1] For example, in the first row above we see exactly 111 organic installs on July 2, 2022, who were playing on version 1.26.5 on Android in a country outside of the US and the Commonwealth. None of those 111 users are counted as part of the installs in any other row with that same date.

Tableau is a pivot table on steroids, and prefers to work with a single dataset containing all the attributes to be visualized and/or required to calculate the KPIs. To facilitate the correct aggregation and weighted average for ARPDAU and churn rate – an average and proportion, respectively – it is important to provide the raw data and let Tableau calculate those values by aggregating over the currently active `platform`, `geo`, `user_type`, and `version` filters. Since ARPDAU = IAP/DAU, and we already have DAU in our relation, we can replace the ARPDAU field with the total revenue contributed by that cohort on that date. Likewise, the churn rate is the ratio of the DAU who last played on that date, so rather than have the query calculate the churn *rate* we instead include the *count* of churned users and leave the calculation to Tableau.

Now that we know what our dataset should look like, let's turn our attention to writing the SQL to generate it. The daily players on each date come from the `session_begin` table. The `platform`, `version`, and `last_date` (to indicate the last day a user played, used in the calculation of the churn count) attributes are also available from this table. However, a user

[1] Some of you might recognize this as third normal form (3NF), where every attribute depends on the key, the whole key, and nothing but the key. In this case, the unique key is the composite of `<date, platform, geo, user_type, version>`.

can start a day playing on a specific `version` of the app, upgrade, and play again. To avoid counting the player twice, we use a window function to only consider the `version` active in their last session of the day:

```
SELECT DISTINCT date,
            user_id,
            platform,
            LAST_VALUE(version) OVER
                (PARTITION BY user_id, date ORDER BY timestamp
                 ROWS BETWEEN UNBOUNDED PRECEDING AND UNBOUNDED
            FOLLOWING) AS version,
            LAST_VALUE(date) OVER
                (PARTITION BY user_id ORDER BY date
                 ROWS BETWEEN UNBOUNDED PRECEDING AND UNBOUNDED
            FOLLOWING) AS last_date
        FROM session_begin
            WHERE date BETWEEN '2022-07-01' AND '2022-07-31'
```

Consider the following raw data for a specific user on a date where they played on two different versions of the client:

date	user_id	platform	version	timestamp
2022-07-25	1000465	ios	1.26.5	2022-07-25 13:45:26
2022-07-25	1000465	ios	1.26.5	2022-07-25 13:49:45
2022-07-25	1000465	ios	1.26.5	2022-07-25 21:41:50
2022-07-25	1000465	ios	1.26.5	2022-07-25 21:42:22
2022-07-25	1000465	ios	1.26.6	2022-07-25 22:13:41
2022-07-25	1000465	ios	1.26.6	2022-07-25 22:15:16
2022-07-25	1000465	ios	1.26.6	2022-07-25 22:16:08
2022-07-25	1000465	ios	1.26.6	2022-07-25 22:18:13

These rows make up the `PARTITION BY` clause. After ordering by `timestamp`, the last value of the `version` column contains the appropriate data. The `DISTINCT` clause ensures only a single row per user per date, regardless of the number of sessions played.

There are two window functions in this query, with the second used to calculate the date of the player's last session (`last_date`). In this case, the window function only partitions by `user_id` and orders by the `date` of every session for that user. The `LAST_VALUE` of the `date` column is the date of that user's last known play date. However, if the query uses a `WHERE` clause to only consider sessions within a specific end point (e.g., July of 2022 as we have done here), our logic is defeated: our partition is truncated, resulting in a `last_date` that can never be greater than July 31st regardless of whether users played in August or later.

To remedy this, we use a CTE to define a set of session dates unbounded by the future:

```
WITH users AS
(SELECT DISTINCT date,
            user_id,
            platform,
            LAST_VALUE(version) OVER (PARTITION BY user_id, date
ORDER BY timestamp ROWS BETWEEN UNBOUNDED PRECEDING AND UNBOUNDED
FOLLOWING) AS version,
            LAST_VALUE(date) OVER (PARTITION BY user_id ORDER BY
date ROWS BETWEEN UNBOUNDED PRECEDING AND UNBOUNDED FOLLOWING) AS
last_date
        FROM session_begin
        WHERE DATE >= '2022-07-01')
```

This ensures the `last_date` is correct at the time of query execution, even if we box the results to a specific date or range of dates:

```
SELECT COUNT(DISTINCT user_id)
FROM users
WHERE DATE BETWEEN '2022-07-01' AND '2022-07-31'
  AND last_date > '2022-07-31'
```

count
75049

Mission accomplished. There were 75,049 players (so far) who played in July of 2022 and have played at least one day *after* July 31, 2022.

To grab the other required attributes (the player's `user_type` and `country/geo`) for each of our DAU, we need to join with the `user_source` view. To count `installs` we also require each player's `install_date`. We can simply add that to the CTE as follows:

```
WITH users AS
(SELECT DISTINCT date,
            install_date,
            user_id,
            s.platform,
            LAST_VALUE(s.version) OVER (PARTITION BY user_id, date
ORDER BY timestamp ROWS BETWEEN UNBOUNDED PRECEDING AND UNBOUNDED
FOLLOWING) AS version,
            LAST_VALUE(date) OVER (PARTITION BY user_id ORDER BY
date ROWS BETWEEN UNBOUNDED PRECEDING AND UNBOUNDED FOLLOWING) AS
last_date,
            country, type
        FROM session_begin s
LEFT JOIN user_source USING (user_id)
        WHERE date >= '2022-07-01')
```

With that added we now have all the attributes required to calculate the installs and DAU for every combination:

```
SELECT date,
       platform,
       version,
       country,
       type,
       COUNT(DISTINCT user_id) AS dau,
       SUM(CASE WHEN install_date = date THEN 1 END) AS installs
FROM users
WHERE date BETWEEN '2022-07-01' AND '2022-07-31'
GROUP BY date, platform, version, country, type
```

However, we don't want to `GROUP BY` every possible value for `type` and `country`; instead, we only need to differentiate the paid and organic users from three distinct geos. This is accomplished[2] through `CASE` statements:

```
CASE
  WHEN country = 'US' THEN 'US'
  WHEN country IN ('CA','GB','AU','NZ') THEN 'CW'
  ELSE 'ROW'
END AS geo,
CASE
  WHEN type = 'Organic' THEN 'Organic'
  ELSE 'Paid'
END AS user_type
```

Then we group by geo and `user_type` instead.

The `churned` are measured with one more `CASE` statement that adds up all the instances where the session date is a player's last play date:

```
SUM(CASE WHEN date = last_date THEN 1 ELSE 0 END) AS churned
```

All that is left to do is calculate the daily IAP revenue for each cohort. This is facilitated by adding an additional CTE to aggregate each payer's total IAP by date:

```
payers AS
(
```

---

[2] This could also be accomplished in Tableau with *Sets* or *Groups*, in which case the SQL could be left as-is. Moreover, the `DECODE` function in SQL is an alternative to the use of `CASE` statements.

```
    SELECT date,
           user_id,
           SUM(converted) AS iap
    FROM purchases_view
    WHERE date BETWEEN '2022-07-01' AND '2022-07-31'
    GROUP BY date,
             user_id
  )
```

then joining payers with users on both date and user_id. Joining by user_id is required to bucket the revenue according to the payer's cohort. The completed query (and some sample rows) is thus:

```
SELECT date,
       platform,
       version,
       CASE
         WHEN country = 'US' THEN 'US'
         WHEN country IN ('CA','GB','AU','NZ') THEN 'CW'
         ELSE 'ROW'
       END AS geo,
       CASE
         WHEN type = 'Organic' THEN 'Organic'
         ELSE 'Paid'
       END AS user_type,
       COUNT(DISTINCT user_id) AS dau,
       SUM(CASE WHEN install_date = date THEN 1 ELSE 0 END)
         AS installs,
       SUM(CASE WHEN date = last_date THEN 1 ELSE 0 END) AS churned,
       SUM(iap) AS iap
FROM users
  LEFT JOIN payers USING (user_id, date)
WHERE date BETWEEN '2022-07-01' AND '2022-07-31'
GROUP BY date,
         platform,
         version,
         geo,
         user_type
```

date	platform	version	geo	user_type	dau	installs	churned	iap
2022-07-01	android	1.26.3	CW	Organic	1178	5	19	753.06
2022-07-01	android	1.26.3	CW	Paid	728	0	14	748.78
2022-07-01	android	1.26.3	ROW	Organic	1210	22	48	498.21
2022-07-01	android	1.26.3	ROW	Paid	1747	17	67	1027.60

date	platform	version	geo	user_type	dau	installs	churned	iap
2022-07-01	android	1.26.3	US	Organic	2563	27	64	1975.35
2022-07-01	android	1.26.3	US	Paid	2070	3	30	2599.82
2022-07-01	android	1.26.4	CW	Organic	5	0	0	
2022-07-01	android	1.26.4	CW	Paid	3	0	1	
...	...	...	...	...	...	...	...	...

Step 3: Create the Dashboard

Now that the query is debugged and ready to go, we can move it to Tableau[3] with a connection to our Amazon Redshift instance.

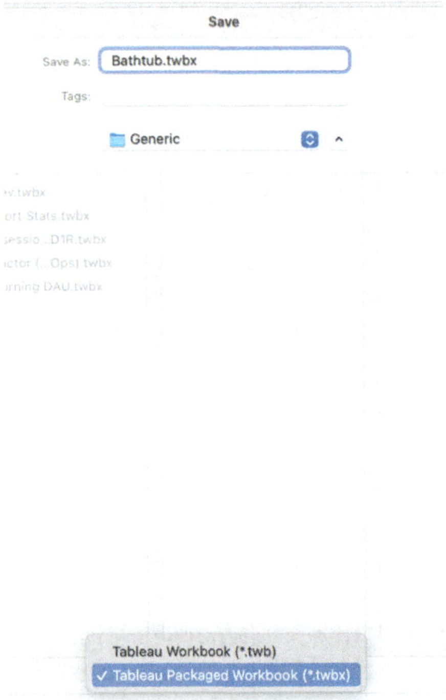

After entering our credentials and landing in the Data tab of a new workbook, the very first thing we do is *Save As...* and change the filetype to a *Packaged Workbook (*.twbx)*.

This saves the extracted dataset from any query executed against Redshift within the workbook itself.

We name the packaged workbook file `Bathtub`.

Next, use the *Schema* dropdown to select the appropriate schema where the analytics tables reside. In our case, it's in the `public` schema.

Double-click on *New Custom SQL* at the bottom of the list of the tables in the schema and copy-and-paste the debugged query from your SQL desktop tool into Tableau's editor.

[3] The examples in this chapter are from Tableau Desktop version 2022.4.

This next step is very important when dealing with large datasets and queries that can take minutes to complete. Choose *Extract* instead of a *Live* connection to the data source. Click *Save* to run the query, create the extract, and save it within your packaged workbook. A *Live* connection is fine if you are dealing with a trivial query or a spreadsheet/CSV, but otherwise can severely impede your work.

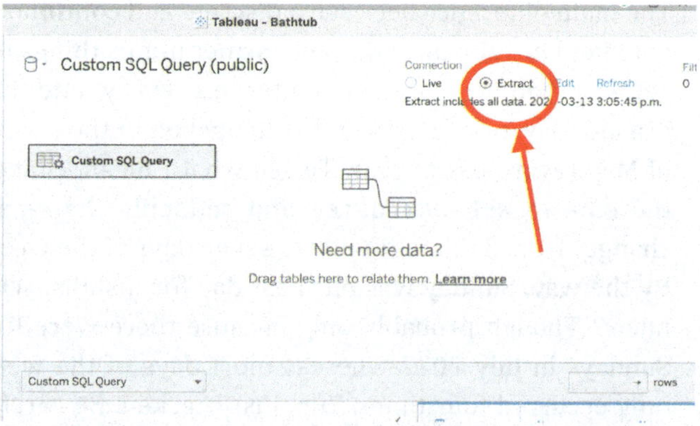

With our data saved, we are ready to begin creating the charts. Let's start with a simple installs-by-date line chart. Click on *New Worksheet* at the bottom next to *Data Source* to create a new tab and rename it `Players`. Everything we are going to visualize in this exercise is a time-series line chart with the date as a column (i.e., the *x*-axis). However, when you drag a date field from the *Measure Names* section, Tableau's default behaviour is to treat the data as a *Discrete* rather than *Continuous* measure; i.e., it's a blue pill instead of green. You end up with a single data point instead of a line chart.

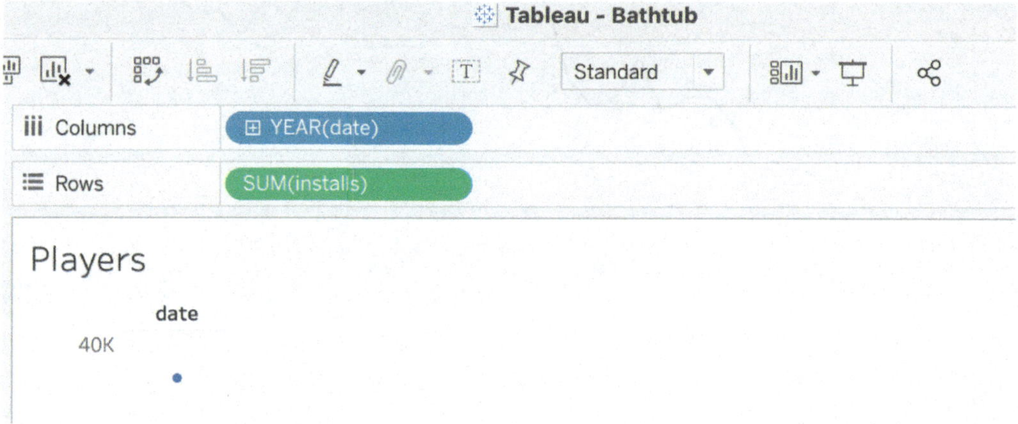

This drove me nuts when I was trying to learn Tableau on my own, but the fix is easy once you are shown how. Click on the right side of the blue pill to activate its drop-down (not the + sign on the left… that will lead you into a whole other world of pain) and change the date's datatype from the currently selected discrete *Year* to a continuous *Day* (indicated by the red arrow in the next figure).

The main difference between a discrete and continuous date field in Tableau is that the former lumps things together based on shared attributes; e.g., every date that is a Monday, or everything that happened in the month of May regardless of year. To see what I mean, change the date to `WEEKDAY(date)` and suddenly the *x*-axis changes from 31 dates in July to seven days of the week. By the way, Sunday was our best day for installs. Who knew? Though probably only because there were five Sundays in July 2022 whereas most days of the week only occurred four times. Yup, just checked. Be careful you don't get fooled into false assumptions.

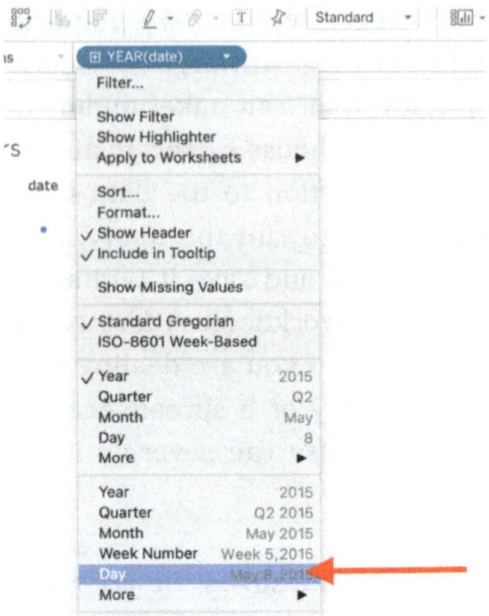

After making this change of type, we have a more reasonable graph of installs-by-date for the month of July:

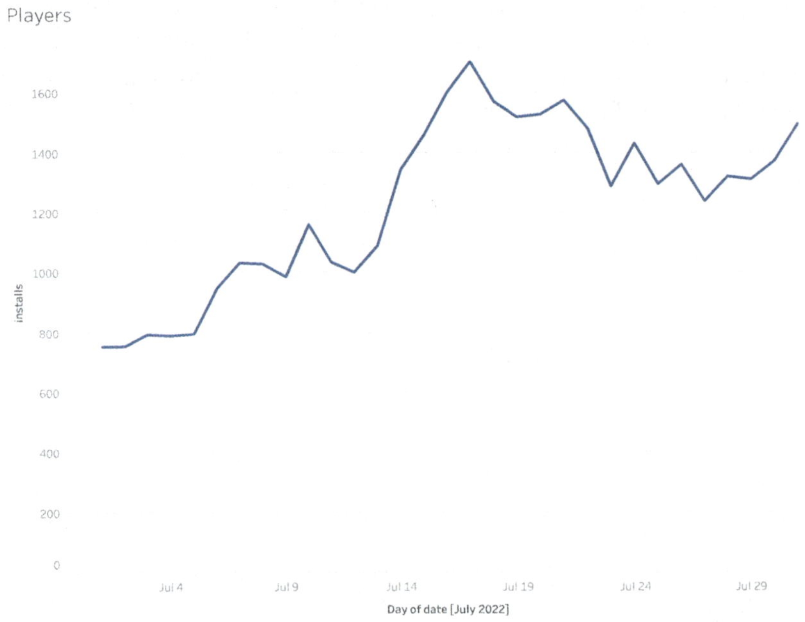

We Really Need to Talk About Aggregates

Recall that our dataset is made up of several rows for each calendar date. When a *Dimension* like `installs` is dragged onto the *Rows* shelf to create a chart, Tableau needs to aggregate the different values for `installs` that appear in the many rows that make up a single point in a line chart. The default behaviour is to `SUM` them together, which is normally what you want, but not always. It worked for `installs`, but it is vital you choose the correct aggregate function when graphing data and/or creating your own *Calculated Fields.*

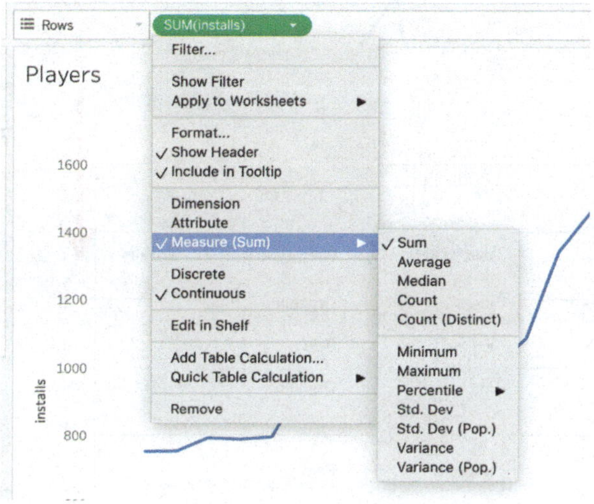

To see why this is important, change the aggregation from *Sum* to *Average* by right-clicking on the `installs` pill in the shelf (see left). Instead of adding up the installs that share the same date, Tableau now takes the average of those same values. The nature and shape of the line chart changes significantly, as shown below.

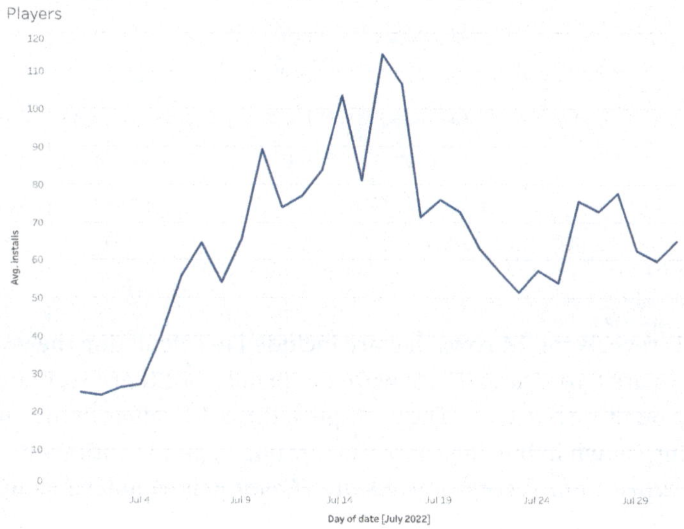

Our daily installs have gone from a high of 1600+ to a peak of < 120. The scale of the *y*-axis has changed significantly. Where did the installs go? They are still there, just being treated differently.

To see what's happening, I find it useful to refer to the raw data, which you can always find by right-clicking on any point in a chart and selecting *View Data...* Let's look at the highest point in this chart and check out some of the columns of the *Full Data*:

View Data: Players (1 mark)

Tabs

Summary

Full Data

Full Data 14 rows 5 fields

Custom SQL Query **Day of date**	Custom SQL Query **geo**	Custom SQL Query **platform**	Custom SQL Query **user_type**	Custom SQL Query **installs**
July 16, 2022	ROW	ios	Organic	31
July 16, 2022	CW	ios	Paid	78
July 16, 2022	CW	ios	Organic	96
July 16, 2022	US	ios	Paid	141
July 16, 2022	US	android	Paid	249
July 16, 2022	CW	android	Organic	97
July 16, 2022	ROW	android	Organic	175
July 16, 2022	ROW	android	Paid	104
July 16, 2022	ROW	ios	Paid	18
July 16, 2022	CW	ios	Paid	0
July 16, 2022	US	ios	Organic	264
July 16, 2022	US	android	Organic	223
July 16, 2022	CW	android	Paid	0
July 16, 2022	CW	android	Paid	125

10,000 → rows

This reveals the 14 rows that are included in calculating the *y*-value. In the `installs` column, there are two zeroes: there were no installs, but there were dau on a specific `version` of the app on those two days. The average of these 14 values in the `installs` column is what is now being shown in the line chart. The *y*-value depends entirely on the aggregation applied. If you switched from *Average* to *Median* to *Count* you would get completely different charts.

Filters

Now let's start adding *Filters*. Whereas the aggregation function defines how the values across rows are combined, filters decide which rows are included/excluded in the calculation. As mentioned right at the start of this chapter, we know that PMs like to drill down into specific time periods (date ranges) by platform, geo, user type, and version. This is effectively every

Measure in the workbook. Dragging those five measures into the *Filters* box, clicking on *Use all* to include every value, then choosing to *Show Filter* provides a way for users of the dashboard to restrict the displayed data to specific cohorts; e.g., only US, organic, Android users on version 1.26.5, as follows:

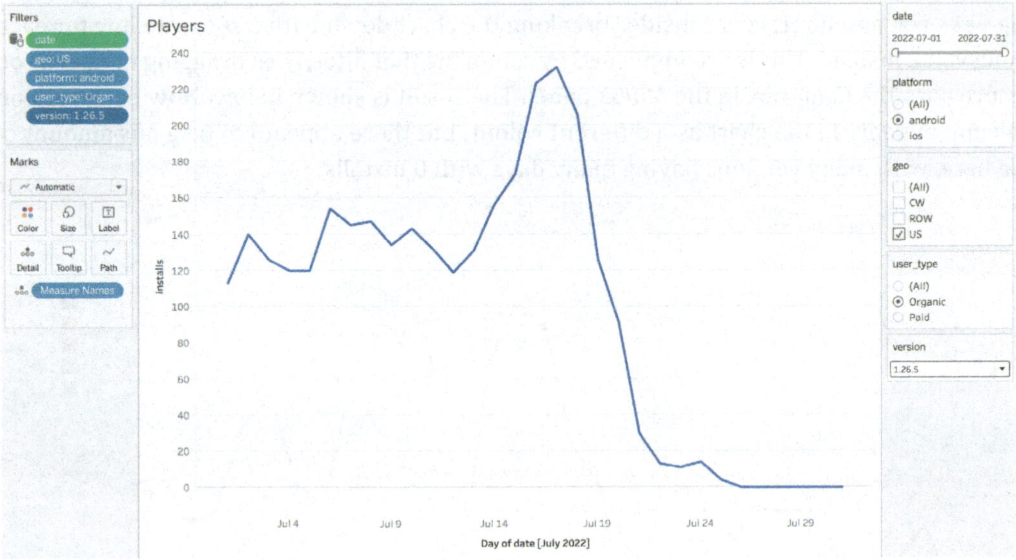

I have changed the setting to *Single Value (List)* for those filters with only two choices: `platform` and `user_type`. There are a lot of different versions of the game in play during this timeframe, so the best choice for the `version` filter is *Multiple Values (dropdown)*.

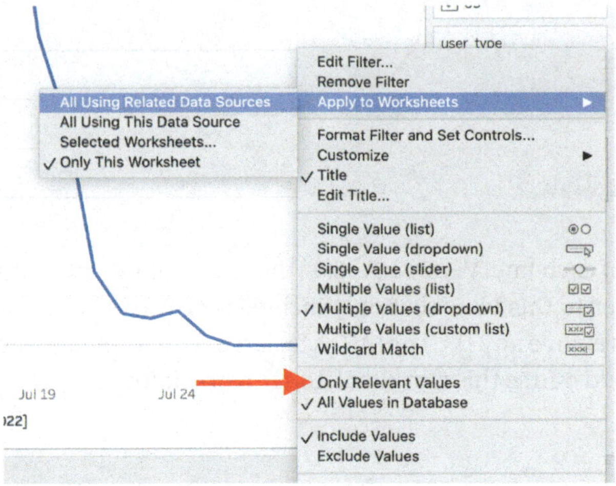

Two settings that you should consider applying to all filters are:

1. *Apply to Worksheets — All Using Related Data Sources*; and,

2. *Only Relevant Values.*

The former ensures that as your users switch from tab to tab, any choices for filters remain in place. The latter helps reduce the number of options in a drop-down when other choices render them irrelevant. While in general adopting this setting is good practice, it won't always make the most sense from a usability standpoint.

Breakdowns

Watching how a KPI behaves as new software versions are released is important. Rather than using `version` as a filter, let's consider breaking the chart down with a separate line for each distinct value instead. This is accomplished by removing that filter, then dragging the `version` measure onto the *Color* box in the *Marks* panel. The result is shown below. Now each version of the app appears in the chart as a different colour, but there appears to be a fair amount of noise here, with many versions having many days with 0 installs:

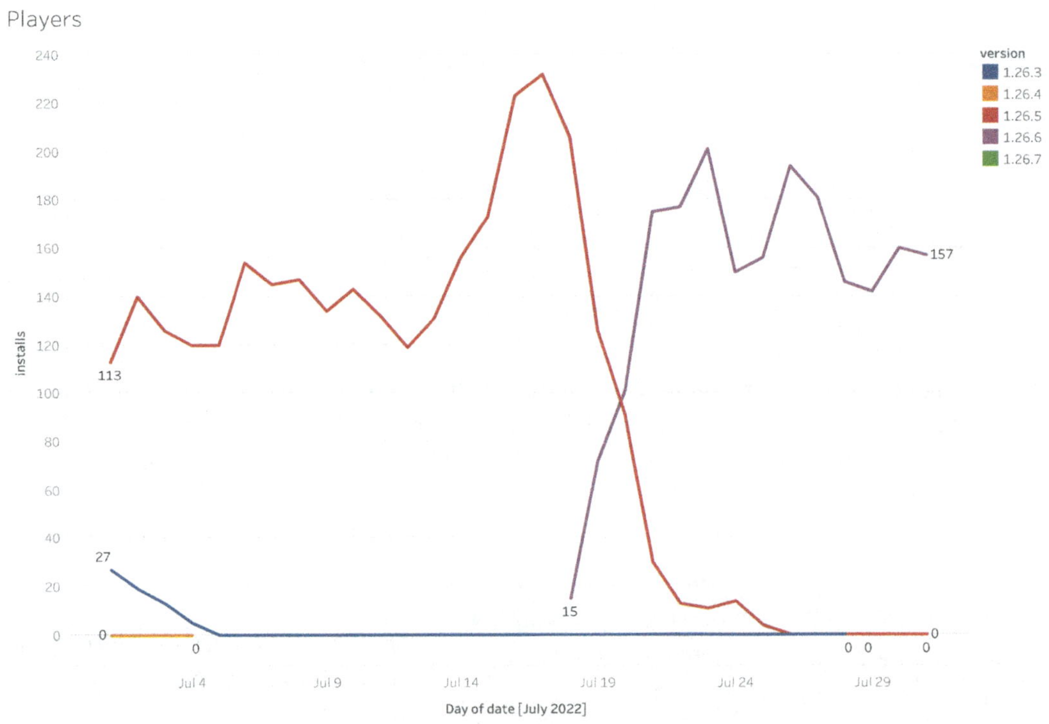

I have added *Labels* to the start and end of each line. Version 1.26.4 (the orange line) only ever has 0 installs. A simple fix is to add a filter to this view that only includes records where `installs > 0`. Though be careful: that will remove any DAU or IAP associated with users playing on that version. Speaking of which, let's add `dau` to this workbook to see a breakdown of active users by `version`:

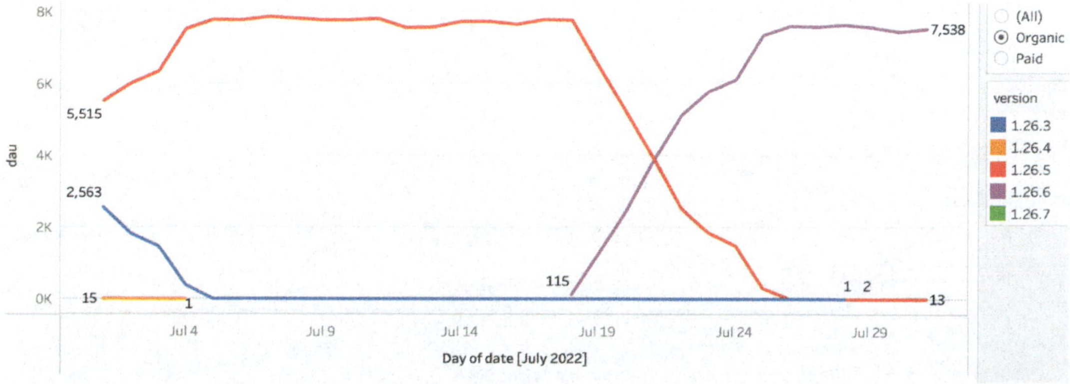

An obvious problem with this visualization is it obscures the total DAU. Is it climbing or falling? What was it on July 1st? Don't make me think! Two possible solutions are to switch the visualization to a stacked bar chart:

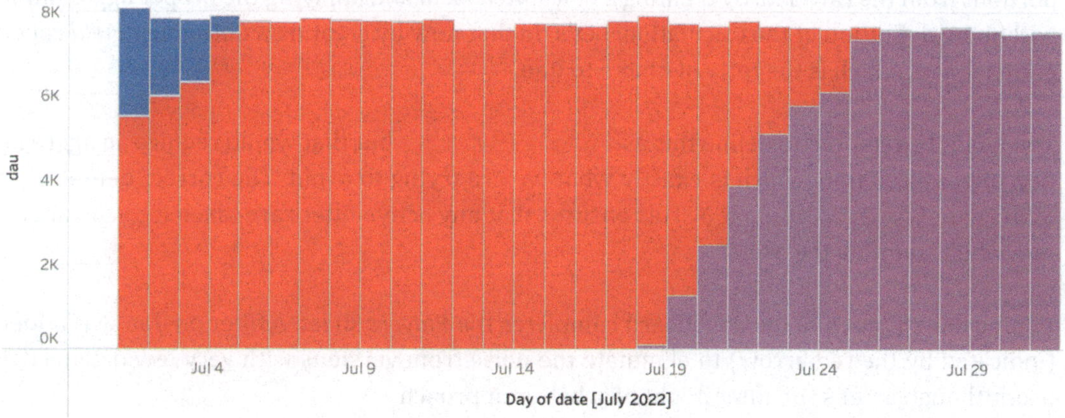

Or, add a second graph of `dau` that is not broken down by version, combining this total DAU graph into a *Dual Axis* with the original DAU graph, and applying *Synchronize Axis* to the total DAU's *y*-axis. The total DAU is the grey line at the top of the following chart:

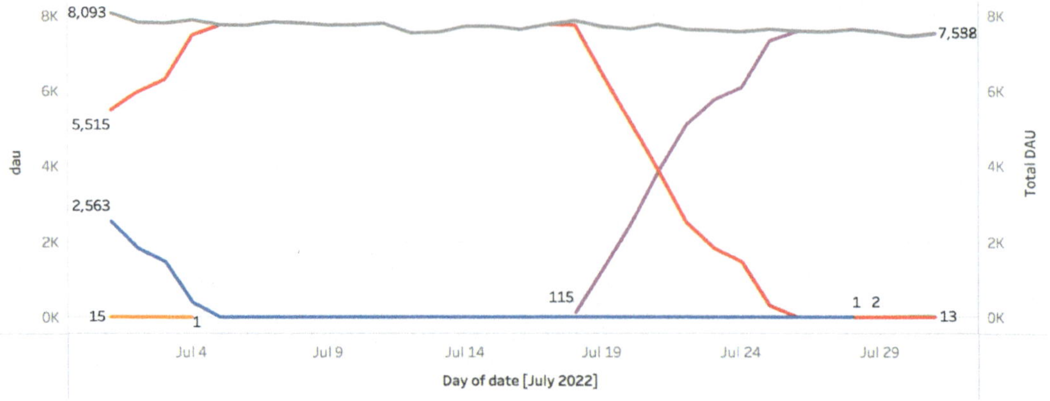

It's a matter of personal preference. Either way, DAU is clearly falling, at least for this cohort defined by the applied filters (i.e., organic, US, Android).

Aggregating Proportions

When it comes to proportions, a common mistake is to use the wrong aggregation function (*Sum* instead of *Average*) or more importantly, to aggregate at all. Summing a proportion will give you bizarre results like D1 retention > 100%. You are better off defining your own proportions from the raw data by creating a *Calculated Field* and applying the proper aggregation within the definition of the calculation. Let's do that now by creating a *Calculated Field* called `churn_rate`, which is the ratio of `churn` to `dau`.

You might be tempted to define this as `[churned]` / `[dau]` but that would require an aggregation after calculation, which is exactly what we are trying to avoid. The correct definition is `SUM([churned])/SUM([dau])`. This ensures that any active filters are taken into consideration when counting the users.

Adding `churn_rate` to the dashboard completes the *Players* sheet. A filter on `dau` was added (indicated by the red arrow) to eliminate the noise from versions with very few daily active users, though a `version` filter might be a better approach:

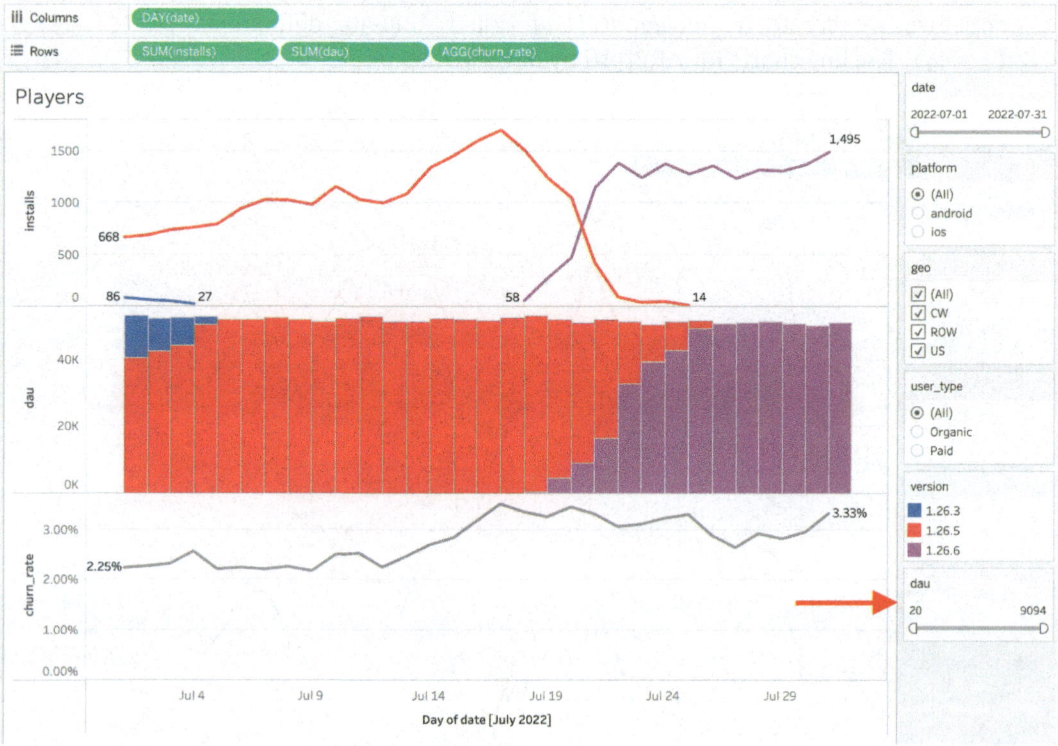

Adding a `version` breakdown to the `churn_rate` chart reveals a common problem when releasing new versions of the code; namely, a spike in churn. When players are forced to update (in this case from 1.26.3 to 1.26.5, then from 1.26.5 to 1.26.6), many will churn rather than visit the platform store to update the app on their device:

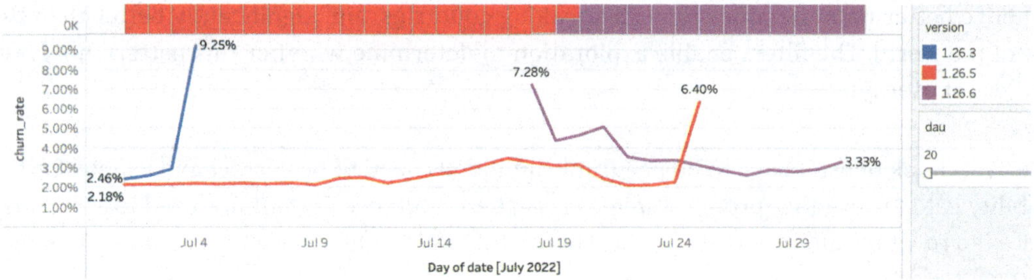

Now let's add the monetization metrics to their own worksheet (tab). This time we want to do a breakdown by `geo` to get a sense of how well the game is monetizing with players from around the world. Likewise, we want to include a breakdown by `platform` in its own chart. Total revenue is not particularly interesting to us: PMs focus on ARPDAU. Like we did with `churn_rate`, we create a *Calculated Field* called ARPDAU, defined as `SUM([iap]) / SUM([dau])`. The line charts for ARPDAU by day are thus:

Note the same filters are included and in the same order as the *Players* sheet. Not surprisingly, we see that iOS players monetize better than Android (bottom). Moreover, players in the US monetize better than the other English-speaking countries, and significantly better than the rest of the world. The filters enable exploration to determine whether this pattern holds regardless of user type.

> Your workbook doesn't have to be beautiful, but it does need to be correct and usable. Part of usability is to ensure that proper *Default Properties – Number Format* are used for *Measures* related to revenue and proportions; e.g., change ARPDAU to *Currency* and `churn_rate` to *Percentage*.

Trend Lines

What about the trend? Is ARPDAU on the rise, or in decline? Adding a *Trend Line* to these graphs is a handy way to visualize where things are headed, especially when the line is very bumpy like the ARPDAU charts.

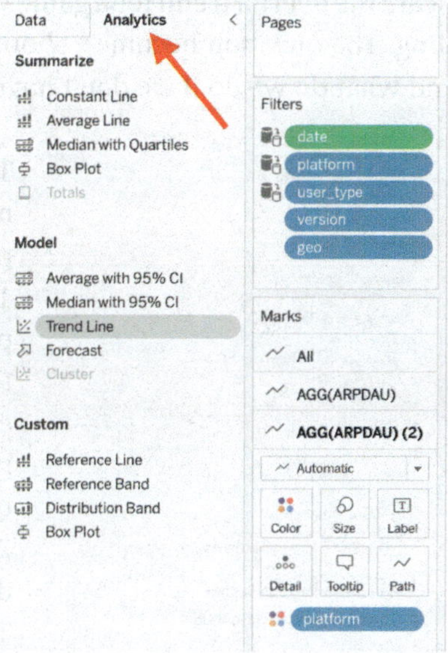

On the *Analytics* tab, there are various *Models* we can add to any time series, including a time-series *Forecast*. To start, drag a *Trend Line* and choose *Linear* as the type. This overlays a straight, dashed line that is a best-fit to the existing data points for the month of July.

We see that in each case, the trend is looking good, with ARPDAU on the rise for each of the five different line graphs. Whether this is indicative of improvements to the game or an artifact of the LiveOps schedule is left to the PM to determine.

Rather than a *Trend Line*, overlaying a seven-day moving average is likely a better way to indicate the overall trend for a game whose monetization is correlated to LiveOps content scheduling. The question becomes, should we incorporate the previous values, or the next values? And what do we do if we don't have a full set of values?

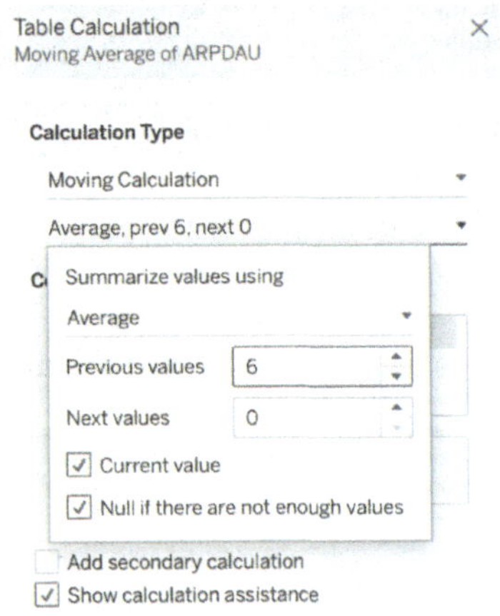

To the left are settings to display a seven-days-previous moving average, including the current data point. To incorporate previous values yet still have our chart begin on July 1st, the query window must be extended further into the past to incorporate the moving average size. Or, alternatively, you can deselect the choice of *Null if there are not enough values,* but that defeats the smoothing inherent in a moving average. Using the settings to the left, and with the query and date filter extended to include data from June 25th, the following chart begins on the 1st as that is the first date with enough values to calculate the moving average. The same trend lines remain:

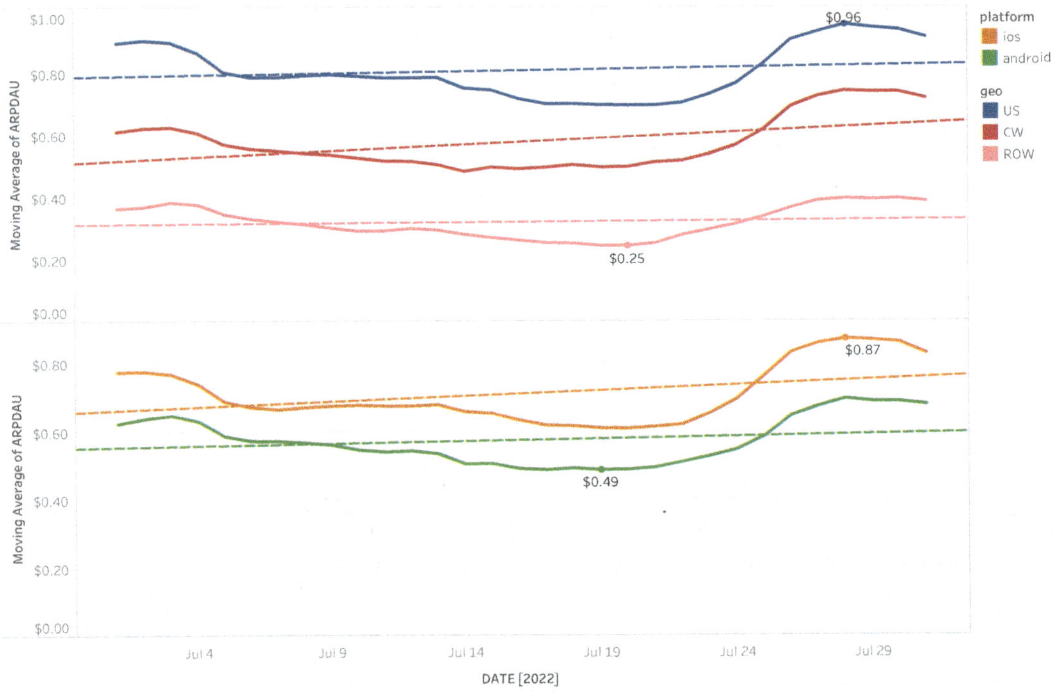

Compare with the previous chart to see the smoothing effect of the moving average.

Step 4: Publish the Dashboard

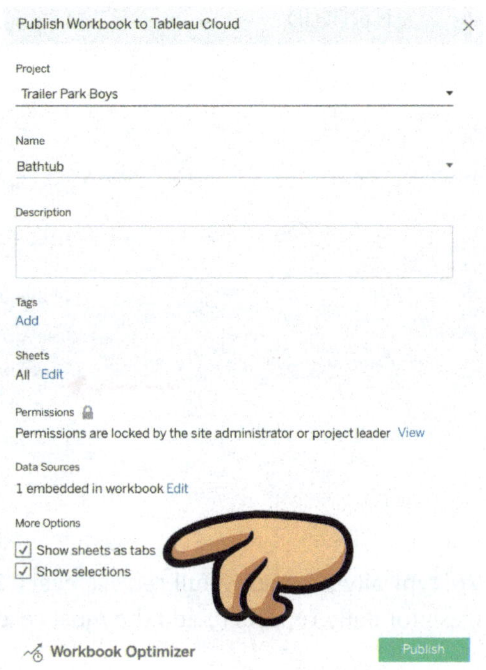

Feeling good about our work so far, it's time to publish the `Bathtub` dashboard so stakeholders can review and provide feedback. Some analysts like to use the *Dashboard* feature of Tableau to consolidate different *Worksheets* before publishing their work, but I prefer to simply share with each *Worksheet* as a tab. From the *Server* menu, *Publish Workbook...* pops up the following dialogue (right), which is where you can specify this option when publishing a workbook containing multiple sheets.

The *Data Source(s)* are embedded in the workbook rather than published separately. To refresh the data, the connection profile and credentials must be made available to Tableau Online. They ask your permission next with the following pop-up:

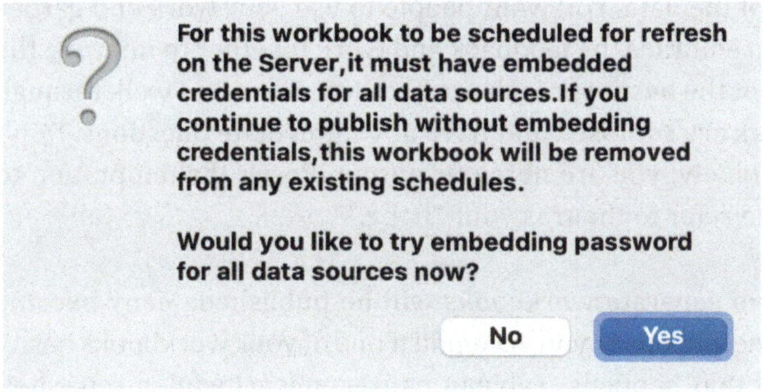

Why "yes," thank you. Having the query and connection profile stored in the Tableau Online workbook enables the data to be refreshed on demand and/or according to a schedule.

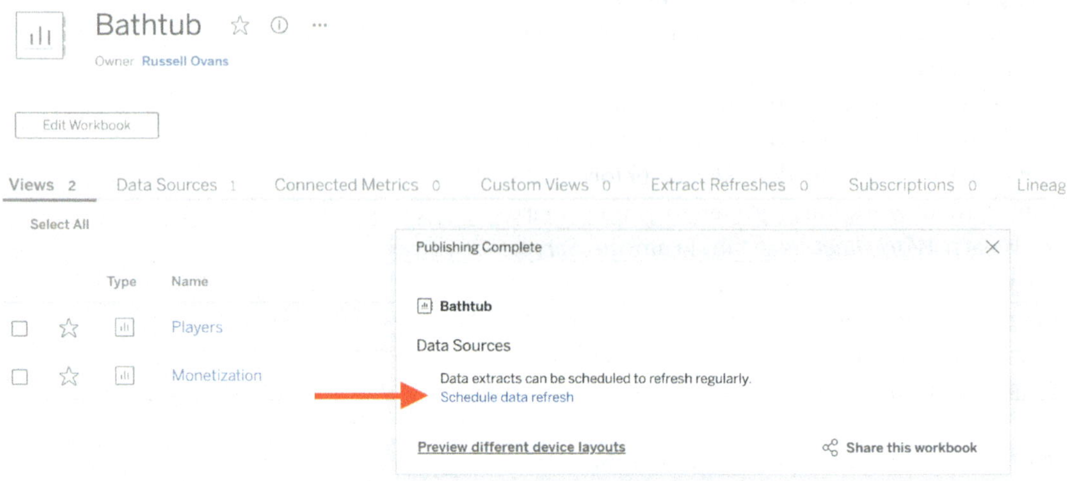

We typically schedule a full refresh every 24 hours for cohort reports and an incremental refresh for daily reports to add the most recent day to the end of the extract.

Step 5: Listen to the Feedback

The work has only just begun. Stakeholders are going to have feedback on usability, and undoubtedly ask for additional views of the data. You want people to use your work and garner insights from these visualizations, so embrace the feedback and work together to improve the dashboard. "Publish and forget" is not the best approach – schedule a demo and walk through the different charts to see if the users are confused and have any immediate questions. Don't take any feedback or criticism personally; you are not your output. Resist the temptation to fall in love with your dashboards and refer to them as your "baby."

Over time, dozens if not hundreds of separate workbooks will be published. Many become forgotten and ignored. Tableau Online will notify you via email if one of your workbooks hasn't recently been viewed by anyone. If that happens, Tableau pauses any scheduled refreshes. This is a great moment to reach out to the team and discuss why nobody has been paying any attention to your baby. (See what I did there?) Perhaps the person who requested this workbook has moved on? Also, it is not uncommon for new team members to be unaware of existing dashboards. This is an opportunity to discuss and decide on the future of any forsaken workbooks, and to remind everyone that nobody puts baby in a corner.

Modeling and Predicting Retention:
LEVEL 4

Retaining customers is the life blood of *any* business, let alone a game studio. Generating new customers is an expensive endeavour, requiring outlays of cash on advertising and signage. As such, it is generally more economical to keep the customers you have than it is to buy new ones. Or, as my Uncle Bob explained to me years ago, "Once the customer enters your business, all of your effort shifts to selling them one thing: a return visit."

To illustrate the importance of customer retention, I want you to imagine for a moment that we are no longer in the games industry. Instead, we have fulfilled a life-long dream and just opened a new hipster coffee shop. Welcome to Le Café d'Arpdau!

Retaining Customers at *Café d'Arpdau*

It's our grand opening. As a means of attracting new customers, we offer a free coffee to the first 100 patrons who sign up for our loyalty program. In exchange for the free java, customers provide us with their phone number to be used as their unique loyalty club identifier, which our staff enter into our cloud-based point-of-sale system. We now have a convenient way to track these customers future visits, which is extremely useful for measuring retention.

The next day – thanks to our loyalty program – we notice that 50 of these original 100 patrons returned to Café d'Arpdau. Our D1 retention for this cohort of customers is 50%. Not bad. However, the following day, only 25 of the customers return: some of those 25 were from yesterday and are frequenting our café for the third day in a row, but not all. Some had skipped a day. Regardless, D2 retention is now only 25%. By day three, only 12 remain. By day seven all our original 100 customers have churned and returned to their habitual Starbucks or Tim Horton's visitations.

Suspecting a pattern, we fire up Excel and graph retention by day since opening. If we add a trendline to the graph (the dotted line), a curve emerges in the form of a decaying exponential function.

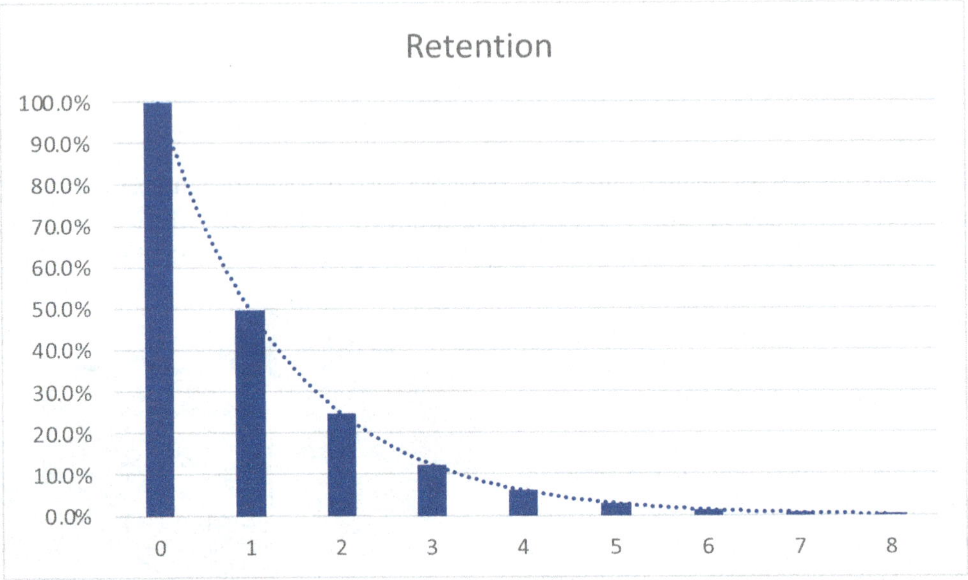

It turns out that the number of returning customers is always half of the previous day's customers. The retention rate for our loyalty club signups is estimated by the trendline fit to our data. In this case, the exponential function:

$$r(n) = 0.5^n$$

where n is any day after enrolment. Since fractional consumers don't exist, the number of customers that return on day n is the floor of $100 * r(n)$.

However, all is not lost at Café d'Arpdau, for we continue to run the free coffee promo, resulting in a new cohort of 100 loyalty club members each day. Unfortunately, these customers all appear to follow this same retention profile. What is the cumulative effect of adding 100 new customers whose retention rate follows this same rate of decay? How many daily customers are we going to end up with, and how many days will it take to get there? Still in Excel, you build a table where the days since opening are the columns, and each row indicates a cohort of customers. A bottom row totals up the customers by day. You end up with something like this:

	D0	D1	D2	D3	D4	D5	D6	D7
Customers:	100	50	25	12	6	3	1	
		100	50	25	12	6	3	1
			100	50	25	12	6	3
				100	50	25	12	6
					100	50	25	12
						100	50	25
							100	50
								100
TOTAL:	100	150	175	187	193	196	197	197

Opening day is our day zero. On D1 we have 50 returning loyalty customers from D0 plus 100 new signups for a total of 150 customers. On D2, 25 of our opening day cohort return, plus 50 from D1's cohort, plus another 100 newbs. And so on. By day six a steady state of 197 total daily loyalty customers is reached. This is the most we can ever expect with 100 new customers per day and a retention profile that sees our returning customers cut in half as each day passes. Especially troubling is that more than half of our daily customers are new, enticed only by the free coffee.

If our customer service and coffee were better, we would see increased customer loyalty manifest as a retention curve that doesn't decay as rapidly. Our daily active customers would grow. For example, if the base of our exponential function was 0.6 instead of 0.5, our steady state rises to 244 by day nine. And if our café truly delights and we only lose 20% of our customers per day (i.e., the base is 0.8), our total customer base peaks at 485 after 20 days. If each customer visit generates roughly the same amount of revenue, retaining customers has a huge impact on the viability of our business.

So, what does all this bricks-and-mortar café nonsense have to do with mobile games? Well, everything. Being able to model historical player (customer) retention with a formula like $r(n)$ is foundational, for it is used to predict engagement for new installs, DAU, and LTV. In the remainder of this chapter, we learn how to build a retention curve from historical data and discuss how the curve's formula is used to calculate the expected number of unique player engagement days. We then present an alternative to your spreadsheet that is a better, faster, and cheaper way of predicting DAU given a retention formula and a constant number of daily new customers.

Don't forget about our beloved Café d'Arpdau. We will revisit it in subsequent chapters to see how LTV is related to retention, and whether buying users by giving away free coffee may or may not be a profitable business model.

The Retention Profile

In the previous chapter on KPIs, we defined day *n* retention (D*n*R) as the percentage of users from a cohort who play exactly *n* days after install. Retention is therefore an aggregate measure applied to a group of players. But at the individual user level, D*n* retention is simply a binary variable: the user either played on that day (indicated by the value 1), they did not play (indicated by a 0), or we don't know yet (indicated by null). For each player, the `user_retention` view contains a binary column for a small set of predefined days after install for which we commonly calculate retention; namely, 1, 7, 30, 90, and 180.

Here is sample retention data for some random *TPB* players.

```
SELECT user_id,
       install_date,
       d1,
       d7,
       d30,
       d90
FROM user_retention
ORDER BY RANDOM() LIMIT 7
```

user_id	install_date	d1	d7	d30	d90
858993	2017-04-23	0	0	0	0
2630131	2017-06-28	0	1	1	0
8554854	2021-11-19	0	0	0	0
226962	2017-04-20	1	1	0	0
7706121	2021-02-06	0	0	0	0
9025650	2022-09-28	0			
3221035	2017-08-19	1	1	0	0

D*n* retention by day is calculated in SQL with the AVG aggregate grouped by all the users with the same install date.

```
SELECT install_date,
       AVG(d1::FLOAT) AS D1R,
       AVG(d7::FLOAT) AS D7R,
       AVG(d30::FLOAT) AS D30R
FROM user_retention
WHERE install_date BETWEEN '2022-07-01' AND '2022-07-09'
GROUP BY install_date
```

install_date	d1r	d7r	d30r
2022-07-01	0.3054	0.1368	0.0784
2022-07-02	0.3586	0.158	0.0876
2022-07-03	0.3619	0.1879	0.0921
2022-07-04	0.3739	0.1838	0.0811

install_date	d1r	d7r	d30r
2022-07-05	0.3839	0.1644	0.079
2022-07-06	0.3941	0.157	0.0727
2022-07-07	0.3878	0.1605	0.0696
2022-07-08	0.3563	0.1495	0.0845
2022-07-09	0.4043	0.1692	0.0689

Rather than a time series of daily retention values, a **retention profile** for the app as a whole is constructed by taking a weighted average of D*n* retention values over multiple install cohorts. Typically, this is a range of consecutive dates on which the install date is at least *n* days old to ensure only fully-baked cohorts are included, but if not, the nulls are conveniently skipped over and not included in the calculation of the average. The daily retention metrics for the nine discrete cohorts above can be aggregated into a single retention profile by dropping the `install_date` column and its `GROUP BY` clause.

```
SELECT AVG(d1::FLOAT) AS D1R,
       AVG(d7::FLOAT) AS D7R,
       AVG(d30::FLOAT) AS D30R
FROM user_retention
WHERE install_date BETWEEN '2022-07-01' AND '2022-07-09'
```

d1r	d7r	d30r
0.3712	0.1626	0.0787

Removing the `WHERE` clause would incorporate every player and calculate all-time retention.

The Retention Curve

For convenience, the days 1, 7, 30, 90, and 180 after install are contained within the `user_retention` view. But what about all the other days in between or after these five specific days? We could measure every D*n*R from the cohort data, but is there a closed-form function that can tell us with reasonable accuracy what D*n* retention is for any day *n*? It turns out there is, and this function defines the retention curve. The **retention curve** is a mechanism to fully describe a historical retention profile *and* predict the expected number of days each new user will engage with the app before churning.

Retention curves are an estimate built from a set of observations. The observations are the true retention values measured for a cohort of installs, defined previously as:

$$\mathrm{D}n\mathrm{R} = \frac{\mathrm{DAU}_n}{\text{cohort size}}$$

Each observation is a dot, and the retention curve connects the dots:

Fitting a Retention Curve to DnR Observations

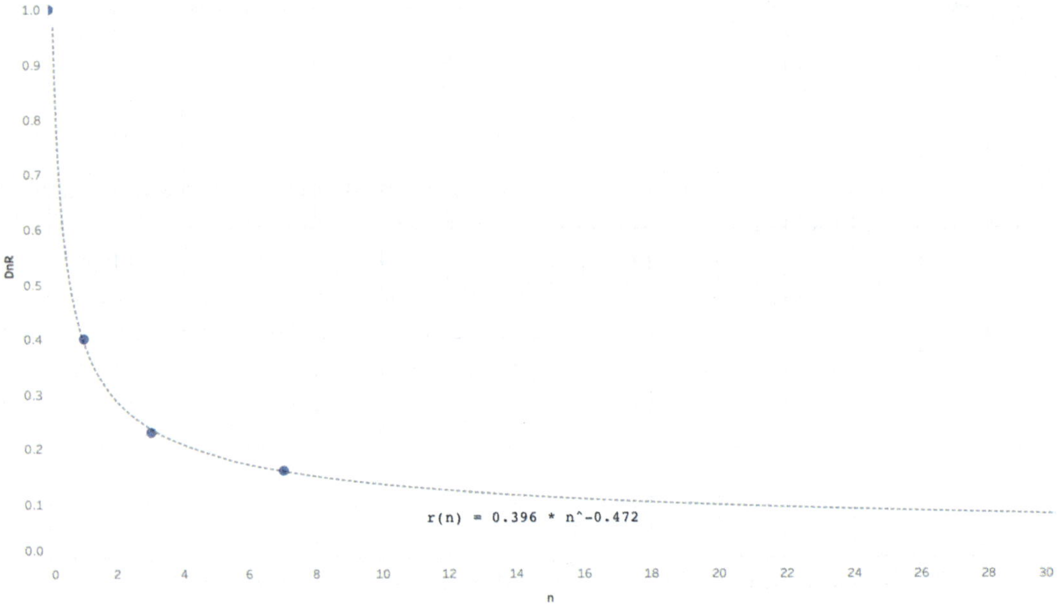

Unlike the exponential function introduced earlier as the retention curve for Café d'Arpdau, mobile game retention is best described by a real-valued **power function**. Whereas an exponential function has a variable exponent and constant base, a power function has a constant exponent and variable base. The generic form of a retention power curve r is a function $r: \mathbb{N} \rightarrow [0, 1]$ of days since install n:

$$r(n) = an^b$$

where

$$a \in (0, 1]$$
$$b < 0$$
$$r(0) = 1.0$$

The real-valued parameters a and b are referred to as the coefficient and exponent, respectively. The exponent is negative, which means that retention starts out high but decays over time. Values returned by the function are proportions between 0 and 1.

For example, a typical retention curve for a mobile game might be:

$$r(n) = 0.4n^{-0.5}$$

This specific function evaluates to a D1 retention of 40.0%, D7R of 15.12%, and D180R of 2.98%. But it can also calculate retention for any arbitrary day after install; e.g., D53R is 5.49%.

> If the negative exponent causes you some anxiety, recall the negative exponent rule: a term with a negative exponent is equal to the reciprocal of that term with the corresponding positive exponent:
>
> $$r(n) = 0.4n^{-0.5} = \frac{0.4}{n^{0.5}}$$

Fitting a retention curve $r(n) = an^b$ to a set of DnR observations is an exercise in statistical regression: determine values for a and b that minimize the residual error between the observations and the predictions. In this chapter, we describe two methods a data analyst can employ to derive the form of the retention curve: regression using Tableau's *Trend Line* feature; or with the `LINEST` function in Excel. We also introduce an algebraic estimation using only two observations of Dn retention. Despite their difference in the details, these methods share the same idea: fit a power function to a set of historical daily retention values.

> Professor Arpdau has kindly automated this process in the *Retention Curve Creator* found at arpdau.com. Enter values for D1R, D3R, D7R, and (optionally) D30R and the professor fits a function $r(n)$ using the same regression technique as Excel and Tableau.

Fitting a Retention Curve in Tableau

Assume we have the following observed retention profile for a game in soft launch, which we have entered into an Excel spreadsheet. The observations are for D1, D3, and D7 retention.

	A	B
1	n	DnR
2	0	1
3	1	0.4
4	3	0.23
5	7	0.16

What is a power function $r(n) = an^b$ that best fits these data points? Open Tableau and paste the values from the spreadsheet into the home screen, then plot retention `DnR` (the rows) as a function of days since install `n` (the columns) to produce a time series of four points. However, after dragging those *Measures* onto your sheet, you may end up with the following:

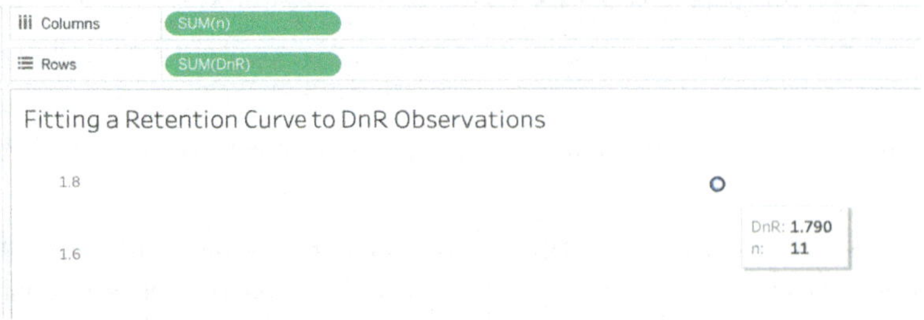

Both dimensions have been aggregated with `SUM`, resulting in a single point. To create a line chart, we need to tell Tableau not to aggregate these measures:

Under the *Analysis* menu, deselect *Aggregate Measures*. Problem solved: you now have four distinct data points, one for each of $n \in \{0, 1, 3, 7\}$.

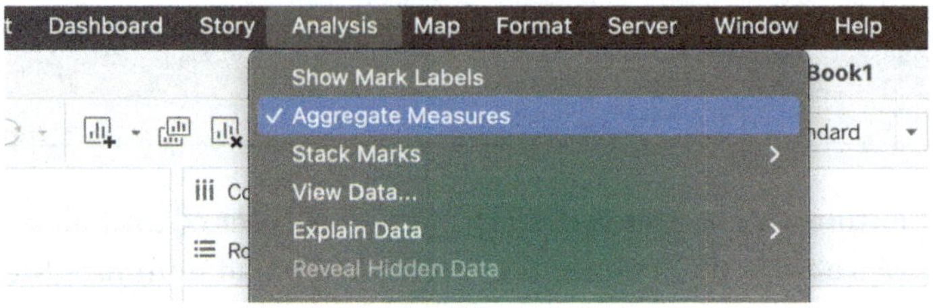

Choose a *Line* graph in the *Marks* pane. The visualization now looks reasonable:

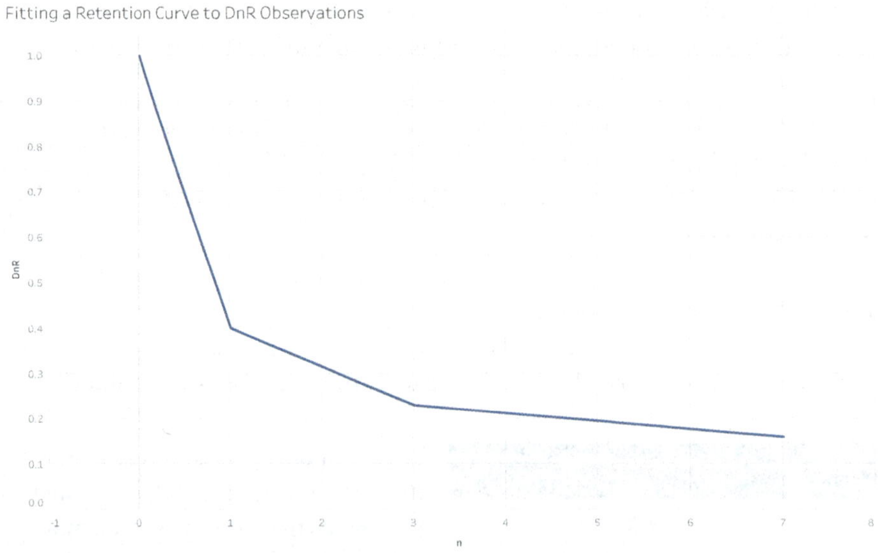

Some of the nit-pickier analysts reading this might object to the use of a line chart instead of a bar chart given that the *x*-axis is discrete and not continuous; i.e., we don't deal in fractional days since install. My use of a continuous line is not meant to imply that something is happening between samples; it is simply an aid to help visualize a trend in the data.

Next, we fit a power function to this data. From the *Analytics* tab, drag a *Trend Line* onto this graph, and select *Power* as the function type.

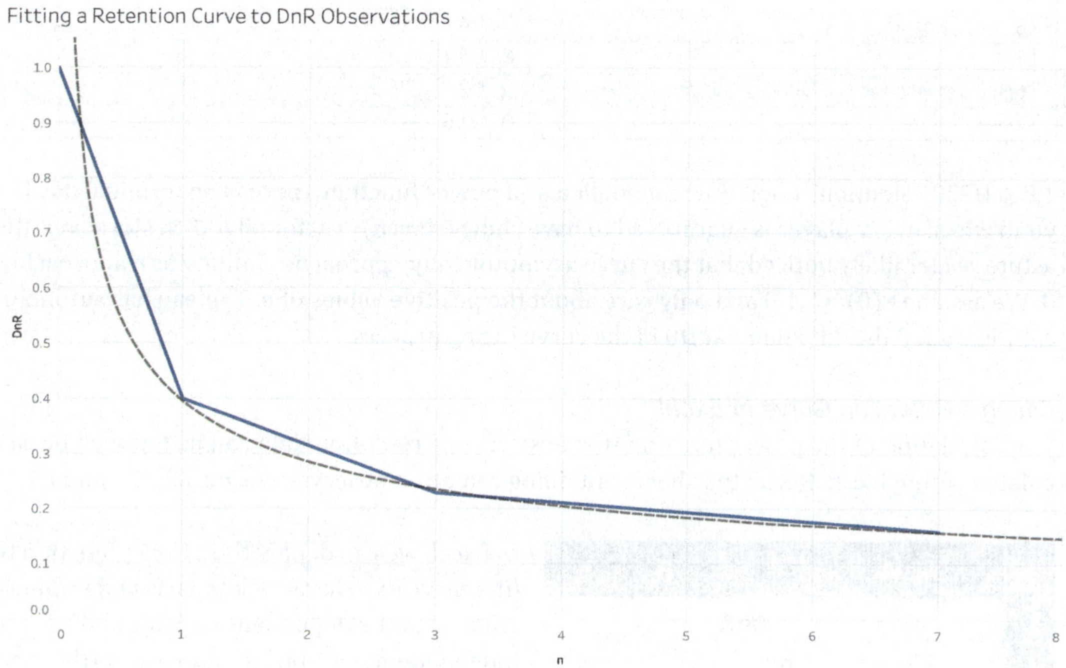

Tableau uses the method of least-squares to find values for the coefficient a and exponent b that best fits these observations. If we hover over the dashed line, a pop-up indicates the formula that Tableau has decided is the best fit for our data. Rounded to three decimal places, the function is:

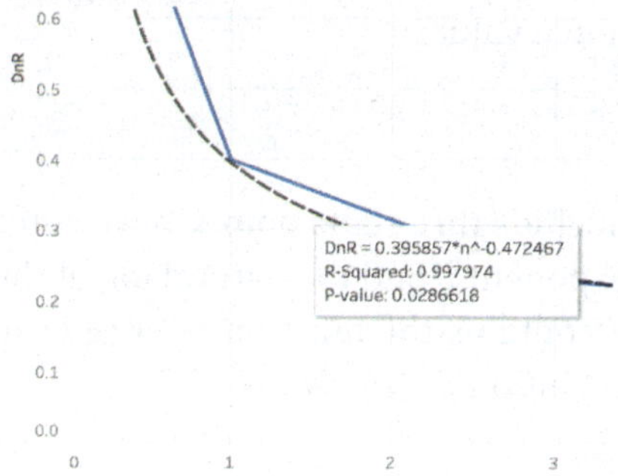

$$r(n) = 0.396n^{-0.472}$$

The slope of the curve is determined by the exponent b, which controls how quickly retention decays. The more negative b is, the faster players churn. As for the coefficient a, its value determines how high up the y-axis the curve starts at D1.

This retention curve – based on observed D1, D3, and D7 retention metrics only – predicts the following values for long-tail retention:

Day n	Predicted Dn Retention
14	0.114
30	0.080
60	0.057
90	0.047
180	0.034
360	0.025
720	0.018

1.8% D720 retention? Cool! When modelled as a power function, there is no terminal day beyond which every player is guaranteed to have churned: $r(n) > 0$ for all $n \in \mathbb{N}$. Moreover, the astute reader likely noticed that the curve asymptotically approaches infinity as n approaches 0. We assume $r(0) = 1.0$ and only care about the positive values of n. Tableau has automatically excluded the data point at D0 in the curve fitting process.

Fitting a Retention Curve in Excel

The calculation of the power function that best fits our retention data can just as well be calculated within Excel. Recall the sheet containing retention observations for D1, D3, and D7.

	A	B
1	n	DnR
2	0	1
3	1	0.4
4	3	0.23
5	7	0.16

In Excel, we can deploy the `LINEST` function to fit a curve to an array of known y- and x-values, where y is the dependent variable and x is the independent variable. In our case, n (the days since install) is the independent variable. As its name suggests, the `LINEST` function – by default – fits a line and returns an array (two adjacent cells) containing the slope and y-intercept of the formula that best fits the data. To instead fit a power function to our data, we need to pass `LINEST` the logarithm (`LN`) of the array of known values:

```
=LINEST(LN(B3:B5),LN(A3:A5))
```

And because the logarithm of 0 is undefined, we can only include three data points. If we enter that function into cell A7 (see below), Excel returns the exponent b and the natural log of the coefficient a in the cells A7 and B7, respectively. Cell C7 contains the function `=EXP(B7)` in order to convert the coefficient to the correct form. Our retention curve is thus:

$$r(n) = 0.396n^{-0.472}$$

	A	B	C
1	n	DnR	
2	0	1	
3	1	0.4	
4	3	0.23	
5	7	0.16	
6	b	ln_a	a
7	-0.472	-0.927	0.396
8	n	Predicted DnR	
9	30	0.079	
10	90	0.047	
11	180	0.034	

If that formula looks familiar it's because it was exactly what Tableau said a couple of pages ago.

Using this curve, cells B9:B11 contain predictions of D30, D90, and D180 retention, respectively; e.g., the formula in B9 is:

```
=$C$7*POWER(A9,$A$7)
```

And that is how you use Excel to determine a formula for a game's retention curve based on a small sample of D*n*R values. Congratulations – achievement unlocked!

Constructing a Retention Curve from (More) Historical Data

These estimates for D90+ retention seem a little optimistic, perhaps owing to the very early and limited number of data points. With more and later observations of retention, the regression analysis should become more accurate. What happens if we measure retention every day instead of just 1, 3, and 7? Intuitively this should result in a curve that fits the data more accurately and provides for more accurate predictions beyond the training set.

Let's consider a game with a full 90-day history of install cohorts and start by building a query to capture retention for every day since install up to D30. To enable this, we envision a relation of the following form, populated here with some sample data:

days_since_install	players
0	38091
1	14628
2	10230
3	8568
4	7453
5	6903
...	...
30	3033

Notice we do not cohort by install date – all we care about is how many users still played *n* days after install, regardless of each user's specific install date. We could have further broken this down by platform or version, but for now we are treating all installs the same. The first row (`days_since_install` = 0) is the total number of installs sampled over some arbitrary date range, or perhaps every install to date. In this case, 38,091 installs are included in our analysis; this is the size of the cohort. Five days after install we see that 6,903 of those 38,091 installs played: D5 retention is 6,903/38,091 = 18.12%. Note that the `players` column is monotonically decreasing by day. If the sample size is large enough, this is to be expected. For very small sample sizes, the `players` column may not behave in the same strict manner.

> We can apply this technique to any range of install dates; by doing so we are effectively taking a weighted average of daily retention. But be careful: you can only include fully-baked installs when building this relation. For example, if you are interested in measuring retention for every day from install to day 30, you can only include players who installed more than 30 days ago and therefore actually had the chance to play every one of those days. Failing to do so will penalize the long-tail retention values.

The query to build this relation is surprisingly simple. Here is the first 30 days of retained players for every new user who installed between 90 and 31 days ago:

```
SELECT datediff(day, install_date, play_date) AS days_since_install,
       COUNT(DISTINCT user_id) AS players
FROM
  (SELECT s.user_id,
          install_date
   FROM user_source s
   WHERE install_date BETWEEN CURRENT_DATE - 90 AND CURRENT_DATE -
31)
LEFT JOIN
  (SELECT DISTINCT user_id,
            date AS play_date
   FROM session_begin
   WHERE date >= CURRENT_DATE - 90)
USING (user_id)
WHERE days_since_install BETWEEN 0 and 30
GROUP BY days_since_install
```

Since we are only interested in the first 30 days after install, the `WHERE` clause filters out the behaviour beyond 30 days for the older players that are included in the subquery of `user_source`.

Notice we aren't calculating the actual retention rate for each of the days since install. This will be left to Tableau (see below) but, if necessary, we could do this in SQL with a window function that takes the `FIRST_VALUE(players)` – the day 0 players – as the number of installs. Let's return to the cohort of players who installed from July 1 – 9, 2022 to illustrate this technique:

```
SELECT datediff(day,install_date,play_date) AS days_since_install,
       COUNT(DISTINCT user_id) AS players,
       FIRST_VALUE(players) OVER (ORDER BY days_since_install ROWS
UNBOUNDED PRECEDING) AS installs,
       players / installs::FLOAT AS retention
FROM (SELECT user_id,
             install_date
      FROM user_source
      WHERE install_date BETWEEN '2022-07-01' AND '2022-07-09')
  LEFT JOIN (SELECT DISTINCT user_id,
                    date AS play_date
             FROM session_begin
             WHERE date BETWEEN '2022-07-01' AND '2022-07-09' + 30)
USING (user_id)
WHERE days_since_install BETWEEN 0 AND 30
GROUP BY days_since_install
```

days_since_install	players	installs	retention
0	7891	7891	1
1	2929	7891	0.3712
2	2120	7891	0.2687
3	1769	7891	0.2242
4	1559	7891	0.1976
5	1409	7891	0.1786
6	1326	7891	0.168
7	1283	7891	0.1626
...	...	...	...
26	704	7891	0.0892
27	680	7891	0.0862
28	658	7891	0.0834
29	651	7891	0.0825
30	621	7891	0.0787

Notice that the values for D1, D7, and D30 retention match with those calculated previously as the retention profile for this same set of installs:

d1r	d7r	d30r
0.3712	0.1626	0.0787

With the query debugged and ready to go, the next step is to visualize within Tableau. Let's apply this technique to the first 30 days of the July 1-9 cohort. Our connection to Redshift from Tableau specifies the following query:

```
SELECT datediff(day, install_date, play_date) AS days_since_install,
       COUNT(DISTINCT user_id) AS players
FROM (SELECT user_id,
```

```
                install_date
            FROM user_source
            WHERE install_date BETWEEN '2022-07-01' AND '2022-07-09')
        LEFT JOIN (SELECT DISTINCT user_id,
                          date AS play_date
                   FROM session_begin
                   WHERE date >= '2022-07-01') USING (user_id)
    WHERE days_since_install BETWEEN 0 AND 30
    GROUP BY days_since_install
```

If we plot `players` as a function of `days_since_install`, we see the familiar retention profile in the form of a decaying power function.

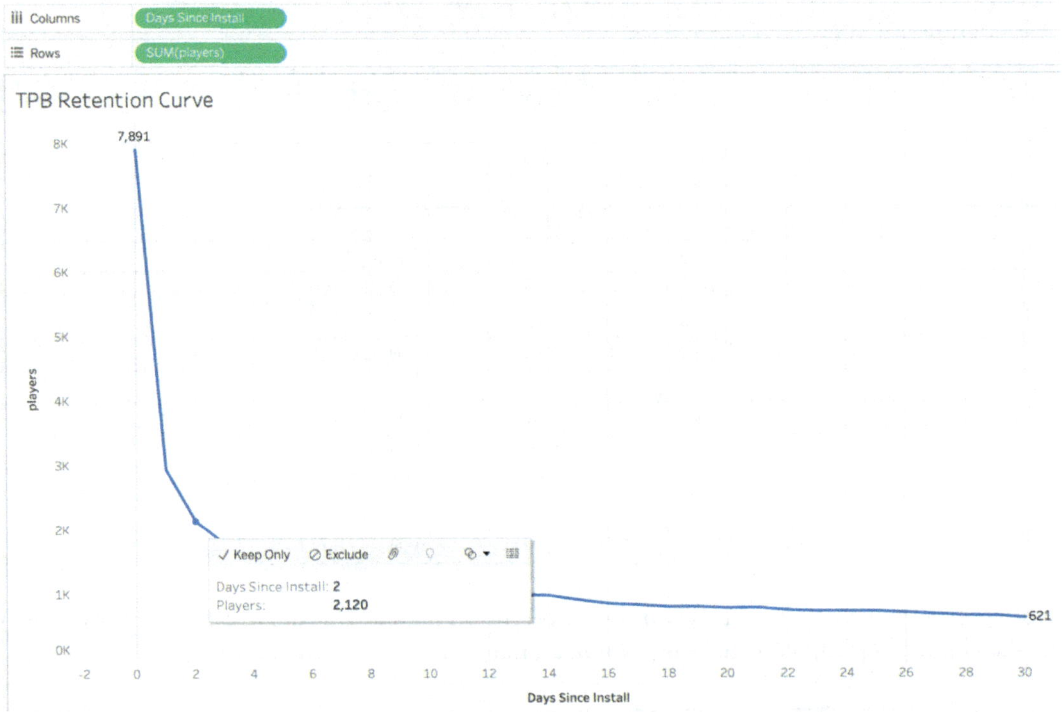

We could fit a curve to this profile, but since each data point is not normalized as a percentage, this wouldn't be useful. To calculate retention as a percentage of installs, we need to divide the `players` by the cohort size; i.e., 7,891, the number of players when days since install is zero. Using the function `MAX([players])` to calculate the cohort size isn't going to cut it as Tableau always wants to apply aggregates while adhering to any dimensions in the current view. The trick is to `EXCLUDE` the `days_since_install` dimension when calculating the aggregate, thus forcing Tableau to take the maximum over all records in the dataset. To do this, create a calculated field called `Cohort Size` and define it as:

```
{ EXCLUDE [days_since_install] : MAX([players]) }
```

and then define `Retention` as a calculated field defined as:

```
SUM([players])/SUM([Cohort Size])
```

Strictly speaking, the `SUM` aggregation isn't required since there are no measures such as platform or version in the dataset, but we have included it here in case we change our mind and want to create separate curves for Android vs. iOS or paid vs. organic.

Now we can plot `Retention` as a function of `Days Since Install` and fit a power curve to create the retention function. Hovering over the dotted line gives us the following estimate for this cohort of players:

$$r(n) = 0.372n^{-0.442}$$

Compare this retention curve with $r(n) = 0.396n^{-0.472}$, the function fit to the first three data points only, which predicted D90R of 4.7%. This curve based on a full set of observations from days 1 to 30 predicts that D90R will be 5.1%. It is higher because of the exponent is less negative.

For the remainder of this book, functions indicate curves fit to a set of observations, whereas the observations are indicated with subscript notation. For example, $r(n)$ is the function that defines the curve fit to a set of $\text{D}_n\text{R} = (\text{DAU}_n)/(\text{cohort size})$ observations.

We use "hat notation" to distinguish an estimate based on evaluation of a regression function from an observation; e.g., D90R is an observed historical value whereas $\widehat{\text{D90R}} = r(90)$ is a prediction.

A Heuristic Estimation of the Power Function

There is a simple heuristic approach to fitting a retention curve using any two observed data points. This might come in handy on those occasions where you can't rely on an external tool like Tableau or Excel (or Professor Arpdau!) to calculate the coefficient a and exponent b. To illustrate this technique, we return to our soft-launch retention profile given by the following table.

N	DnR
0	1.00
1	0.40
3	0.23
7	0.16

As a reminder, the retention curve fit to these four data points was:

$$r(n) = 0.396n^{-0.472}$$

Start by setting a to the observed value for D1 retention – in this case, 0.40. This forces the formula to exactly fit our data point at D1:

$$r(1) = 0.4(1^b) = 0.40$$

Next, the value for b can be estimated using one other observation: in this case, either D3R or D7R. We force the formula (with $a = 0.40$) to exactly fit one of those data points, then solve for b using the laws of exponents. For example, to force the function to exactly fit our observed value for D3R (23%), we proceed as follows:

$$\begin{aligned}
&r(3) = 0.23 = 0.40(3^b) \\
&\rightarrow \frac{0.23}{0.40} = 3^b \\
&\rightarrow \ln\left(\frac{0.23}{0.40}\right) = \ln(3^b) \\
&\rightarrow -0.5534 = b\ln(3) \\
&\rightarrow b = \frac{-0.5534}{\ln(3)} \\
&\rightarrow b = -0.504
\end{aligned}$$

Using only observed values for D1 and D3 retention we have derived a formula to estimate retention on any day after install:

$$r(n) = 0.4n^{-0.504}$$

We can use this function to interpolate values for Dn retention between observations (e.g., $\widehat{\text{D2R}} = 0.28$), or we can use this function to predict retention for values beyond the observations (e.g., predicted $\widehat{\text{D90R}} = 0.042$).

Evaluating this function at D7, we get $\widehat{\text{D7R}} = r(7) = 0.15$. But wait a second... we observed D7R = 0.16, not 0.15. If we had used our D7 retention observation instead of D3R to estimate the exponent b, the function r would exactly match our observed D7R instead. In general, with any observation DnR, the value for the exponent b that solves DnR = D1R(n^b) is:

$$b = \ln(\text{D}n\text{R}/\text{D1R})/\ln(n)$$

If observed D7R is 0.16, we have $b = \ln(0.16/0.4)/\ln(7) = -0.471$. The resulting formula $r(n) = 0.4n^{-0.471}$ is very close to the curve fit previously using least-squares; namely, $r(n) = 0.396n^{-0.472}$. The heuristic function is slightly more optimistic, resulting in higher predicted values of long-tail retention.

Which estimate of b is better to use: the one we get forcing the function to fit D3R, or D7R? In general, the further-out observation is preferred, so in this case D7R. But there are alternatives. If you want to be conservative, use the value for b that is closer to negative 1; optimistic, use the other. You could also take the average of the b estimates.

User Duration as Sum of Retention

The retention curve defines the probability a user drawn at random from the set of installs plays exactly n days after their install date. As such, an important use of the retention curve is in predicting future engagement of new and existing players. In particular, the number of distinct dates we can expect each new user to play the game during their first n days after install.

A **play date** occurs when a user has at least one session on a specific date. The **user duration** is the count of the number of distinct play dates a user plays between install and churning. Quantifying user duration is an important tool in predicting LTV, which we discuss in a later chapter on how LTV is just user duration multiplied by ARPDAU.

We can count the number of play dates for each user within a specific historical range of install dates with a query of the following type. In this case, the number of distinct calendar days played by each new user who installed between July 1st and July 9th of 2022, but limited to within their first 30 days after install. We are going to reuse this query, so let's define it as a CTE called pd for "player days":

```
WITH pd AS
(SELECT a.user_id,
        COUNT(DISTINCT b.date) AS play_dates
FROM user_source a
LEFT JOIN (SELECT DISTINCT user_id,
                           date
           FROM session_begin
           WHERE date >= '2022-07-01') b
     ON (a.user_id = b.user_id AND b.date <= a.date + 30)
WHERE a.date BETWEEN '2022-07-01' AND '2022-07-09'
GROUP BY a.user_id)

SELECT * FROM pd ORDER BY user_id
```

user_id	play_dates
8915877	1
8915878	1
8915879	1
8915880	2
8915881	23
8915882	9
8915883	3
...	...

Values for play_dates range from 1 (the user never returned to the game after playing on their install date) to 31 (the user played every single day of their first 30 days after install). A histogram of play_dates is derived by wrapping pd in the following aggregation:

```
SELECT play_dates,
       COUNT(*) AS players,
       players::FLOAT/SUM(players) OVER
         (ROWS BETWEEN UNBOUNDED PRECEDING AND UNBOUNDED FOLLOWING)
    AS proportion
FROM pd
GROUP BY play_dates
```

play_dates	players	proportion
1	3939	0.4992
2	1236	0.1566
3	591	0.0749
4	314	0.0398
5	203	0.0257

play_dates	players	proportion
6	169	0.0214
...	...	...
29	58	0.0074
30	71	0.009
31	225	0.0285

If we plot this as a histogram with `play_dates` on the *x*-axis and `proportion` on the *y*-axis, we find a distribution that is heavily skewed to the left, but with a sizeable amount going on out in the long tail where the hardcore players live. A surprising 2.85% of all installs played every day! Distributions of this kind – a valley between peaks on the left and right extremes – are a common feature of games.

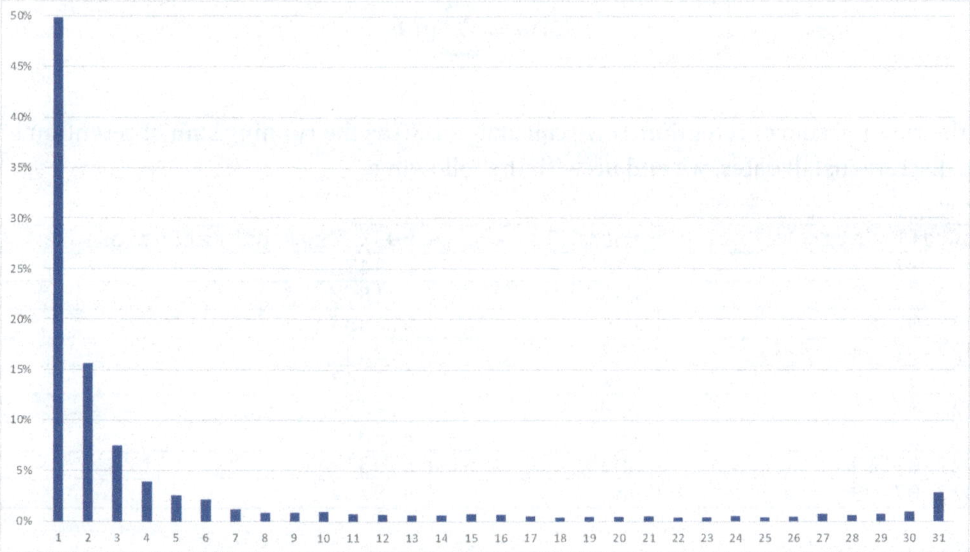

The average number of play dates (PD) within 30 days of install (PD30) for users in this cohort is the weighted (by `players`) average of the `play_dates` column in the histogram result set, or more simply:

```
SELECT SUM(play_dates) AS total_days,
       COUNT(*) AS players,
       total_days / players::FLOAT AS PD30
FROM pd
```

total_days	players	PD30
39594	7891	5.018

For the cohort of installs from July 1-9, users on average played 5.018 distinct dates within their first 30 days. This does not necessarily mean the first five consecutive days after install; any days between 0 and 30 count towards this total. The higher this number is, the better, since a player can only be monetized on the days they play!

We can generalize our PD30 result to any days since install. Let PD*n* be the average number of play dates within *n* days of install for a cohort of users. We have shown how to calculate this value in SQL from the raw data using a weighted average. But equivalently:

$$\text{PD}n = \sum_{i=0}^{n} \text{D}i\text{R}$$

i.e., the running sum of retention. If we calculate PD30 as the running sum of retention for the nine discrete install dates, we end up with the following:

install_date	installs	PD30 (sum of retention)
2022-07-01	754	4.3475
2022-07-02	755	5.1868
2022-07-03	794	5.2594
2022-07-04	790	5.2342
2022-07-05	797	5.1443
2022-07-06	950	5.2421
2022-07-07	1034	4.8017
2022-07-08	1030	4.9816
2022-07-09	987	4.9757

The weighted (by `installs`) average of these nine values is 5.018, which is exactly the same value calculated for PD30 previously using the histogram of play days.

As a cohort metric, PD*n* is a random variable with an expected value (E) defined by the summation[1] of the retention curve $r(i)$ that best fits the retention profile of historical installs:

---

[1] In the literature you will often see reference to the "area under the curve", or "the integral of the retention curve." Strictly speaking this is incorrect, as the retention function is only defined for integer values of *n*. If you plug a retention curve formula into a symbolic integration tool, you will find the answer is typically inflated compared to a discrete summation.

$$E(\text{PD}n) = \sum_{i=0}^{n} r(i)$$

Once you have a function *r* that describes the retention profile of your game, you can use this curve to predict the user duration of new installs (and LTV if you multiply by average ARPDAU). This is why retention and ARPDAU are so important.

Using Tableau, we previously fit a retention curve to the first 30 days of data for the cohort of installs over the period July 1-9th as $r(n) = 0.372n^{-0.442}$. Calculating the running sum of this function over some range of values for *n* can be accomplished within a spreadsheet. While tedious, the spreadsheet approach – left as an exercise to the reader – is appropriate for one-offs. From Excel you will find the summation is 5.021, which differs slightly from 5.018. Recall that the retention curve is a best-fit estimate based on the actual D*n*R observations. Therefore, it is not guaranteed to exactly align with the weighted average, but in this case agrees within two decimal places.

In the same manner that the retention curve predicts cohort DAU of new installs, 5.021 is the user duration that we expect for installs from July 10th onwards, over their first 30 days, playing the same version of the game.

We now present two other means of calculating user duration: iterate programmatically; or, fit a curve to the running sum of retention.

Calculating Expected User Duration Programmatically

Since summation involves iteration, we can write a program to keep a running sum of *r* evaluated for any range of values of *n*. Here is a recursive function[2] in R to create a vector of daily retention values for any power function defined by coefficient *a* and exponent *b* over the first *n* days:

```
ret_curve <- function(a, b, n)
{
  if (n <= 0) return (1.0)
  return (c(ret_curve(a, b, n-1), a * n^b))
}
```

---

[2] There is no reason why I chose to use recursion instead of iteration other than I am a recovering computer scientist.

```
R> ret_curve(a=0.372, b=-0.442, n=30)

 [1] 1.00000000 0.37200000 0.27383420 0.22890503 0.20157303 0.18264097 0.16850007
 [8] 0.15740177 0.14838061 0.14085353 0.13444447 0.12889835 0.12403517 0.11972366
[15] 0.11586556 0.11238558 0.10922496 0.10633703 0.10368418 0.10123574 0.09896638
[22] 0.09685499 0.09488381 0.09303776 0.09130395 0.08967130 0.08813019 0.08667227
[29] 0.08529019 0.08397752 0.08272854
```

From there, a running sum of these daily retention values is computed as follows:

```
sum_ret_curve <- function(a, b, n)
{
  if (n >= 0)
    ret_curve(a, b, n) + c(0, sum_ret_curve(a, b, n-1))
}

R> sum_ret_curve(a=0.372, b=-0.442, n=30)

 [1] 1.000000 1.372000 1.645834 1.874739 2.076312 2.258953 2.427453 2.584855
 [9] 2.733236 2.874089 3.008534 3.137432 3.261467 3.381191 3.497056 3.609442
[17] 3.718667 3.825004 3.928688 4.029924 4.128890 4.225745 4.320629 4.413667
[25] 4.504971 4.594642 4.682772 4.769445 4.854735 4.938712 5.021441
```

Deriving a Formula for Expected User Duration

Alternatively, the expected value can be modelled by fitting a curve to the *running sum* of observed daily retention. Instead of building a retention curve from the daily retention rates, we fit a curve to the running sum of these same retention rates. The resulting closed-form function PD(n) can estimate expected user duration for any value of n. *Nice!*

Returning to Tableau where we previously derived the retention curve for this cohort, we plot the running sum of `Retention` and fit a curve to that data instead. We could simply add a *Quick Table Calculation* to the `Retention` pill, but then we would have to change the default number format from percent to number. Instead, we first create a calculated field called `Player Days` defined as `RUNNING_SUM([Retention])`. Then we plot `Player Days` as a function of `days_since_install`. Refer to the following chart.

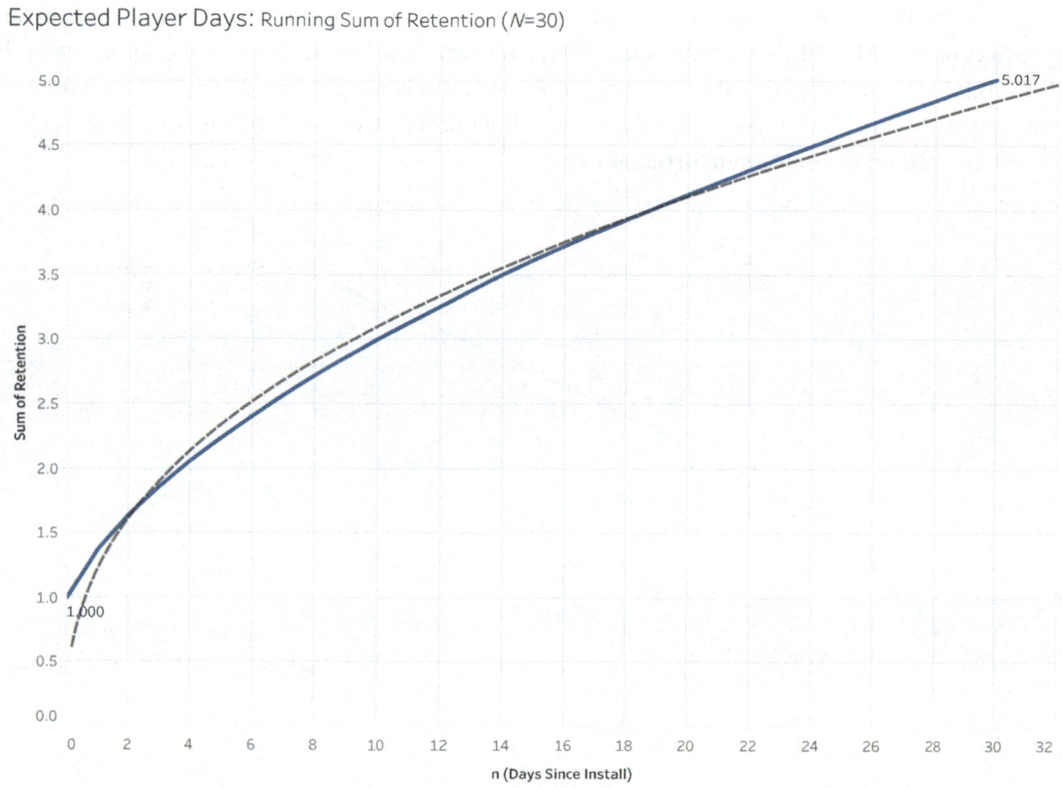

This curve is explicitly built by summation over the individual retention metrics. At day zero, we have 1.00 player day. By day 30, the sum is 5.017. The dashed line is a *Trend Line* of type *Power*, resulting in the following closed-form estimate of PD*n*:

$$\mathrm{PD}(n) = 1.21n^{0.41}$$

Note that while the curve has a very strong R-squared[3] of 0.99, it appears to be on a rather poor trajectory. Predicted player days beyond D30 are likely to be under-estimated. Indeed, if we compare the predicted number of player days by D180 calculated in R versus Tableau's regression curve, the results are quite different. The recursive function in R, which iterates

---

[3] In statistical regression, **R-squared** is the **coefficient of determination**, an indicator of the strength with which the trend line fits the data. R-squared describes the proportion of the variance in the dependent variable data points (*y*-axis) that are explained by the independent variable (*x*-axis). The closer to 1.0 the better the fit.

over the retention curve, predicts 12.6 player days by D180, whereas the curve fit by Tableau predicts only $1.21 * 180^{0.41} = 9.98$ days. Why are they so different? The two graphs are built from the same underlying data, but the curves fit to their graphs are distinct. Here are both the retention and sum of retention data, plus their power curves fit to the data (the dashed lines), plotted on the same synchronized axes:

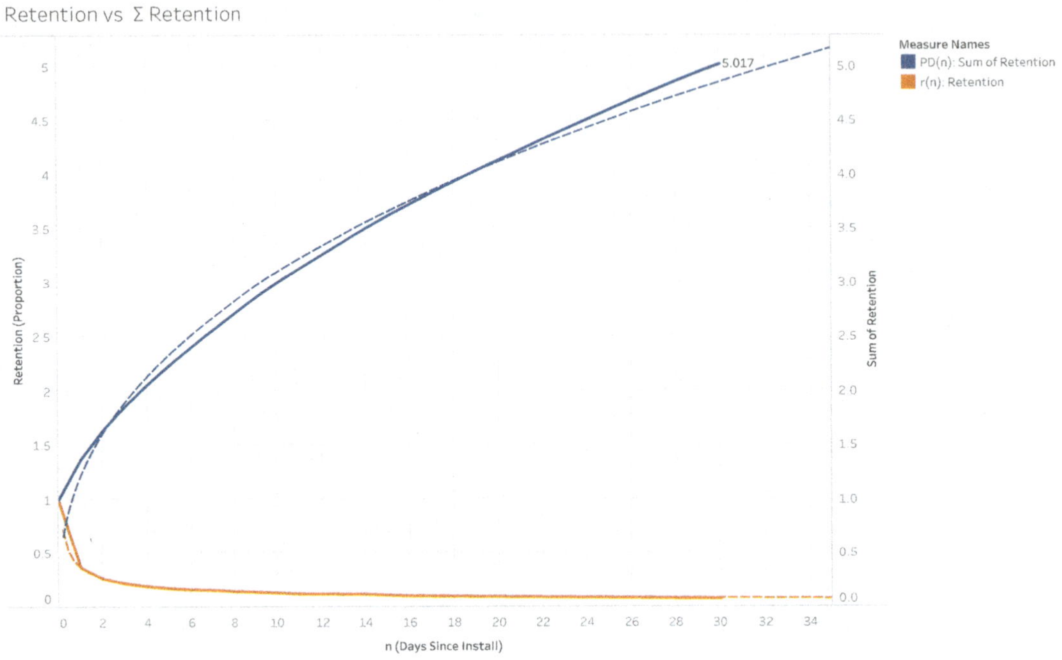

The function $r(n)$ seems to be a much better fit (at least visually) to the first 30 days of data, and indeed the R-squared value is slightly better at 0.996 compared to only 0.99 for $\mathrm{PD}(n)$, but at that point we're really just splitting hairs.

Which is the better predictor of user duration beyond D30? We won't know until this cohort is 180 days fully baked. But at the time of writing, this cohort is now more than 180 days old, so I can tell you that the actual PD180 was 11.62. Refer to the following chart from Tableau, with the *x*-axis extended to D180:

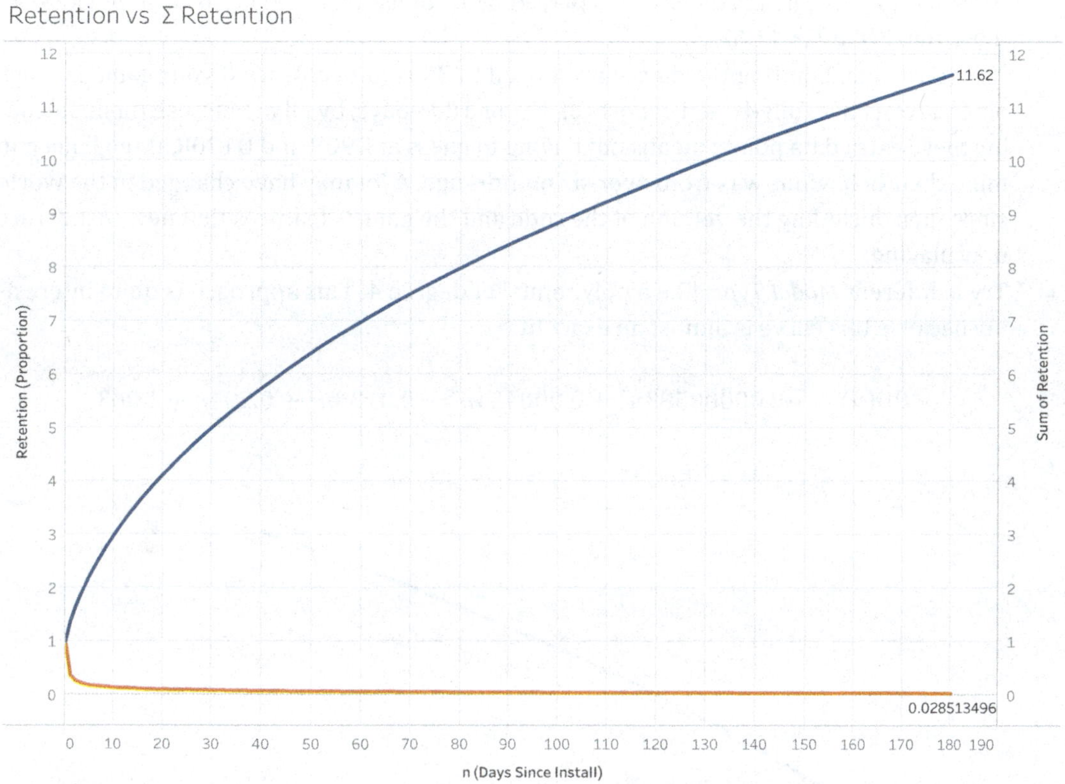

The function $\mathrm{PD}(n)$, fit to the first 30 days of data, predicted only 9.98 player days by D180, whereas $\sum r(n)$ predicted it would be 12.6. Parenthetically, D180R landed at 2.85%, but the curve fit to 30 days of data predicted it would be $0.372(180)^{-0.442} = 3.75\%$. This optimism is the cause of the over-estimation of PD180 by the summation of $r(n)$.

Perhaps there is a way to derive a $\mathrm{PD}(n)$ curve that is a better fit to the running sum of retention values? Tableau's dotted line seems particularly sensitive to the fact that a simple power formula is always 0 at the y-intercept. To remedy this, we could try any of the following:

- Use a *Filter* on `days_since_install` to eliminate the day zero data point where the error is greatest. We know that player days at D0 is 1.0, which we can add to the function as a constant. Using this approach in Tableau gives us $\mathrm{PD}(n) = 1 + 0.404n^{0.685}$. The predicted days played by D180 becomes 15.16.
- A similar idea is to shift the data over by adding one to each `days_since_install`. Day zero becomes day one, etc. The formula for this running sum gives us $\mathrm{PD}(n) =$

$0.97(n+1)^{0.476}$. The predicted days played by D180 is thus 11.46. This is a lot closer to the actual PD180 of 11.62.

- Use more data. Limiting the days since install to 30 is unnecessary if your game is much older. If you have fully-baked cohorts of 90+ or 180+ days, by all means, use them. Including these extra data points means not having to guess at D90R and D180R, though keep in mind their behaviour was from over six months ago. A lot may have changed in the world since then, including the version of the code and the game's features that new installs are now playing.
- Try a different *Model Type*, like a polynomial of degree 4. This approach is quite interesting because this curve is almost an exact fit:

$$\text{PD}(n) = -0.00000583n^4 + 0.000454n^3 - 0.0138n^2 + 0.294n + 1.063$$

Retention vs Σ Retention: Degree-4 Polynomial Trend Lines (*N*=30)

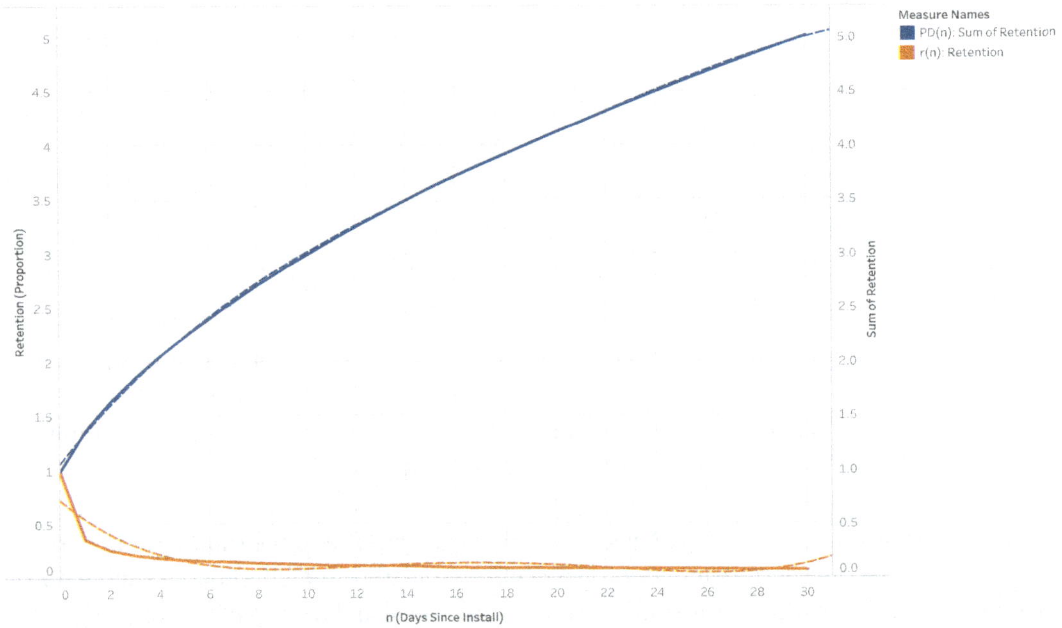

The R-value for the polynomial function's fit to the PD*n* observations is a near perfect 0.9997. But beware the **overfitting pitfall of machine learning**: polynomials can behave very erratically outside of their training set; i.e., for values of $n > 30$. What do these two polynomials predict for retention and user duration? If we extend the *x*-axis out to 90 days since install, we can track the somewhat comical behaviour of the curves:

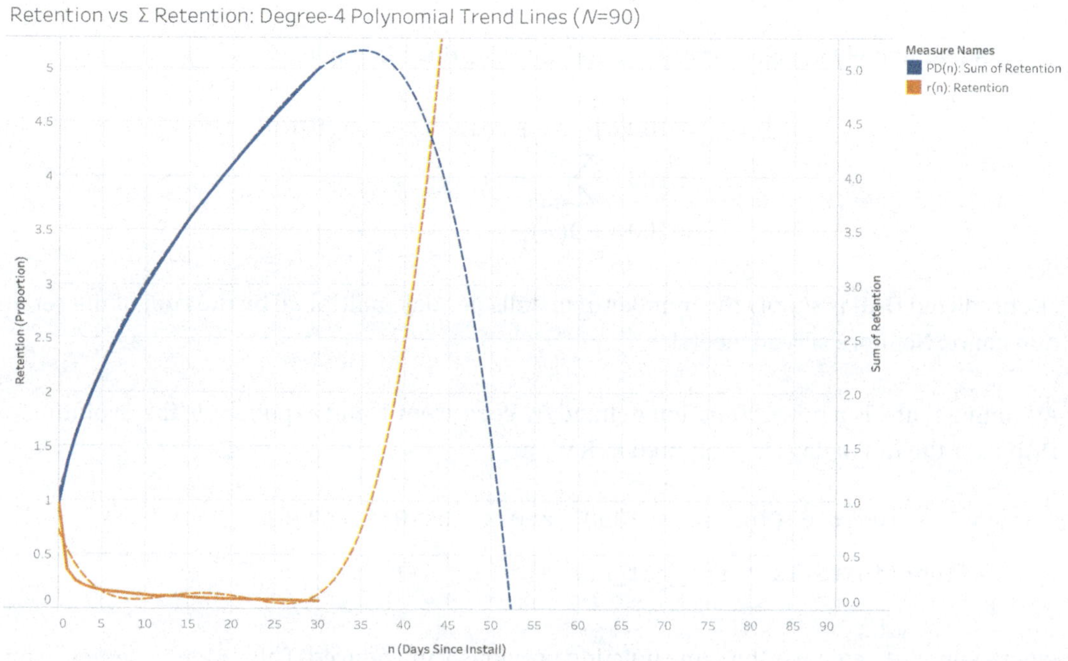

This is why we prefer to stick with power or logarithmic trend lines. You have been warned.

Predicting DAU with a Retention Curve

By now we should all be very comfortable with the idea that a retention curve is a model – derived from historical data – of the probability a player has a session exactly n days after their install date. The retention curve is defined by a power formula $r(n) = an^b$. When applied to a cohort of installs, the expected number of DAU from that cohort on day n after install is $cohort\ size * r(n)$.

A simple prediction of total DAU by day n after game launch can be constructed by extending this concept over a sequence of overlapping daily install cohorts. Consider the following table to illustrate the phenomenon assuming 100 installs per day.

Days After Launch	Expected DAU
0	100*r(0)
1	100*r(1) + 100*r(0)
2	100*r(2) + 100*r(1) + 100*r(0)
...	...
n	100*r(n) + 100*r(n-1) + ... + 100*r(1) + 100*r(0)

The number of daily installs factors out and we have the following:

$$\begin{aligned}\mathrm{DAU}_n &= 100 * [r(n) + r(n-1) + \cdots r(0)] \\ &= 100 * \sum_{i=0}^{n} r(i) \\ &= 100 * \mathrm{PD}(n)\end{aligned}$$

i.e., predicted DAU is simply the number of installs per day multiplied by the sum of the retention curve. No more spreadsheets!

Assuming that *r* is a power function defined by coefficient *a* and exponent *b*, the evolution of DAU over the first *n* days is computed in R with:

```
dau <- function(installs=1000, a=0.4, b=-0.5, n=90)
{
  floor(installs * sum_ret_curve(a, b, n))
}
```

where `sum_ret_curve` is the same function previously introduced. This model assumes a constant number of `installs` (the cohort size) per day. For example, the predicted DAU after 30 days for a new game with 500 installs per day and a retention profile of $a = 0.372, b = -0.442$ is 2,510:

```
R> dau(installs=500, a=0.372, b=-0.442, n=30)
 [1]  500  686  822  937 1038 1129 1213 1292 1366 1437 1504 1568 1630 1690 1748
[16] 1804 1859 1912 1964 2014 2064 2112 2160 2206 2252 2297 2341 2384 2427 2469
[31] 2510
```

```
R> plot(dau(installs=500, a=0.372,
b=-0.442, n=30),type="l",xlab="n")
```

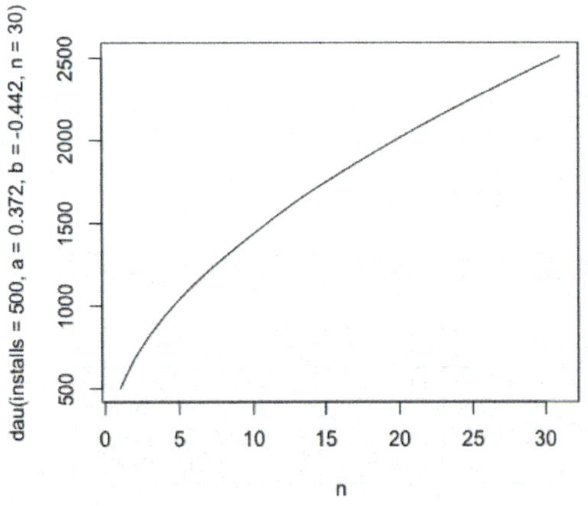

This approach to predicting DAU never settles on a steady state; the retention curve asymptotically approaches 0 as $n \to \infty$, therefore this DAU model grows forever. (Compare with the heuristic we defined as part of the bathtub analogy, which employs the daily churn rate and does stabilize.) A simple fix is to define a terminal date after which all players are assumed churned. For example, 365 days after install:

```
ret_curve <- function(a, b, n)
{
  if (n <= 0) return (1)
  if (n >= 365) Dn = 0 else Dn = a * n^b
  return(c(ret_curve(a, b, n-1), Dn))
}
```

Summary

We covered a lot of material in this chapter. The key take-aways are:

- The retention profile for a game is a non-linear regression function fit to a set of observed D*n*R values for installs over a range of historical dates. This function is referred to as the retention curve.
- The retention curve is a power formula $r(n) = an^b$, which defines a retention rate as a function of n, the days since install. This formula also defines the probability that a user plays exactly n days after install. It follows that D0R $= r(0) = 1.0$ and D*n*R $\cong r(n)$.
- The user duration is the number of distinct dates an install engages with (plays) the app over the user's lifetime (i.e., until churn) or within the first n days after install. The expected value of user duration by day n is the summation of the retention curve from days 0 to n. This summation can be performed both iteratively with a programming language or estimated analytically by fitting a curve PD(n) to the running sum of D*n*R.
- A prediction of total DAU by day n after game launch is the number of daily installs multiplied by the summation of the retention curve.

After fitting a curve to observed D*n*R values, Professor Arpdau iterates over that retention function to calculate the expected user duration. A curve is fit to define PD(n). The professor then predicts DAU (and daily revenue) using the same technique described in this chapter. Try it out at arpdau.com.

Modeling and Predicting Revenue:
LEVEL 5

Coffee's on at Le Café d'Arpdau. We are still running our free coffee give-away to the first 100 customers who sign up for our loyalty program each day, but we're not sure how well this promotion is doing. How many customer visits can we expect from each loyalty signup? We know from the prior chapter that user duration in player days (i.e., customer duration in café visits) is the summation of retention. For our café patrons, daily retention is:

$$\mathrm{D}n\mathrm{R} = 0.5^n$$

D1R is 50%, D2R is 25%, etc., which indicates that all customers churn within seven days of signing up. Therefore, the expected number of café visits before churn is:

$$\sum_{n=0}^{6} 0.5^n$$

We run that summation through Excel and find the answer is 1.98. We conclude that each free coffee generates 0.98 additional visits to our store. Repeat customers are great, but how much money does that make us? What is the total revenue from each cohort of loyalty customers before they churn? To find out, we download daily CSVs for our loyalty customers from our POS system and load them into Excel, starting with the day we opened (July 10th). Most of the 100 signups only took the free coffee, but some added a baked good or other beverage to their order. The data looks something like this, with a record for each signup that made an additional purchase beyond simply taking the free coffee:

Date	Customer ID	Customer Since	Purchase
2022-07-10	555-555-1234	2022-07-10	$2.50
2022-07-10	555-555-4218	2022-07-10	$7.50
2022-07-10	555-555-1255	2022-07-10	$2.50
2022-07-10	555-555-2345	2022-07-10	$3.00
2022-07-10	555-555-9876	2022-07-10	$5.25
...	...	...	...

Total revenue (the sum of the `Purchase` column) was $201.00, for an average of $2.01 per loyalty signup.

The next day, 50 customers returned and made a purchase. Total revenue from those 50 loyalty members was $305.50. Average revenue per daily customer for this cohort on this day is $6.11, mainly due to no more free coffee for this group. Average lifetime revenue is now $(201 + 305.50)/100 = \$5.07$.

That's all well and good, but how much revenue do the customers who signed up on opening day generate before they stop buying their coffee from us? We know that none of the original 100 patrons remain after six days; i.e., July 16 is the last day this cohort will generate revenue. After downloading the data for the next five days, we plug the figures into Excel and construct the following chart.

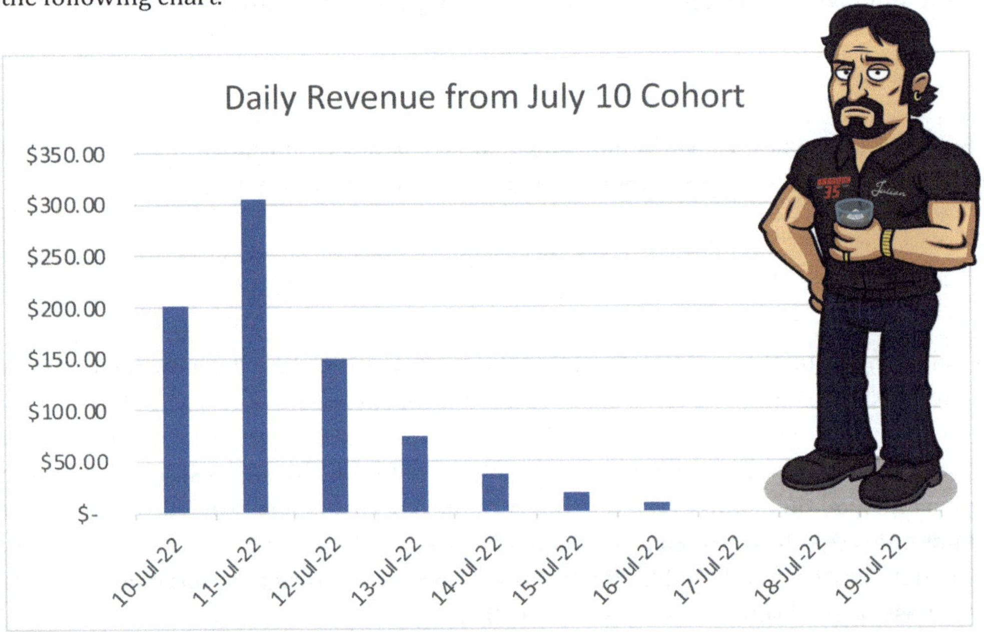

How much is that in total? We need an alternative visualization of this data to make that clear. A **revenue curve** is the *running sum* of daily revenue derived from a cohort. Instead of $305.50 as the revenue for July 11, the total revenue to date of $201.00 + $305.50 is plotted. We also switch to a line chart rather than bars. See Figure 5.1. It is a *curve* because the revenue starts to taper off as customers churn or cease to monetize. Total revenue for this cohort taps out at just shy of $800.

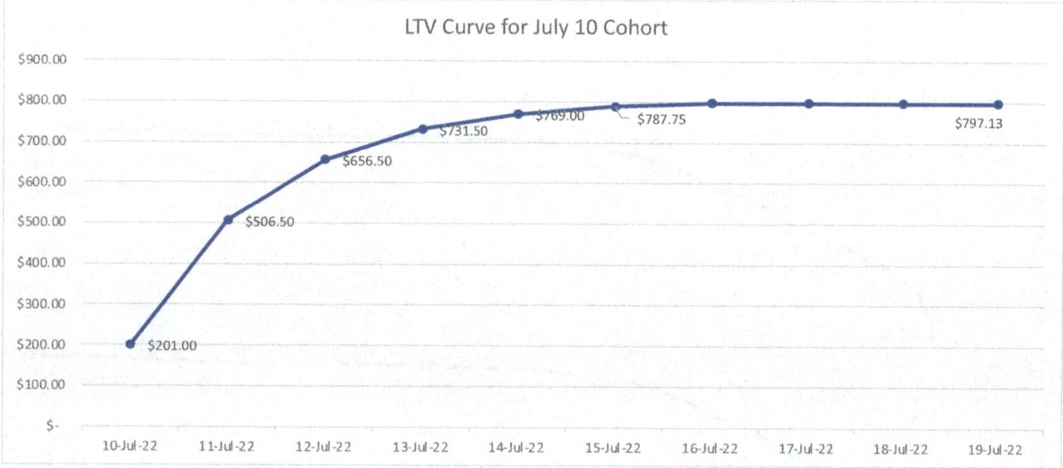

Figure 5.1 A revenue curve for the July 10th cohort of 100 Café d'Arpdau loyalty club customers from signup to churn. Final LTV is $797.13/100 = $7.97.

Each day of loyalty signups exhibit their own unique revenue curve. But will they be similar? Just like we did with retention, can we fit a curve to this data and derive a formula for revenue as a function of days since signup? And can we use this curve's function to predict revenue for new customers?

In this chapter, we seek answers to these and other questions regarding how to model and predict LTV. In particular, we learn to build revenue curves based on cohort IAP over the first n days since install. To foreshadow, Figure 5.2 (top) is a revenue curve for a single install date of *BFIT* players. The y-axis is a running sum of IAP revenue. The curve starts to flatten at 175 days since install, but revenue continues to trickle in until $n = 343$, generating $8,982.52 in total revenue. At this point the cohort of players has either fully churned, or those that remain have stopped monetizing.

An **LTV curve** is a revenue curve where the y-axis is scaled to customer lifetime value by dividing the cumulative revenue by the size of the cohort; i.e., plotting average revenue per player. Recall that:

$$\text{LTV}_n = \frac{\sum_{i=0}^{n} \text{revenue}_i}{\text{cohort size}}$$

The numerator is the running sum of observed cohort revenue; i.e., the revenue curve. An LTV curve indicates how the cohort's LTV grows over time. In the case of Figure 5.2 (middle), from $0.14 at D0 to $5.54 by D365.

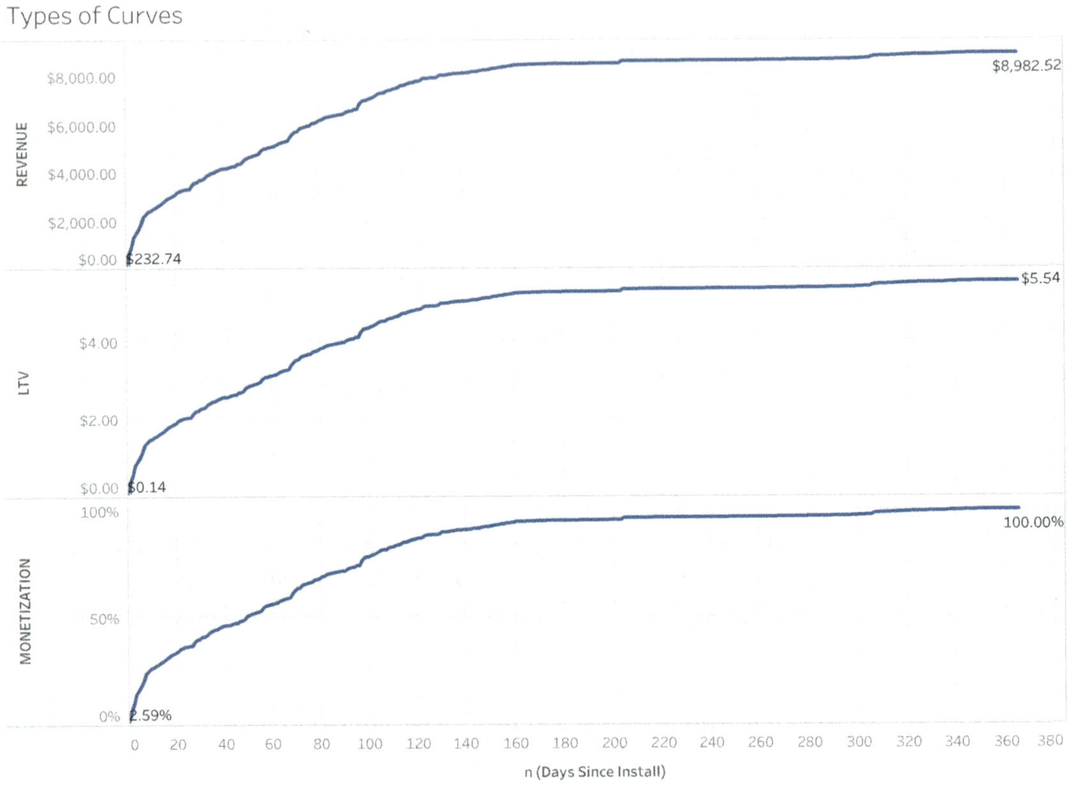

Figure 5.2 Three types of *running sum of IAP* curves for a cohort of installs. The shape of the curve is the same in each case – only the y-axis has changed. A *revenue* curve (top) is the running sum of daily revenue. The y-axis is absolute IAP revenue. An *LTV* curve (middle) indicates how average LTV for the cohort's players grows over time. A *monetization* curve (bottom) normalizes the y-axis to the percentage of total revenue achieved by a terminal day after install (in this case 365).

Individual cohorts exhibit a high degree of variance when it comes to IAP revenue, whether converted to LTV or left absolute. As such, the techniques introduced in this chapter mainly concern how best to combine revenue curves and derive a closed-form function to model and predict LTV. The monetization curve in Figure 5.2 (bottom) is indicative of the approach, which mirrors our development of the retention profile and its function $r(n)$ in the previous chapter. Our focus now is on fitting a monetization curve $m(n)$ to historical data, then using $m(n)$ to predict LTVn for new install cohorts.

But first, let's observe the nature of LTV from IAPs in free-to-play games.

LTV From IAP

In this chapter, we only consider IAPs in our modeling and prediction of revenue. With access to user-level ad monetization data (i.e., ad revenue attributed to specific users in your game) it is possible to accurately include ad revenue. But in our experience, models of revenue based on ad monetization alone are straightforward and their predictions more likely to be accurate compared to models based on IAP. In games where IAP revenue is a much greater share of total revenue, it is more important – and more difficult – to derive accurate models of LTV. Why? Two reasons.

1. Most active players watch rewarded video ads, but < 5% of players typically make an IAP. If a player is active, they are highly likely to contribute ad revenue but not contribute IAP revenue. Therefore, there is less data upon which to build an IAP LTV model.
2. There is very little variance in ad revenue between users whereas IAP revenue per paying user can vary wildly, resulting in a wide range of IAP LTV between install cohorts. This variance is an artifact of the high spenders, which we call *whales*.

"Welcome to the Ocean, We've Got Fun and Games"

There is a tendency amongst data analysts with a background in other industries to want to exclude outliers. When it comes to IAP, don't do that. Always remember that *any* IAP is an outlier, and amongst those outliers, some of your spenders are likely paying what you might consider an obscene amount of money to partake in a free game.

Don't believe me? Let's look at the distribution of IAP-only LTV90 for the installs who make up the cohort of players pictured back in Figure 5.2. This is from the ESG game *BFIT*, and represents actual customer data. Refer to the next chart, where the *y*-axis is a count of the number of users whose LTV90 falls within the buckets defined by the *x*-axis. Seufert (2014) refers to this histogram as a *monetization curve*. While it is usually clear from context which type of curve you are measuring and discussing, we deviate from Seufert and refer to this chart as an **LTV distribution**. Keep in mind that the average LTV90 is $3.99 for this cohort.

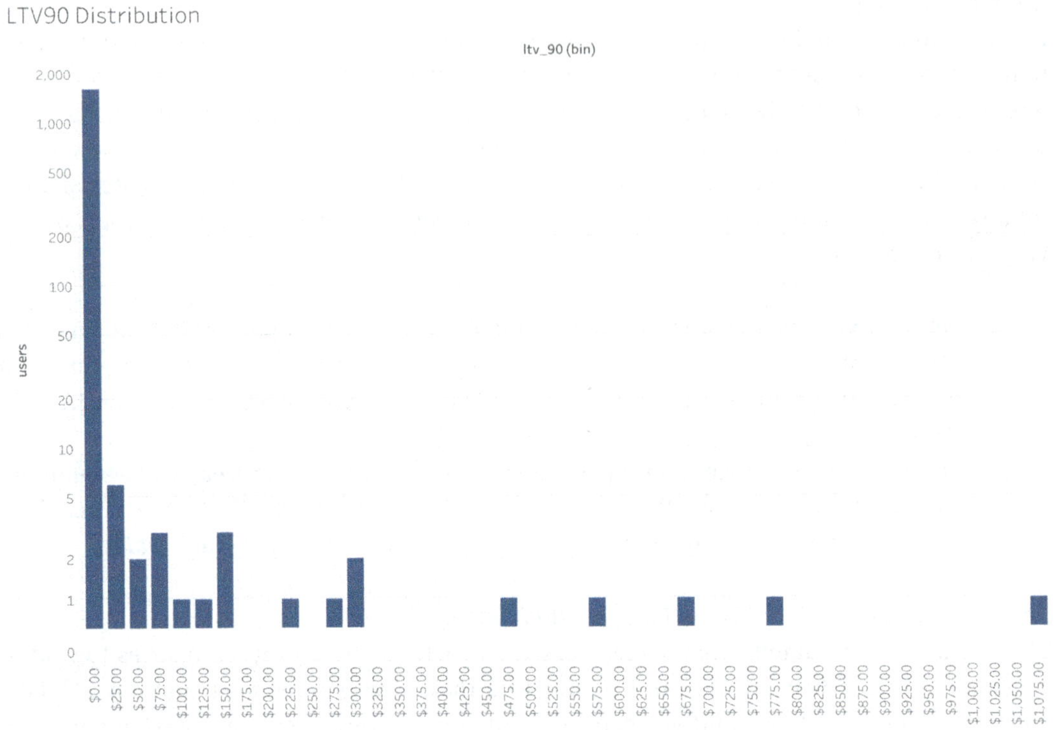

For readability, the *y*-axis is logarithmic. Only 61 of the 1,622 installs made an IAP within their first 90 days; D90 conversion is fairly low at only 3.76%. The first bin of the histogram, which includes all 1,561 non-monetizers plus 36 spenders with LTV90 < $25, contains 98.5% of the cohort. Only 25 users spent more than $25.00 during their first 90 days. But look at the five spenders out on the right! Of the $6,478.15 in IAP revenue, those five individuals accounted for $3,639.52 or 56% of the total. The single player at the tail end spent $1,096.17, accounting for 17% of the cohort's total revenue.

While impressive, spending $1,000 within 90 days of installing a game does not qualify this customer as a whale. A *dolphin*, maybe. To find the whales in our sea of players, we need to cast a wider net. If we plot a histogram of LTV90 from every monetizing install over a six-month period, some of the whales begin to breach the surface:

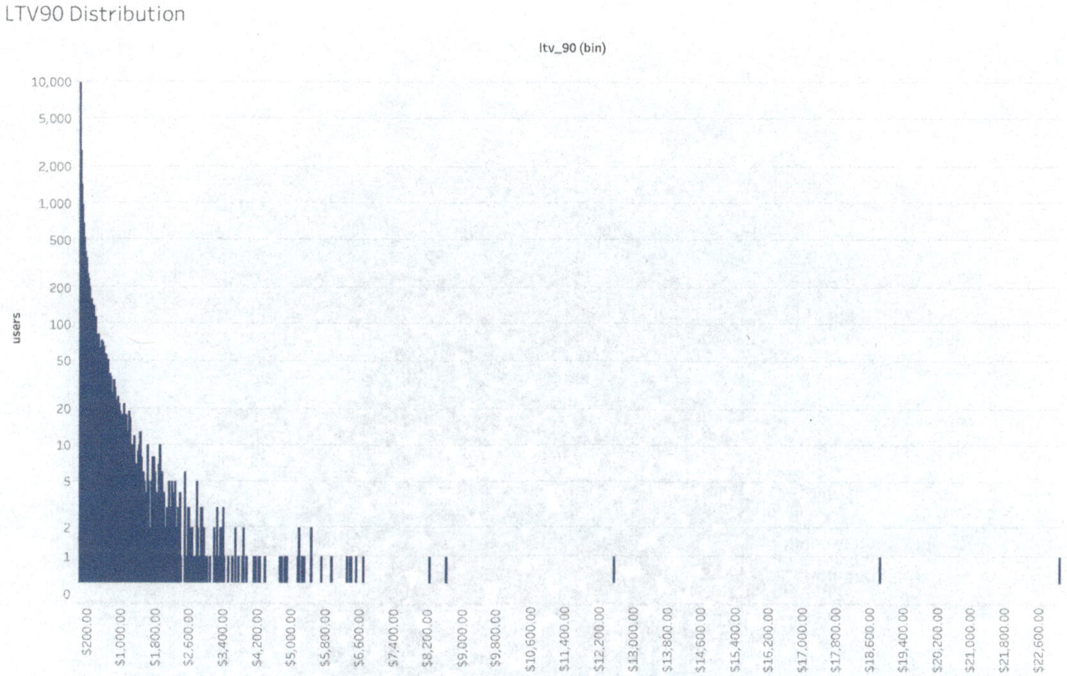

The one player on the extreme right spent just over $23,000 in their first 90 days of game play.

To get a sense of the extent to which whales dominate total revenue, let's build a bubble chart in Tableau from this same set of monetizing players. A bubble chart, where each bubble represents an individual monetizing user's LTV90, is depicted in Figure 5.3. There are five colour bands, each host to a different category of monetizers. From darkest to lightest, the categories are whales, dolphins, salmon, minnows, and shrimp. A whale is not defined by their absolute spend on IAP but rather by which band of 20% they land when sorted by percentage of total IAP revenue. The whales in the center of the chart – the largest bubbles with the darkest colour – account for a combined 20% of revenue, even though there are only 244 of them. Likewise, the dolphins on the next band account for a total of 20%, and so on. We call this visualization a **Janin Chart**, named for its creator and our colleague, Francois Janin.

Looking at Figure 5.3, trying to find that one user we met on the previous page whose LTV90 is $1,096.17 is like trying to find a needle in a haystack. (I know – I tried finding them by mousing over countless bubbles and hoping for that figure to pop-up.) In the broader picture, that level of LTV90 revenue places them in the 60-80% of total revenue band, making them a dolphin. But just barely.

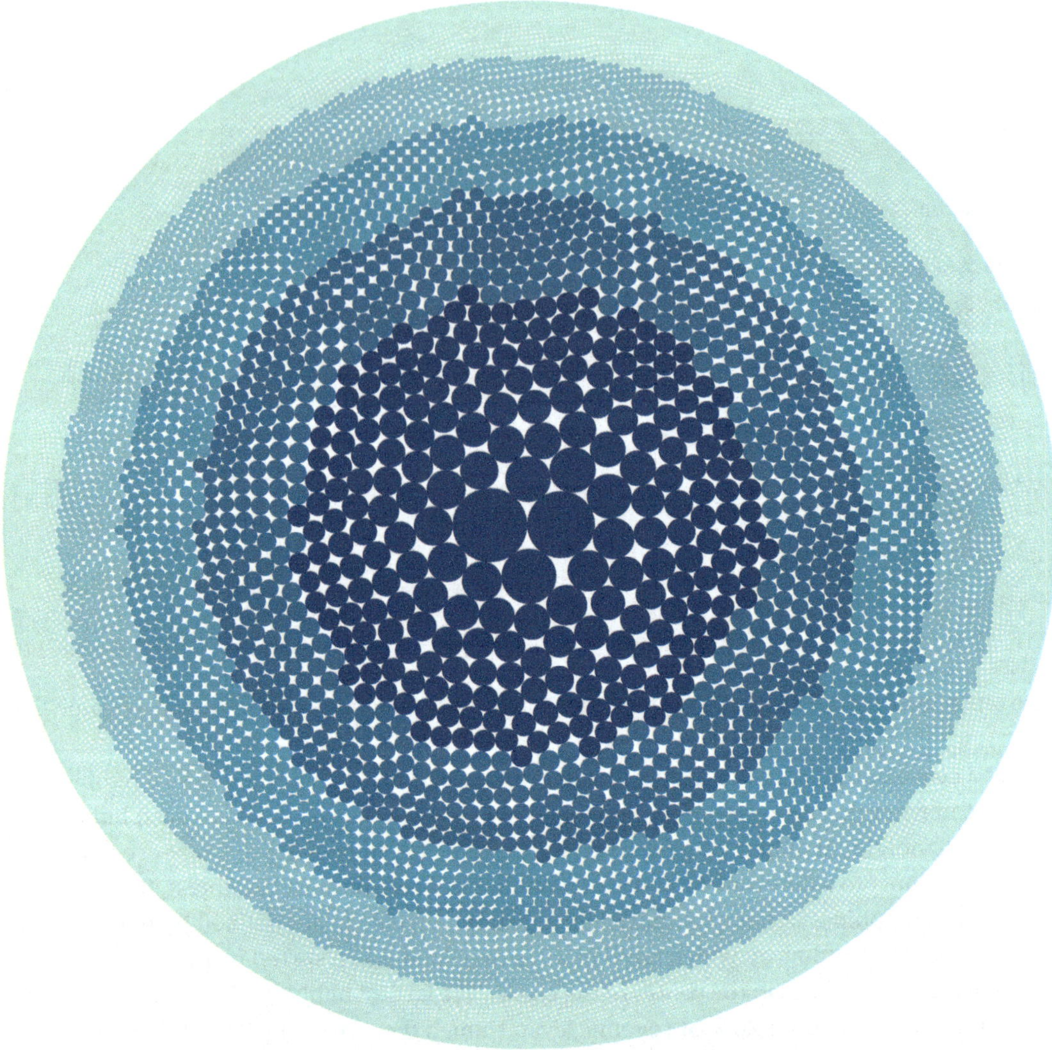

Figure 5.3 A Janin Chart assigns a distinct colour gradient to groups of users that contribute a combined 20% of the total cohort IAP revenue. Each bubble represents a single monetizing user. The size of the bubble indicates that player's absolute LTV90 relative to the others. The sum of LTV90 across all users in each band of colours accounts for 20% of total revenue.

The query used to build a Janin Chart requires user-level monetization data, including each monetizing player's share of the total revenue:

```
WITH monetizers AS
(
SELECT user_id,
       ltv_90,
       install_date,
       SUM(ltv_90) OVER
       (ROWS BETWEEN UNBOUNDED PRECEDING AND UNBOUNDED FOLLOWING) AS
total_ltv,
       ltv_90::FLOAT / total_ltv AS share_of_revenue
FROM  user_ltv
WHERE install_date BETWEEN '2022-07-01' - 365 AND '2022-07-01' - 91
  AND ltv_90 > 0
)
```

Further, a running sum of each payer's share of total revenue is necessary to band individuals into their respective "20% of total revenue" buckets. This is accomplished by ordering the result set by `ltv_90` within the window function:

```
SELECT *,
       SUM(share_of_revenue) OVER (ORDER BY ltv_90
             ROWS BETWEEN UNBOUNDED PRECEDING AND CURRENT ROW)
       AS sum_sor
FROM monetizers
ORDER BY ltv_90
```

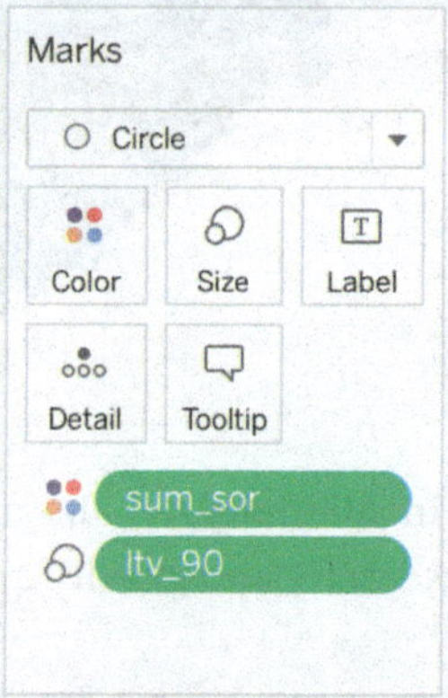

From there it's simply a matter of configuring the *Marks* panel as shown to the right.

A Janin chart indicates the diversity of a game's ecosystem of paying users. It also tells you what level of expenditure separates a whale from a dolphin, etc.

An interesting alternative bubble chart is built by ordering and colouring the bubbles (users) by their `install_date` rather than share of total revenue. The resulting visualization is reminiscent of the old fractal-geometric Mandelbrot sets that were super popular when I was an undergrad. The older installs are in the center of the chart and are of a lighter colour. Whales appear randomly in time, surrounded by schools of minnows.

It's beautiful, but not necessarily actionable.

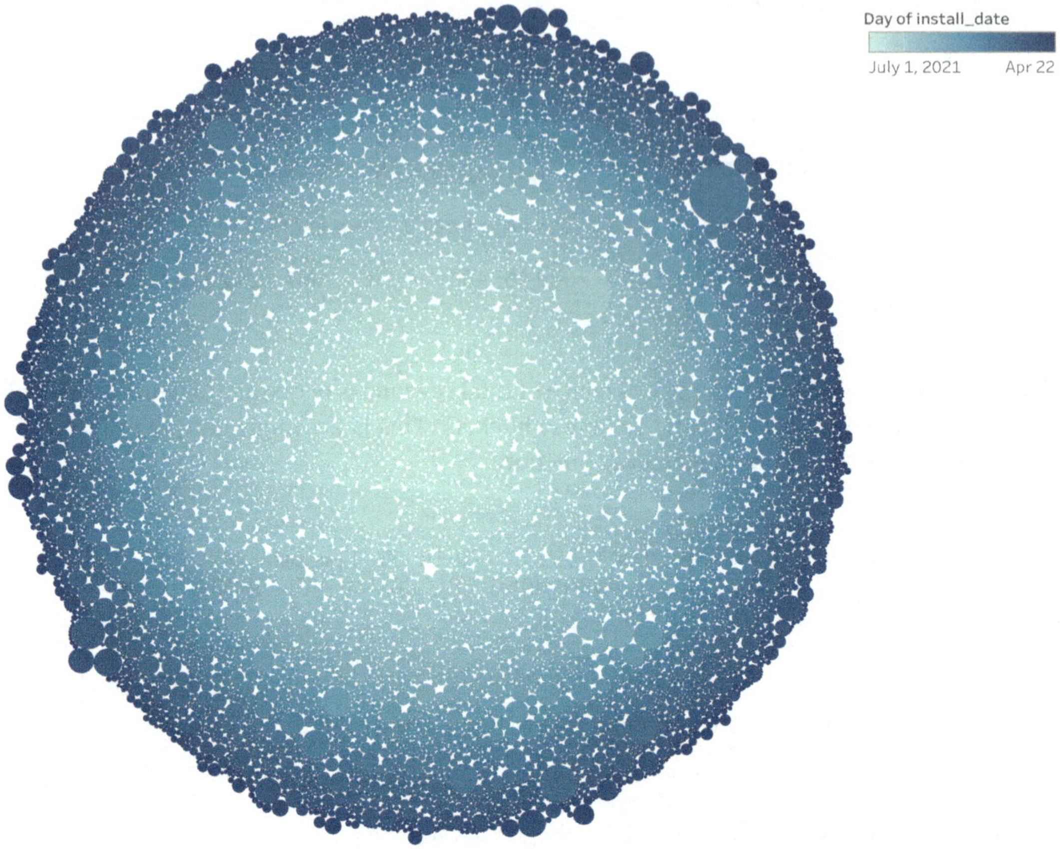

In summary, whales are real, and an important part of how games monetize. Their combined scarcity and gravity are what makes modeling IAP LTV difficult.

The Monetization Curve

As defined previously, a revenue curve is the running sum of daily revenue derived from a cohort of players, where the *x*-axis is days since install. Conversely, in a **monetization curve**, the *x*-axis extends only to a chosen terminal day (typically 90 or 180 days) and absolute revenue ($) on the *y*-axis is replaced with the percentage of total revenue by terminal day. A monetization curve is a normalized revenue (or LTV) curve, and answers important questions like, "what percentage of total revenue by day 90 can we expect by day seven?" And with a little algebra, the monetization curve can also predict the absolute revenue we can expect by day 90 given the observed revenue generated by day seven.

These are the steps involved in generating a 90-day monetization curve based on an IAP history of 90D fully-baked players taken from 365 to 91 days prior to July 1, 2022. Like we did with retention, Tableau is used to fit a trendline of type power to this data to derive a closed-form function. We then apply this function to predicting LTV90 for installs in the month of July 2022.

Step 1: Collect the purchase history (by date) for each monetizing player who installed during that timeframe. We start by imagining a relation with the following columns:

```
<user_id, install_date, purchase_date, revenue>
```

where `user_id` identifies the spender, `install_date` is the date they started playing, and `revenue` consists of the total IAP revenue attributed to that user on that `purchase_date`. A CTE for this relation is:

```
WITH monetizers AS
(
SELECT user_id,
        install_date,
        purchase_date,
        revenue
FROM (SELECT user_id,
             install_date
     FROM user_source
     WHERE install_date BETWEEN '2022-07-01' -365 and '2022-07-01' -
   91)
   INNER JOIN (SELECT user_id,
                      date as purchase_date,
                      SUM(converted) as revenue
               FROM purchases_view
               GROUP BY user_id,
                        purchase_date) USING(user_id)
)

SELECT *
FROM monetizers
ORDER BY RANDOM() LIMIT 7
```

user_id	install_date	purchase_date	revenue
8358656	2021-09-08	2021-09-18	12.64
8668524	2022-01-24	2022-01-25	4.20
8157611	2021-07-20	2021-08-22	20.53
8280987	2021-08-24	2021-11-08	6.30
8229557	2021-08-12	2021-08-12	2.49
8368810	2021-09-10	2021-09-27	4.02
8329831	2021-09-03	2021-09-25	2.53

Our interest does not lie in specific purchase dates, however, but rather in how many days since install it was when that player made a purchase. We replace the `purchase_date` column with the difference in days since install. Moreover, we only need purchases made within the first 90 days of install to build our model. The modified CTE is:

```
WITH monetizers AS
(
  SELECT user_id,
         install_date,
         DATE_DIFF('day', install_date, purchase_date) AS
days_since_install,
         revenue
  FROM (SELECT user_id,
               install_date
        FROM user_source
        WHERE install_date BETWEEN '2022-07-01' - 365 AND '2022-07-
01' - 91)
    INNER JOIN (SELECT user_id,
                       DATE AS purchase_date,
                       SUM(converted) AS revenue
                FROM purchases_view
                GROUP BY user_id,
                         purchase_date) USING (user_id)
  WHERE days_since_install BETWEEN 0 AND 90
)
```

user_id	install_date	days_since_install	revenue
8358656	2021-09-08	10	12.64
8668524	2022-01-24	1	4.20
8157611	2021-07-20	33	20.53
8280987	2021-08-24	76	6.30
8229557	2021-08-12	0	2.49
8368810	2021-09-10	17	4.02
8329831	2021-09-03	22	2.53
...	...	...	...

Step 2: Aggregate by `days_since_install` to eliminate individual users from the result set. The monetization curves are based on *cohort* purchases by days since install, so we combine the contributions of individuals. We also include the `install_date` to distinguish between specific cohorts.

```
SELECT install_date,
       days_since_install,
       SUM(revenue) AS revenue
FROM monetizers
GROUP BY install_date,
         days_since_install
```

Move this data into Tableau and create a plot of `revenue` (*Rows*) by `days_since_install` (*Columns*). This lumps all the IAP together based only on what day after install the purchases occurred. We see that the revenue is front-loaded: most occurs in the first 10 days of a cohort's lifetime. From D1 onwards it resembles the retention curve.

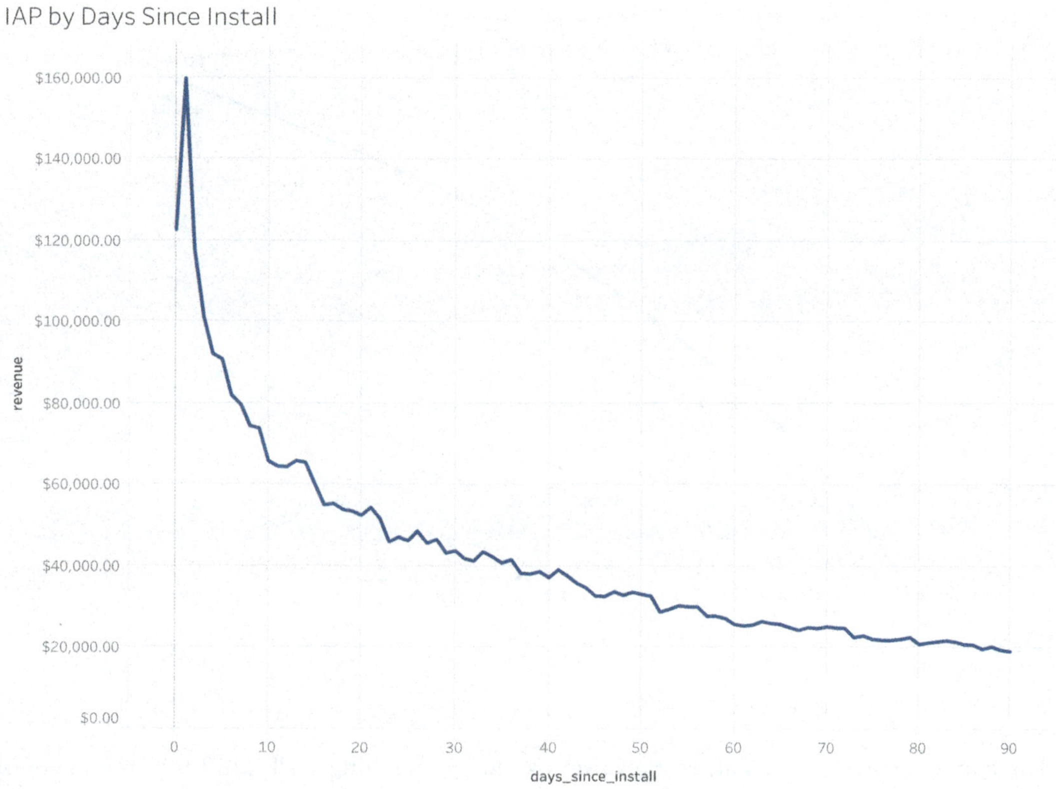

Step 3: Create a revenue curve by applying a *Quick Table Calculation* to the `SUM(revenue)` pill and selecting *Running Total.*

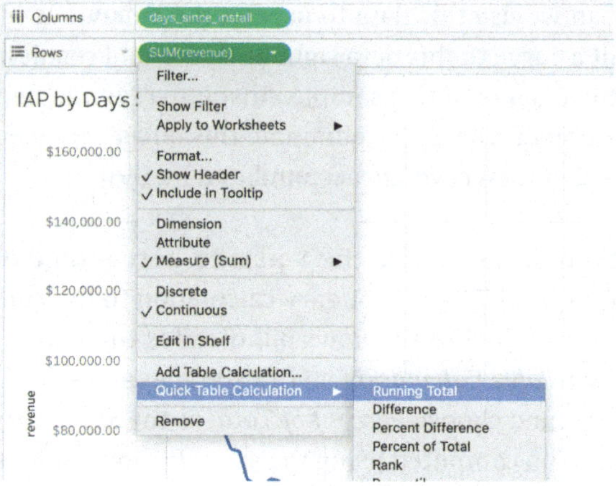

Note that `SUM` is the correct aggregation to apply to `revenue` since the data is broken down by `install_date` – a breakdown we haven't used yet, but soon will.

First, let's examine the (absolute) revenue curve that results from applying the running total to the IAP data. The *y*-axis now becomes the *Running Sum* of revenue.

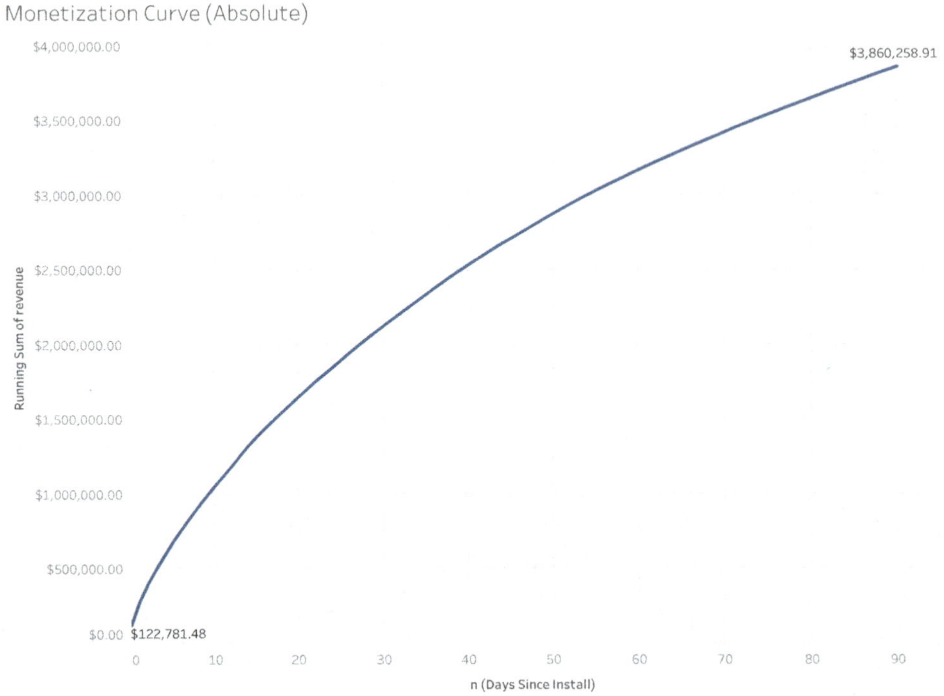

The curve is surprisingly flat: (some) users keep on spending well into D90 (and beyond). However, more than 50% of the revenue is collected by D30.

Can we use this data to predict the behaviour of future cohorts? We could, but if we were to fit a curve to this data right now it would result in a function based on the absolute revenue of the players in this sample. Absolute revenue depends entirely on the cohort size and composition of whales. To eliminate this effect, we need to normalize the *y*-axis and look at percentage of total revenue accumulated by D90.

Step 4: Normalize the *y*-axis to percentage of total. This step is a little tricky since it requires adding a secondary calculation to the running total. Remember that the *Table Calculation* applied to the *Rows* pill dictates the *y*-axis, which we now want to be 0...100%. Choose *Edit Table Calculation* on the `SUM(revenue)` pill, check the box next to *Add secondary calculation*, and choose *Percent of Total* as the *Secondary Calculation Type*. The secondary calculation is to be computed using the specific dimension `days_since_install`.

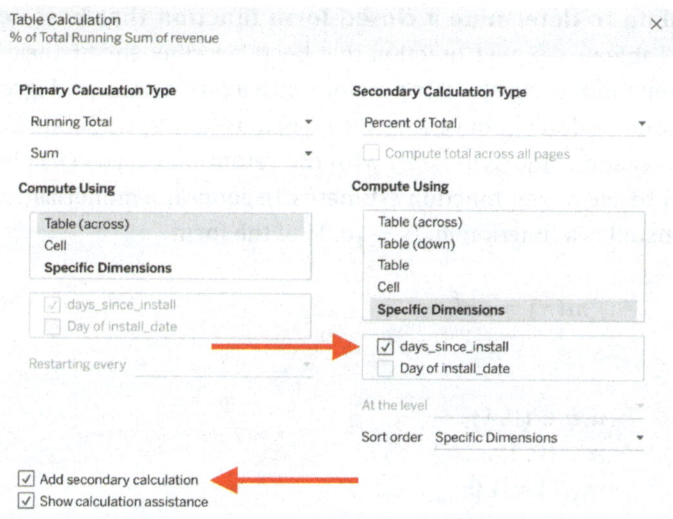

This bit of magic doesn't change the shape of the curve, but it does change its meaning rather significantly. Whereas before the last point in the graph was (90, $3,860,258), that point is now (90, 100%). It no longer matters how much revenue the users generated; it now matters *when* the revenue was generated.

What we know now is the proportion of the total D90 revenue that was generated on days 0 to 89. For example, by D30, 55.13% of the total revenue. Therefore, if the total revenue by D90 was only $100, then $55.13 happened by D30, as evidenced by selecting the point where `days_since_install` = 30:

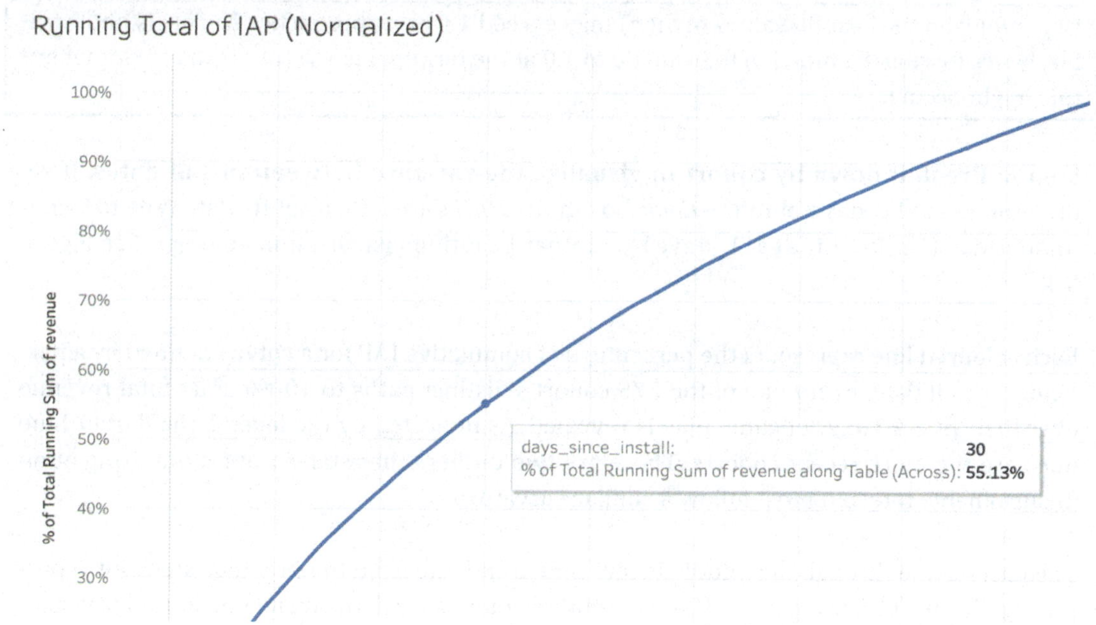

Step 5: Fit a trend line to the data to determine a closed-form function that best describes this curve. According to Tableau, a power function that best describes the historical data is $m(n) = 0.07n^{0.6}$, but an even more accurate fit is possible with a polynomial of degree three (or higher). However, polynomials don't behave very well when used to extrapolate beyond the terminal day *N*. For this reason – and symmetry with the retention curve $r(n)$ also being a power function – we prefer to use power function estimates. In general, a monetization curve over the first *N* days since install is a function $m: \mathbb{N} \rightarrow [0, 1]$ of the form

$$m(n) = an^b$$

where

$$a, b \in (0, 1]$$
$$n \in \{0, 1, \dots, N\}$$
$$m(N) = 1.0$$

The real-valued parameters a and b are referred to as the coefficient and exponent, respectively. Note the similarity to the retention curve, but in this case the exponent is positive. Values returned by the function are proportions between 0 and 1.

> Depending on the best fit, values of $m(n)$ may exceed 1.0 as n approaches *N*. This is undesirable, hence forcing the function to evaluate to 1.0 at the terminal day *N* (or any day prior where this might occur).

Step 6: Break it down by cohort to visualize the variance between install dates. If we drag the `install_date` onto the *Color* box in the *Marks* area, then set its date type to a continuous day (i.e., `DAY(install_date)`), a rather beautiful visualization emerges. See Figure 5.4.

Each coloured line represents the percentage of cumulative IAP for a cohort defined by a particular install date. Every one of the 275 cohort's distinct paths to 100% of its total revenue over their first 90 days of game play is revealed. As indicated by the legend, the darker blue lines are the more recent cohorts. There are two outliers that started out monetizing at an unsustainable rate, but most follow a similar curvature.

The dashed line through the middle is the same trend line from the previous step, but representing the most typical path to 100% of total revenue. We call the trend line fit to this visualization the **Bondy curve**, named after our colleague Justin Bondy, who first developed this technique.

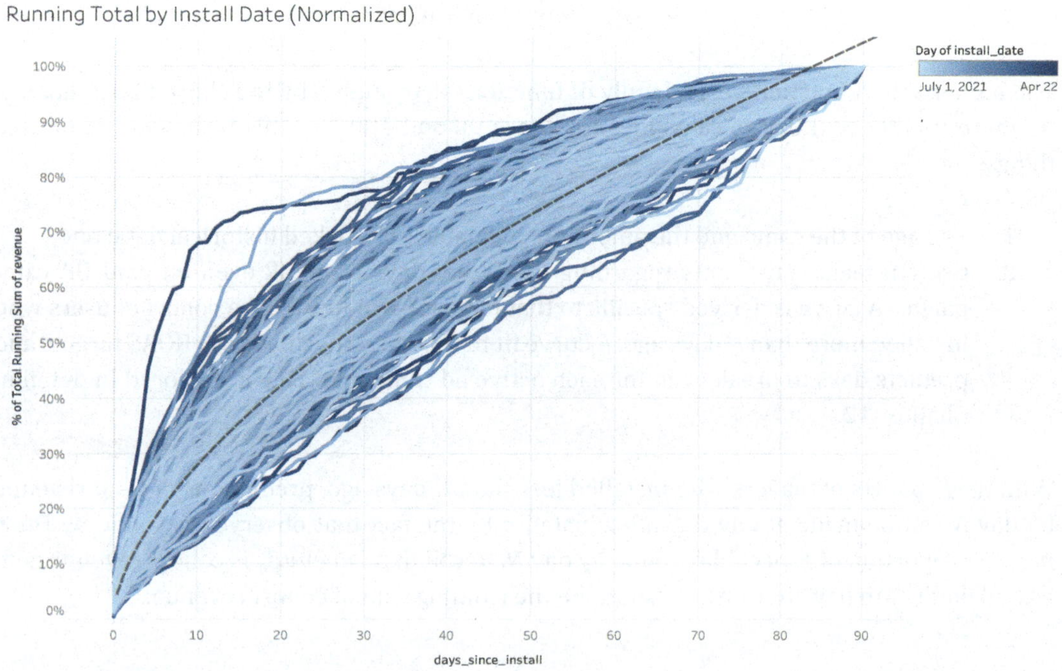

Figure 5.4. A Bondy curve is the trend line that best describes the path of daily install cohorts from 0 to 100% of their IAP revenue within the first *N* days since install.

The variance between individual cohorts is manifest in the Bondy curve and are suggestive of confidence intervals one can expect when used as an LTV prediction tool. The Bondy curve's R-squared is only 93.9% when best fit to each cohort's normalized revenue simultaneously. Conversely, when all the data was lumped together into a single monetization curve made up of a weighted average of the 275 cohorts, the function $m(n) = 0.07n^{0.6}$ fit the data with an R-squared of over 99.8%. With this dataset, however, the power function coefficient and exponent are the same to within three decimal places, likely due to the large sample size of individual cohorts. Hereafter, "monetization curve" is used to describe either approach unless explicitly stated otherwise.

Monetization curves model past behaviour, but can they predict future cohort monetization?

Making Predictions with the Monetization Curve

Knowing how previous cohorts of installs have behaved with respect to IAP is useful in predicting the purchasing behaviour of new installs. For a mature game with enough fully baked historical data, the approach we take is to fit a monetization curve to the first *N* days after install:

$$m_N(n) = an^b \qquad n \in 0..N$$

The monetization function m is a family of functions determined by the chosen terminal day N where $m_N(N) = 1.0$. Typical values for N are 90 and 180, but this is dependent on two things:

1. The age of the game and the amount of available fully-baked historical data; and,
2. Growth team constraints regarding the target days to break even on paid UA campaigns. A curve is derived specific to that payback window from a cohort of users who installed more than N days ago. A curve fit to that data specifies both ROAS targets and predicts days to break even for each active ad campaign. This is explored in detail in Chapter 12.

With new cohorts of players who installed less than N days ago, predictions of total revenue by day N can be made at any day after install n by the fact that observed revenue by Dn is $m_N(n)$ proportion of expected revenue by day N. Recall that $revenue_n$ is cohort revenue generated on the nth day after install. Let R_n be the running sum of cohort revenue:

$$\mathrm{R}_n = \sum_{i=0}^{n} \mathrm{revenue}_i$$

With observed monetization by day n, our prediction for total revenue by day N is given by:

$$\hat{\mathrm{R}}_N = \frac{\mathrm{R}_n}{m_N(n)}$$

Dividing R_n by cohort size, we can also predict LTV by day N:

$$\widehat{\mathrm{LTV}}_N = \mathrm{LTV}_n / m_N(n)$$

In practice, we use this technique to predict LTV90 for new *weekly* install cohorts based on observed LTV7. We lump the installs into weekly cohorts to increase the accuracy of the predictions, which tend to vary widely when applied to the smaller daily cohorts (see below). Predictions are updated frequently based on revenue to date and the days since install; i.e., as LTVn evolves. As cohort age approaches 90 days since install, predicted becomes actual.

A monetization curve's utility extends to predictions of R_i for any day i between the present-day n and terminal day N. With observed R_n, predicted R_i is:

$$\widehat{R}_i = m_N(i) * \frac{R_n}{m_N(n)}$$

$$= m_N(i) * \widehat{R}_N$$

$R_n/m_N(n)$ is predicting terminal $\widehat{R}_N$, then that number is scaled by the predicted percentage of that revenue we expect to see by day i.

> You might be tempted to extrapolate beyond day N. However, a monetization curve bounded by a maximum number of days since install N results in a function that is not to be trusted for predictions for $i > N$. For instance, we can't accurately predict LTV180 as $\widehat{\text{LTV}}_{90} * m_{90}(180)$. In our experience, this will overestimate LTV180.

Let's use the monetization curve defined by $m_{90}(n) = 0.07n^{0.6}$ to test its predictive power on the 31 install cohorts in the month of July. The actual LTVs for n=7, 30, 60, and 90 are given by the following query:

```
SELECT install_date,
       AVG(ltv_7) AS ltv7,
       AVG(ltv_30) AS ltv30,
       AVG(ltv_60) AS ltv60,
       AVG(ltv_90) AS ltv90
FROM user_ltv
WHERE install_date BETWEEN '2022-07-01' AND '2022-07-31'
GROUP BY install_date
```

This query was run 90 days after July 31, 2022, so all data is fully baked. We seek to examine how accurately LTV90 is predicted by $\text{LTV}_n/m_{90}(n)$ for $n \in \{7, 30, 60\}$. Adding predictions to our query (columns `ltv90_Dn` to indicate predicted LTV90 based on observed LTVn) is simply a matter of dividing by evaluation of the function $0.07n^{0.6}$. In SQL this is:

```
SELECT install_date AS date,
       AVG(ltv_7) AS ltv7,
       ltv7/(0.07*power(7,0.6)) AS ltv90_D7,
       AVG(ltv_30) AS ltv30,
       ltv30/(0.07*power(30,0.6)) AS ltv90_D30,
       AVG(ltv_60) AS ltv60,
       ltv60/(0.07*power(60,0.6)) AS ltv90_D60,
       AVG(ltv_90) AS ltv90
FROM user_ltv
WHERE install_date BETWEEN '2022-07-01' AND '2022-07-31'
GROUP BY install_date
```

date	ltv7	ltv90_d7	ltv30	ltv90_d30	ltv60	ltv90_d60	ltv90
2022-07-01	2.60	11.56	5.92	10.99	10.87	13.31	12.18
2022-07-02	1.91	8.49	4.88	9.06	7.20	8.82	8.03
2022-07-03	1.75	7.78	3.59	6.66	4.96	6.07	5.69
2022-07-04	0.77	3.42	1.33	2.47	1.82	2.23	2.19
2022-07-05	0.59	2.62	1.97	3.66	2.99	3.66	3.97
2022-07-06	1.71	7.6	5.54	10.28	8.55	10.47	10.62
2022-07-07	3.88	17.25	6.39	11.86	6.67	8.17	6.71
2022-07-08	1.33	5.91	3.74	6.94	5.64	6.91	6.94
...	...	...	...	...	...	...	...

The last column is the actual LTV90; compare with the predictions based on observed LTV at days 7, 30, and 60. Typically the predictions improve as *n* increases. Some of the predictions are excellent, but others are way off; e.g., the July 7 cohort started out strong with an LTV7 of \$3.88 putting it on pace to reach a juicy \$17.25 LTV90. In reality, it fell flat and landed at only \$6.71. To visualize the source of these errors, let's construct a Bondy curve for just these July install cohorts:

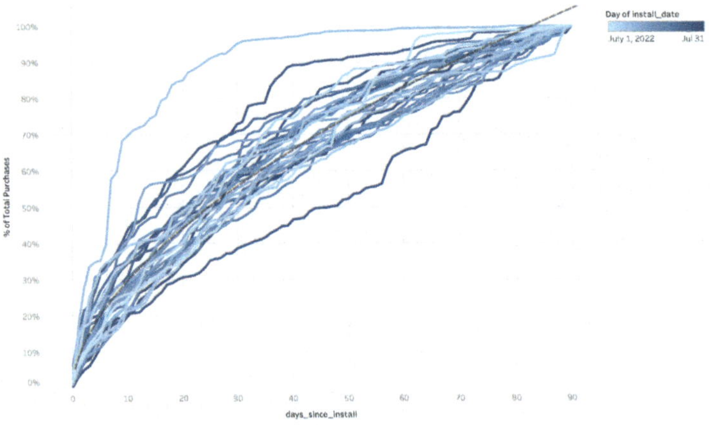

There are three bad actors; i.e., cohorts that stray far from the average path. The July 7th cohort is that light-blue line at the top that starts out fantastic but falls off a cliff by D30. Conversely, the dark-blue line at the bottom is a late bloomer; the specific data for that cohort in our query is:

date	ltv7	ltv90_d7	ltv30	ltv90_d30	ltv60	ltv90_d60	ltv90
2022-07-28	0.62	2.76	1.38	2.56	2.35	2.88	3.59

All three estimates (\$2.76, \$2.56, and \$2.88 made at D7, D30, and D60, respectively) are significantly lower than actual (\$3.59), which you would expect for any cohort whose monetization curve follows a path below the fitted curve.

The Bondy curve fit by Tableau to these 31 July cohorts alone is $m_{90}(n) = 0.079n^{0.58}$, which is slightly different than the historical curve we used to make the predictions. Either the game has changed, or the users acquired in this timeframe are not indicative of past monetizers. This is one of the caveats of this approach to predicting LTV, which we summarize here:

- "Past performance is no guarantee of future outcomes." In the Bondy visualization, it is clear that individual cohorts don't care about the past. Each will take its own path to 100% of revenue by day N. The predictions based on early observations, particularly D7, might land far off target.
- The coefficient and exponent change over time. As features of the game evolve, so will the shape of the monetization curve. It is important to refit the curve periodically as new installs become fully baked. A sliding window of cohort install dates should be used to replace stale cohorts with more recent players. However, the monetization from players who installed less than N days ago is never included.
- Predictions are more robust for larger cohorts that span a range of install dates.
- Burelli (2019) refers to our approach as an *average model based on historical data*, which he criticizes for its inability to predict LTV for individual customers who have yet to make a purchase. This is a valid critique but given our ultimate use case – predicting ROAS for ad campaigns – not particularly relevant.
- Monetization curves are different for each game. The overall shape is typically a power function, but each game has its own unique bend to the curve.
- Predictions of LTV beyond day N are not trustworthy.

Summary

The main idea introduced in this chapter is the monetization curve as a tool to model past IAP revenue and to predict future LTV. The construction of a monetization curve begins with a revenue curve, which is the running sum of daily revenue derived from a cohort of players, where the x-axis is days since install. The monetization curve modifies the revenue curve in two important ways:

1. the x-axis extends only to a chosen terminal day N, typically 90 or 180 days; and,
2. absolute revenue ($) on the y-axis is replaced (normalized to $[0, 1]$) with the proportion of total revenue by day N.

A monetization curve is described by a power function $m_N(n) = an^b$ defined for $n \in \{0, 1, \dots, N\}$ that is a best-fit to the observed historical data of N-day fully-baked users. The function m can answer important questions like, "what percentage of total revenue by day N can we expect by day n?" And with a little algebra, can also predict the absolute revenue we can expect by day N given the observed revenue generated by a cohort n days after install.

However, the function m is based on the historical monetization of users who installed the app more than N days ago. Therefore, the prediction techniques developed in this chapter have assumed a mature game and the existence of historical data to build a normalized LTV curve. Without a sizable cohort of N-day fully-baked installs, we are faced with the task of trying to estimate each cohort's absolute LTV curve based on early LTV signals only. This is addressed in a later chapter.

The *LTV Predictor* at arpdau.com is a quick and easy tool for simulating LTV curves for new (or hypothetical) games without the benefit of historical data. The underlying approach employed is described in the next chapter.

LTV = Σ (Retention) × ARPDAU:
LEVEL 6

The monetization curve is not the only popular method of modeling revenue in freemium products. An alternative LTV model is based on the summation of *retention* × ARPDAU. To see, let's check back in with our revenue curve at Café d'Arpdau.

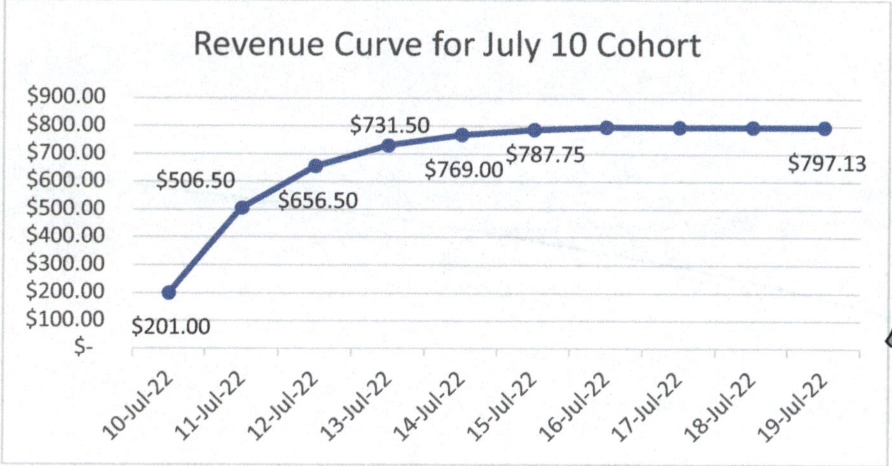

Total revenue of $797.13 from 100 customers indicates that LTV for this cohort was $7.97. From the running sum of retention, we know this LTV was generated by 1.98 café visits per customer. If customer LTV is $7.97 from an average of 1.98 visits each, the average revenue per café visitor must be $7.97/1.98 = $4.03. In the parlance of freemium, average ARPDAU must be LTV divided by the sum of retention:

$$\text{Average ARPDAU} = \frac{\text{LTV}_n}{\sum_{i=0}^{n} \text{D}i\text{R}}$$

Shuffling terms, we have:

$$\text{LTV}_n = \text{Average ARPDAU} * \sum_{i=0}^{n} \text{D}i\text{R}$$

In Figure 6.1, we foreshadow the relationship between the retention curve, average ARPDAU, and LTV.

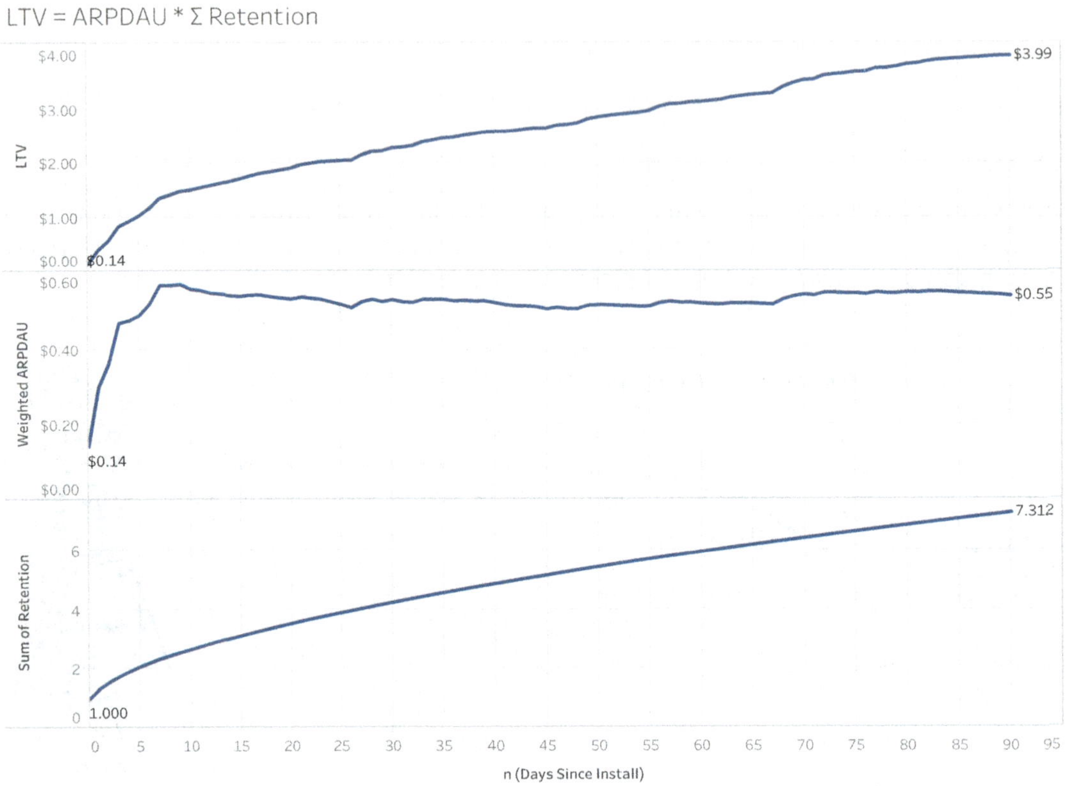

Figure 6.1 LTV (top), weighted average ARPDAU (middle), and the running sum of retention (bottom) as a function of days since install. The first 90 days for a small cohort of players is shown. At D90, average ARPDAU = $3.99/7.312 = $0.5456.

But how do we calculate ARPDAU as a cohort metric, and how exactly should we calculate average ARPDAU by days since install? To address that question, we consider the equivalence of the two LTV models. When presenting the monetization curve as our preferred model of LTV, we defined LTV as the running sum of cohort revenue divided by the cohort size.

$$\mathrm{LTV}_n = \frac{\sum_{i=0}^{n} \mathrm{revenue}_i}{\mathrm{cohort\ size}}$$

If LTV is also just *retention*×ARPDAU, then this equivalence must hold:

$$\frac{\sum_{i=0}^{n} \text{revenue}_i}{\text{cohort size}} = \text{Average ARPDAU} * \sum_{i=0}^{n} \text{D}i\text{R}$$

By solving for *Average* ARPDAU we can determine how it should be calculated to maintain this identity. In doing so we conclude that the two models of LTV and their predictive powers are identical. Without further ado…

Same LTV, Different Channel

As just noted, an alternative model of LTV you often hear about is the summation of retention multiplied by ARPDAU.

$$\text{LTV}_n = \text{ARPDAU} * \sum_{i=0}^{n} \text{D}i\text{R}$$

The summation of daily retention, DiR, over n days since install is nothing new. In the previous chapter, we defined the running sum of retention as PDn. The other term, however, is ARPDAU. In free-to-play games, ARPDAU is not constant, regardless of whether you look at it as a play-day metric or as a cohort metric. A formal definition of how ARPDAU should be computed in this context is regularly lacking in the literature. If this formula for LTVn is not a heuristic, but rather an equivalent way of expressing customer lifetime value, then the duality should inform our approach to defining "ARPDAU" in this context.

In other words, we have two competing definitions of LTVn, that if equivalent, tell us:

$$\text{ARPDAU} * \sum_{i=0}^{n} \text{D}i\text{R} = \frac{\sum_{i=0}^{n} \text{revenue}_i}{\text{cohort size}}$$

$$\text{ARPDAU} = \frac{\frac{\sum_{i=0}^{n} \text{revenue}_i}{\text{cohort size}}}{\sum_{i=0}^{n} \text{D}i\text{R}}$$

By definition, DiR $= \text{DAU}_i/(\text{cohort size})$.

$$\text{ARPDAU} = \frac{\frac{\sum_{i=0}^{n} \text{revenue}_i}{\text{cohort size}}}{\frac{\sum_{i=0}^{n} \text{DAU}_i}{\text{cohort size}}}$$

$$= \frac{\sum_{i=0}^{n} \text{revenue}_i}{\sum_{i=0}^{n} \text{DAU}_i}$$

That is what "ARPDAU" must mean in this context; namely, it is the running sum of daily cohort revenue divided by the running sum of daily cohort active users. The two models of LTV are identical if ARPDAU is defined this way. We use the term $\boldsymbol{w}\mathbf{ARPDAU}_n$ to denote this "weighted average ARPDAU for a cohort by day n after install," and LTV is thus:

$$\mathrm{LTV}_n = w\mathrm{ARPDAU}_n * \sum_{i=0}^{n} \mathrm{D}i\mathrm{R}$$

$$= w\mathrm{ARPDAU}_n * \mathrm{PD}_n$$

This is not (yet) a predictive model of LTV, but simply another way to describe what has happened historically.

We now describe an alternative derivation of $w\mathrm{ARPDAU}_n$ by following the data.

Cohort ARPDAU

Until now, we have only considered ARPDAU as the ratio of revenue to active players on a specific calendar day; i.e., as a time series based on play dates. But "daily active users" doesn't have to mean *every* person who plays on exactly the same date. In the same way that retention and LTV curves consider a cohort of players and follow the cohort's users from day 0 to n since install, we can do the same with ARPDAU. The DAU in this case are only the active users who belong to the same initial cohort; i.e., the retained players used in the calculation of daily retention.

$$\mathrm{ARPDAU}_n = \mathrm{revenue}_n / \mathrm{DAU}_n$$

To facilitate calculation, we first augment the relation (and its CTE) defined previously when building monetization curves. Whereas before we were only concerned with monetizing players, we now broaden our scope to include *all* players and include days where users play but do not make a purchase. This enables counting all active players for the denominator (DAU). The structure of the relation remains the same, namely:

```
<user_id, install_date, days_since_install, revenue>
```

But now, the `revenue` field is null on days where the user played but did not make a purchase. We define a new CTE by making the following modifications to the `monetizers` CTE: joining with `session_begin`.

```
WITH cohort AS
(
```

```
SELECT inst.user_id,
       install_date,
       DATE_DIFF('day',install_date,play_date) as days_since_install,
       revenue
FROM
    (
     SELECT user_id,
            install_date
     FROM user_source
     WHERE install_date BETWEEN '2022-07-01'-365 and '2022-07-01'-91
    ) inst
    LEFT JOIN
    (
     SELECT sb.user_id,
            play_date,
            revenue
     FROM (
            SELECT DISTINCT user_id,
                   date AS play_date
            FROM session_begin
            WHERE date >= '2022-07-01'-365) sb
            LEFT JOIN
           (
            SELECT user_id,
                   date as purchase_date,
                   SUM(converted) as revenue
            FROM purchases_view
            WHERE purchase_date >= '2022-07-01'-365
            GROUP BY user_id, purchase_date
           ) pur ON sb.user_id = pur.user_id
                 AND sb.play_date = pur.purchase_date
    ) play USING(user_id)
)
```

To create a graph of ARPDAU by days since install for this rather large cohort requires the following aggregation:

```
SELECT install_date,
       days_since_install,
       SUM(revenue) AS revenue,
       COUNT(*) AS players,
       FIRST_VALUE(players) OVER (PARTITION BY install_date
         ORDER BY days_since_install ROWS UNBOUNDED PRECEDING)
         AS cohort_size
FROM cohort
GROUP BY install_date,
         days_since_install
```

The column `players` is a count of active players on `days_since_install` for the cohort who share the same `install_date`. A window function is used to derive the initial size of the cohort defined by `install_date`; it's not strictly necessary but does simplify some of the calculations we are going to ask Tableau to perform. You hopefully noticed that retention is `players/cohort_size`. In fact, this CTE and the aggregate query generates the "Swiss-army-knife" dataset of game analytics: it facilitates calculating pretty much everything, as we are about to see as we use it to build some charts in Tableau.

First, we need a *Calculated Field* called `ARPDAU` defined as `SUM([revenue])/SUM([players])`. Creating a time series of ARPDAU by days since install helps visualize a response to the question "does ARPDAU remain constant as a cohort matures?" Short answer is no, it bounces around. Looking at a cohort of 1,622 players with the same install date, the first 90 days of ARPDAU ranges from $0.00 to $2.50, with an average value of $0.58.

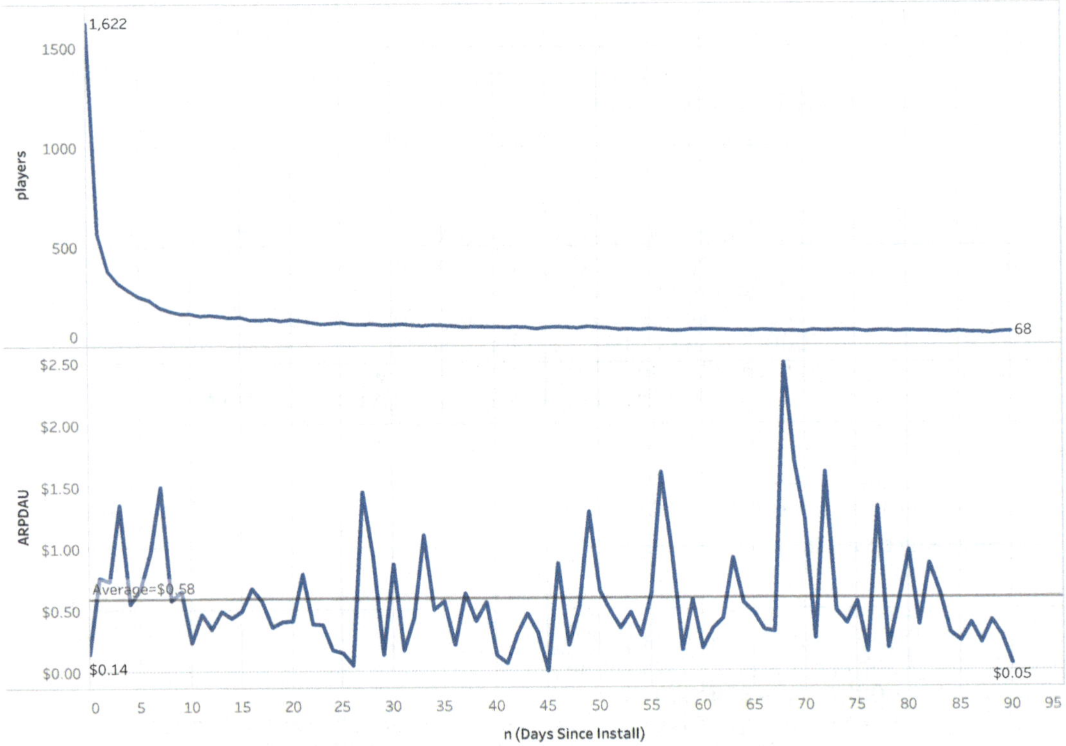

Still, the fact that ARPDAU remains somewhat consistent with only 68 players remaining is counter intuitive. One might expect that ARPDAU would increase as the unengaged players churn and the cohort shrinks, but this is not the case. What we notice when charting ARPDAU as a function of days since install is that ARPDAU on D0 is typically low ($0.14 in this case)

relative to the other days. This is because the installs are too new to have committed to the game and found a reason to make an IAP.

If we expand the size of the cohort to include several install dates, the fluctuations in the ARPDAU chart are smoothed. Here is the same graph but including four months of installs.

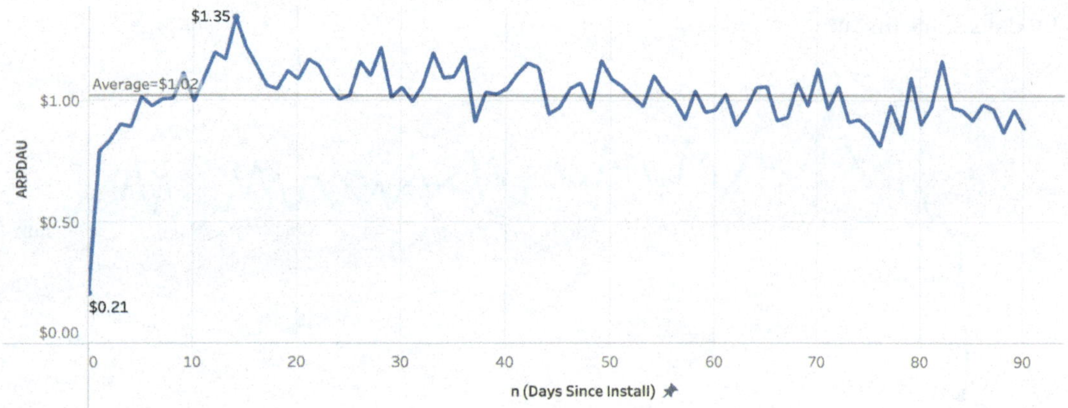

In this case, ARPDAU is at its lowest on D0 when the number of active players is at its peak.

The average ARPDAU is $1.02, and the variance from the mean seems low. But as I've said ad nauseam, an average of an average is never a good idea. We should be tracking how weighted ARPDAU evolves over time. Why? Because it's not as if that $1.35 peak ARPDAU blows away the drag of that $0.21 ARPDAU on D0. As *n* increases, ARPDAU is contributed by fewer and fewer active users and should not carry as much weight as those days with more active players.

Weighted average ARPDAU – where the weights are the size of the cohort's active users (DAU) – is:

$$\frac{\sum_i (\mathrm{ARPDAU}_i * \mathrm{DAU}_i)}{\sum_i \mathrm{DAU}_i}$$

But by definition $\mathrm{ARPDAU}_i = revenue_i/\mathrm{DAU}_i$, so multiplying by DAU_i in the numerator results in just $revenue_i$. Therefore, weighted ARPDAU by day *n* since install ($w\mathrm{ARPDAU}_n$) is

$$w\mathrm{ARPDAU}_n = \frac{\sum_{i=0}^{n} \mathrm{revenue}_i}{\sum_{i=0}^{n} \mathrm{DAU}_i}$$

i.e., the running sum of revenue divided by the running sum of active players. In Tableau, this can be implemented with the following calculated field.

```
RUNNING_SUM(SUM([revenue]))/RUNNING_SUM(SUM([players]))
```

Here is the weighted ARPDAU version (bottom) beneath daily cohort ARPDAU over the first 90 days since install:

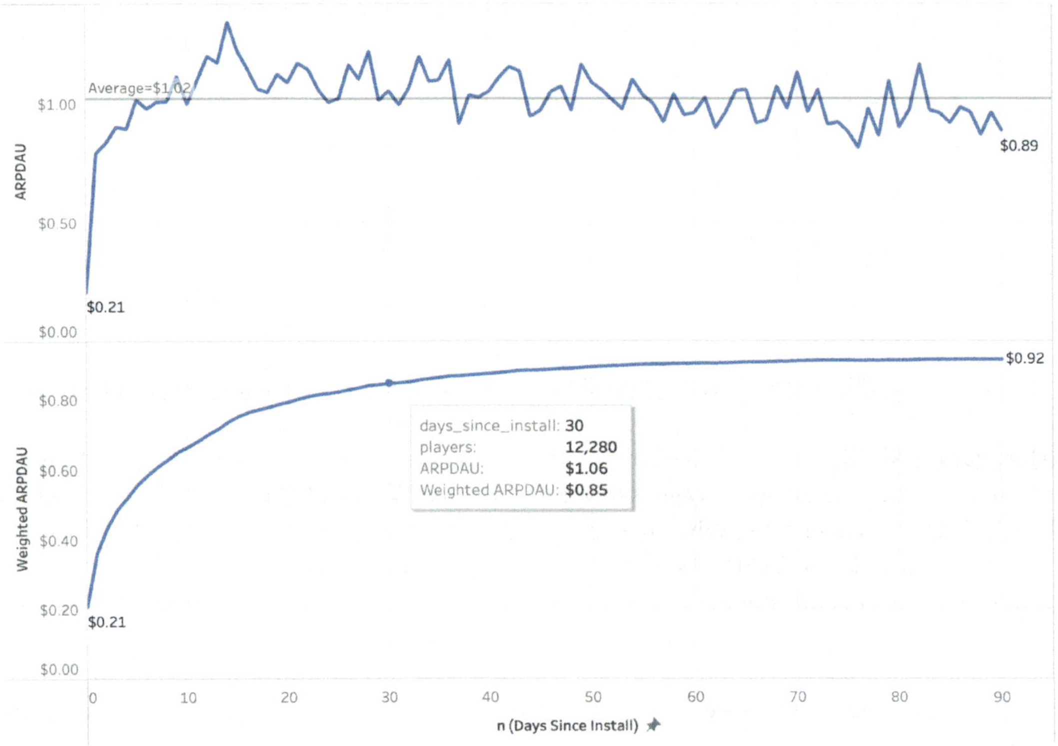

Besides being a smooth power (or logarithmic) curve, weighted ARPDAU is an accurate model of prior monetization, and once the curve flattens, a better predictor of future revenue. The wARPDAU$_{90}$ of \$0.92 is a more likely predictor of what we can expect for days 91 to 180 than the arithmetic mean of daily ARPDAU (\$1.02). The smoothing effect on daily fluctuations is manifest in the pop-up at D30, where the specific ARPDAU on that day was \$1.06. But taking every day's weight into account up to and including D30, wARPDAU$_{30}$ is only \$0.85.

And finally, here is a chart of weighted ARPDAU for the same cohort of players but extended to the first 180 days after install. The top chart is the running sum of revenue. The middle chart is the running sum of daily active players. Weighted ARPDAU at the bottom is the top chart divided by the middle chart. Weighted ARPDAU peaks at $0.92 at 82 days after install before starting to fall slightly.

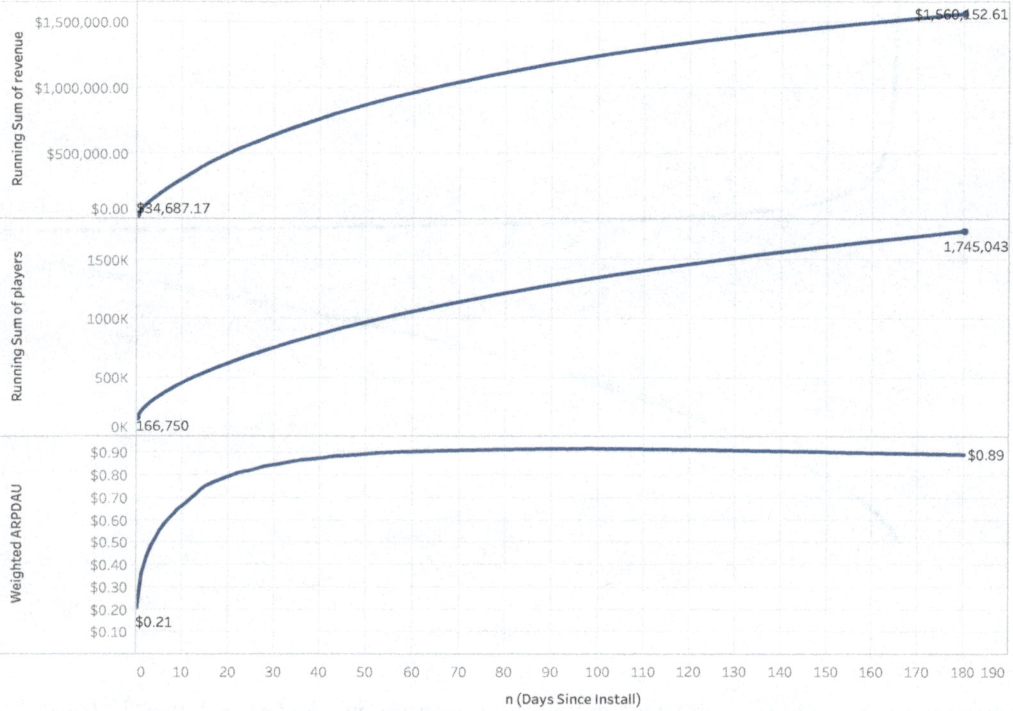

Predicting LTV with Normalized Retention and ARPDAU

The monetization curve fits the normalized running sum of revenue and models how cohort spending evolves over the first *N* days after install. Given the duality of the two LTV models, a similar technique is possible using the alternative formula for LTV; i.e., normalized *sum of retention * weighted cohort ARPDAU* instead. We now repeat the creation of the monetization curve from the previous chapter, but instead of revenue as the source data, we will use retention and weighted ARPDAU. Our intention is to reveal how the normalized curve based on monetization is identical to the normalized curve based on retention and ARPDAU; predictions based on either approach are the same.

Our analysis is applied to all users who installed *BFIT* 365 to 91 days prior to July 1, 2022. The retention profile for this group of users over their first 90 days after install is as follows.

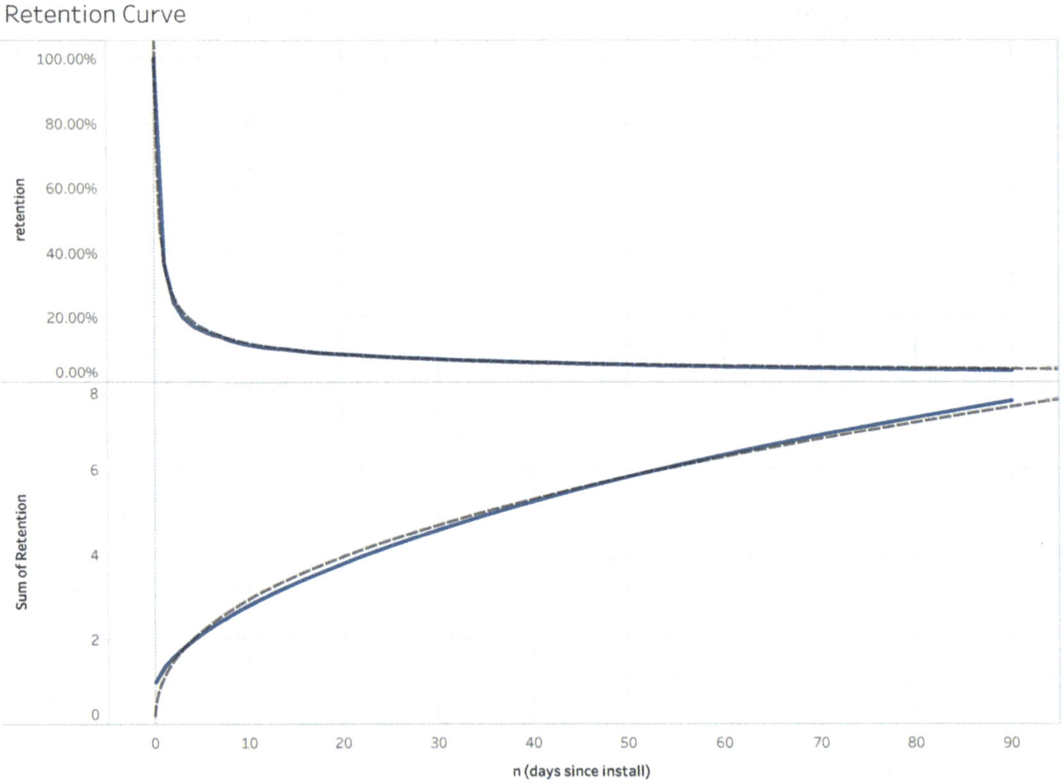

The power functions fit to each curve define the retention curve $r(n) = 0.38n^{-0.5}$ (top) and the running sum of retention curve $\mathrm{PD}(n) = 1.1n^{0.425}$ (bottom). The latter function is the best fit to the sum of retention applied to the weighted historical average over all installs from June 30, 2021, to April 1, 2022, and defines the expected user duration in player days for new installs. For example, $\mathrm{PD}(90) = 1.1(90)^{0.425} = 7.45$ is the expected number of player days for new users within their first 90 days after install.

Likewise, the ARPDAU and weighted ARPDAU graphs for this cohort are as follows.

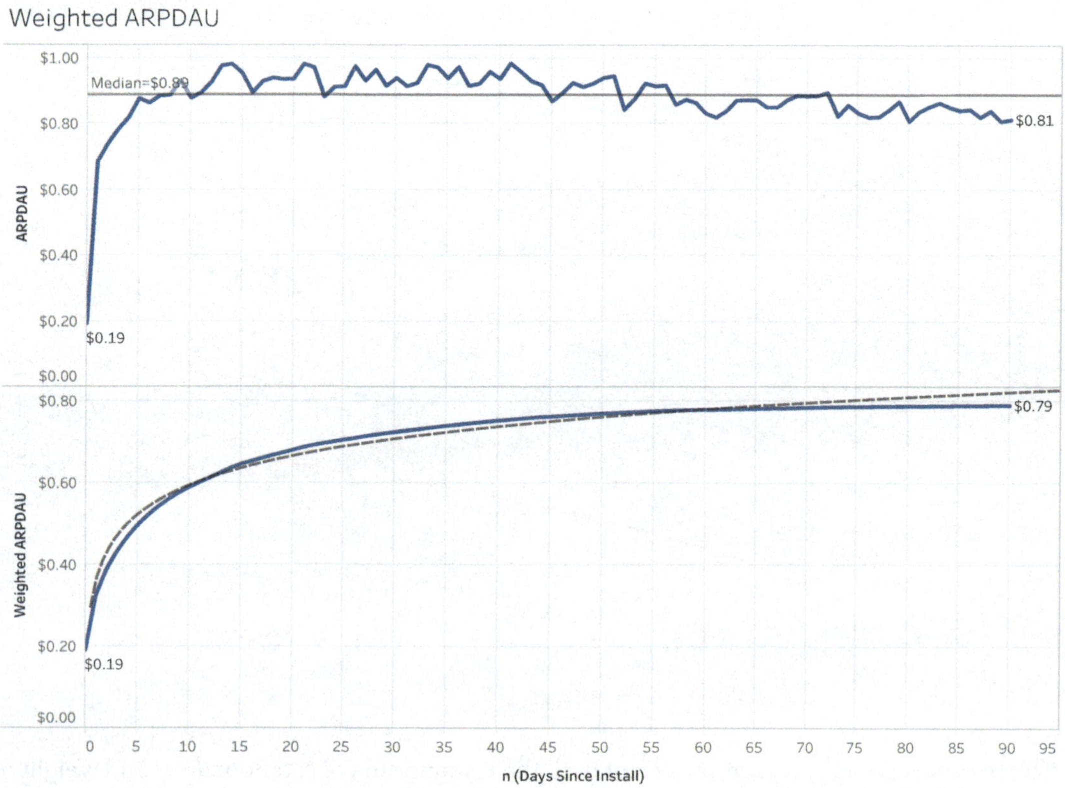

Median ARPDAU (top) is $0.89 for the 90 days of data, but the weighted average (bottom) maxes out at $0.79. The dashed logarithmic trend line is a good fit for how the ARPDAU grows asymptotically, but it fails to model declining ARPDAU as the cohort's players age.

To predict LTV90 for new install cohorts based on observed early retention and ARPDAU requires a normalized version of *both* the PD*n* and weighted ARPDAU curves. The construction of these graphs in Tableau is identical to how we built the monetization curve, only the variables `[players]` and `[arpdau]` are used instead of `[revenue]`.

Refer to the following Tableau visualization.

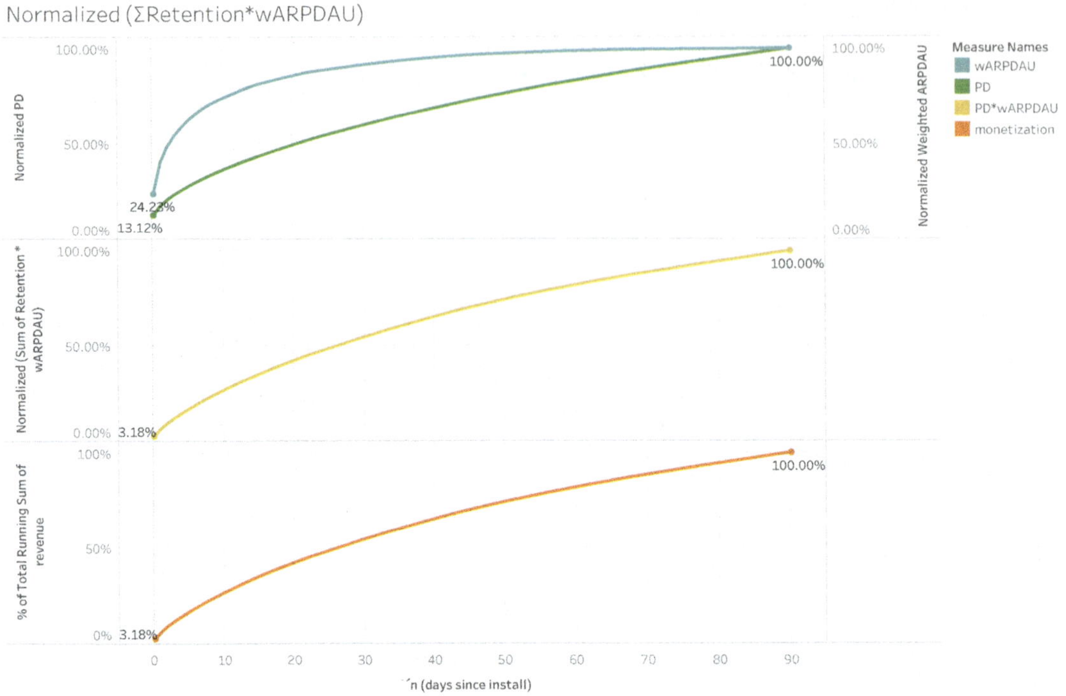

The top chart is a normalized version of both the running sum of retention (`PD`) and weighted ARPDAU (`wARPDAU`). The *y*-axis is percentage of total by D90. Multiplying these two curves from the top chart together gives us the yellow curve (`PD*wARPDAU`) in the middle chart. The monetization curve (bottom chart, in orange) is constructed in the usual manner as a *Running Total* table calculation of `[revenue]` with *Percent of Total* added as a secondary calculation. The monetization curve is identical to the `PD*wARPDAU` curve.

As predicted by the duality, whether you use the monetization curve or the normalized sum of *retention* × ARPDAU, the derived function $m(n)$ is the same.

Normalized *w*ARPDAU

The normalized version of the weighted ARPDAU curve is interesting, since the highest accumulation of *w*ARPDAU isn't necessarily at the terminal day. Some of the install cohorts exhibit diminishing ARPDAU as the cohort ages. This is more likely to occur with smaller cohorts.

Normalization of the observed values of $w\text{ARPDAU}_n$ is through division by $w\text{ARPDAU}_N$. To facilitate calculation of a normalized version of $w\text{ARPDAU}_n$, we define a *Calculated Field* called `Normalized Weighted ARPDAU` as:

```
[Weighted ARPDAU]/WINDOW_MAX([Weighted ARPDAU], LAST(), LAST())
```

The window function – which could have been average, median, min, or sum since it only applies to one element – is applied only to `LAST()`, which is $w\text{ARPDAU}_N$. To illustrate, here is a graph of *w*ARPDAU (top) as a function of days since install for a single cohort of installs, and its normalized version (bottom) with terminal day $N = 90$. The lowest and highest points are labelled. The peak *w*ARPDAU for this cohort is $0.81, which occurs when *n*=36. This is 115.65% of the *w*ARPDAU at D90, the terminal day for this chart. Whereas the percentage of total revenue by day *N* in a monetization curve is always monotonically increasing as a function of *n*, this is not necessarily the case with *w*ARPDAU.

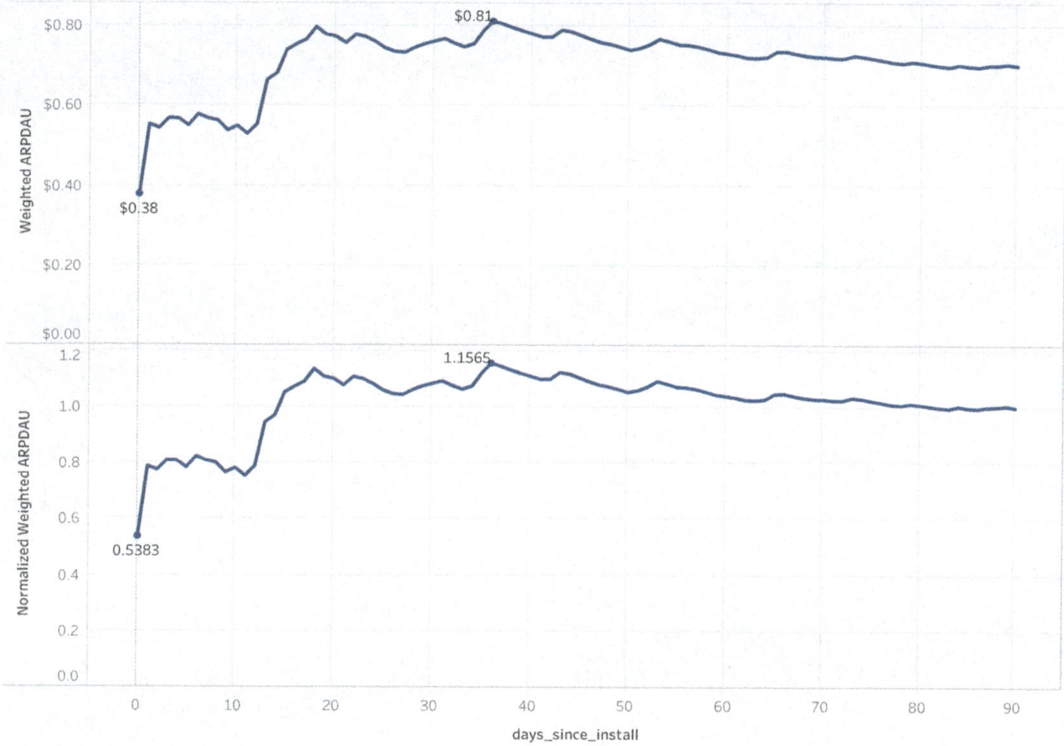

Summary

The main topic of this chapter was exploring *retention* × ARPDAU as an alternative model of LTV. The monetization function *m* is the same whether one models LTV as the running sum of average cohort revenue, or as the running sum of *retention* × ARPDAU. But this duality only holds if ARPDAU is defined as the running sum of cohort revenue divided by the running sum of cohort DAU. Predicting LTV for new install cohorts based on other heuristic definitions of cohort ARPDAU – or likewise without a sizable cohort of *N*-day fully-baked installs with which to model retention and ARPDAU – are likely to lead to different results. This is an idea explored in the final chapter of this book when we seek to predict LTV without the use of a monetization curve.

A simple, interactive tool to predict LTV*n* for new installs based on a game's retention curve and estimated ARPDAU can be found at arpdau.com. The *LTV Predictor* is particularly adept at illustrating the impact early retention has on the LTV curve.

Churn:
LEVEL 7

Businesses that rely on subscriptions tend to obsess over customer churn. Specifically, on identifying the customers that are probably not going to renew, then focusing every effort on enticing those customers to stick around. For example, whenever my current mobility plan comes up for renewal, I am bombarded with email offers, text messages, phone calls, and sometimes even unwelcome visitations to my home by customer service reps looking to lock me up for another term. Perversely, these intrusions make me more likely to switch to a competitor, but "better the devil you know" as they say.

Player churn in a free-to-play mobile game is quite a different beast, but still an important concept to model. At ESG, we often create lists of users that are at risk of churning, then target them with specific reengagement ads, email campaigns, or push notifications. This is very much a marketing activity, but the marketers invariably require the help of a data analyst to generate the list of users to target. In extreme cases, specific in-game promos are shown only to users who might be on the fence about quitting; a purchase will hopefully keep them engaged. If not, maybe we can squeeze a last dollar out of them before they leave for good.

In this chapter, we consider the likelihood of player churn as a function of last day played; i.e., $P(\text{churn} \mid D_n)$. This is a special case of building a complete model of what a player is most likely to do next given they just played on their nth day since install. To facilitate this calculation, we model the problem as labeling the arcs in a Markov chain. We also revisit the problem of classifying a particular user as churned based solely on the number of days since they last played. The relationship between churn and the retention curve is complex, so our investigation starts there.

Retention Curves Are Memoryless

Retention metrics are based on playing exactly n days after install. Each set of players for any day n consists of a blend of players whose previous play day was anywhere between 0 and $n - 1$. Sometimes people misinterpret the retention curve as modelling players who play every day (i.e., D2 retention is the ratio of installs who played on D1 *and* D2) or modelling the proportion who play on any day after *n* (i.e., D*n* retention is the proportion of installs who played on any day >= *n*). Neither is the case. All we know about the players counted in the numerator of D*n* retention is that they played on D0: we don't know which other days they played.

That is a rather long-winded way of stating that the retention curve is **memoryless** and does not capture any information regarding prior player history. What we think of as the "retention curve" is the probability a user will play on day *n* given they played on D0. In terms of conditional probability, the retention curve function *r* is equivalent to:

$$r(n) \equiv P(\mathrm{D}_n \mid \mathrm{D0})$$

But what about the probability a user will play on day *n* given they played on D1? Intuition suggests that a retention function modeling $P(\mathrm{D}_n \mid \mathrm{D1})$ is very different and much better in terms of long-tail retention. Let's find out by modifying our raw retention curve query by limiting the cohort to only those who played on D1.

```
SELECT datediff(day,install_date,play_date) AS days_since_install,
       COUNT(DISTINCT user_id) AS players,
       MAX(players) OVER (ORDER BY days_since_install ROWS UNBOUNDED
PRECEDING) AS installs,
       players/installs::FLOAT AS retention
FROM (SELECT user_id,
             install_date
      FROM user_retention
      WHERE install_date BETWEEN '2022-07-01' AND '2022-07-09'
      AND   d1 = 1)
   LEFT JOIN (SELECT DISTINCT user_id,
                     date AS play_date
             FROM session_begin
             WHERE date BETWEEN '2022-07-01' AND '2022-07-09' + 30)
USING (user_id)
WHERE days_since_install BETWEEN 0 AND 30
GROUP BY days_since_install
```

days_since_install	players	installs	retention
0	2929	2929	1
1	2929	2929	1
2	1736	2929	0.5927
3	1470	2929	0.5019
4	1331	2929	0.4544
5	1211	2929	0.4135
6	1142	2929	0.3899
7	1099	2929	0.3752

days_since_install	players	installs	retention
...	...	...	...
28	571	2929	0.1949
29	563	2929	0.1922
30	534	2929	0.1823

As expected, the retention rate is significantly better. For example, the probability that a user plays on D7 given they played on D1 is much higher (37.52% in this case) than regular old D7 retention (16.3%). Heck, D30 retention for D1 players at 18.23% is even higher than D7R for all players.

Generalizing this notion leads to a family of retention curve functions, one for having first played on every possible day D*i* after install:

$$r_i(n) \equiv P(\mathrm{D}_n \mid \mathrm{D}_i), n \geq i$$

Given any two days after install *i* and *n*, where $n \geq i$, the function $r_i(n)$ defines the probability that a user plays on D*n* given they played on D*i*. Up until now, what we have defined as the retention curve is the special case of $r_0(n)$.

Knowing the full family of retention curves enables – in theory – improved predictions about player retention, churn, and DAU. But which curve should be used? If a specific install played on days 1, 3, 6, and 7 over their first week after install, but skipped all the others, what is the expectation they will play on days 8, 21, or 180? How do we combine five retention curves – each with a different prediction for D8 – into a single likelihood this user will play tomorrow? Moreover, none of the curves contains any explicit history of player state. The function $r_7(n)$ only embeds knowledge about users who happened to play on D7; it doesn't discriminate those who played every day since install from those who skipped every day between D1 and D6 or from those like our specific user who played on days 1, 3, 6, and 7.

At this point, we are left with a choice: build a machine learning model that takes an entire user's play history as an argument and returns individual predictions for future retention; or get pragmatic and use only the last day played to predict each player's future behaviour. In other words, since the specific user above last played on D7, it makes sense to use $r_7(n)$ to predict the likelihood they play on $n = 8, 21, \text{or } 180$.

This latter approach is reminiscent of the Markov memoryless property in stochastic modeling. We don't care how the user ended up playing on D7, all that matters is they did. Their future behaviour only depends on the fact they played on D7. Speaking of Markov...

Predicting Churn: Retention as a Markov Chain

If we know a game's entire family of retention curves, and the last day played (in days since install) of every user, we can calculate the expected number of players remaining tomorrow, the day after, or even 100 days from now.[1] But determining every one of those curves is a lot of heavy lifting. I am pretty lazy, so instead we will settle for a simple model of churn and retention based only on the last day played. We turn our attention to determining the probability that a user who plays on D*n* will never play again. That is, we want to determine:

$$P(\text{churn} \mid \mathrm{D}_n)$$

Also, the probability that a user who plays on D*n* will return to play the very next day:

$$P(\mathrm{D}_{n+1} \mid \mathrm{D}_n)$$

Both probabilities can be modelled with a discrete-time Markov chain. A **Markov chain** (or Markov process) describes a state-space and a sequence of possible events, where the probability of the next event is only a function of the current state. An event is a transition from one state to another. Chains are represented as a directed graph, where the states are the nodes, and the edges connect states where transitions may occur. The directed edges (i, j) are labeled with the probabilities that define the likelihood of transitioning from state i to state j, written as $i \rightarrow j$.

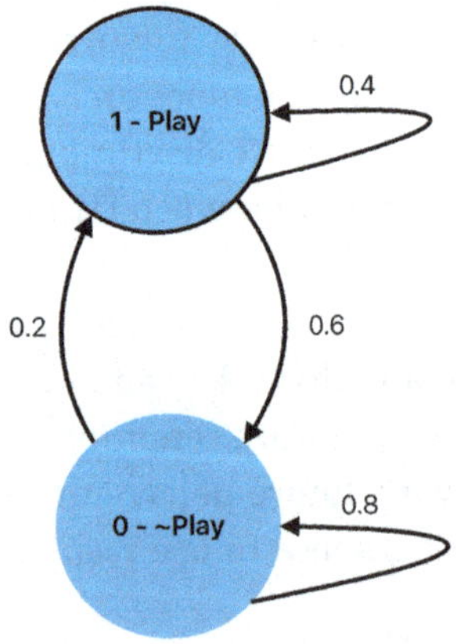

A very simple chain (left) to model daily user retention has two states. State 1 represents playing, while state 0 represents *not* playing. The time intervals are discrete days. Players begin in state 1, which is equivalent to D0. The history of state transitions forms a vector, where each element *i* is a binary value with 1 indicating *played* and 0 *did not play* on D*i*. Our hypothetical user who played on days 1, 3, 6, and 7 is represented by the vector <1, 1, 0, 1, 0, 0, 1, 1>.

The edges are labeled with probabilities of transitioning from a play day to a missed day (0.6) or deciding to play after missing a day (0.2). Continuing to play the next day (0.4) or continuing to not play (0.8) are also modeled in this chain. The sum of the edges

[1] With one caveat: we don't know the retention curve at the frontier of the player base; i.e., those whose last day played is at the maximum possible given the number of days since launch.

leading out of both nodes equals 1. A random walk through this graph creates a simulated play history for a user. But would this play history accurately reflect the retention profile of a free-to-play game?

No, not really. In reality, users tend to get stuck playing every day, or stuck not playing every day; i.e., they churn. For example, if a user has played for 10 consecutive days, they are extremely likely to extend that streak to 11. However, a fundamental tenet of a Markov process is that the transition probabilities depend only on the current state, and not on the way the state was reached. We know from our study of retention that player behaviour as a function of days since install does not share this memoryless feature of a Markov process. Indeed, this simple two-state model of retention does not result in a retention curve anything like the power function we know and love. We require a more sophisticated model of player retention.

A More Sophisticated Markov Model

An alternative Markov chain to model daily player retention is comprised of separate states $\{0, 1, \ldots, n\}$ for each day after install, where state *i* represents the event "play on D*i*." With this chain, we can model what a player is most likely to do next (including churn) given they just played on their *n*th day since install. The state transition from $i \rightarrow j$ represents playing on D*i* then next on D*j* with no intervening days of game play. The edge (i, j) is labeled with the probability that a user who plays on D*i* will next play on D*j*. The probability of transitioning from 0 → 1 is what we have defined previously as "D1 retention."

To illustrate, the possible transitions from states $i \rightarrow j$ for the first three days after install for a new user are represented in Figure 7.1. The state *i* is labelled D*i* to remind us that it means "played on D*i*." Probabilities are omitted for now. The chain begins in state D0. D2 players are made up of two mutually exclusive sets: those who played on D1, and those who skipped D1. Meanwhile, for those who played on D3, the route to get there is even more complicated, with a total of four unique paths (i.e., **retention histories**) through the directed, acyclic graph: (D0, D1, D2, D3); (D0, D1, D3); (D0, D2, D3); and (D0, D3). The *churn* state represents never playing again, and is said to be an *absorbing* state: once you enter, you can never leave. This state is different than playing again on some future day after D3; those states and their transitions are not included in Figure 7.1., so keep in mind that D3 is not an absorbing state.

Paths through the graph in Figure 7.1 enumerate the possible retention histories for new installs up to D3. But what is the probability of each transition occurring, and thus each retention history? In other words, how do we label the arcs in Figure 7.1? Quite simply, by considering the historical data of player behaviour during their first *n* days since install.

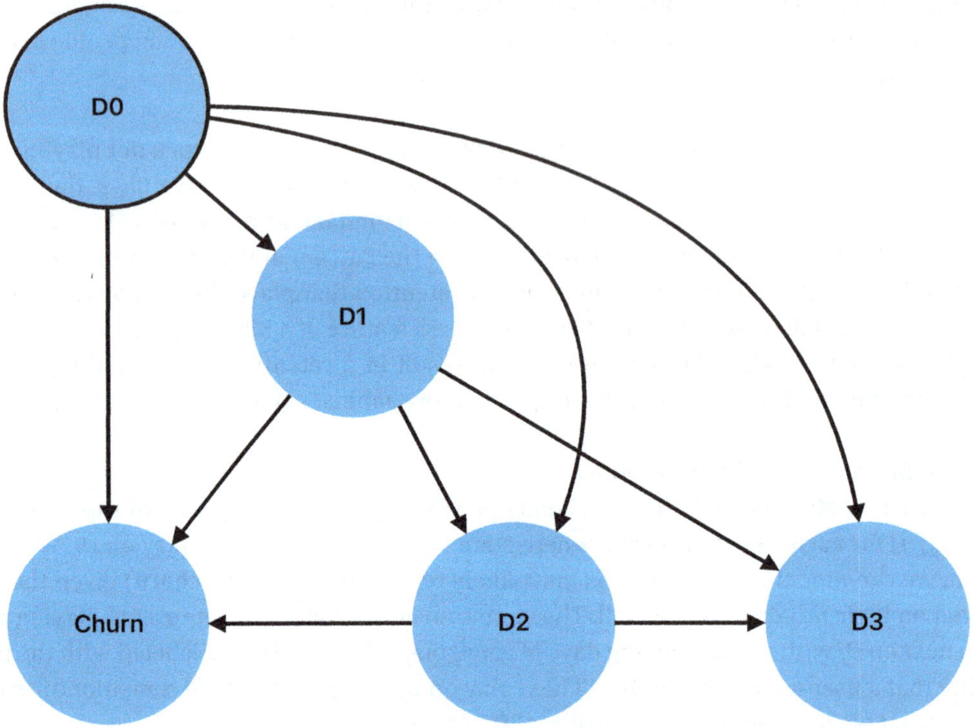

Figure 7.1 A Markov chain for the first three days after install. The nodes represent playing on day D*i* or leaving the game (*Churn*). All players start in state D0. Edges represent the possible transitions from state to state. States for playing on D*i* where $i > 3$ are excluded.

Calculating the Transition Probabilities

Traditionally, a Markov chain is represented as a matrix **T** where $\mathbf{T}[i, j]$ contains the probability of transitioning from state i to state j. Indices are zero-based, with the first row indexed as $[0, j]$ and the first column as $[i, 0]$. An algorithm (inspired by Burelli (2019)) to calculate each element of an $n \times n$ matrix representing the transition probabilities during the first $n - 1$ days after install for any historical cohort is as follows:

1. Initialize all elements of **T** to 0.
2. Increment $\mathbf{T}[i, j]$ if a player was observed transitioning from state i to j; i.e., played on D*i* then next on D*j* without any intervening days.
3. Increment $\mathbf{T}[i, i]$ if D*i* is the last observed play day for a user; i.e., $\mathbf{T}[0, 0]$ is the count of all installs who played on D0 but never played again, whereas $\mathbf{T}[0, 1]$ is the count of all installs who next played on D1.

4. After all data is collected, normalize each row by dividing each element by the sum of the row's values; e.g., **T**[0, 1] is now equivalent to D1R for this cohort.

$\mathbf{T}[i, j]$ now contains the likelihood a player transitions from D*i* to D*j*, or in the case of $[i, i]$ the probability of churning after playing on D*i*. The values in each row sum to 1.0. The matrix is sparse, with $\mathbf{T}[i, j] = 0 \; \forall \; i > j$; i.e., it's all zeroes below the diagonal. This is a side-effect of not being able to travel backwards in time.

Tread Carefully Here
The matrix elements $[i, j]$ only contain the probability of directly transitioning from states *i* to *j*, and do not contain the more general $P(\mathrm{D}j \mid \mathrm{D}i)$ where $j > i$, which may include stops along the way playing on D*k* where $j > k > i$. For example, element [0, 2] does not represent the $P(\mathrm{D2} \mid \mathrm{D0})$. The element [0, 2] is only the probability of playing on D2 after skipping D1; i.e., directly moving from D0 to D2 with no intervening play dates. In other words, the element [0, 2] represents $P(\mathrm{D2} \cap {\sim}\mathrm{D1} \mid \mathrm{D0})$.

As an exercise, we now label the edges in Figure 7.1 using the trusty cohort of players from July 1 to 9th. The algorithm for calculating the elements of the transition matrix is our inspiration, but we won't explicitly create a matrix. Instead, we use SQL to derive the data and calculations required to label the edges by building a relation with one row per non-zero element of what would be the matrix **T**.

To start, the following `Markov` CTE creates a single row for each unique date played for each user in the cohort. This is the user's retention history. The difference in days between each play date and their install date is included as `i`. The window function `LAG` determines `j`, the next day played by that user.

```
WITH Markov AS
(
SELECT user_id,
       install_date,
       play_date,
       play_date - install_date AS i,
       LAG(i) OVER
          (PARTITION BY user_id ORDER BY play_date DESC) AS j
FROM user_source s
LEFT JOIN (SELECT DISTINCT date AS play_date,
                           user_id
             FROM session_begin
             WHERE date >= '2022-07-01') p USING (user_id)
WHERE s.install_date BETWEEN '2022-07-01' AND '2022-07-09')

SELECT * FROM Markov
```

user_id	date	play_date	i	j
8915877	2022-07-01	2022-07-01	0	
8915878	2022-07-01	2022-07-01	0	
8915879	2022-07-01	2022-07-01	0	
8915880	2022-07-01	2022-07-01	0	7
8915880	2022-07-01	2022-07-08	7	
8915881	2022-07-01	2022-07-01	0	1
8915881	2022-07-01	2022-07-02	1	2
8915881	2022-07-01	2022-07-03	2	3
8915881	2022-07-01	2022-07-04	3	4
8915881	2022-07-01	2022-07-05	4	5
8915881	2022-07-01	2022-07-06	5	6
8915881	2022-07-01	2022-07-07	6	7
8915881	2022-07-01	2022-07-08	7	8
8915881	2022-07-01	2022-07-09	8	9
8915881	2022-07-01	2022-07-10	9	10
8915881	2022-07-01	2022-07-11	10	11
8915881	2022-07-01	2022-07-12	11	12
8915881	2022-07-01	2022-07-13	12	13
8915881	2022-07-01	2022-07-14	13	14
8915881	2022-07-01	2022-07-15	14	15
8915881	2022-07-01	2022-07-16	15	16
8915881	2022-07-01	2022-07-17	16	17
8915881	2022-07-01	2022-07-18	17	18
8915881	2022-07-01	2022-07-19	18	19
8915881	2022-07-01	2022-07-20	19	20
8915881	2022-07-01	2022-07-21	20	21
8915881	2022-07-01	2022-07-22	21	26
8915881	2022-07-01	2022-07-27	26	
8915882	2022-07-01	2022-07-01	0	2
8915882	2022-07-01	2022-07-03	2	3
8915882	2022-07-01	2022-07-04	3	5
8915882	2022-07-01	2022-07-06	5	6
8915882	2022-07-01	2022-07-07	6	7
8915882	2022-07-01	2022-07-08	7	8
8915882	2022-07-01	2022-07-09	8	10
8915882	2022-07-01	2022-07-11	10	11
8915882	2022-07-01	2022-07-12	11	
...	...	...	...	...

The history of state transitions is given above for the first six users in the cohort. Each row in this result set indicates an instance where the specific user played on D*i* then next played on D*j*. In records where `j` is null, `i` is the last day that user played: they had yet to transition out of state *i* when the query was run.

Before normalization, each entry $[i, j]$ in the matrix **T** is a count of the number of players who transited from $i \rightarrow j$. The following aggregation over our CTE calculates this value for each pair i, j.

```
SELECT i,
       j,
       COUNT(DISTINCT user_id) AS players
FROM Markov
GROUP BY i, j
```

To label every edge in Figure 7.1, there are two more columns we need to add to this query. First, we need to calculate the total number of players who played on D*i* regardless of their next state *j*. This is given by an additional column called `entered`, defined by the window function `SUM(players) OVER (PARTITION BY i)`. Dividing each element in the row by this count normalizes the transition as a probability (`prob`).

```
SELECT i,
       j,
       COUNT(DISTINCT user_id) AS players,
       SUM(players) OVER (PARTITION BY i) AS entered,
      players / entered::FLOAT AS prob
FROM Markov
WHERE i <= 3
GROUP BY i, j
ORDER BY i, j
```

If we limit the result set to only those rows where `j <= 3`, we end up with the following labels (the column `prob`) for each of the edges (*i, j*) in Figure 7.1:

i	j	players	entered	prob
0	1	2929	7891	0.371
0	2	384	7891	0.049
0	3	162	7891	0.021
1	2	1736	2929	0.593
1	3	200	2929	0.069
2	3	1407	2120	0.664

The first row is D1 retention (37.1%) for this cohort, as we have calculated several times previously. The second row indicates that 384 players of the 7,891 installs skipped D1 and played on D2. The probability of that happening is only 4.9%. And so on.

Observe that $P(\text{D3} \mid \text{D2}) > P(\text{D2} \mid \text{D1}) > P(\text{D1} \mid \text{D0})$. Playing begets playing. The sum of the edges leading out of any state is < 1.0 as not only do some of the players next play on some day D4+, but we have yet to calculate the $P(\text{churn} \mid \text{D}n)$ and label the edge that leads to the *churn* state.

How do we do that? Failing to transition out of state *i* is a proxy for churning on D*i*. Wrapping our CTE with an aggregation by *i* provides a simple mechanism for approximating this probability. Of the players who `entered` state *i*, some never play again (as indicated by `j IS NULL`), and the rest will play on a later date (`transited` to indicate they transition from state *i* to any later state *j*). The $P(\text{churn} \mid \text{D}i)$ for $i \in \{0, 1, 2, 3\}$ is given by:

```
SELECT i,
       COUNT(*) AS entered,
       SUM(CASE WHEN j IS NULL THEN 1 END) AS churned,
       SUM(CASE WHEN j IS NOT NULL THEN 1 END) AS transited,
       churned / entered::FLOAT AS p_churn,
       SUM(CASE WHEN j = i + 1 THEN 1 END) / entered::FLOAT as p_next
FROM Markov
WHERE i <= 3
GROUP BY i
```

i	entered	churned	transited	p_churn	p_next
0	7891	3778	4113	0.4788	0.3712
1	2929	678	2251	0.2315	0.5927
2	2120	361	1759	0.1703	0.6637
3	1769	209	1560	0.1181	0.7145

For example, if a user plays on D3, there is only an 11.81% chance they churn and never play again. A quick look at the first row should reinforce the concept that (1.0 – D1R) is *not* the percentage of players who churn on D0. While D1 retention is only 2929/7891 = 37.12%, a further 4113 − 2929 = 1184 installs skipped D1 and played on a later date. The $P(\text{churn} \mid \text{D0})$ is 47.88%, meaning that just over 52% of the installs from July 1 to 9th played at least one more day after install.

Figure 7.2 is the labeled version of Figure 7.1. The labeled arcs inform us that if a user played on D1, there is a 59.3% chance they played on D2, and a 23.2% chance they churned. Again, none of the transitions beyond D3 are included thus the sum of the edges leaving each node is less than unity.

Finally, to calculate the probability of playing on D_{n+1} given that a player was active on D_n is simply a matter of counting the number of times that *j* is equal to $i + 1$. This was already snuck into the query as:

```
SUM(CASE WHEN j = i + 1 THEN 1 END) / entered::FLOAT as p_next
```

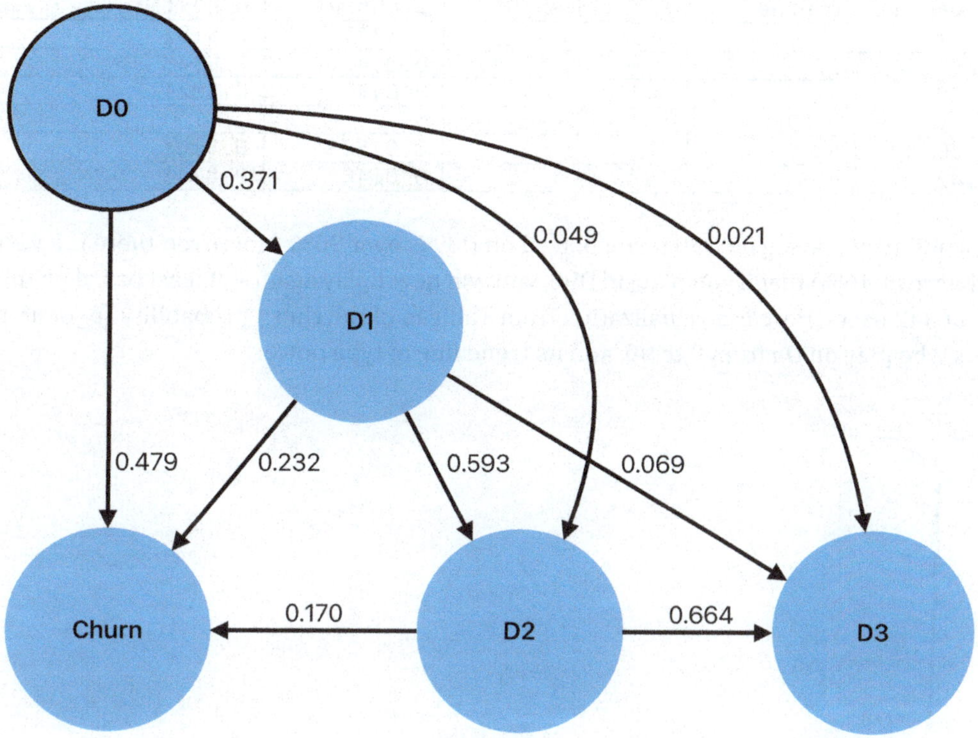

Figure 7.2 Once again, but with probabilities. The likelihood of transitioning from state-to-state based on the observed behaviour of the cohort of installs from July 1 to July 9, 2022. For example, if a user played on D2, the probability they played on D3 was 0.664.

Extending the result set out to 90 days after install provides some interesting context:

i	entered	churned	transited	p_churn	p_next
0	7891	3778	4113	0.4788	0.3712
1	2929	678	2251	0.2315	0.5927
2	2120	361	1759	0.1703	0.6637
3	1769	209	1560	0.1181	0.7145
4	1559	173	1386	0.1110	0.7242
5	1409	132	1277	0.0937	0.7516
6	1326	105	1221	0.0792	0.7655
7	1283	104	1179	0.0811	0.7615
...	...	...	...	...	...
14	970	64	906	0.066	0.7711
15	901	48	853	0.0533	0.7913
16	844	40	804	0.0474	0.8069
17	822	42	780	0.0511	0.7968
18	794	29	765	0.0365	0.8312

i	entered	churned	transited	p_churn	p_next
19	792	27	765	0.0341	0.8182
20	775	30	745	0.0387	0.8348
21	778	34	744	0.0437	0.8021
...	...	...	...	...	...
89	330	5	325	0.0152	0.9061
90	342	5	337	0.0146	0.8743

The probability of playing on D90 if you played on D89 is over 90%. Moreover, there is a very small chance (1.46%) that if you play on D90, you will never play again – at least based on this sample of 342 users. Here is a visualization from Tableau of the churn probability (p_churn) for users who play on D*n* from 0 to 90, and its trend line of type power:

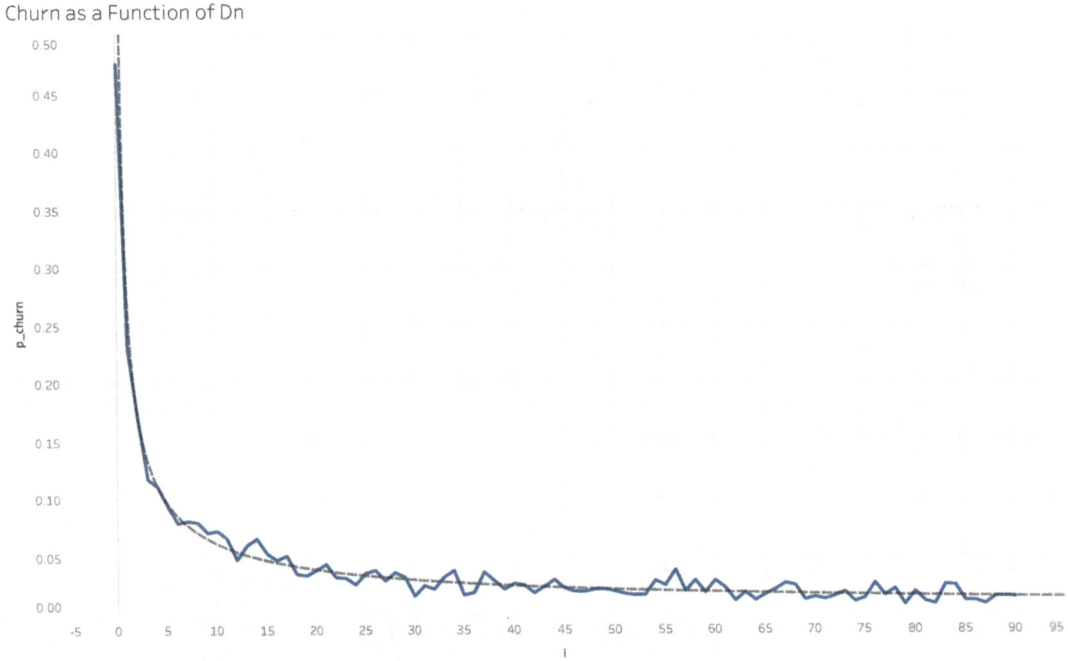

The curve fit to that data predicts the probability a player churns given they just played on D*n*.

In summary, the probability of an active player returning the next day is highly dependent on their age in days since install. We revisit this concept and its predictive value in a later chapter when we look at improving retention.

Revisiting Churn as "Has Not Played in *N* Days"

In the chapter on KPIs, we indicated that ESG defines the daily churn rate as:

$$\text{churn}_d = \text{count(users who churned on } d)/\text{DAU}_d$$

A daily churn rate chart is a time series like the following.

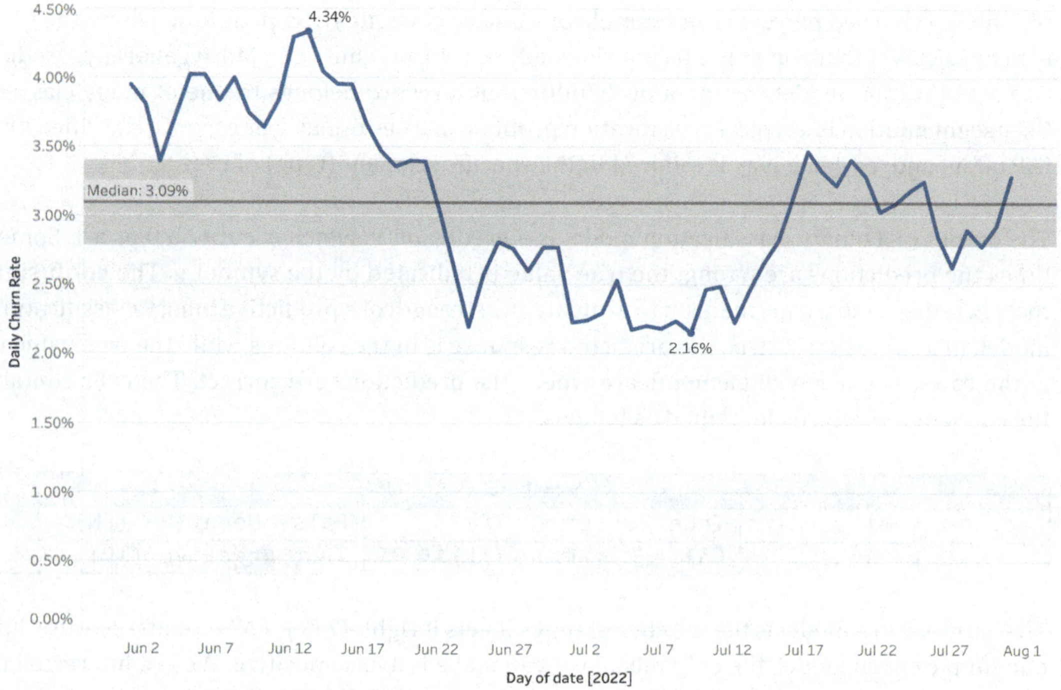

However, we do not employ any user-level feature analysis in our determination of players we believe have churned. Instead, it is simply:

$$\text{churn}_d = \text{count(users } \textbf{who last played} \text{ on } d)/\text{DAU}_d$$

We think users who haven't played in 14+ days have churned. As such, we only calculate this KPI for dates that are at least 15 days old.

Our model is extremely simple, taking only one user feature (days since last played) into account. Adding additional features such as the age of the user in days since install, level completed, and LTV are likely to increase the efficacy of the model substantially.

We chose two weeks as the cut off without ever quantifying the probability of making an incorrect determination; i.e., labeling a player as churned who wasn't done playing. How good of an estimate is 14 days? Another way of putting that question is, how often do we falsely identify players as churned when N is the number of lapsed days used in the determination?

Classification Problems

Identifying churned players is an example of a binary **classification problem**, where the goal is to predict whether a user is a 0 (not churned) or a 1 (has churned). More generally, predictive classification models assign a probability that a record belongs to one of many classes. User segmentation is a typical classification problem in free-to-play games; once classified, the IAP offers and/or game play is tailored to the specific segment (type) of user.

The output of a binary classification model is a prediction $\hat{y}$, which is either a 0 or a 1. Sometimes the predictions are wrong; the true value is indicated by the symbol y. The **confusion matrix** is the standard mechanism to evaluate the strength of a predictive binary classification model. In a confusion matrix, the predicted response is in the columns while the true value is in the rows. The diagonal elements are where the predictions are correct. The cells contain the count of the records identified as follows.

	$\hat{y} = 1$	$\hat{y} = 0$
$y = 1$	True Positive (TP)	False Negative (FN)
$y = 0$	False Positive (FP)	True Negative (TN)

The accuracy of a model is the number of times it gets it right: $(TP + TN)/\text{count(records)}$. For our simple churn model, the only mistake it can make is a false positive. We are interested in the false positives as a function of N, the number of lapsed days used to identify a player as churned. If a player predicted to have churned returns to play another day, then the original diagnosis was a **false positive**. Our task is to quantify the false positive rate (FPR), which we define as $FP/(FP + TP)$.

How Long is Long Enough?

Currently, with $N = 14$, the churn rate is a retroactive DAU metric defined for play days that are at least 14D fully baked. The numerator in our daily churn rate calculation is the number of users who last played on that date. Therefore, churn rate is a daily metric that can retroactively diminish as time passes. However, with each passing day, it becomes less and less likely that any of the remaining lapsed players are going to return. Eventually the churn rate will stabilize. How long do we have to wait before we can accurately calculate the churn rate for a past date?

As a case study, let's imagine it is 00:00:01 on July 10, 2022. At that moment, we are first able to calculate a churn rate for the calendar date 14 days prior; i.e., June 26, 2022. The June 26th lapsed players are the June 26th DAU that have not played since. Of those lapsed players, some are going to surprise us and play again, either later on July 10th, or any other day in the future. Those are the false positives (FP). The true positives (TP) are those lapsed players that have yet to return to the game whenever the churn rate is calculated. Therefore, over time, FP will climb while TP decreases.

The FPR for June 26, 2022, is initially 0% – when first calculated, none of the lapsed players have been given a chance to return. But what does the FPR ultimately become as time passes? To facilitate this analysis in SQL, it helps to build a CTE like `Markov`, but one that contains a complete play history in calendar dates for every install since world-wide launch:

```
WITH play_history AS
(
  SELECT user_id,
         install_date,
         play_date,
         LAG(play_date) OVER
            (PARTITION BY user_id ORDER BY play_date DESC) AS next_pd
  FROM user_source s
    LEFT JOIN (SELECT DISTINCT date AS play_date,
                               user_id
               FROM session_begin
               WHERE date >= '2017-04-20') p USING (user_id)
  WHERE install_date >= '2017-04-20'
)

SELECT *
FROM play_history
```

user_id	install_date	play_date	next_pd
1000016	2017-04-25	2017-04-25	2017-04-26
1000016	2017-04-25	2017-04-26	2018-01-09
1000016	2017-04-25	2018-01-09	
1000017	2017-04-25	2017-04-25	2017-04-26
1000017	2017-04-25	2017-04-26	
1000018	2017-04-25	2017-04-25	2017-04-26
1000018	2017-04-25	2017-04-26	2017-04-27
1000018	2017-04-25	2017-04-27	2017-04-28
1000018	2017-04-25	2017-04-28	2017-04-29
1000018	2017-04-25	2017-04-29	2017-05-01
1000018	2017-04-25	2017-05-01	2017-05-03
1000018	2017-04-25	2017-05-03	
...	..	...	...

The last date played for each user is the row where `next_pd` is null. The beauty of this relation is its ability to place us at any historical date in time by looking only at those rows where the `play_date` has a specific value; e.g., June 26, 2022. These rows indicate which users comprised the DAU on that date, and when each of them next played (if at all).

On any date *d*, we can define two mutually exclusive sets of lapsed players by finding the users with a record that is either:

1. a false positive (`fp`): those `WHERE play_date = d AND next_pd >= d +14`; or,
2. a true positive (`tp`): those `WHERE play_date = d AND next_pd IS NULL`.

Each user in `play_history` will match at most one of those two conditions.[2] We want to know what we thought when `play_date = '2022-06-26'`. A query to determine the cardinality of the two sets naturally follows from their definition:

```
SELECT SUM(CASE WHEN next_pd >= play_date+14 THEN 1 END) AS fp,
       SUM(CASE WHEN next_pd IS NULL THEN 1 END) AS tp,
       fp + tp AS lapsed,
       fp / lapsed::FLOAT as FPR
FROM (SELECT *
      FROM play_history
      WHERE play_date = '2022-06-26')
```

fp	tp	lapsed	fpr
609	1569	2178	0.2796

On July 10, 2022, it was believed that 2,178 lapsed players had newly churned; i.e., hadn't played since June 26th. But when we run that query now, months later, 609 of those lapsed users have ended up playing again at some future date. Our FPR for June 26, 2022, is a rather terrible 27.96% – and potentially climbing with each passing day. What should *N* be if we want the FPR to be less than 20%? The following table reflects the change in FPR for June 26, 2022, as a function of the size of the lapsed duration *N* in days.

N	FPR
7	0.48
10	0.37
14	0.28
21	0.20
28	0.14
35	0.13

---

2 For completeness, the other records with a matching `play_date` are the true negatives: those `WHERE play_date = d AND next_pd < d +14`.

As expected, the longer we wait to first calculate a churn rate, the lower the FPR, but note the diminishing returns. Based on this result, it looks like $N = 21$ days of inactivity results in a 20% FPR, at least for that date in history. We can expand our query to look at the historical daily FPR by joining the `play_history` CTE with each unique day of game play, which we grab from the `session_begin` table:

```
SELECT d.date,
       SUM(CASE WHEN next_pd >= d.date+14 THEN 1 END) AS fp,
       SUM(CASE WHEN next_pd IS NULL THEN 1 END) AS tp,
       fp + tp AS lapsed,
       fp / lapsed::FLOAT AS FPR
FROM (SELECT DISTINCT date
     FROM session_begin
     WHERE date BETWEEN '2017-04-20' AND '2022-07-10') d
  LEFT JOIN play_history ph
ON ph.play_date = d.date
GROUP BY d.date
```

date	fp	tp	lapsed	fpr
2017-04-20	2635	41336	43971	0.0599
2017-04-21	4697	78913	83610	0.0562
2017-04-22	5085	82577	87662	0.058
2017-04-23	6097	95813	101910	0.0598
2017-04-24	5519	85154	90673	0.0609
2017-04-25	5293	82539	87832	0.0603
2017-04-26	5194	76101	81295	0.0639
2017-04-27	4825	67492	72317	0.0667
2017-04-28	4560	60710	65270	0.0699
2017-04-29	4572	61233	65805	0.0695
2017-04-30	4963	61085	66048	0.0751
2017-05-01	4404	52317	56721	0.0776
...	...	...	...	...

The FPR with $N = 14$ starts out reasonably well (<6%), but steadily increases as the sample sizes of newly `lapsed` players decreases. The accuracy of churn prediction using 14 days of absence is sensitive to the sample size and the maturity of the player base. The weighted average FPR from launch up to June 26, 2022, is 21% for N=14. At N=21, the weighted average drops to 16.4%. We conclude that for ESG games, 21 days of inactivity is a superior method of classifying churned players.

Summary

In this chapter, we extended our exploration of retention by looking more deeply into the meaning of a retention curve. We concluded that retention curves are memoryless predictors of future engagement, based solely on a single precondition: the user played on D0. As a conditional probability, $r(n)$ is $P(\mathrm{D}n \mid \mathrm{D0})$. Distinct retention curves exist for cohorts made up of users who play on D*i*, *i* > 0, defined as $r_i(n) = P(\mathrm{D}n \mid \mathrm{D}i), n > i$. What we have defined as the "retention curve" is the special case of $r_0(n)$.

A Markov chain can model the probability of churn and the probability of playing the next day, both given a user plays on D*n*. The probability of an active player returning the next day is highly correlated to their age in days since install.

Finally, we discussed how to measure the daily false-positive rate for churned players. This technique is useful for determining an optimal number of consecutive days of inactivity to use when identifying churned players.

Congratulations on completing Level 7. We now switch gears for a bit, as the next four chapters consider the myriad ways that analytics and data analysts are involved in making more money from games in LiveOps. As we have learned so far, in order to increase LTV (i.e., "make more money"), you have to improve one of ARPDAU and retention, but without harming the other.

One of the primary roles of a data analyst in freemium games is working with product managers and game designers to improve retention and monetization. In addition to measuring and reporting on KPIs, this teamwork involves running experiments called A/B tests that compare competing versions of the game presented to distinct customer segments. Evaluating the results of an A/B test is perhaps the most important way that data analysts derive actionable insights. The material on this topic is spread over the next two chapters starting with a review of the connection between A/B testing and the academic discipline of statistics.

A/B Testing and Statistics:
LEVEL 8

A/B testing is simply another name for the topic of hypothesis testing *you hopefully learned about in stats class; this chapter is a review of the material on interval estimation, bootstrapping, and permutation testing. This is going to be a whirlwind, and much of the material is math-heavy and meant for the data analysts – the people who really need to master the concepts. If your role is more on the soft-side of production and game development, don't worry if a lot of this doesn't immediately make sense. It is more important that you get a sense of the vocabulary and the big picture.*

A/B testing is a data-driven technique used to compare and measure potential changes to products. An **A/B test** is a marketing experiment where customers are split into two groups, where each group is presented with a different version of a product. Based on how the customers respond, variant A or B is declared the winner and its salient difference incorporated into the product. The product can be pretty much anything: a mobile app, e-commerce website, advertisement, novel, film, etc. The different product versions tested might include things like a different app icon; whether the image of a puppy appears on the checkout page; a different call-to-action on an online ad; the font used on the cover of a book; and, which guy Molly Ringwald ends up with at the end of *Pretty in Pink*. The behaviour of the two customer groups is monitored and statistics collected regarding their actions, clicks, preferences, likelihood to buy, sentiment, and overall positive or negative experience with their version of the product. Do customers prefer A or B? Changes to the product are made based on the results of these tests.

A/B testing is an important endeavour meant to improve the KPIs of games in LiveOps. Existing players (or new installs) are split into two groups and play competing versions of the game. The different product experiences tested might be subtle, like the timer interval between availability of rewarded video ads, or major, like different price points for IAPs. Typically, the A/B test is measuring a change to the existing version of the app, in which case the group shown the new version is called *test* or *treatment* while the other group subjected to the status quo is called *control*. The purpose of an A/B test is to verify that a change to the game results in a significant improvement to the game's KPIs.

But what exactly qualifies as "significant?" This is where statistics has a role to play. A fundamental skill required of a game data analyst is the ability to evaluate the results of an A/B test and declare a winner. Statistics is the tool we use to determine whether any observed difference between the groups is real or inconsequential. Being "real" means it was not a fluke; the difference between the KPIs of the two groups is statistically significant. A **statistically significant** result of an experiment is a fancy way of saying the difference is not purely an artifact of the random allocation of players into the two groups, but a direct result of the *treatment* experience being truly different than *control*.

We start our review with a motivating example. Thanks to Jes Simkin for this scenario, which she developed into a technical screening question when interviewing data analyst candidates. But first, some context. A **push notification** (PN) is a pop-up consisting of an icon and text that alerts your mobile device to something of interest, e.g., a timer trunk is ready to be opened in *TPB*. Here are two examples.

The top PN is from Zillow, which thinks I might be interested in buying a winter home in California. Tempting, but I'm not quite ready to become a snowbird. Below that is a reminder from the game *Idle Distiller* (by our friends at Kano) that a time-limited event is underway. Clicking on a PN opens the associated app. The click-through rate (CTR) of a PN is its proportion of clicks to impressions.

The Motivating Example
A PM describes an experiment their team ran comparing two different versions of a PN used to alert players that a time-limited event has started. One PN has a higher CTR than the other: 11% vs 10%. The PM has decided that from now on they will use the PN that saw an 11% CTR because it performed better at bringing users back to the game. But first they would like the blessing of the analytics team. How would you respond to the PM's conclusion? What questions would you have for them? Would you suggest any further investigation?

What has just been described is an A/B test comparing two versions of a game's PN. The observed difference in CTR (11% vs. 10%) may be statistically significant or may be a fluke. The purpose of this chapter is to explain how the formal discipline of statistics provides the tools you need to make that determination. At the end of the next chapter, we put our learnings into practice by revisiting and discussing this motivating example.

There Will Be R

This chapter utilizes the programming language R, which I don't really know particularly well. I am an old-school C/C++ and Java software engineer who long ago lost his zeal for learning yet another programming language. I do think R is cool, though. I apologize in advance for any inelegant code, and I welcome your feedback.

Teach Yourself Stats in 24 Hours

Statistics is the branch of mathematics that deals with collecting and analyzing numeric data with the intention of inferring generalizations about large datasets (called **populations** for historical reasons) by making only a small number of observations (called **samples**, an activity referred to as **sampling**). The practice of statistics involves two types of logical reasoning: deduction and inference. Sampling from a known population (e.g., drawing playing cards from a standard, shuffled deck of 52) follows the laws of probability and is deductive. Sampling from an unknown population (e.g., the intention of voting-age Canadians in the next federal election) uses inference to make conclusions about the population as a whole, but with a margin of error.

For example, the traditional formula used by opinion pollsters defines a **confidence interval** of the form:

$$\mu = X \pm (\text{critical value} * \text{ standard error})$$

where:

- μ is an estimate of the population proportion who answer "yes" to a proposition[1], e.g., "Do you plan to vote for the New Democratic Party (NDP) in the upcoming election?"
- X is the sample proportion who said "yes."
- the **critical value** is a constant defined by the standard normal distribution. The specific value determines how confident you can be in the estimate of the population proportion. Typically, you want to be 95% certain, in which case the critical value is 1.96: the number of standard deviations from X, both positive and negative, where 95% of the data lies in a standard normal distribution. Critical values are in units of standard deviations.
- the **standard error** is:

---

[1] I am deviating from the standard use of the symbol π to represent a population proportion and instead will use μ and X for the population mean and sample mean, respectively, regardless of whether the arithmetic average is applied to a set of binary numbers (a *proportion*) or scalar numbers (a *mean*).

$$\sqrt{\frac{X(1-X)}{n}}$$

where n is the sample size, the number of randomly selected voting-age Canadians who answered the question. This formula approximates the standard deviation (i.e., how spread out the observations are relative to X) of the sampling distribution. It's called an *error* because the difference between the sample mean and the true population mean is a measurement error.

For example, a sample of $n = 2{,}000$ voting-age Canadians revealed that 345 plan to vote for the NDP: $X = 345/2000 = 0.1725$, or 17.25%. We can't assume that 17.25% is true of the entire population. Plugging the numbers into the formula above gives us

$$\begin{aligned}\mu &= 0.1725 \pm 1.96\sqrt{\frac{0.1725(1-0.1725)}{2000}}\\ &= 0.1725 \pm 0.0166\\ &= [0.1559, 0.1891]\end{aligned}$$

The confidence interval is the range between $0.1725 - 0.0166$ and $0.1725 + 0.0166$. The true proportion of NDP voter support is very likely to be somewhere in this [0.1559, 0.1891] interval. How likely? If we conducted this sample another 19 times, each with a different group of randomly chosen 2,000 voters, the true population proportion is expected to fall within the confidence interval in all but one of those 20 samples. This is where the ubiquitous "19 times out of 20" caveat originates when you hear the results of opinion polls read on the news.

The following graph illustrates. The *x*-axis is the proportion of voting-age Canadians that support the NDP, with the red line our observed sample proportion at 0.1725. The dotted black lines bracket the confidence interval, and both are 1.96 standard deviations from the red line. The bell curve of the normal distribution is overlaid in dark blue. We don't know for sure that 17.25% is correct, but based on the size of our sample, we are 95% (19/20) sure the actual level of NDP voter support lies somewhere between the dotted black lines; namely, between 15.59% and 18.91%. If we increase our sample size, the confidence interval shrinks.

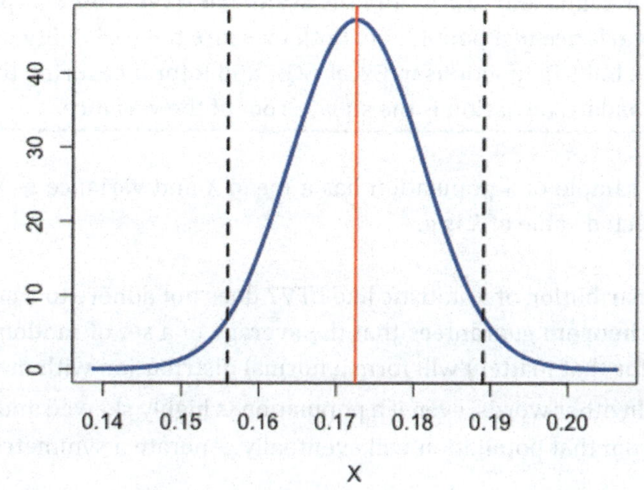

Properties of the standard normal distribution enable us to reason quantitatively about the differences in game KPIs between the two groups in an A/B test. In particular, KPIs like LTV7, D1 retention, and daily conversion rate are calculated for groups A and B after the test has completed. The difference in these averages (*means*) is tested for significance. Underpinning this reasoning is a feature of sample means; namely, they are normally distributed around the true mean of the population. By extension, so are any differences in sample means.

> **Nevermind**
> Those of you in the know have probably surmised that my approach to hypothesis testing is decidedly frequentist, not Bayesian. While Bayes was brilliant and his theories are useful, I've never taken the time to master them. I like to joke that, "Thomas Bayes is the Kurt Cobain of data science: popular with a specific demographic, and highly overrated." But as Jes Simkin always reminds me, not understanding something is never a good reason to have an opinion about it.

The Central Limit Theorem: A Data Analyst's Best Friend

A mobile game's current set of active players is a sample of an unknown population consisting of the set of all possible game players. We don't know the truth about the underlying population, but we use inference to generalize about all future players by observing a sample of current and historical players. For example, a statistic like LTV7 is estimated by taking the mean over a cohort of users. The true LTV7 is represented by μ and its variance by σ^2. Those are universal and unknown parameters that we can only estimate via sampling; i.e., collecting analytics data from our players.

> σ is the Greek letter sigma and represents the **standard deviation** of a population. Sigma's relative, σ^2, is the **variance** of a population. Both measure the variability or "spread" in a distribution. There are built-in functions in Excel, SQL, and R for measuring the variance of a set of numbers. The standard deviation is the square root of the variance.

To differentiate, a sample of a population has a mean X and variance s^2, which are random variables. The expected value of X is μ.

Even though the distribution of a statistic like LTV7 does not adhere to a normal distribution, the **central limit theorem** guarantees that the average of a set of random sample means of LTV7 (or any KPI for that matter) will form a normal distribution with mean μ and standard deviation $\sqrt{\sigma^2/n}$. In other words, even if a population is highly skewed and non-normal, sample means taken from that population will eventually generate a symmetric normal distribution.

To illustrate, let's look at the distribution of LTV7 for all paying players for one of ESG's games, which shall remain anonymous for privacy reasons. We apply our analysis to all monetizing users (`ltv > 0`) who installed in 2021 with the following CTE.

```
WITH monetizers AS
(
  SELECT platform,
         ltv_7,
         ltv_90,
         ltv
  FROM user_ltv
  WHERE install_date BETWEEN '2021-01-01' AND '2021-12-31'
  AND   ltv > 0
)
SELECT * FROM monetizers
```

platform	ltv_7	ltv_90	ltv
android	72.95	362.14	362.14
ios	64.90	710.54	2460.76
ios	0.00	27.58	27.58
android	50.77	109.05	109.05
android	16.53	16.53	16.53
...	...	...	...

The results of this query, with one row per user, are exported to a file called `ltv.csv` for use throughout this chapter. We are temporarily going to consider this cohort and the contents of this CSV file as the "population" of this game's players who installed in 2021 and converted.

At the time of query execution, there were 15,210 monetizing players. There may be more as time goes on as some of those laggards still playing finally decide to convert.

Plotting a normalized histogram of `ltv_7` from this CSV dataset in Tableau reveals a common feature of free-to-play games: a non-normal distribution skewed by whales.

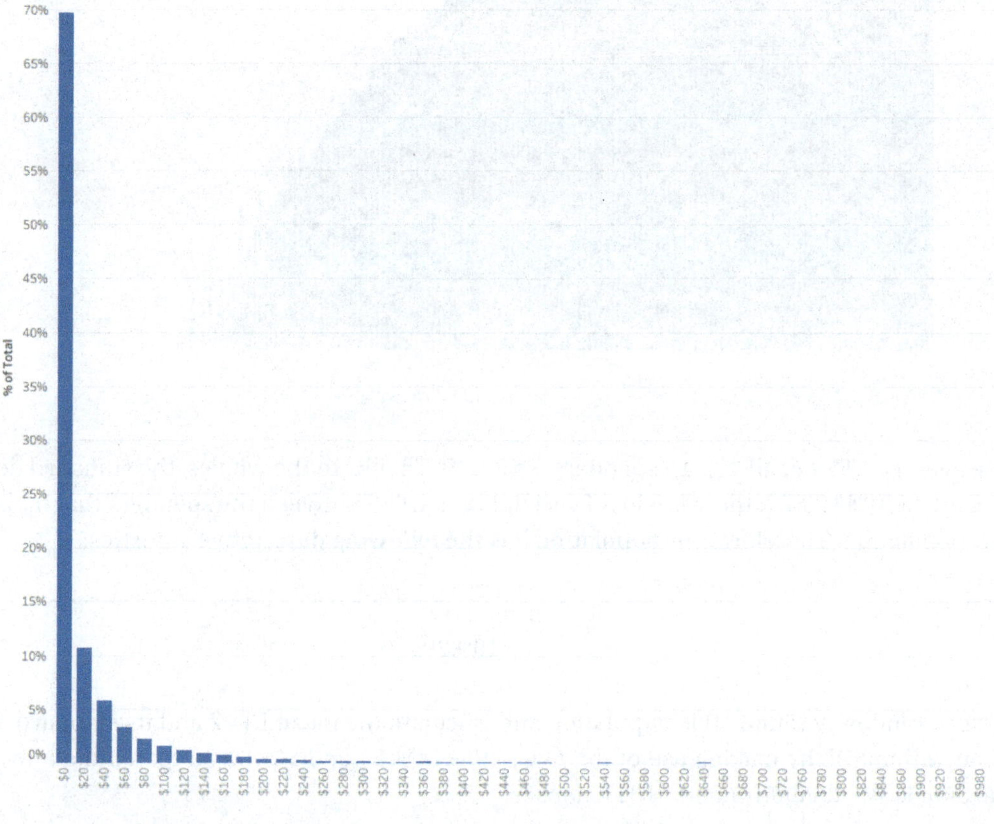

The vast majority (91.8%) of the monetizing users spent less than $100 by D7, but the whales out on the right provide a long tail. The *x*-axis on this chart is truncated: one player spent more than $6,000 in their first seven days! (Please don't judge.) If we switch both axes to logarithmic, the whales surface.

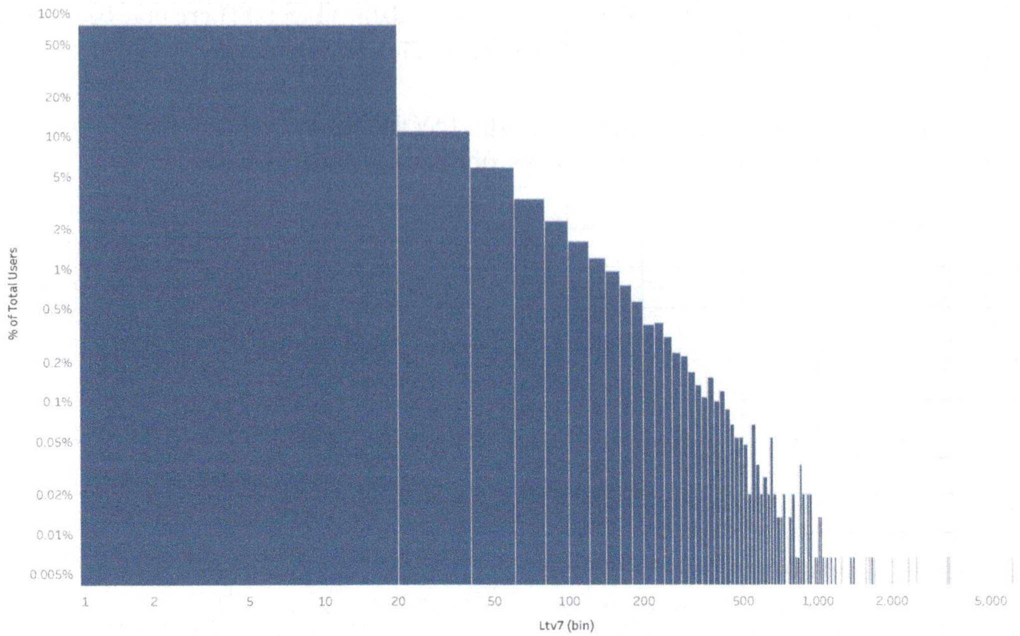

The average LTV7 of all 15,210 spenders is $33.99. Thanks to the whales, the standard deviation is a hefty $109.29; there is a lot of variability in LTV7 between the spenders that make up this population. Therefore, our population has the following descriptive statistics:

$$\mu = 33.99$$
$$\sigma = 109.29$$

We can randomly sample this population and calculate the mean LTV7 and its standard deviation within SQL by making use of the `AVG`, `VARIANCE`, and `SQRT` aggregate functions, and the `ORDER BY RANDOM()` and `LIMIT` clauses:

```
SELECT AVG(ltv_7) AS mean,
       SQRT(VARIANCE(ltv_7)) AS standard_deviation
FROM (SELECT ltv_7
      FROM monetizers
      ORDER BY RANDOM() LIMIT 100)
```

If we run this query a few times with different values for the sample size (`LIMIT n`), we end up with a set of data something like this:

sample size (LIMIT *n*)	mean	standard_deviation
10	25.46	32.82

sample size (LIMIT *n*)	mean	standard_deviation
50	25.91	61.27
100	38.46	84.75
500	33.41	90.30
1000	29.89	72.01
5000	33.94	91.75

The mean of the sample with size 5,000 is within 0.05 of μ. None of the samples appear to have caught any/many whales, as indicated by the low standard deviation relative to the population (109.29). The $n = 1{,}000$ sample was particularly unlucky.

While the parent LTV7 distribution is very non-normal, we know from the central limit theorem that any sample mean taken from this population is a random variable with a normal, bell-shaped distribution. To convince ourselves this is true, we shall now sample only some of these 15,210 data points over and over and calculate a large set of sample means. We could use the SQL above, but it's clunky and difficult to automate. Instead, we use the following `bootie` function in R to resample with replacement.

Our `bootie` function – as its name suggests – is similar to the **bootstrap** technique.[2] The bootstrap is a way to simulate the effect of the central limit theorem and estimate the variance in a population mean when your sample is of a particular size. Whereas a bootstrap starts with a single sample of size n and takes multiple resamples (with replacement) of size n of this same sample, the `bootie` function takes random samples (with replacement) of a specified size m of an underlying parent sample of size n. This approach is referred to as the "m out of n bootstrap." The code is as follows, and don't feel ashamed if you skip right over it. Consistent with the discourse to this point, the underlying parent sample is referred to as the "population" and defined by the dataset of n records in the CSV file passed as the first argument to the function.

---

[2] Everything I know about the bootstrap and permutation testing I learned from reading *Practical Statistics for Data Scientists* by Bruce and Bruce (2017). The R functions introduced in this chapter are inspired by their code.

```
bootie <- function(file, stat_col, sample_size, R=2000)
{
  data <- read.csv(file)

  # treat the entire dataset as the population
  n <- nrow(data)
  pop_val <- round(mean(data[[stat_col]]),3)
  pop_std <- round(sqrt(var(data[[stat_col]])),3)
  cat(sep="","Number of records: ", n, " ", stat_col,": ", pop_val, "
SD: ", pop_std)

  # randomly resample the data R times and calculate the mean
  boot_fun <- function(x, size, m)
  {
    idx <- sample(1:size, m, replace = TRUE)
    return (mean(x[idx]))
  }

  cat("\nResampling", R, "times...")
  resamples <- rep(0, R)
  for (i in 1:R) {
    resamples[i] = boot_fun(data[[stat_col]], n, sample_size)
  }

  # plot a histogram of these R measurements
  hist(resamples, freq=FALSE, density=25, main=paste("Bootstrap with R
=", R,"and m/n =", sample_size, "/", n), col="blue", xlab=stat_col)

  mu <- round(mean(resamples),3)
  std <- round(sqrt(var(resamples)),3)

  cat("\nAvg sample mean:", mu, " SD:", std, " Theoretical SD:",
round(pop_std/sqrt(sample_size),3))
  cat(sep="", "\n95% Confidence interval: ", round(mu-1.96*std,3),
"...", round(mu+1.96*std,3))
  abline(v = mu + 1.96*std, col="black", lwd=2, lty=2)
  abline(v = mu, col="red", lwd=3)
  abline(v = mu - 1.96*std, col="black", lwd=2, lty=2)
  lines(density(resamples), lwd=2, col="yellow")
}
```

The `bootie` function calculates R sample means of the numeric values stored in the `stat_col` column. Each sample is of size `sample_size`. Let's use `bootie` to take 2,000 random samples of size 500 and calculate 2,000 means of the values from the `ltv_7` column. The result is a **sampling distribution** of 2,000 different LTV7 means clustered around the expected value of 33.99.

```
R> bootie("ltv.csv", stat_col="ltv_7", sample_size=500, R=2000)

Number of records: 15210 ltv_7: 33.992 SD: 109.287
Resampling 2000 times...
Avg sample mean: 34.007  SD: 5.047  Theoretical SD: 4.887
95% Confidence interval: 24.115...43.899
```

`bootie` is also kind enough to plot these 2,000 values, resulting in the following sampling distribution for LTV7:

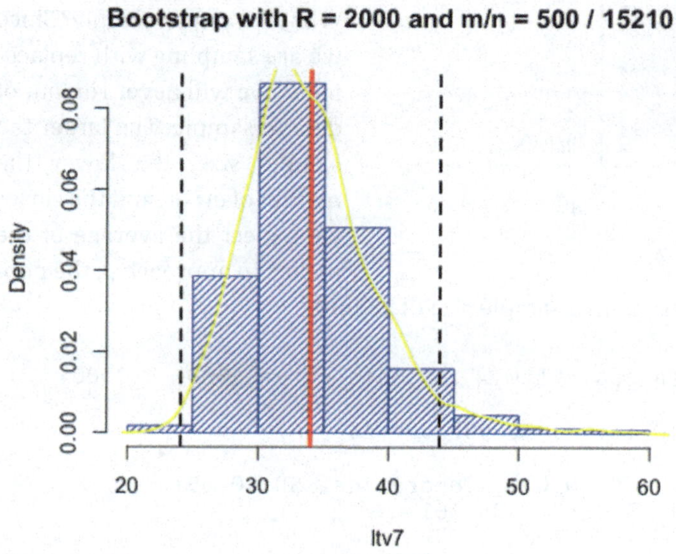

As predicted by the central limit theorem, this distribution already looks somewhat normal. The average of the 2,000 samples ($34.007, in red) is also very close to the "population" mean of $33.992.

Even though the underlying population has a wide variance, samples of the mean will not. The theoretical value is the standard error: the population variance divided by the square root of the sample size, or in this case, $109.2867/\sqrt{500}$. The measured standard deviation of our 2,000 samples is 5.047, compared to the theoretical value of 4.8874. The 95% confidence interval of [24.115, 43.899] – as indicated by the vertical black dashed lines in the histogram – is 1.96 standard deviations from the average of the sample means.

The standard deviation of the sampling distribution is dependent on the size of each sample. If we increase the sample size to 2,000, we expect the standard deviation to fall to the theoretical standard error of $109.287/\sqrt{2000} = 2.444$ and shrink the confidence interval accordingly. Let's try:

```
R> bootie("ltv.csv", stat_col="ltv_7", sample_size=2000, R=2000)

Number of records: 15210 ltv_7: 33.992 SD: 109.287
Resampling 2000 times...
Avg sample mean: 34.044  SD: 2.422  Theoretical SD: 2.444
95% Confidence interval: 29.297...38.791
```

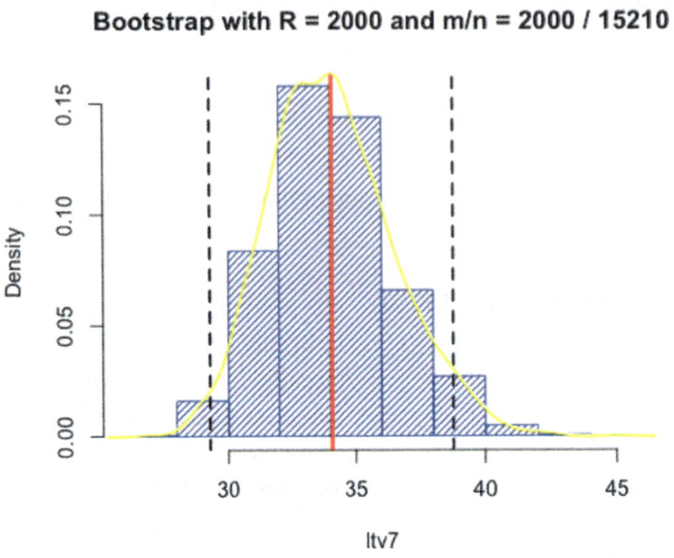

Indeed, this works. Increasing the sample size to 2,000 per resample has shaved about $5 off each end of the mean LTV7 confidence interval.

What happens if we keep increasing the sample size? What if we over-sample? Since we are sampling with replacement, we will never run out of data to sample. The larger the sample size, the lower the margin of error, and the closer we expect the average of the means to approach μ, the population mean. Let's get crazy and try with a sample size of 25,000:

```
R> bootie("ltv.csv", stat_col="ltv_7", sample_size=25000, R=2000)

Number of records: 15210 ltv_7: 33.992 SD: 109.287
Resampling 2000 times...
Avg sample mean: 33.972  SD: 0.678  Theoretical SD: 0.691
95% Confidence interval: 32.643...35.301
```

The average of the means worked out to be within $0.02 of the LTV7 average μ from the entire dataset, which is to be expected as we increase the number of iterations and/or the sample size. Finally, if we also increase the number of resamples to 10,000, a nearly perfect bell-shaped curve (super-imposed in blue in the figure to the right) results.

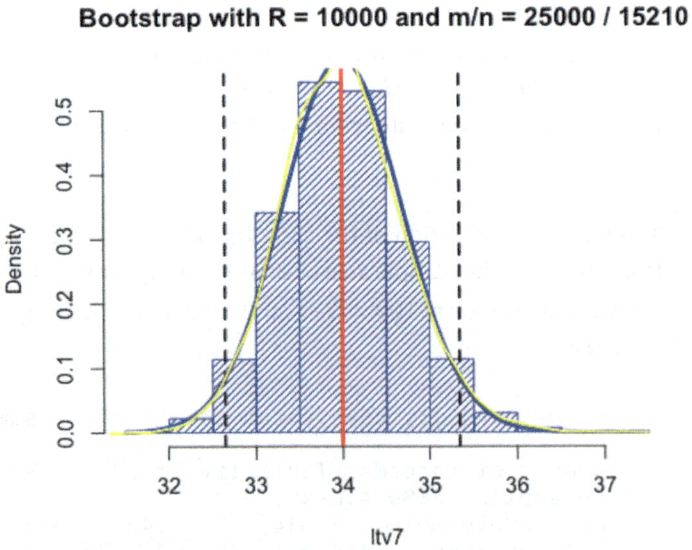

The Difference in Sample Means

We just witnessed how a sample mean for a metric like LTV7 bounces around within a confidence interval dictated by the theoretical standard error. We now extend this idea by considering how the **difference between two sample means** likewise behaves according to the central limit theorem. Whereas we used bootstrapping before to compare the standard deviation of the sampling distribution for a statistic like LTV7 with its theoretical standard error, this time we are going to consider how the difference in LTV7 between two random partitions of the users behaves.

To illustrate, we proceed as follows.

1. Randomly split the users in the `ltv.csv` file into two groups, A and B.
2. Measure the average `ltv_7` for the users in groups A and B.
3. Save the difference between the two means: $\text{ltv\_7}_A - \text{ltv\_7}_B$.
4. Repeat steps 1 to 3 a total of 5,000 times, then plot a histogram of the 5,000 differences in means.

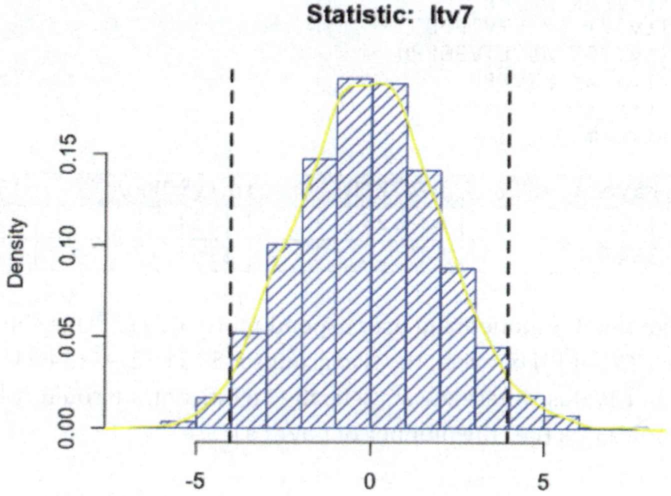

See above. The *x*-axis is the difference in means. The average difference between the two means is 0, with a standard deviation of 2.03. Extreme values for the difference range from about −6 to +6. The data is normally distributed with 95% of the 5,000 values landing between the dashed vertical black lines. The 95% confidence interval is $[-1.96 * 2.03, +1.96 * 2.03]$.

This random shuffling of players into groups for the purpose of calculating a confidence interval for the difference in means is a key component of permutation testing, which is one of the techniques for hypothesis testing we shall now explore.

Hypothesis Testing

As a case study in statistical theory, we are going to prove or disprove the following hypothesis: "iOS ARPPU is greater than Android ARPPU." The two groups of users are those who play on iOS versus those who play on Android. Rather than randomly assigning players to two groups, the users have self-selected by their choice of mobile device. As such, this is not exactly an A/B test, but the statistical theory we use to analyze the difference in means between the two groups is the same as when assessing the results of a true A/B test.

To begin, let's consider the average revenue per paying user (ARPPU), quantified as LTV7, LTV90, and total LTV per paying user (PPU) who installed this anonymous ESG game in 2021. These players were defined previously by the `monetizers` CTE.

```
SELECT platform,
       count(*) as payers,
       AVG(ltv_7) as LTV7PPU,
       AVG(ltv_90) as LTV90PPU,
       AVG(ltv) as LTVPPU
FROM monetizers
GROUP BY platform
```

platform	payers	LTV7PPU	LTV90PPU	LTVPPU
android	11363	$33.25	$134.21	$221.42
ios	3847	$36.16	$164.72	$299.24

It certainly looks like the iOS monetizing users spend more. LTV7PPU is similar, but the observed difference in LTV90PPU between the two groups is \$164.72 – \$134.21 = \$30.51. That's 23% more on iOS, but is this difference statistically significant, or could it be a reasonable result given the sample sizes (i.e., the number of `payers`)?

A statement such as "iOS LTV90 PPU is greater than Android LTV90 PPU" is a **hypothesis** that is either true or false. In statistical testing, a hypothesis is paired with its **null hypothesis**, which assumes that any difference between sample means is due to the errors inherent in random sampling. In this case, the null hypothesis is "there is no difference in LTV90 PPU between iOS and Android." More formally we have:

The null hypothesis, $H_0: LTV90PPU_{ios} = LTV90PPU_{android}$

The alternative hypothesis, H_A : $LTV90PPU_{ios} > LTV90PPU_{android}$

The burden of proof lies with the alternative hypothesis. Let's assume we are convinced if the evidence in favour of the null hypothesis is 5% or less. In other words, if the observed difference in means ($30.51) is outside a 95% confidence interval for the true difference in LTV90PPU, we reject the alternative hypothesis and conclude that iOS LTV90PPU is higher than Android. We now consider two different approaches to testing this hypothesis.

1. Use statistical inference by calculating a 95% confidence interval for the difference in means. If the confidence interval includes the null value (0 when assuming the means are equal), the null hypothesis is accepted.
2. Use a permutation test to determine a sampling distribution of the difference in means from repeated, random shuffles of the users into the iOS and Android groups. Then we consider where our observed difference in means lands on this distribution. If our observation falls within the 95% confidence interval, the null hypothesis is accepted.

The Confidence Interval Approach

Comparing the difference in means of a value like LTV90PPU is one of two standard types of A/B tests a data analyst is likely to encounter in games.[3] The types are:

1. A ***t*-test of a difference in two means**. When the statistic is a continuous variable (ARPU, LTV) or a count (number of sessions per day), the standard error is calculated by pooling the variance of the two samples. This assumes the variance of the two populations is equal, which is a reasonable assumption in randomly assigned A/B groups of game players. Pooled standard deviation for the two sample groups of size n_1 and n_2, respectively, is:

$$s_p = \sqrt{\frac{s_1^2(n_1 - 1) + s_2^2(n_2 - 1)}{(n_1 - 1) + (n_2 - 1)}}$$

And a 95% confidence interval for the difference in the two means is:

[3] A third, but rare, scenario is the **matched** or **paired sample**, where the same users are in both groups. A paired sample is used to evaluate a *before-and-after* scenario.

$$(X_1 - X_2) \pm t_{.025} * s_p \sqrt{\frac{1}{n_1} + \frac{1}{n_2}}$$

The critical value $t_{.025}$ is the t-statistic, the value of which depends on the sample size. But for sample sizes greater than 120, the standard normal z-value is a reasonable substitute: 1.96. However, if the hypothesis is **one-sided** (i.e., that one group is strictly greater than the other rather than simply different), we want all 5% of the normal distribution tail to be at one end, and not split evenly between the two tails. In that case, the t-statistic becomes $t_{.05}$. For 95% confidence with a large (> 120) sample size, $t_{.05}$ is estimated by $z_{.05}$, which is 1.645.

2. A **difference in two proportions.** When a statistic is binary for each user in the sample, as in the case of D*n* retention and D*n* conversion, the average is a proportion between 0 and 1. The standard error calculation is different when the means are proportions. When comparing two means that are proportions averaged over sample sizes n_1 and n_2, respectively, a 95% confidence interval is:

$$(X_1 - X_{2)} \pm 1.96 \sqrt{\frac{X_1(1 - X_1)}{n_1} + \frac{X_2(1 - X_2)}{n_2}}$$

> It is important to keep this in mind when planning and evaluating the results of an A/B test: even though they are both averages, comparing two *proportions* is different than comparing two *means*. In particular, the power calculation used to determine sample sizes is sensitive to small proportions. More about this in the next chapter.

Returning to the task at hand, we recognize that comparing the variable LTV90PPU between the Android and iOS groups is a t-test of the difference in two means. Our alternative hypothesis states that on average iOS monetizers *spend more* by D90. Therefore, this is a one-sided test: we are only interested in measuring whether $\text{LTV90PPU}_{\text{ios}}$ is strictly greater than $\text{LTV90PPU}_{\text{android}}$ and not simply different.

Our two observed sample means and the sample sizes are known. All that remains is to determine the pooled variance[4] of the two groups to calculate the confidence interval. We use the

[4] We assume the variance is roughly the same for the Android and iOS populations of monetizing players, which is validated by the ratio of the two standard deviations from our samples. Alternatively, *non-pooled* variance could be used to build the error term. The results are similar.

VARIANCE aggregate function to calculate the ltv_90 variance by platform, then wrap that with an aggregate to calculate pooled variance (sp), standard error (se), and the one-sided 95% confidence interval (ci):

```
SELECT SQRT(SUM(w_s90) / SUM(n-1)) AS sp,
       sp * SQRT(SUM(1.0 / n)) AS se,
       1.645 * se AS ci
FROM (SELECT platform,
             COUNT(*) AS n,
             VARIANCE(ltv_90) AS s90,
             s90*(n-1) AS w_s90
      FROM monetizers
      GROUP BY platform)
```

sp	se	ci
429.7068	8.015	13.19

The resulting confidence interval for the difference in LTV90PPU is 30.51 +/- 13.19 = [17.33, 43.70]. The population's actual difference between iOS and Android is 95% likely to fall within $17.33 and $43.70. Since zero does not lie within this interval, the null hypothesis is rejected. We conclude with 95% confidence that LTV90 per paying user for iOS is greater than Android.

What about LTV7 instead of LTV90? We measured an observed difference in LTV7PPU between iOS ($36.16) and Android ($33.25) of $2.91, which may not be significant at the 95% level of confidence. If we change our query to use the ltv_7 column instead of ltv_90, we get a confidence interval of [-0.448, 6.258], which spans 0. Therefore, the null hypothesis is accepted: there appears to be no significant difference in LTV7PPU between iOS and Android.

Let's try a proportion. Is there a difference in D7 conversion rates between the two platforms? In this instance, we consider the D7 conversion rate of all installs in 2021 – not just the monetizers. The query is:

```
WITH d7conversion AS
(
  SELECT platform,
         COUNT(*) AS installs,
         SUM(CASE WHEN ltv_7 > 0 THEN 1 END) AS d7converts,
         d7converts / installs::FLOAT AS d7cvr
  FROM user_ltv
  WHERE install_date BETWEEN '2021-01-01' AND '2021-12-31'
  GROUP BY platform
)

SELECT * FROM d7conversion
```

platform	installs	d7converts	d7cvr
android	213412	7473	0.035
ios	70401	2485	0.0353

The observed difference between our two groups is only 0.0003. This is a two-sided test of a difference in two proportions, therefore the confidence interval is calculated differently than our previous one-sided difference in means. The aggregation over the d7conversion CTE is:

```
SELECT 1.96 * SQRT(SUM(d7cvr*(1-d7cvr)/installs))
FROM d7conversion
```

which returns a value of 0.00157. The resulting confidence interval is [-0.00127, 0.00187], which includes 0. We conclude that there is no significant difference in D7 conversion between the two platforms.

Permutation Test

A **permutation test** – like bootstrapping – is a randomized, repeated sampling of a dataset. When used to evaluate the results of an A/B test, users from the original sample are randomly assigned to the *test* and *control* groups thousands of times while maintaining the original size of each group. After each random assignment, the difference in means between *test* and *control* is measured and recorded. A histogram of the resulting set of differences is plotted to estimate the sampling distribution and its variance. A confidence interval of ±1.96 standard deviations from the average of the difference in sample means (or +1.645 in the case of a one-sided test) is calculated and overlaid on the plot. If the observed difference in means from the original sample falls within the confidence interval, the null hypothesis is accepted.

We now present a function in R called p_test that conducts a hypothesis test using both the confidence interval and permutation test approaches. The data is in the form of a CSV file containing one record for each sample (user) in the A/B test. The source code for the function is spread over the next two pages. The p_test function calculates the observed difference in means (if t_test=TRUE) or proportions (if t_test=FALSE) of the stat_col values between the records where the group_col=test_group and those where the group_col<>test_group. That is a mouthful, so it's best to explore its use with an example.

```
p_test <- function(file, stat_col, group_col, test_group, R=2000,
sided=1, t_test=TRUE)
{
  results <- read.csv(file)

  # put the test into group_1 and the control into group_2
  group_2 <- results[results[[group_col]] != test_group, ]
  control_size <- nrow(group_2)
  control <- mean(group_2[[stat_col]])
  control_var <- var(group_2[[stat_col]])
  cat("Control group size: ", control_size, stat_col, "=", control)

  group_1 <- results[results[[group_col]] == test_group, ]
  treatment_size <- nrow(group_1)
  test_val <- round(mean(group_1[[stat_col]]),4)
  test_var <- var(group_1[[stat_col]])
  cat("\nTreatment group size:", treatment_size, stat_col, "=",
test_val)

  # what is the difference between test and control?
  observed <- test_val - control
  cat("\nObserved difference in")
  if (t_test) {
    sp = sqrt((test_var*(treatment_size-1) + control_var*(con-
trol_size-1))/((treatment_size-1)+(control_size-1)))
    std_error = sp * sqrt(1/treatment_size + 1/control_size)
    cat(" means ")
  } else {
    std_error <- sqrt((test_val*(1-test_val)/treatment_size) +(con-
trol*(1-control)/control_size))
    cat( " proportions ")
  }
  cat("between test and control:", observed, "\n\tPct difference =",
round(100.0* (observed/control),2),"%")

  z <- observed / std_error
  # 95% confidence interval
  if (sided == 1) {
    z_value <- 1.645
    p_value <- 1-pnorm(z)
  } else {
    z_value <- 1.96
    p_value <- 2*(1-pnorm(abs(z)))
  }

  ci <- round(z_value * std_error,4)
  cat(sep="","\nStandard error = ", std_error,"\n\t95% confidence in-
terval: ",observed - ci, "...", observed+ci)
  cat("\nz-score =", z, "p-value", p_value)

  # randomly shuffle the data into treatment and control and measure
```

```
the difference
  perm_fun <- function(x, treat, control)
  {
    n <- treat + control
    idx_t <- sample(1:n, treat)
    idx_c <- setdiff(1:n, idx_t)
    return(mean(x[idx_t]) - mean(x[idx_c]))
  }

  cat("\n\nPermutation testing with R =", R)
  perm_diffs <- rep(0, R)
  for (i in 1:R) {
    perm_diffs[i] = perm_fun(results[[stat_col]], treatment_size, con-
trol_size)
  }
  m <- mean(perm_diffs)
  std <- sqrt(var(perm_diffs))
  cat("\n\tSampling distribution mean = ",m,"SD = ",std)

  # plot a histogram of these differences
  hist(perm_diffs, freq=FALSE, density=15, main=paste("Statistic: ",
stat_col), col="blue", xlab=paste("Difference Between",test_group,"and
Control"))

  # where does our actual observed difference lie in this distribu-
tion?
  abline(v = observed, col="red", lwd=3, lty=2)

  # fit a line to the distribution
  lines(density(perm_diffs), lwd=3, col="yellow")

  # add the confidence interval(s)
  abline(v = m + z_value*std, col="black", lwd=2, lty=2)
  if (sided == 2) {
    abline(v = m - z_value*std, col="black", lwd=2, lty=2)
    p_value <- mean(abs(perm_diffs) > abs(observed))
  }
  else {
    p_value <- mean(perm_diffs > observed)
  }
  curve(dnorm(x, mean=m, sd=std), add=TRUE, col="blue", lwd=2)

  # what pct of random trials saw a difference greater than our ob-
served difference?
  cat("\n\tPermutation test est. p-value:", p_value)
}
```

To facilitate our test for a difference in ARPPU between iOS and Android, we can use the same `ltv.csv` file we generated previously. The `p_test` function assumes the CSV has a header with column names, and that there are no null (or `NA`) values. Since all players in this cohort were more than 90 days fully baked, we don't have to worry about nulls in the result set. In every case, LTV ≥ LTV90 ≥ LTV7 ≥ 0. Here again are a few rows of the CSV, sorted by `ltv` descending:

platform	ltv_7	ltv_90	ltv
android	791.38	4967.75	25173.68
ios	130.89	5589.7	21255.65
android	1687.54	11450.48	21178.76
ios	556.76	4813.12	20364.76
...	...	...	...

A sample call to our function in R looks something like this:

```
R> p_test(file="ltv.csv", group_col="platform", test_group="ios",
stat_col="ltv_90", sided=1, t_test=TRUE)
```

The parameters to our `p_test` function begin with the name of the CSV `file` followed by the name of the column used to differentiate the two groups (`group_col="platform"`) and within that column the value that identifies the *treatment* (or *test*) group (`test_group="ios"`). We could have specified "android" instead, but in a one-sided test, the function assumes that the `test_group` is expected to be greater than the control group. The parameter `stat_col` specifies the name of the column in the CSV that contains the statistic to be measured. In this case, `ltv_90`. The observed difference in average `ltv_90` between the *treatment* and *control* groups is tested for significance at a 95% confidence level. Here is the output:

```
R> p_test("ltv.csv", group_col="platform", test_group="ios",
stat_col="ltv_90")

Control group size:  11363 ltv_90 = 134.2181
Treatment group size: 3847 ltv_90 = 164.7292
Observed difference in means between test and control: 30.51108
   Pct difference = 22.73 %
Standard error = 8.015474
   95% confidence interval: 17.32558...43.69658
z-score = 3.806522 p-value 0.00007046728

Permutation testing with R = 2000
   Sampling distribution mean =  -0.04240762 SD =  8.088412
   Permutation test est. p-value: 0
```

Most of the textual output is from the traditional confidence interval approach to hypothesis testing. As already calculated with SQL, we see that the sample sizes are 11,363 for Android (the control group size) and 3,847 for iOS (treatment). The average LTV90 and observed difference in means also jives. The additional information in the output includes the standard error and its corresponding confidence interval at the 95% level. Since zero does not lie within this interval, the null hypothesis is rejected.

The output also includes a *z*-score and its corresponding *p*-value. Being able to explain what those are – especially in a job interview – are critical skills for any data analyst, so I am about to give it my best shot. But first, there is a plot we need to discuss.

Just like its friend `bootie`, the `p_test` function generates a powerful visualization. In this case, a histogram of the differences in means from randomly assigning the users into the *treatment* and *control* groups 2,000 times. The distribution is centered at ~0. As expected, the standard deviation (SD) of this sampling distribution is very close to the standard error used to generate the confidence interval. The observed difference of $30.51 between users in iOS versus Android is plotted in red on top of this histogram.

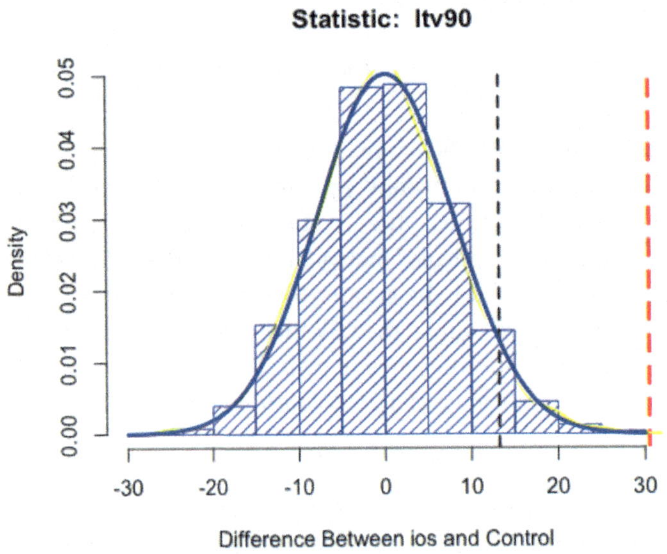

Note our observed value hanging out way over in the right tail, way past the one-sided 95% confidence interval indicated by the black dashed line. The *p*-value of a permutation test is the proportion of randomizations that exceed the observed value. If the observed difference in means is easily beat by a random reshuffle of the users, then there is nothing very special about the original allocation of players to groups and the different game treatments they were subjected to. But in the case of LTV90, the estimated *p*-value is 0, meaning that *none* of the 2,000 random permutations found a difference between *treatment* and *control* that was greater than 30.51. Each time we run the `p_test` function a new set of randomized trials is conducted. Therefore, the exact numbers won't be the same between runs, but the overall conclusion should remain stable.

Another interpretation of the *p*-value is this: if the null hypothesis is true and there is no difference in iOS and Android paying users, what is the probability (*p*-value) that a random sample's difference in means could be as large as 30.51? To calculate its value, we first need to quantify how rare a value of 30.51 is given the distribution of our sample means; i.e., what is the *z*-score for 30.51 given the standard error?

The ***z*-score** for a statistic is how many standard deviations its value is from the mean. In the `p_test` function, the *z*-score is calculated as:

$$z = \frac{X_{treatment} - X_{control}}{\text{standard error}}$$

This formulation assumes the null hypothesis is always "there is no difference in means" and thus the true mean should be zero. In this instance, $z = 30.511/8.015 = 3.807$. Landing almost four standard deviations from the mean is an extremely unlikely event. By definition, the ***p*-value** is the area under the standard normal curve that is beyond the *z*-score. In this case, a *z*-score of 3.807 corresponds to a $p\text{-value} < 0.0001$. In general, if the *p*-value is below a predefined threshold α, the null hypothesis is rejected. In `p_test`, we set $\alpha = 0.05$ and build a $1 - 0.05 = 95\%$ confidence interval for the difference in means.

Let's try a metric where the two groups are closer in value. What about LTV7 instead of LTV90? We can easily switch the test to any other column by specifying a different `stat_col` parameter:

```
R> p_test("ltv.csv", group_col="platform", test_group="ios",
stat_col="ltv_7")

Control group size:  11363 ltv_7 = 33.25683
Treatment group size: 3847 ltv_7 = 36.1615
Observed difference in means between test and control: 2.904666
   Pct difference = 8.73 %
Standard error = 2.038496
   95% confidence interval: -0.4486336...6.257966
z-score = 1.424907 p-value 0.07709206

Permutation testing with R = 2000
   Sampling distribution mean =  -0.05995709 SD =  2.029585
   Permutation test est. p-value: 0.085
```

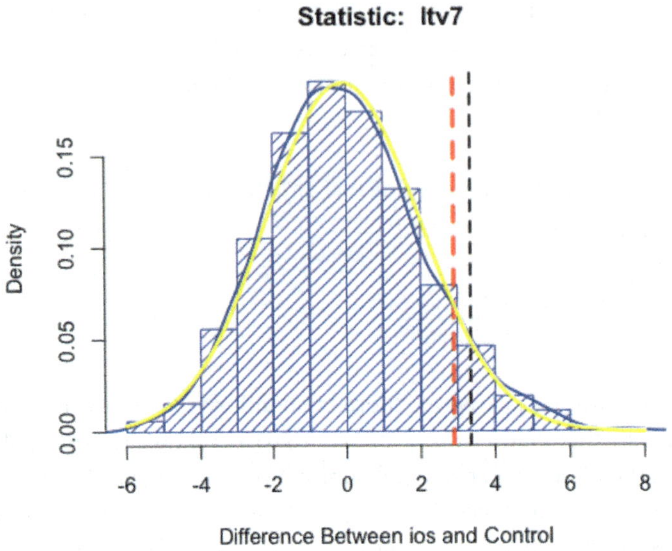

Note that the confidence interval spans zero, and the *p*-value of 0.0771 is greater than 0.05. This time, the null hypothesis is accepted: there appears to be no significant difference in LTV7 between iOS and Android spenders.

As for the permutation test, this histogram (left) reveals that while we detected a difference of \$2.90 between the two groups, that difference is not large enough to accept the alternative hypothesis that LTV7 for iOS spenders is greater than LTV7 for Android spenders. This result is consistent with the classical test. The *p*-value reported in the R console (`est. p-value: 0.085`) is the proportion of randomized permutations where the difference in means exceeded the observed value of \$2.90. If the *p*-value were less than 0.05, we would reject the null hypothesis at a 95% confidence level.

Beware the Bias Monster

Simply stated, a **biased sample** is an unreliable estimate of the underlying population metric. From a theoretical standpoint, bias is avoided if:

1. the samples are truly random; and,
2. the samples are independent of any prior sample. In practice, this means you should sample with replacement, but with large enough *n* the difference between sampling with or without replacement is negligible.

In a freemium game, not all players are created equal. Players from certain countries (Switzerland and the USA) enjoy stronger purchasing power and tend to monetize better. This is sometimes true of the Scandinavian countries, especially Norway.[5] Many of ESG's games are not localized (i.e., translated), which means that we tend to see very poor retention amongst non-English speaking players. And as we just saw, it is often the case that players on iOS monetize better than players on Android. Finally, it is sometimes the case that paid users perform better than organic installs, through the magic of ad network algorithms that target players more likely to take desirable actions (i.e., an IAP) in your game.

To avoid a biased sample when calculating any KPI, watch out for country, platform, and user type (organic vs. paid). As such, we often restrict our analysis to only organic Android users in the USA.

LTV by Platform for US Players Only

We previously found a statistically significant difference in LTV90 between iOS and Android players. But what if our sample was biased? We know that iOS adoption is much higher in North America, and that Android is much more common elsewhere. Indeed, the sample size difference between the two platforms indicate that many more of the spenders were on Android. Prices for the same SKU on Android are often lower than on iOS due to the idiosyncrasies of how Apple sets prices in non-US countries. This means that conversion could be higher on Android, but ARPPU is lower simply due to price differences between the platforms. However, SKU prices are identical in the USA on iOS and Android. So, what happens if we only include spenders from the USA in our samples?

```
SELECT s.platform,
       ltv_7 AS ltv7,
       ltv_90 AS ltv90,
       ltv
FROM user_ltv l LEFT JOIN user_source s USING (user_id)
WHERE l.install_date BETWEEN '2021-01-01' AND '2021-12-31'
AND   ltv > 0
AND   country = 'US'
```

Saving this data as `ltv_us.csv`, if we re-run a significance test for LTV7 and LTV90, we get very different results than our prior assessment.

```
R> p_test("ltv_us.csv", group_col="platform", test_group="ios",
stat_col="ltv7")
```

---

[5] Ah, the coveted Scandinavian market. Everyone uses Norway, Sweden, Denmark, and Finland in the conversion testing phase of soft launch because of the mythology surrounding the Nordic consumer: English speaking and loaded with discretionary income.

```
Control group size:  7208 ltv7 = 37.50845
Treatment group size: 2810 ltv7 = 37.7079
Observed difference in means between test and control: 0.1994538
   Pct difference = 0.53 %
Standard error = 2.629415
   95% confidence interval: -4.125946...4.524854
z-score = 0.07585484 p-value 0.4697673

Permutation testing with R = 2000
   Sampling distribution mean =  -0.06999345 SD =  2.626007
   Permutation test est. p-value: 0.4395
```

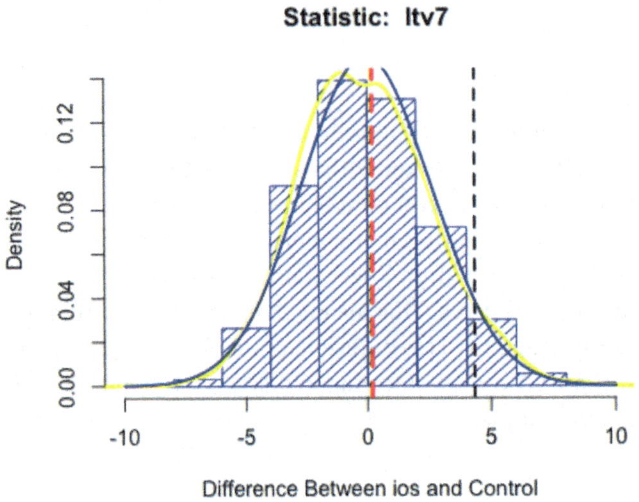

For LTV7 the difference in means is nearly identical. However, a gap starts to widen when we consider LTV90.

```
R> p_test("ltv_us.csv", group_col="platform", test_group="ios",
stat_col="ltv90")

Control group size:  7208 ltv90 = 153.4563
Treatment group size: 2810 ltv90 = 171.7227
Observed difference in means between test and control: 18.26637
   Pct difference = 11.9 %
Standard error = 10.13948
   95% confidence interval: 1.586965...34.94577
z-score = 1.80151 p-value 0.0358113

Permutation testing with R = 2000
   Sampling distribution mean =  0.06852996 SD =  10.06635
   Permutation test est. p-value: 0.0365
```

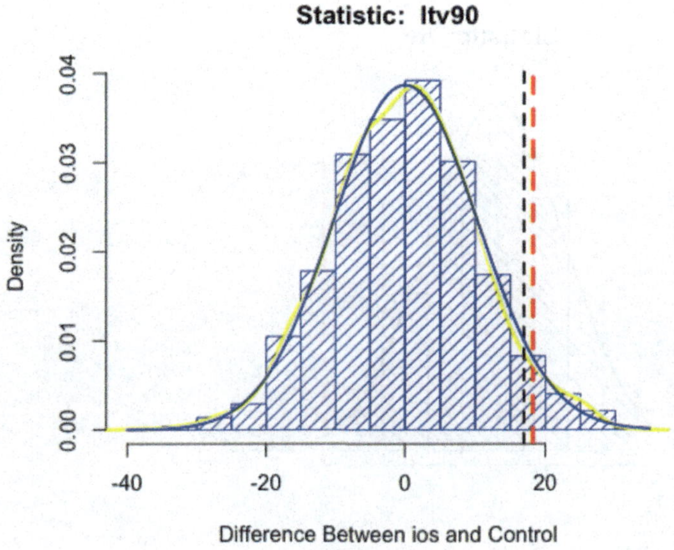

Both the classical test and the permutation test reject the null hypothesis, with *p*-values ~0.036. The confidence interval begins at 1.59, missing the inclusion of zero. We conclude, with 95% confidence, that US monetizing players spend more by D90 on iOS compared to their Android counterparts.

And finally, if we look at ongoing LTV uncapped by any days since install, we definitely see those iOS payers in the US spending like drunk data scientists at a Python conference in Las Vegas:

```
R> p_test("ltv_us.csv", group_col="platform", test_group="ios",
stat_col="ltv")

Control group size:  7208 ltv = 253.8157
Treatment group size: 2810 ltv = 303.5496
Observed difference in means between test and control: 49.73395
   Pct difference = 19.59 %
Standard error = 20.07915
   95% confidence interval: 16.70375...82.76415
z-score = 2.476895 p-value 0.006626537

Permutation testing with R = 2000
    Sampling distribution mean =  -0.2541656 SD =  20.52884
   Permutation test est. p-value: 0.0105
```

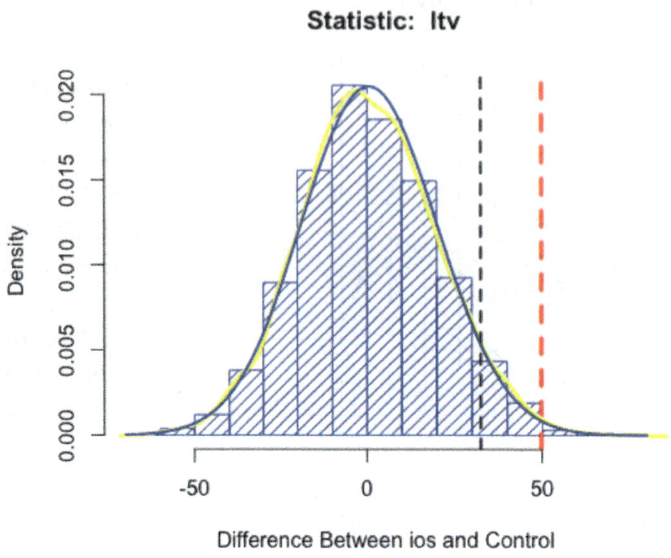

What we don't know definitively is *why* this is happening. Further investigation could look at the effect of whales, or if long-tail retention for Android spenders is significantly lower than on iOS.

Summary

In the preceding discussion, we reviewed the central limit theorem and the properties of sampling distributions. We put this theory into practice by analyzing the difference in ARPPU between users on iOS vs. Android. While this wasn't a traditional A/B test, the statistical analysis we used to check for significance is the same as how you would analyze the difference between two means in an actual A/B test: is the difference between the two groups of players shown competing game treatments truly different or simply due to the random assignment of players to each group?

There are two types of averages that are compared between groups in an A/B test. A proportion is an average of a set of binary numbers, where the 1s are the successes like "played" or "purchased." Conversely, a mean is an average of a set of scalar values like LTV7. The difference in averages between groups A and B is compared using either a difference in two proportions, or a *t*-test of the difference in two means. Regardless, the null hypothesis is always "there is no difference: $X_A - X_B = 0$." A confidence interval is constructed for $X_A - X_B$, and if the interval contains 0, then the null hypothesis is accepted. This entire analysis is possible using only SQL, but does require implementation of the formulas for standard error within the query. The programming language R includes functions for doing either type of test with a single line of code, but we built our own function to conduct both a 95% confidence interval using the theoretical standard error, and the standard deviation of a sampling distribution constructed through permutation testing. The *p*-value is the probability that the null hypothesis is true given the data at hand. If the *p*-value is below a predefined threshold – usually 0.05 or 0.01 – the null hypothesis is rejected and the alternative hypothesis is accepted as more probable.

In the next chapter, we delve into further detail regarding how to plan, conduct, and evaluate A/B tests within the context of free-to-play games.

A/B Testing in Practice:

LEVEL 9

In this chapter we cover how to design, run, and evaluate a free-to-play game A/B test. We start by introducing the ESG Playbook – a checklist for data analysts to follow when working with a game's team on designing a test. We cover the important topic of **statistical power***: determining how much data we need to ensure we draw the right conclusions. Some specific case studies are presented from actual A/B tests run at ESG. Finally, we recap what we have learned by revisiting and discussing the push notification scenario introduced at the start of the previous chapter.*

An A/B Testing Playbook

The sequence of steps required when running and measuring any A/B test are as follows.

1. **Define the hypothesis.** What is being changed or introduced to the game, and what is the expected outcome of the change or new feature on the game's KPIs? What do we want to learn? How will this help us make decisions and take actions? For example, "Lowering the price of the first-time buyer pack (FTBP) from $9.99 to $5.99 will increase D3 conversion." This is our hypothesis. The null hypothesis typically asserts that the difference in KPIs between the two groups is zero; in this instance, D3 conversion between the two groups is the same.
2. **Choose your KPIs.** Determine the statistic(s) used to measure success or failure of the experiment. What determines a winner? Usually this is obvious from the hypothesis (e.g., D3 conversion rate), but consider measuring for other foreseen or unforeseen consequences of the change like long-term retention (D7R, D30R) and monetization (e.g., ARPU, LTV30). For example, if the FTBP is perceived by the player after purchase as poor value and a bad consumer decision, increasing the probability that it becomes the first item purchased may lead to a decrease in second purchases, or an increase in churn.
3. **Segment the players.** Decide on an assignment of the players into groups, e.g., A (or *test*) is presented with a FTBP of $5.99, and B (*control*) is shown a price of $9.99. Do you need to limit the test to specific demographics (e.g., US, Android, organic), or is a random sample of all eligible players a better approach? Should this test be run with new installs only, or can the test include existing players? In the latter case, any player who has never made

a purchase, or has never purchased the FTBP, could be eligible to participate in the study. However, to be free of any bias regarding the existing players (who have chosen not to purchase the FTBP and not to churn for some reason), it makes sense to only include new installs from the start of the experiment. This is especially necessary if D3 conversion is the primary statistic to measure, though one could look at conversion within three days of starting the test rather than three days after install.

4. **Decide on what the stakeholders consider significant.** How big of a change are you looking to see in the KPIs? Is a 10% increase in D3 conversion worth making this change to the product? How about a 5% change in LTV30? The detectable change is called the **effect** and is stated as a +/- percentage from the baseline or control. Be careful not to confuse absolute vs. relative changes: a lift in D3 conversion from 3.0% to 3.3% is a 10% change, *not* a 0.3% change. Conversely, a change in LTV30 from $5.00 to $5.25 is a 5% lift. Percentage changes to small proportions, like conversion rate, result in very small absolute effects.
5. **Determine the sample size.** How do we know when we have gathered enough information? Calculate the required sample size using the power formula. The smaller the effect you want to detect (e.g., a 2% lift in D3 conversion) at a specific *p*-value (e.g., 95% confidence), the larger the sample size required and the longer your test might have to run. Consider the trade-off between accuracy and time. If you need to run a test for six months before you can reach a conclusion, that is probably not the best use of analyst resources. Moreover, when a statistic is a proportion and the values are typically very small, this will seriously impact the power calculation. For conversion tests, a general rule of thumb is that any dataset must include 10 successes to be valid. For metrics like D1 conversion, where the number of successes is very small, this can be particularly relevant. See the discussion *We Need More Power!* below.
6. **Start your engines!** Randomly segment the users into groups A and B. Run the experiment until the requisite sample size for both groups is reached, and enough time has passed for the samples to become fully baked with respect to the KPIs of interest.
7. **Generate the dataset.** Use SQL to query the database and generate a CSV file that contains one record per user in the experiment.[1] One of the columns must indicate whether this sample is from group A or B. Each record normally contains relevant statistics for

---

[1] The specific details of how users are assigned to groups are highly dependent on the segmentation tool utilized to set up and run an A/B test. At ESG we have used SWRVE, Firebase, and our own internal segmentation tool driven by each game's backend. Regardless, our Redshift Mentor databases each contain a table called `ab_test` where the specifics reside. In the case of third-party tools like SWRVE or Firebase, this table is hydrated by a batch ETL process, the primary requirement of which is to ensure that user IDs are mapped properly to facilitate recognizing which users were assigned to which group (and when). The details – while important to get right – are irrelevant to the discourse.

each unique user involved in the test. Avoid daily aggregated statistics like ARPDAU that encompass all players in the same cohort – it will take forever to generate enough data. Instead, for monetization, track LTV for each user *after* they enter the test, and compare ARPU (average LTV by the *n*th day after entering the test) between A and B.

8. **Clean the dataset.** Be sure to exclude nulls in the dataset by either removing them from the file or by setting a default value (e.g., 0.00 for LTV if the user made zero purchases). The approach you take depends on the context of the test statistic. For example, if you are measuring D1 and D7 retention, some of the rows may have nulls for D7 but not for D1 – players who have installed within the past week. Those rows should be removed since we can't assume any value for the missing D7 until after those players are fully baked. While this should never happen, check for users who somehow managed to end up in both groups. Generate a list of user IDs that exist in both groups and remove those entirely from the dataset with a `NOT IN` clause.
9. **Test for statistical significance.** There is a difference in means (or proportions) between groups A and B, but is it significant or simply due to chance? To find out, construct a confidence interval centered on the observed difference using the standard error calculation based on the type of test. If the interval includes the value 0, accept the null hypothesis. Alternatively, fire up R and analyze the data in the CSV generated and cleaned in the previous steps. The `p_test` function introduced last chapter uses both traditional statistics (hypothesis testing with confidence intervals) and permutation testing to determine significance with 95% confidence. Is your test two-sided (looking for any difference) or one-sided (looking for an improvement only)? By default, `p_test` assumes one-sided, but this can be overridden by passing the parameter `sided=2`.
10. **Act.** Communicate the results to the stakeholders. If the experiment improved the game in a significant way, roll out the change to all players.

"We Need More Power!"

Statistical power is simply the probability that we can detect statistical significance when looking for a particular effect (e.g., a 5% lift in D1R). The smaller the effect we want to detect, the larger the sample size required. But watch out: not all effects are created equal. A 5% lift in conversion from 3.0% to 3.15% is quite a different animal than a 5% lift in D1 retention from 40% to 42%.

Before conducting any test, we should consider the minimal effect we want to measure by starting with a baseline – the current value of a KPI like 40% D1 retention – and a change considered relevant or significant – like a 5% increase to 42% D1R. From there, the `pwr` package in R can determine the sample sizes required to detect this amount of change with a specific probability.

The pwr package includes functions where you supply all but one of parameters representing the effect, alpha, sample size, and power, and the function returns the calculated value for the missing parameter. The most common use case is to determine the requisite sample size. For example, if we want to detect a 10% effect (h=0.1) with 95% confidence (sig.level=0.05) in a two-sided test of difference in proportions:

```
R> pwr.2p.test(power = 0.8, h = 0.1, sig.level = 0.05)

     Difference of proportion power calculation for binomial
distribution (arcsine transformation)

              h = 0.1
              n = 1569.772
      sig.level = 0.05
          power = 0.8
    alternative = two.sided
```

we need a sample size n of 1,570 for both groups. The power parameter indicates the likelihood (80%) of correctly rejecting the null hypothesis when the alternative hypothesis is true, i.e., avoiding a type II error.

A **type I error** occurs if you incorrectly reject the null hypothesis: you think the difference is significant, but it was due to chance. The probability of this happening is α. For example, if α =0.05, this is the one case in 20 where a 95% confidence interval fails: the *p*-value is less than 0.05 but it was due to chance.

A **type II error** occurs when you incorrectly accept the null hypothesis. The probability of this happening is β. The best way to reduce β is to increase the sample size.

The **power** of a hypothesis test = $P(\text{reject } H_0 \mid H_1 \text{ is true}) = (1 - \beta)$.

The most relevant functions in the pwr package for our purposes are pwr.2p.test (for comparing proportions like retention and conversion) and pwr.t.test (for comparing quantities like LTV) to determine a required sample size before an experiment begins, then pwr.2p2n.test and pwr.t2n.test after the dataset is generated to confirm that both n_1 and n_2 were appropriately sized.

Case Studies

Enough of the theory – let's review some of the A/B tests you are likely to find at a game studio. The R function p_test introduced in the previous chapter is the primary tool used to conduct the analysis.

Case Study 1: Promo 220 A/B Test

A case study was run at ESG to compare two versions of a promo in a time-limited weekend event. A summary of the data is as follows:

group	size	converted	cvr
control	5107	163	0.0319
test	45319	1369	0.0302

The full dataset with one row per user is in a file called `e220AB.csv`. The first few rows of the data appear as follows:

egp_event_220_1	country	install_date	eltp	eltv	converted
1	CA	2020-08-19	0	0	0
1	US	2018-01-21	0	0	0
1	US	2020-10-30	2	8.62	1
1	US	2020-11-19	0	0	0
0	AU	2017-09-20	0	0	0
...	...	...	...	...	...

The hypothesis was that the treatment group (`egp_event_220_1=1`) was more likely to convert than the control group. The statistic tested was the difference in proportions (`-0.0017`) of the column `converted`.

```
R> p_test("e220AB.csv", group_col="egp_event_220_1", test_group="1",
stat_col="converted", t_test=FALSE)

Control group size:  5106 converted = 0.03192323
Treatment group size: 45318 converted = 0.0302
Observed difference in proportions between test and control: -
0.001723228
   Pct difference = -5.4 %
Standard error = 0.002588202
   95% confidence interval: -0.006023228...0.002576772
z-score = -0.665801 p-value 0.7472308

Permutation testing with R = 2000
   Sampling distribution mean =  -0.00001071747 SD =  0.002531636
   Permutation test est. p-value: 0.76
```

The result was a *p*-value of 0.75 (single-sided test) and we accept the null hypothesis (no difference in conversion). In fact, the treatment group performed worse than control.

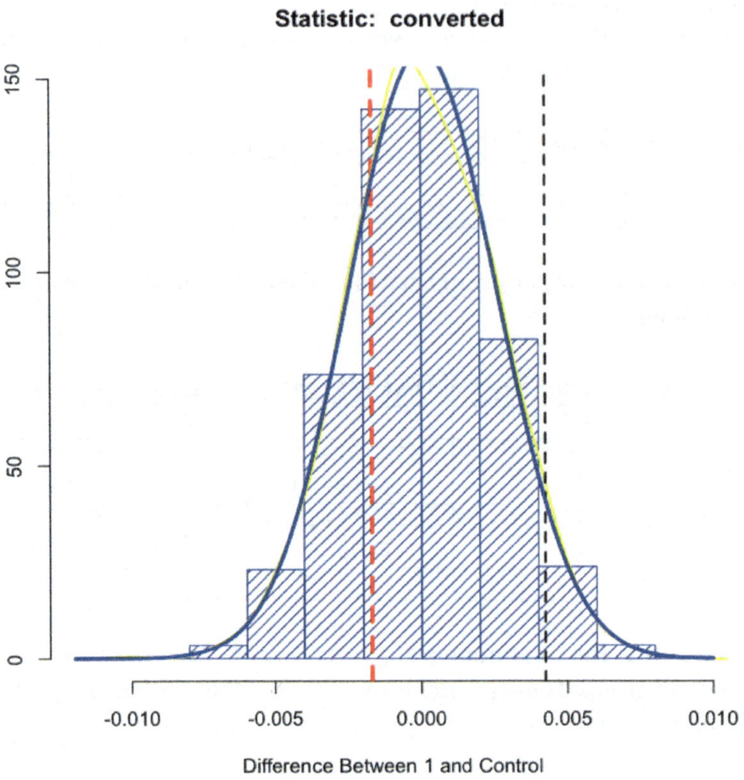

But was our sample size large enough? This was a "two sample test for proportions with different sample sizes." According to the function `pwr.2p2n.test` we are 99% sure (`power`) that our sample sizes were big enough to detect a 10% effect in conversion.

```
R> pwr.2p2n.test(h=0.1, sig.level=0.05, n1=5107, n2=45319,
alternative="greater")

     difference of proportion power calculation for binomial
distribution (arcsine transformation)

              h = 0.1
             n1 = 5107
             n2 = 45319
      sig.level = 0.05
          power = 0.9999999
    alternative = greater
```

But let's be careful with how effect (`h`) works. We can use the `ES.h` function to specify the exact absolute values of the proportions from our two samples:

```
R> ES.h(.0319, .0302)
[1] 0.009801833
```

That's a lot smaller than 0.1. Effect is not a linear calculation. Therefore, before starting a test, specify the parameter for effect, `h=ES.h(p1,p2)`, with a guesstimate for what we believe the control group proportion is (e.g., 0.03) and what we hope our test group will be (e.g., 0.035). If we saw a lift in conversion from 3 to 3.5% for this test, I think we'd be happy, right? So how big would our sample sizes need to be to detect that with 80% confidence (`power=0.8`) with a one-sided (`alternative="greater"`) test?

```
R> pwr.2p.test(h=ES.h(p1=.035,p2=.03), power=0.8, sig.level=.05,
alternative="greater")

     Difference of proportion power calculation for binomial
distribution (arcsine transformation)

              h = 0.02821746
              n = 15529.67
      sig.level = 0.05
          power = 0.8
    alternative = greater
```

15,530 people in each group. Note the non-linear calculation of the effect in the output based on the two proportions given as arguments. Algebraically, improving from 3% to 3.5% is a 16.7% increase, but this does not translate into the effect size when calculating statistical power of tests involving small proportions.

We now realize that our control group was probably too small. What effect could we have detected reliably with the actual sample sizes in our one-sided test?

```
R> pwr.2p2n.test(power=0.8, n1=5107, n2=45319, sig.level=0.05,
alternative="greater")

     difference of proportion power calculation for binomial
distribution (arcsine transformation)

              h = 0.03667845
             n1 = 5107
             n2 = 45319
      sig.level = 0.05
          power = 0.8
    alternative = greater

NOTE: different sample sizes
```

An effect of 0.037. What's that work out to when dealing with a tiny baseline proportion of 0.03? After some trial-and-error, it looks like 0.0365:

```
R> ES.h(0.0365, 0.03)
[1] 0.03629691
```

The sample sizes were large enough to correctly reject the null hypothesis if the true difference in proportions was at least 0.0065, but too small to have reliably detected anything tinier. In other words, if the promo did increase conversion, we weren't likely to reject the null hypothesis unless the treatment group's conversion rate was that much larger than the baseline. However, our sample sizes would have been just fine if instead we were comparing D1 retention between two groups where our baseline is 35% and we are looking for a change of ±3 basis points:

```
R> pwr.2p2n.test(n1 = 5107, n2 = 45319, sig.level = 0.05,
h=ES.h(p1=0.35,p2=0.38))

     difference of proportion power calculation for binomial
distribution (arcsine transformation)

              h = 0.0623268
             n1 = 5107
             n2 = 45319
      sig.level = 0.05
          power = 0.9881682
    alternative = two.sided
```

In this case, we can be confident that our sample sizes are more than adequate to have correctly rejected the null hypothesis if D1R changed by ±0.03.

Case Study 2: Idle Stonks *Tech Tree Feature*

Early metrics collected when the ESG game *Idle Stonks* was in soft launch indicated poor D7 retention. To remedy this situation, the game designers introduced a new feature called the *Tech Tree*, which included a clear and visible set of medium- and long-term goals to pursue while fully complementing the game's idle mechanic. Stakeholders at the studio wanted to know, did it work?

An A/B Test was run targeting new installs only from Jan 13, 2022, until Jan 26, 2022. There was an even split between *control* (Tech Tree disabled) and *treatment* (Tech Tree enabled).

The hypotheses to test were broken down into retention and monetization KPIs:

H_0: There is no difference in D7 retention (D7R) between new installs who have the Tech Tree enabled and those that have the Tech Tree disabled.

H_A: New installs with the Tech Tree feature exhibit higher D7R.

Further, we have:

H_0: There is no difference in LTV7 between new installs who have the Tech Tree enabled and those that have the Tech Tree disabled.

H_A: New installs with the Tech Tree feature exhibit higher LTV7.

After all participants were D7 fully baked, a query was run to generate a dataset (`stonks_tech_tree.csv`) that included one row per user in the study. The resulting CSV looks something like the following:

group_name	start_time	ltv_7	d7
variant_tech_tree_disabled	2022-01-26 3:44	0	0
variant_tech_tree_enabled	2022-01-17 2:06	0	0
variant_tech_tree_enabled	2022-01-19 18:33	0	1
...	...	...	...

There were 18,579 total users in the experiment, roughly split 50-50 between the two groups. With 80% power, we can detect a *t*-test difference in means of 3.6% for LTV7:

```
R> pwr.t.test(n=9300, power=0.8, type="two.sample",
alternative="greater")

     Two-sample t test power calculation

              n = 9300
              d = 0.03648989
      sig.level = 0.05
          power = 0.8
    alternative = greater

NOTE: n is number in *each* group
```

But for D7R (two proportions), the power of the test is only 72% when the effect is specified as a change from 10% D7R to 11% D7R:

```
R> pwr.2p.test(n = 9300, alternative="greater", sig.level = 0.05,
h=ES.h(0.11,0.10))
```

```
     Difference of proportion power calculation for binomial
distribution (arcsine transformation)

                h = 0.0326294
                n = 9300
        sig.level = 0.05
            power = 0.7191016
      alternative = greater

NOTE: same sample sizes
```

The p_test function was used to evaluate ltv_7 and d7 differences for significance. The primary goal of this new feature was to increase D7R, so we start with stat_col="d7".

```
R> p_test("stonks_tech_tree.csv",
test_group="variant_tech_tree_enabled", stat_col="d7",
group_col="group_name", t_test=FALSE)

Control group size:  9243 d7 = 0.1057016
Treatment group size: 9336 d7 = 0.0996
Observed difference in proportions between test and control: -
0.006101612
   Pct difference = -5.77 %
Standard error = 0.004453412
   95% confidence interval: -0.01340161...0.001198388
z-score = -1.370098 p-value 0.9146719

Permutation testing with R = 2000
   Sampling distribution mean =  0.000005406509 SD =  0.004465491
   Permutation test est. p-value: 0.9175
```

However, we see that the *treatment* group performed worse than *control*, with D7R dropping from 10.57% to 9.96%. Since we expected retention and monetization to improve within the *treatment* group, we used a one-sided test. If we re-run the test and specify sided=2, we see that the difference in D7 retention is insignificant.

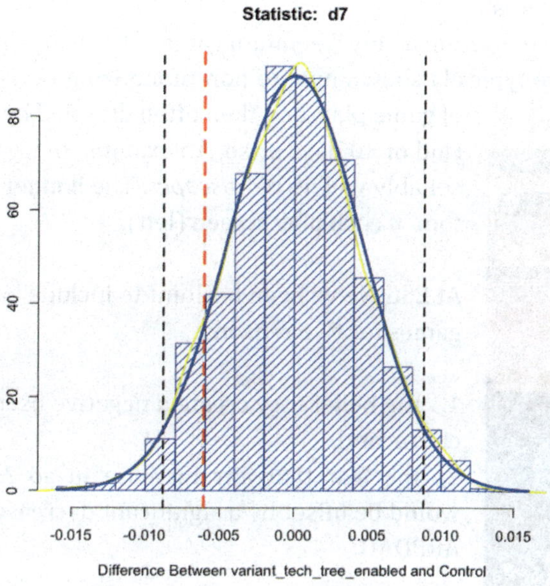

Completing the analysis with `stat_col="ltv_7"` also suggests that despite a 1.44% increase in LTV7 in the *treatment* group, there is very little reason to reject the null hypothesis:

```
> p_test("stonks_tech_tree.csv",
test_group="variant_tech_tree_enabled", stat_col="ltv_7",
group_col="group_name")

Control group size:  9243 ltv_7 = 0.3657287
Treatment group size: 9336 ltv_7 = 0.371
Observed difference in means between test and control: 0.00527134
   Pct difference = 1.44 %
Standard error = 0.07697422
   95% confidence interval: -0.1213287...0.1318713
z-score = 0.0684819 p-value 0.472701

Permutation testing with R = 2000
   Sampling distribution mean =  0.0004278176 SD =  0.07605177
   Permutation test est. p-value: 0.473
```

In summary, we dismissed the Tech Tree as a viable feature for improving D7R and LTV7. But given there was very little evidence to suggest the feature harmed either KPI, removing or adopting the Tech Tree was left to the discretion of the PM.

Case Study 3: Banner Ads

A simple way to increase revenue in any freemium game is to include **banner ads** in the user interface. These ads are typically shown only to non-monetizing users after a certain period of game play, and then often disabled by any purchase for a period of 30 days or so. An example of a game that does this reasonably well is *Wordscapes*. The banner ad appears at the bottom of each play screen (left).

At ESG we've been hesitant to include banner ads in any of our games for two reasons:

1. the belief they create a negative user experience leading to churn; and,
2. the fear that any increase in ad ARPDAU from banners would be offset by a significant decrease in rewarded video ad ARPDAU.

However, these assumptions had never been tested. It is worth finding out: game publishers include banner ads because they historically generate about $0.02 in ad ARPDAU. If you have 500,000 non-monetizing DAU, that works out to $10K/day, or *holy moly that's like $3.65M in annual revenue*! And if those non-spenders haven't been willing to make an IAP, maybe they will convert if they know those annoying banner ads will disappear once they do.

Banner ads were A/B tested as follows. The null hypothesis was that showing banner ads to non-paying users starting at level 10 would *not* impact retention nor existing LTV and ad monetization. In other words, adding banner ads would add incremental revenue with no downside. The KPIs deemed important to monitor were retention 1, 3, 7, and 14 days *after* players began level 10. For monetization metrics, the conversion rate, LTV, and number of rewarded video ads watched during the first 14 days after the start of the test were measured.

Any player who entered level 10 and had not made an IAP within the last 30 days was eligible for inclusion in the experiment. These users were split into two groups: *treatment* (shown banner ads) and *control* (no banner ads). If a player in the *treatment* group made any purchase, banner ads were disabled for 30 days. Existing players who were already in level 10 or higher were excluded from the study.

A difference of 5% of any of the monitored KPIs would raise eyebrows. Given that we weren't sure whether the banner ads would have a positive or negative impact, a two-sided test is required.

The requisite sample size was determined using the R library pwr. For retention after start of level 10, historical data indicates that about 50% of users play exactly 14 days after the start of level 10. Therefore, the ES.h(0.525,0.5) parameters are chosen as representative of a 5% change. What sample size is required for a difference of proportions with 95% confidence and power of 80%?

```
R> pwr.2p.test(sig.level=0.05, power=0.8, h=ES.h(0.525,0.5))

     Difference of proportion power calculation for binomial
distribution (arcsine transformation)

              h = 0.05002086
              n = 6273.853
      sig.level = 0.05
          power = 0.8
    alternative = two.sided
```

We want at least 6,274 in both the *treatment* and *control* groups.

SWRVE was used to segment players based on the criteria indicated above. The experiment ran for six weeks. The dataset generated from SQL was contained in a file called bannerads.csv, the first few rows of which appear as follows:

ltv	converted	rewarded_ads	d1	d3	d7	d14	grp
0	0	5964	1	1	1	1	control
12.62	1	1282	1	1	1	1	test
0	0	70	1	1	0	1	test
0	0	291	1	1	1	0	test
0	0	1598	1	1	1	1	test
113.8	1	3012	1	0	1	1	control
...	...	...	...	...	...	...	...

We start by examining D14, which is a 1 if a user played exactly 14 days after reaching level 10 and entering the A/B test, or a 0 otherwise.

```
R> p_test("bannerads.csv", sided=2, group_col="grp", stat_col="d14",
t_test=FALSE, test_group="test")

Control group size:  8304 d14 = 0.57671
Treatment group size: 2739 d14 = 0.5604
```

```
Observed difference in proportions between test and control: -
0.01631002
   Pct difference = -2.83 %
Standard error = 0.01092427
   95% confidence interval: -0.03771002...0.005089981
z-score = -1.493008 p-value 0.1354351

Permutation testing with R = 2000
   Sampling distribution mean =  -0.0003689555 SD =  0.01114822
   Permutation test est. p-value: 0.144
```

The players who saw banner ads exhibited a 56.04% retention rate 14 days after their first exposure, compared with 57.67% for those in the control group. The null hypothesis is accepted.

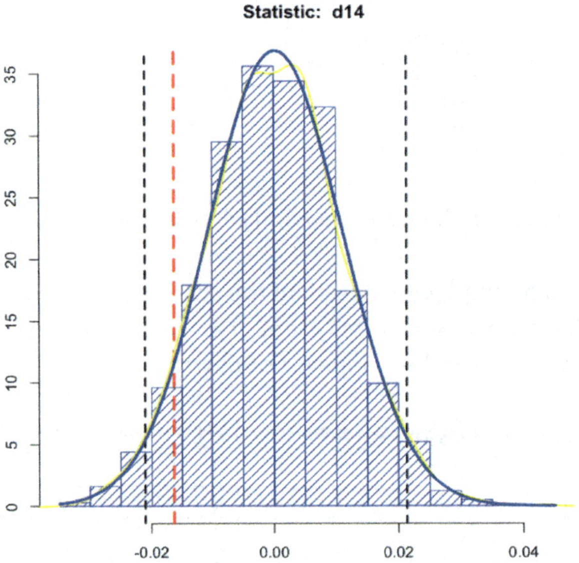

However, that red dashed line is looking pretty far from the mean. If we do a one-sided test to compare D14R for the control group vs. treatment, the extra retention exhibited by the control group is close to being significant, with a *p*-value of 0.068. But again, with a 95% confidence interval, we (arbitrarily) miss the criteria to reject the null hypothesis.

It turns out that none of the ad monetization, IAP conversion, nor LTV metrics checked out as statistically significant, either. We accept every null hypothesis: showing banner ads to non-paying users starting at level 10 does not negatively impact retention nor monetization.

However, note that the test was under-powered. According to the p_test function, SWRVE only assigned 2,739 players to the treatment group, which is too small by over 3,500. Low power means a high probability of incorrectly accepting the null hypothesis. What is that probability exactly?

```
R> pwr.2p2n.test(sig.level=0.05,n1=2739,n2=8304, h=ES.h(0.525,0.5))

     difference of proportion power calculation for binomial
 distribution (arcsine transformation)

              h = 0.05002086
             n1 = 2739
             n2 = 8304
      sig.level = 0.05
          power = 0.6217875
    alternative = two.sided
```

With power=0.62 we have a 38% chance of a Type II error; we accepted the null hypothesis, but that may have been the wrong decision. Indeed, we later backtracked on this action and disabled banner ads after re-running this A/B test six months later.

Summary: The Push Notification Scenario Revisited

At the start of the last chapter, we introduced the topic of A/B testing for mobile games with the following scenario:

The PM shows you the click-through rates (clicks per impression) of the two different PNs they tested. One PN has a higher click-through rate (CTR) than the other: 11% vs 10%. The PM proudly announces that they will now use the PN that saw an 11% CTR moving forward because it has a higher rate and is thus the better option. How should you respond to the PM's conclusion?

You should now recognize this as a simple A/B Test. In particular, a one-sided comparison of two proportions (the CTR). The null and alternative hypotheses are:

> H_0: There is no real difference in CTR between the two groups, i.e., a difference in sample proportions of zero falls within the confidence interval of the test.
>
> H_A: The PN that scored an 11% CTR is not due to chance and is actually the better option, i.e., the extra CTR is significant.

Immediate questions that should spring to mind include:

- Was the sample biased? Were any criteria other than true randomness used to cohort players into groups A and B? Was the test run at the same time using two distinct groups, or were the tests run with the same player segment over different time periods (i.e., a paired sample)?
- How big were the two groups? Are groups A and B large enough or was the test under-powered? You quickly fire up R and check what you would have recommended at the start of the test. You need over 11.6K in both groups to detect whether an increase of this magnitude is significant:

```
R> pwr.2p.test(h = ES.h(0.11,0.10), alternative="greater", sig.level
= 0.05, power=0.8)

     Difference of proportion power calculation for binomial
distribution (arcsine transformation)

              h = 0.0326294
              n = 11613.95
      sig.level = 0.05
          power = 0.8
    alternative = greate
```

- Other than CTR of each campaign, were other game KPIs considered? There appears to have been an implicit hypothesis that neither campaign would impact the player's behaviour once they returned to the game. But is it possible that post-click retention and LTV of the two groups were affected by the contents of each PN?
- Do we have a way to uniquely identify each player that saw PN version A versus B? If so, we can use SQL to generate a dataset with any KPIs we deem important.
- How can we test whether 11% versus 10% is statistically significant? If we can generate a dataset, we could simply use `p_test` to run a permutation test. Or, if the size of the two groups is known (n_1 and n_2 for the group with an 11% CTR and 10% CTR, respectively), we can construct a 1-sided 95% confidence interval for the difference in proportions with:

$$(0.11 - 0.10) \pm z_{0.025} \sqrt{0.11(1-0.11)/n_1 + 0.10(1-0.10)/n_2)}$$

For example, if the PM indicates the two groups contained only 500 players each, the confidence interval is big:

$$\begin{aligned} &= 0.01 \pm 1.645\sqrt{0.0001958 + 0.00018} \\ &= 0.01 \pm 0.032 \\ &= -0.022 \ldots 0.042 \end{aligned}$$

This is not surprising given the power calculation we performed suggested we would need a lot more than just 500 in each group. Since the null hypothesis (the difference in means is zero) is contained within this confidence interval, we reject the PM's claim. But perhaps after buying them a coffee, going over your findings, and brainstorming some better ways to test their great ideas for PN content.

Such is the role of the data analyst: shattering beliefs by poking holes in biases.

Sometimes it's not about A/B testing so much as knowing how to identify areas of weakness in game performance. In the next two chapters, we develop concrete ideas on where to look for these weaknesses in retention and IAP conversion, respectively.

Improving Retention:
LEVEL 10

Meanwhile, back at Le Café d'Arpdau, we are obsessing about customer retention. How can we ensure our patrons keep coming back? During an all-hands brainstorming session, two ideas emerge:

1. reward our loyalty customers with a free coffee every five visits; and,
2. when a loyalty customer's next visit will be their fifth, send them a text message to remind them their next coffee is on us.

We all agree that the first idea is gold, especially given our abysmal churn rate by day six. One of the staff members, François, suggests we A/B test this, but everyone shouts him down. We immediately start notifying our new signups about this incredible benefit. Our retention rate at five-days-after-signup jumps from 3% to 4%, and we celebrate by high-fiving each other in the kitchen. François mentions something about "statistical significance," but we ignore him, as usual. He is also overheard grumbling something about the cost of the free coffee exceeding the revenue from the increase in retention, but nobody likes a party pooper.

We also think the second idea is good, but we realize we don't ask our loyalty customers for permission to send them a text message when they enroll in the program. We immediately incorporate that ask into the signup process. But after a couple of weeks, we discover that only 5% of our signups are opting to receive text messages. We decide they need to first realize the value of receiving notifications, so we change the process slightly. We start asking customers for permission on their *second* visit and incentivize them to opt-in with another free coffee. Even though only about half of our loyalty signups ever make a second visit, nearly all of them agree to opt-in to receive text messages. Our overall signup rate jumps from 5% to 45%.

After a month of sending out text messages to remind customers of the free coffee, we are delighted to find that our long-tail customer retention has increased significantly. We are now seeing customers return to the store weeks after signing up. Even François is impressed.

So, the café is seeing an uptick in customer visits. That's great, but how can a game studio improve retention? Games are not unlike storefronts, and there are lessons to be learned from the basic mechanisms employed by your local coffee shop. Daily login rewards, incentivizing (rewarding) desirable marketing actions, free or heavily discounted first purchases, judicious use of push notifications, increasing the opt-in rate for push notifications, etc., are all proven strategies to increase stickiness. But in this chapter, we focus on three distinct analytical approaches to identifying potential retention problem areas that are beyond the usual product decisions owned by the PM.

The first approach is to look at new installs: how long is their first session, or more broadly, how many minutes do they play on their first day? We look at correlating **D0 minutes** played to D1 retention and why it is a useful tool in determining whether you have a problem with the FTUE.

Next, we look at how many new installs complete the tutorial. The **tutorial** is the part of the FTUE that explains the object of the game, how players achieve that objective, and the rules of the game. Depending on the complexity of the game, the tutorial is often spread out over the first few levels of a game as its features are introduced and explained. Analyzing where users drop out of the tutorial is a way to diagnose possible problems with specific tutorial checkpoints. The tutorial funnel is introduced as a visualization tool for identifying problem spots.

Finally, we look at an advanced retention metric known as **next day return** and how it correlates with the age of your DAU.

Correlating D0 Minutes Played to D1 Retention

Adam Carpenter from Google gave a popular and influential presentation on game data analytics back in 2018 entitled *Identifying Anti-Patterns in Game Data*. The video is up on YouTube and worth the 19 minutes and 36 seconds of your time. In his presentation, Adam shares that amongst the top 200 or so IAP apps on Google Play, 38% D1 retention puts you in the 50th percentile. Anything above 52% puts your game in the 90th percentile.

The most important factor to focus on for retention, engagement, and growth of your player base, is getting today's players to return tomorrow.
Adam Carpenter

One thing Google looks at is the correlation between D0 minutes played and D1 retention. The ideal shape of that correlation is a straight line that is sloped up and to the right: the longer a user plays on their install date, the more likely they should be to play again tomorrow.

The key finding at Google was that the first ten minutes of this correlation to D1R is the most important indicator of game success. The shape of the trend line should not be flat nor dip. If D1 retention does not improve with each minute played, this is indicative of a likely problem with your FTUE such as:

1. a large content download is required to continue playing;
2. the tutorial is not fun and engaging, or simply too long;
3. there are slow loading times between screens, or gameplay is laggy;
4. confusion as to what to do (or where to be) after the tutorial finishes;
5. the game hangs or crashes during initialization; and,
6. the game is nothing at all like the misleading ad suggested.

In this section we will build a visualization of the correlation between D0 minutes played and D1R, and discuss its relevance as a tool for identifying problems with D1 retention.

Building a Query

The required result set to build the correlation is of the form

```
<user_id, install_date, d1r, d0sessions, d0minutes>
```

where `d1r` is a binary value indicating whether the user played on D1. The `user_id` and `install_date` are not strictly necessary, though the date could be useful for filtering based on specific install cohorts. The `d0sessions` is a count of the number of distinct D0 sessions; its inclusion is to facilitate the correlation between the number of D0 sessions and D1R.

The first three attributes are easily derived from `user_retention` over any install cohorts of interest; e.g., the July of 2022 installs:

```
WITH cohort AS
(
  SELECT user_id,
         platform,
         d1,
         install_date AS date
  FROM user_retention
  WHERE install_date BETWEEN '2022-07-01' AND '2022-07-31')
```

Note the inclusion of `platform` as a breakdown. We could also include `version` to test for problems with specific rollouts of software updates, or the ad creative if we are concerned about a specific ad campaign. Before proceeding, we note there is a significant platform discrepancy in D1R for this cohort:

```
SELECT platform,
       COUNT(*),
       AVG(d1::FLOAT) AS d1r
FROM cohort
GROUP BY platform
```

platform	count	d1r
android	22214	0.3280
ios	15867	0.4615

The number of distinct sessions for each user in this same time period is defined as follows:

```
begins AS
(
  SELECT DISTINCT user_id, date, timestamp AS start
  FROM session_begin
  WHERE date BETWEEN '2022-07-01' AND '2022-07-31'
)
```

Joining these two CTEs generates one row per distinct session on D0:

```
d0sessions AS
(
  SELECT *,
           NVL(LEAD(start) OVER
          (PARTITION BY user_id ORDER BY start),date+1) AS next_start
  FROM cohort
    LEFT JOIN begins USING (user_id, date)
)
```

The inclusion of the `next_start` attribute is to facilitate reasoning regarding the order of events when calculating minutes played. Some sample rows look like this:

user_id	date	plat-form	d1	start	next_start
8905251	2022-07-19	android	0	2022-07-19 21:08:47	2022-07-20 00:00:00
8906006	2022-07-15	ios	0	2022-07-15 23:39:06	2022-07-15 23:39:35
8906006	2022-07-15	ios	0	2022-07-15 23:39:35	2022-07-16 00:00:00

user_id	date	plat-form	d1	start	next_start
8909257	2022-07-14	android	1	2022-07-14 18:46:14	2022-07-14 21:11:29
8909257	2022-07-14	android	1	2022-07-14 21:11:29	2022-07-14 21:12:49
8909257	2022-07-14	android	1	2022-07-14 21:12:49	2022-07-14 21:13:35
...	...	...	...	...	...

ESG's Mentor SDK does not, for a myriad of technical reasons, reliably generate *session_end* events. How can we measure D0 minutes played without a *session_end* event? We know from the `d0sessions` CTE when each new session begins, but how do we track when the user quit playing the previous session? A heuristic solution is to choose another table where events are known to occur frequently whenever a user is actively playing the game. A heartbeat, as it were. In ESG games, *action* events are generated with every UI interaction. Therefore, the timestamps of `action` records are a reasonable proxy for player activity.

```
actions AS
(
  SELECT DISTINCT user_id,
         date,
         timestamp AS activity
  FROM action
  WHERE date >= CURRENT_DATE- 30
)
```

But given there are multiple actions within each session, the `MAX(activity)` is taken as the `last_activity`, and the duration of the session (in seconds) is calculated as such:

```
spurts AS
(
  SELECT user_id,
         date,
         platform,
         d1,
         start,
         MAX(activity) AS last_activity,
         datediff(sec, start, last_activity) AS seconds
  FROM d0sessions
    LEFT JOIN actions USING (user_id, date)
  WHERE activity BETWEEN start AND next_start
  GROUP BY user_id,
           date,
           platform,
           d1,
           start
)
```

Each "spurt" is a distinct D0 session. Finally, our query to build the visualization is an aggregation of each user's `spurts` into minutes played:

```
SELECT user_id,
       date AS install_date,
       platform,
       d1,
       COUNT(*) AS sessions,
       SUM(seconds / 60.0) AS minutes
FROM spurts
GROUP BY user_id,
         install_date,
         platform,
         d1
```

Visualizing in Tableau

Creating a graph of the correlation between D0 minutes played and D1R in Tableau is straightforward, but it does require creating a bin for the `minutes` measure.

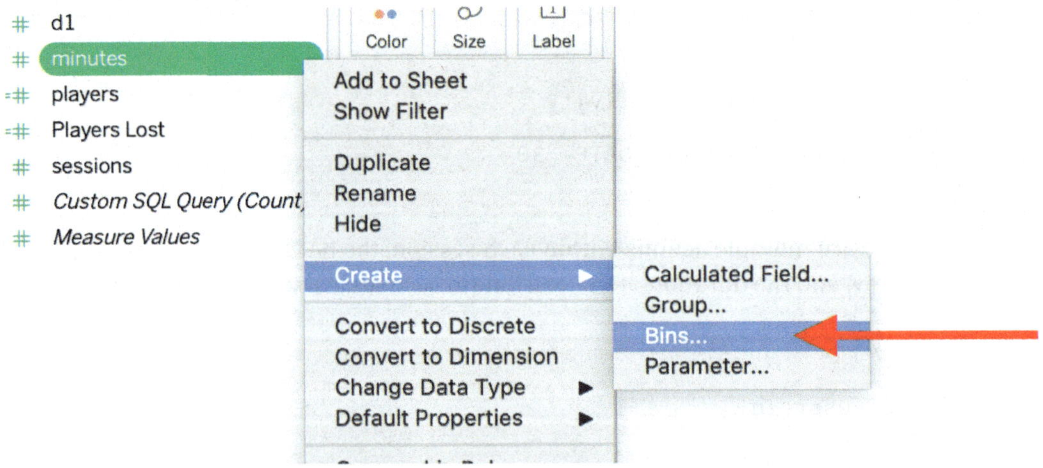

Setting the bin size to 1.0 does the trick nicely. As you can see from the *Measures* pane above, two *Calculated Fields* have been added. The first is called `players`, defined simply as `COUNTD([user_id])`; this gives us an idea of how many unique users make up each bin. The second is called `Players Lost`, defined as `[players]-SUM([d1])`. These players aren't necessarily lost – we know that many will play again, just not on D1. But the name is chosen to coincide with the nomenclature from Carpenter's talk.

To plot the correlation, the `minutes(bin)` is our *Columns* while the `AVG([d1])` is our *Rows*. A reference line at 40% D1R has been added, along with a *Mark* at minute 10 in the histogram.

While the general momentum of the graph is heading in the correct direction (up and to the right), there are some anti-patterns:

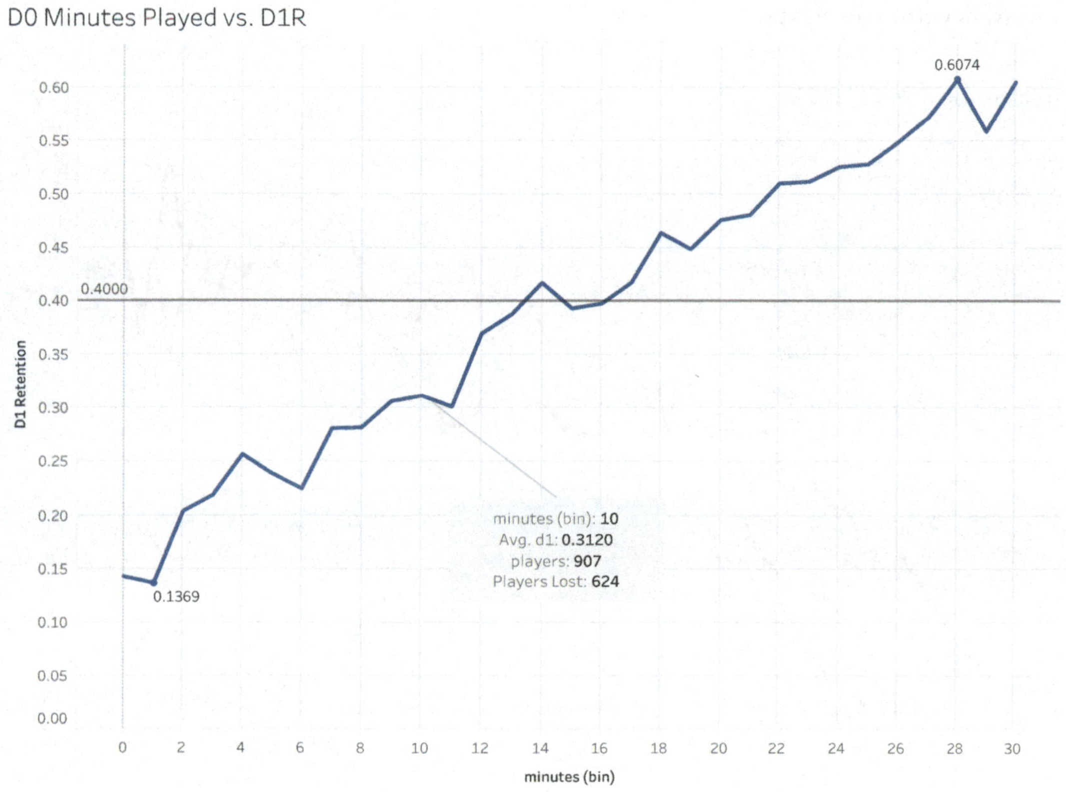

Note that users who spent between 10 and 11 minutes playing on D0 were only 31.2% likely to return on D1. There were 907 unique players who fell into that bin – 624 of them chose not to play the next day. The dips in the graph between minutes zero and one, and again at minutes four and six, are problematic. On average, more than 14 minutes of game play is required before D1R eclipses 40%, a target added as a constant horizontal line in the graph. Users who played for 30 minutes on D0 had a D1R of 60%.

If we break it down by `platform`, a significant discrepancy between Android and iOS is visible. The *x*-axis in the following chart is extended to 55 minutes of D0 game play. Note that Android finally catches up to iOS by minute 49 – prior to that, Android D1R as a function of D0 minutes played is significantly lower than iOS. The dip in Android D1R for users who play between one and two minutes is missing from the iOS graph, indicating a possible issue with loading or asset bundle downloading on the Android platform only. While the iOS graph is much better in terms of both slope and early retention, the anti-pattern dip between minutes four and six mirrors that of Android, suggesting a problem with the tutorial that affects both platforms. Of note, 40% D1R is reached for iOS users by 10 minutes of D0 game play, but followed by a dip for users within the next bin.

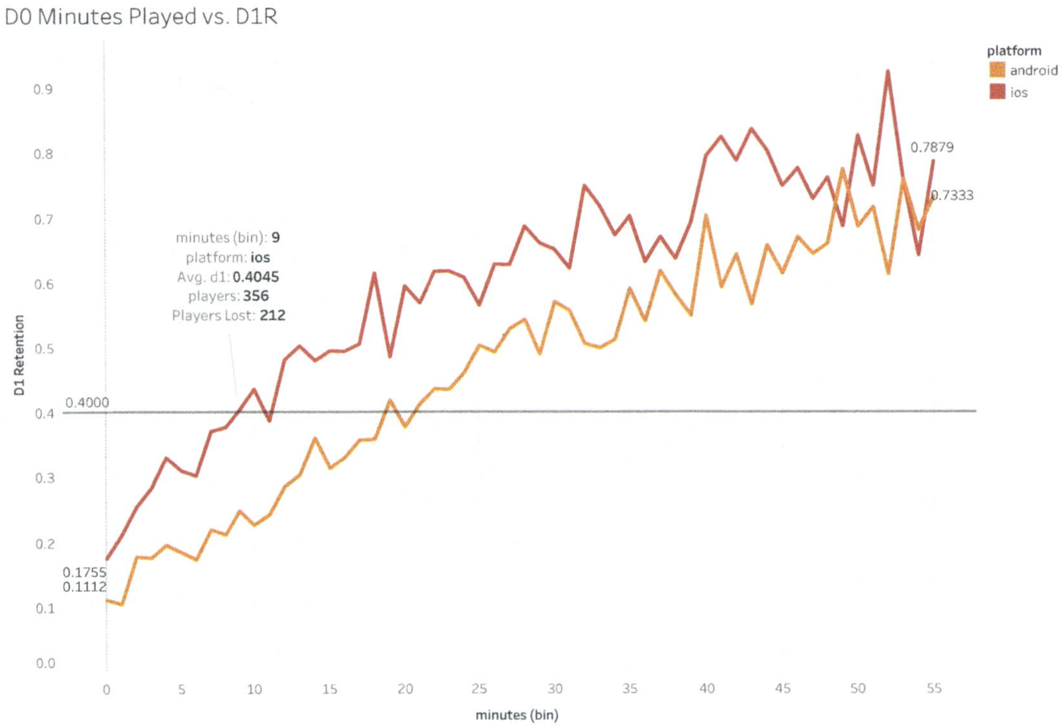

Analyzing where the biggest jumps occur between consecutive minutes played may reveal how the introduction of specific game features correlates with player satisfaction.

Finally, Carpenter also introduced a visualization looking at the cumulative percentage of players lost as a function of D0 minutes played. This visualization serves no purpose other than to demoralize you with how quickly your installs churn. To build it in Tableau requires a *Table Calculation* applied to the *Calculated Field* `Players Lost` described earlier (see right).

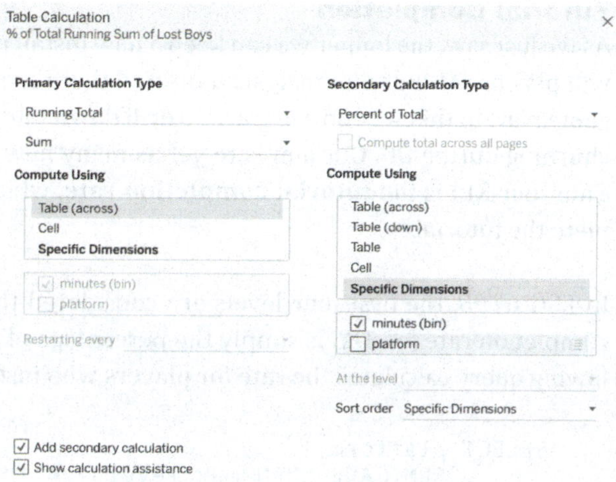

The following chart indicates that over 50% of the Android installs played less than four minutes:

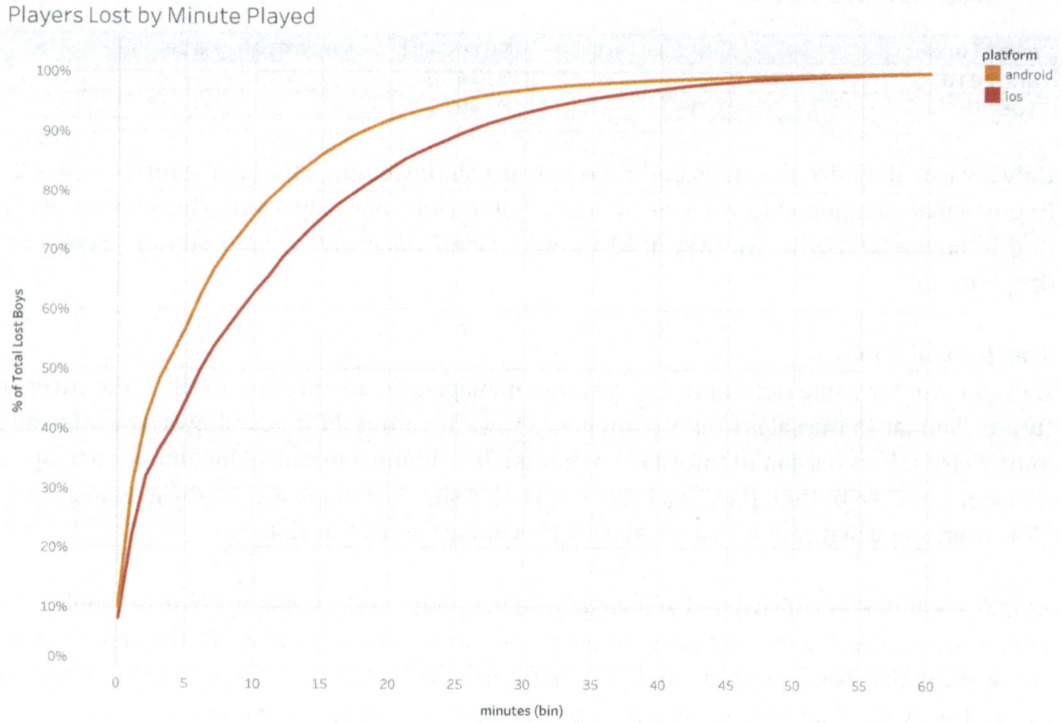

The moral of the story is this: ensure the FTUE is fun, crisp, requires no downloads, and introduces the most satisfying piece of the game mechanic within the first 10 minutes.

Tutorial Completion

As we just saw, the longer we can keep a new install playing on D0, the greater the chance they will play on D1. But our analysis indicated there are some issues with the first 10 minutes of game play. In this section, we learn to drill down into the tutorial to find out where players are churning during D0. Our aim is to get as many new players as possible through the tutorial. Thus, our KPI is the **tutorial completion rate**, which is the proportion of installs who complete the tutorial.

In ESG's *TPB*, the first four levels are considered the entire tutorial. Therefore, the tutorial completion rate for *TPB* is simply the percentage of installs who complete level four. The following query calculates the rate for players who installed in July of 2022:

```
SELECT platform,
       SUM(CASE WHEN max_level > 4 THEN 1 END) / COUNT(*)::FLOAT
   AS tutorial_completion_rate
FROM user_retention
WHERE install_date BETWEEN '2022-07-01' AND '2022-07-31'
GROUP BY platform
```

platform	tutorial_completion_rate
android	0.3458
ios	0.4975

Only 35% of all Android installs bothered to learn all the features that make up the game. To improve that completion rate, we need to understand why our players are churning out early. And to understand why, we first need to understand *where* in the tutorial our players are dropping out.

The Tutorial Funnel

A useful tool for game designers and product managers to analyze the FTUE is the **tutorial funnel**. Similar to the sales funnel from marketing, the tutorial funnel follows a new install's journey from first session to tutorial completion. It is a funnel because the number of players that come out the bottom (i.e., finish the tutorial) is significantly less than those who started. Moreover, some players may churn at each checkpoint in the tutorial.

At ESG, the funnel is constructed and visualized via events collected in a `tutorial` table. This table tracks individual player progression as the user completes a set of discrete steps or checkpoints that comprise the whole of the tutorial. Completing a step generates a *tutorial* event. The events that are instrumented in the code depend on the game and on what milestones the game designer and/or product manager want tracked. Here are the first few rows of data for a specific user as they begin the tutorial for one of ESG's games:

user_id	level	step	detailed_name
1454315936173057	1	1	Story Sequence 1
1454315936173057	1	2	Gameplay 1
1454315936173057	1	3	Tutorial Overlay 1
1454315936173057	1	4	Gameplay 2
1454315936173057	1	5	Story Sequence 2
1454315936173057	1	6	Gameplay 3
...	...	...	...

If a player quits during the tutorial, the last `level` and `step` in this table indicates their churn point:

```
WITH churn_point AS
(
SELECT DISTINCT user_id,
         MAX(level) OVER (PARTITION BY user_id) AS last_level,
         LAST_VALUE(step) OVER (PARTITION BY user_id ORDER BY
level,step ROWS BETWEEN UNBOUNDED PRECEDING AND UNBOUNDED following)
AS last_step
  FROM tutorial
  WHERE date >= CURRENT_DATE - 30
)
```

In this game, the last step in the tutorial is step 14 of level 4 (with some additional optional steps beyond that):

```
SELECT *
FROM churn_point
WHERE last_level <= 4 AND NOT (last_level = 4 AND last_step > 14)
ORDER BY RANDOM() LIMIT 5
```

user_id	last_level	last_step
1586169169967105	1	10
1588599648286721	1	4
1588339990888497	2	6
1587238162676737	3	24
1588302690214913	1	6

To construct a funnel, we only need to calculate the number of players who installed the game and start each step of the tutorial. This is accomplished with an aggregation of the `churn_point` CTE after first selecting an install cohort to track from `user_source`. Note the elegant use of a window function (`SUM`) to count the number of players remaining at each step in the funnel:

```
SELECT last_level,
       last_step,
       COUNT(DISTINCT user_id) AS churners,
```

```
        SUM(churners) OVER
         (ORDER BY last_level,last_step ROWS BETWEEN CURRENT ROW AND
          UNBOUNDED FOLLOWING) AS starters
FROM user_source
  LEFT JOIN churn_point USING (user_id)
WHERE install_date BETWEEN CURRENT_DATE- 30 AND CURRENT_DATE- 14
  AND last_level <= 4 AND NOT (last_level = 4 AND last_step > 14)
GROUP BY last_level,
         last_step
```

last_level	last_step	churners	starters
1	1	619	64548
1	2	716	63929
1	3	905	63213
1	4	3169	62308
1	5	1111	59139
1	6	127	58028
1	7	572	57901
1	8	2680	57329
1	9	844	54649
1	10	1755	53805
...	...	...	...
4	9	41	29452
4	10	59	29411
4	11	47	29352
4	12	325	29305
4	13	133	28980
4	14		28847

This query tells us that of the 64,548 players who entered the funnel (i.e., generated at least one *tutorial* event), only 28,847 fell out of the bottom of the funnel; i.e., started the last step. That's a 44.7% FTUE completion rate. How do we improve it?

The real power of this data is to identify specific checkpoints where players are most likely to churn. What step in the tutorial leads to the most churn? If we simply `ORDER BY churners`, we see the following:

last_level	last_step	churners	starters
3	24	4432	35544
1	4	3169	62308
1	8	2680	57329
2	4	2155	47501
...	...	...	...

The game's PM can then go about addressing the pain points within those steps. For instance, what happens at the end of step 24 in level 3? Is the player confused about what to do next, or are they unwilling to download a 55MB asset bundle?

Visualizing a Tutorial Funnel

Ideally, identification of the highest churning tutorial checkpoint is enabled through a dashboard. The resulting tutorial funnel can then be refreshed daily and monitored by the PM for sudden dropout points. A typical ESG Tableau tutorial funnel looks like the graph below. The player count (the blue bars) decreases with each step in the tutorial. The percentage of change from the previous step is in the far-right column. This could also be the percentage of total players lost in the funnel. Places where those bars extend further left indicate pain points in the tutorial that should be investigated and addressed.

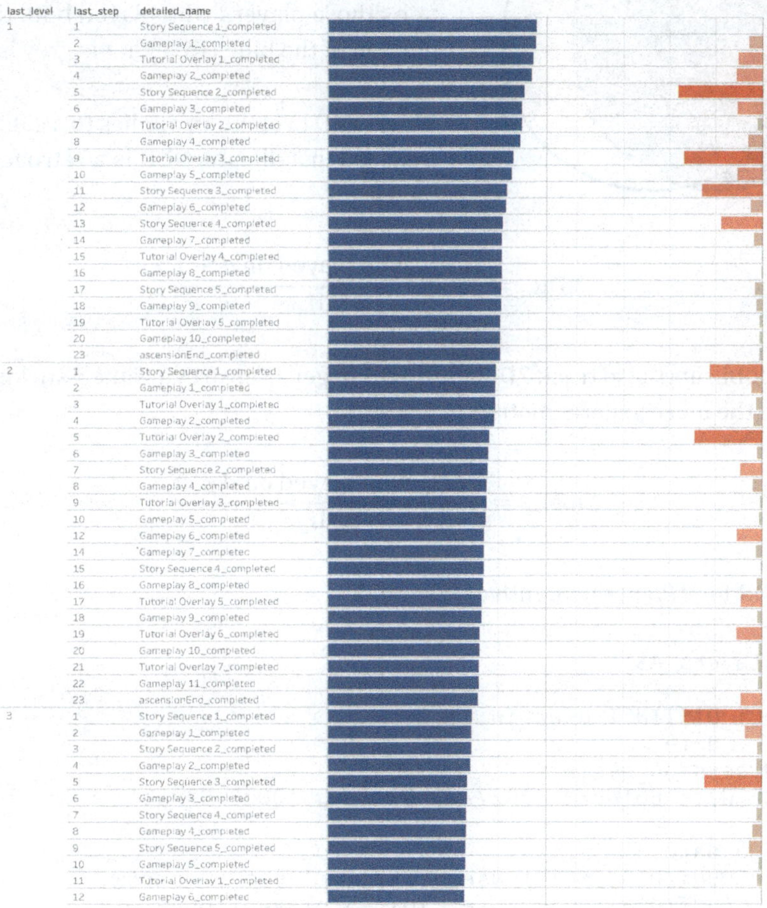

The ability to compare the shape of the funnel between different versions of the game on each platform is particularly important, as it is not uncommon for unintended bugs to creep into the tutorial as a result of changes to the asset bundle. In this case, a "population pyramid" – with version or platform instead of gender – is a useful visualization.

Next Day Return

An alternative measure of retention is **next day return** (NDR), defined as the proportion of DAU who play again the very next day. This is like D1 retention, but instead of defining the cohort as new installs only, NDR considers all currently active players.

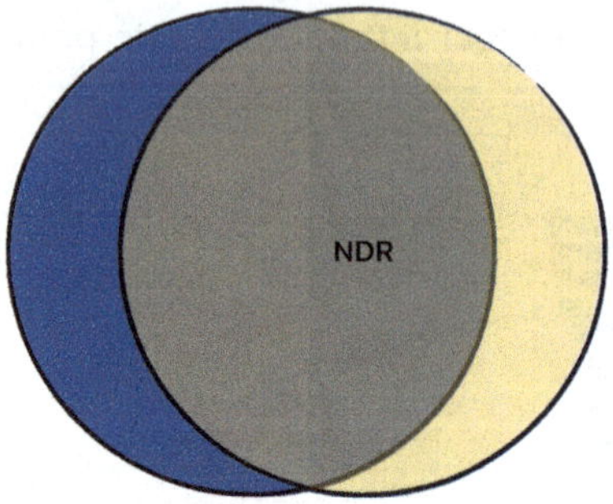

Assume that the blue circle in the Venn diagram to the left represents the set of all active users on some date *d*. The yellow circle is the set of all active users on the day after. The overlapping area (in grey) contains those players who played both days. The proportion of the blue circle that is grey is NDR.

Whereas D1 retention applies to a cohort defined by a shared install date, NDR is a retroactive play date metric:

$$\text{NDR}_d = \frac{\text{DAU}_d \text{ who played on } d+1}{\text{DAU}_d}$$

Some game publishers also track 7DR and 14DR to get a sense of a game's stickiness, in which case we have the more general metric:

$$n\text{DR}_d = \frac{\text{DAU}_d \text{ who played on } d+n}{\text{DAU}_d}$$

What was NDR for *TPB* in the month of July 2022?

```
WITH players AS
(
  SELECT DISTINCT user_id,
         date
  FROM session_begin
  WHERE date BETWEEN '2022-07-01' AND '2022-07-31'
)
SELECT d.date,
       COUNT(DISTINCT t.user_id) AS played_tomorrow,
       COUNT(DISTINCT d.user_id) AS played_today,
       played_tomorrow/played_today::FLOAT AS ndr
FROM players d
  LEFT JOIN players t
         ON d.user_id = t.user_id AND t.date = d.date +1
GROUP BY d.date
```

date	played_tomorrow	played_today	ndr
2022-07-01	46534	53303	0.873
2022-07-02	46206	52311	0.8833
2022-07-03	46591	52549	0.8866
2022-07-04	46387	53103	0.8735
2022-07-05	46139	52148	0.8848
2022-07-06	46324	52085	0.8894
...	...	...	...

About 88%, which is very good. According to metrics also disclosed in Carpenter (2018) for Google Play top grossing games, median NDR is 77%, and an 88% NDR score puts *TPB* in the 90th percentile.

Why is NDR for *TPB* so high? *TPB* is a game that does a good job of giving players a reason to come back every day through daily login rewards, a steady stream of new content, and reminders via push notifications to play limited-time events. But if we look at *TPB*'s NDR at worldwide launch, it was much lower – only in the 10th percentile according to Google.

date	played_tomorrow	played_today	ndr
2017-04-20	97568	156346	0.624052
2017-04-21	165908	281008	0.590403
2017-04-22	204311	324767	0.6291
2017-04-23	243701	385110	0.632809
2017-04-24	265232	395774	0.67016
2017-04-25	275611	405442	0.679779
...	...	...	...

Here is a chart of *TPB* NDR for the first 365 days after world-wide launch. NDR starts to improve as the player base matures. It takes about 145 days for the NDR to reach 88%. The peak lifetime NDR (so far) is 92%, which occurred 345 days into *TPB*'s product life. The median NDR is 87%.

NDR by Days Since Launch: D0 is April 20, 2017

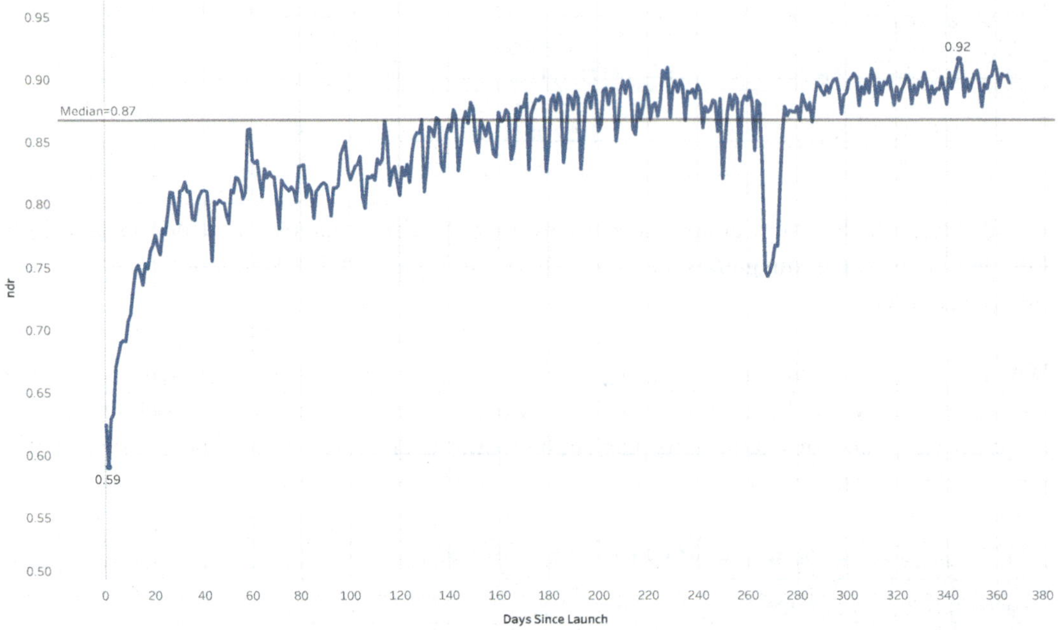

The dip between 260 and 280 days after world-wide launch was due to a feature on Google Play that drove thousands of organic installs to the game, most of whom bounced. This illustrates how sensitive NDR is to an influx of new installs. Based on what we learned when developing a model for predicting churn as a function of D*n*, this is to be expected. Is there a formal relationship between NDR and the maturity of a DAU's player base? Intuition suggests there is a positive correlation between the two. Let's find out.

Player Age Distribution and Game Maturity

Every game has its own distinct mix of daily players. Some of the players are new installs, some have been playing for a while, and others have been playing since the day the game was released. The **age** of a daily active player is the number of days since its install date; this is the *n* in D*n*.

Previously we defined DAU_d as the count of distinct active players on date *d*. This can be broken down by the respective ages of the active users. Let $\mathrm{DAU}_{d,n}$ be the count of distinct active users playing on their D*n*. Then,

$$\mathrm{DAU}_d = \sum_{n=0} \mathrm{DAU}_{d,n}$$

A DAU's **fingerprint** is its distribution of players by age, i.e., how many players make up each of the *n* buckets. Since the propensity to churn is inversely related to player age, the older a game's current fingerprint skews, the higher the NDR and the more stable we can expect its DAU to be.

A fingerprint for a specific date – which we calculate here for the DAU on July 10, 2022 – is derived from a result set that counts the number of players of each possible age. Given that *TPB*'s world-wide launch date was April 20, 2017,

```
SELECT DATE('2022-07-10') - DATE('2017-04-20')
```

?column?
1907

the age of players on July 10th can range from 0 to 1,907. The age of a game is the number of days since its world-wide launch; *TPB* was 1,907 days old on July 10, 2022. It is not unusual for a game to be older than its oldest active player, so it is important to keep the two ages distinct.

The data to plot a histogram of player count by their age in days since install comes from the following query:

```
WITH users AS
(
  SELECT DISTINCT date,
         install_date,
         date - install_date AS age,
         user_id
  FROM session_begin
    INNER JOIN (SELECT user_id, install_date FROM user_source) USING
(user_id)
  WHERE install_date >= '2017-04-20'
)

SELECT age,
       COUNT(*) AS players
FROM users
WHERE date = '2022-07-10'
GROUP BY age
```

Figure 10.1 contains the distribution of player age for the set of DAU on July 10, 2022.

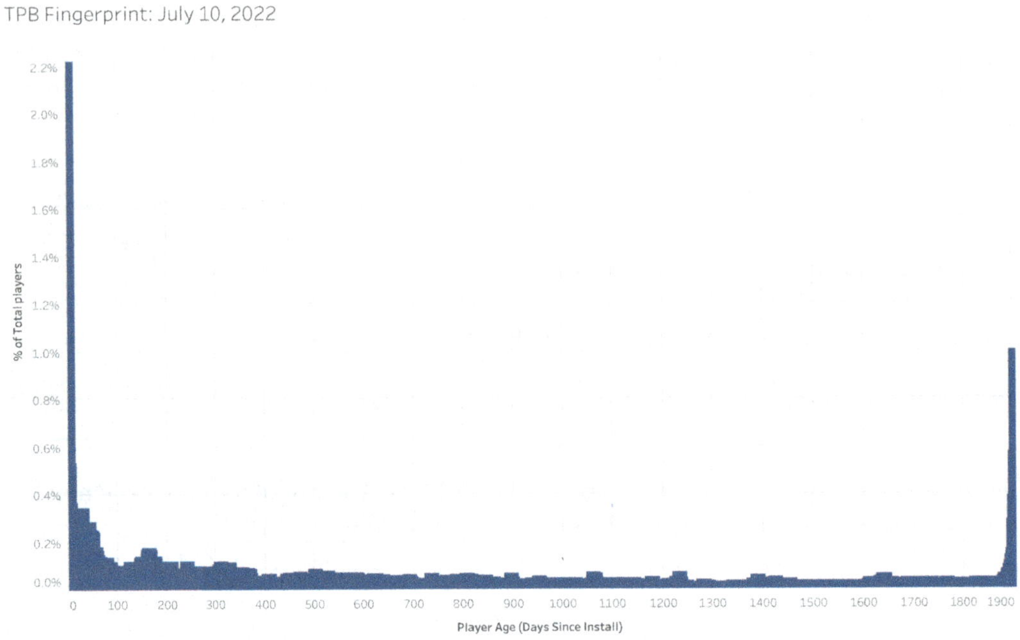

Figure 10.1. A histogram of player age for the *TPB* DAU on July 10, 2022, comprises the game's *fingerprint* for that day. The *x*-axis is days since install for each active player, from 0 to 1,907, where 1,907 is the age of the game in days since world-wide launch. A symmetric, valley-shaped histogram indicates good retention of the golden cohort.

We call distributions of this shape a *valley* or a *half-pipe*. This distribution will vary by date, as will the range of the *x*-axis. When creating a fingerprint, be sure the x-axis extends to the age of the game, not just the age of the oldest player. However, in this instance, the DAU on July 10th is made up of players of every possible age, and the shape of the distribution is remarkably symmetric. While just over 2.2% are new installs (age = 0), over 1% of the DAU are players from the **golden cohort** who started playing the day the game was released over five years prior. Everyone else falls somewhere in the valley between. Sometimes a game's fingerprint is missing the mountain on the right-hand side, which indicates there are no players remaining from the golden cohort.

The histogram in Figure 10.1 is also a probability distribution for the discrete random variable age: pluck an active user at random from the July 10th DAU and the *y*-axis describes the likelihood of that player's specific age being *x*. For example, $P(\text{age} = 0) = 0.022$. The center of gravity of this distribution, which we call **maturity**, is simply the average age of the daily players:

```
SELECT date,
```

```
        AVG(age::FLOAT) AS maturity
  FROM users
  GROUP BY date
```

date	maturity
2022-07-10	693.8621

Like any mean of a discrete random variable, maturity is the balancing point where exactly half of the probability distribution's weight is on either side of the teeter totter defined by the *x*-axis. It is also the expected value of player age. Note that since players on the extremes carry more weight, this fulcrum is not necessarily the point where half of the users are on either side. Here is maturity (the vertical black line) added as a reference line to our fingerprint:

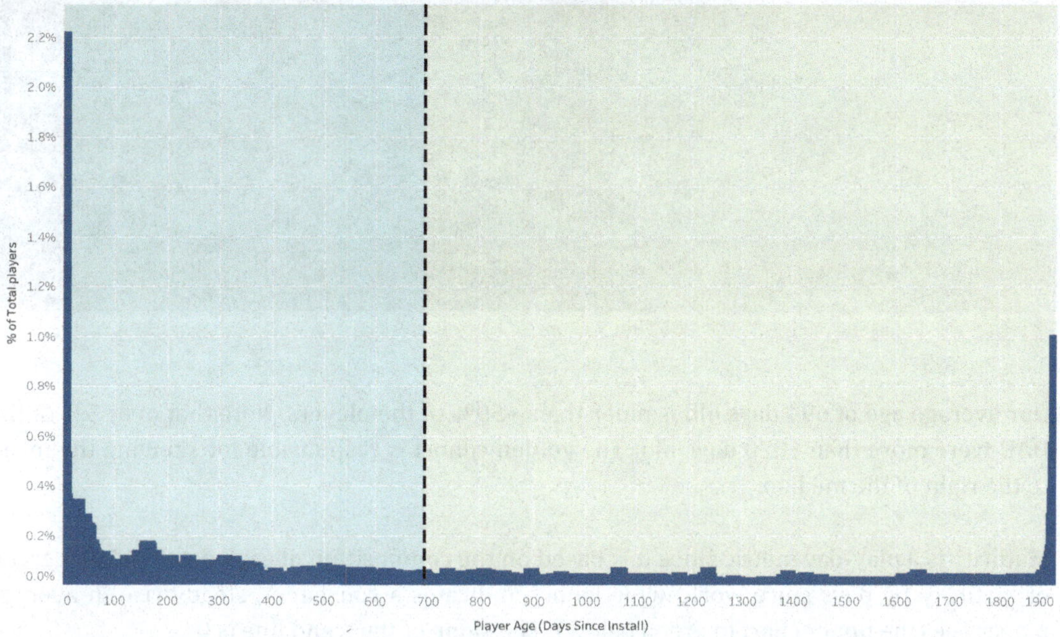

If we convert our histogram to a cumulative distribution (accomplished in Tableau by creating a *Bin* for age and adding a secondary *Table Calculation* for `players`) we see that half the DAU were less than 520 days old:

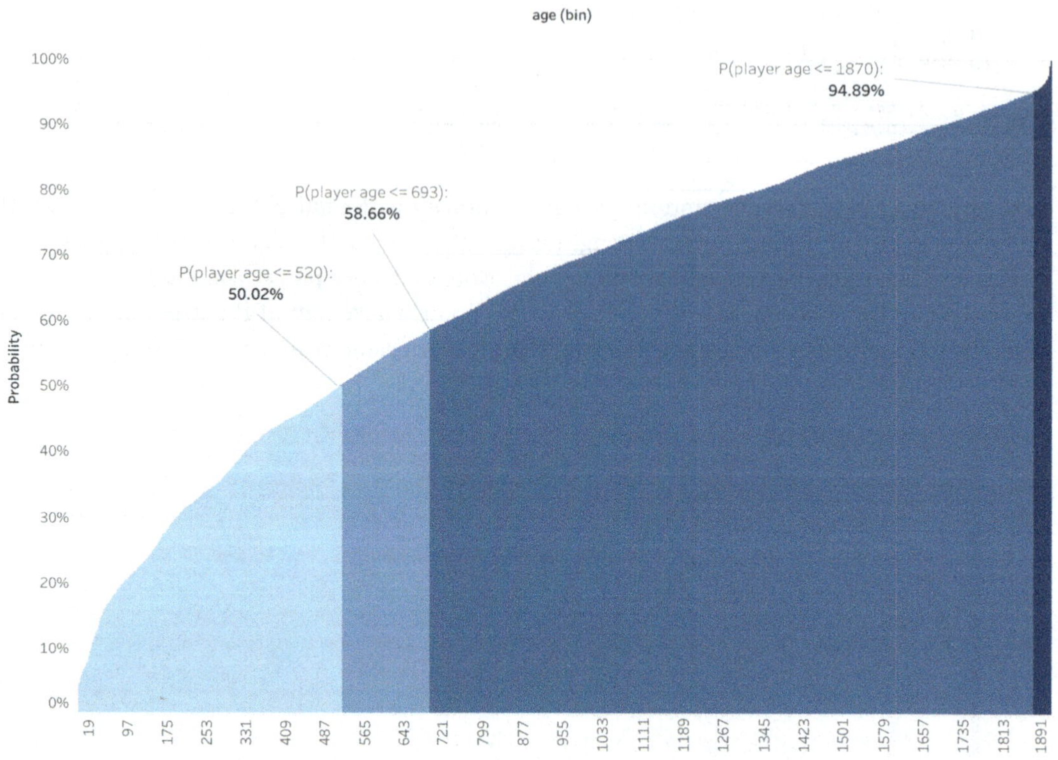

Our average age of 694 days old is older than ~59% of the players. Note that over 5% of the DAU were more than 1870 days old! The golden cohort is responsible for skewing the mean to the right of the median.

Maturity is a play-day metric since it is based on the composition of each date's DAU. A graph of maturity by days since world-wide launch indicates a consistent, steady rise in average player age (the upper chart in green below). The slope of the trend line is 0.5.

The bottom chart is a synchronized, dual graph of two proportions. The orange line is a normalized measure of maturity. Let M_n be a game's maturity n days after launch. Normalized maturity is defined as:

$$\bar{M}_n = \frac{M_n}{n}$$

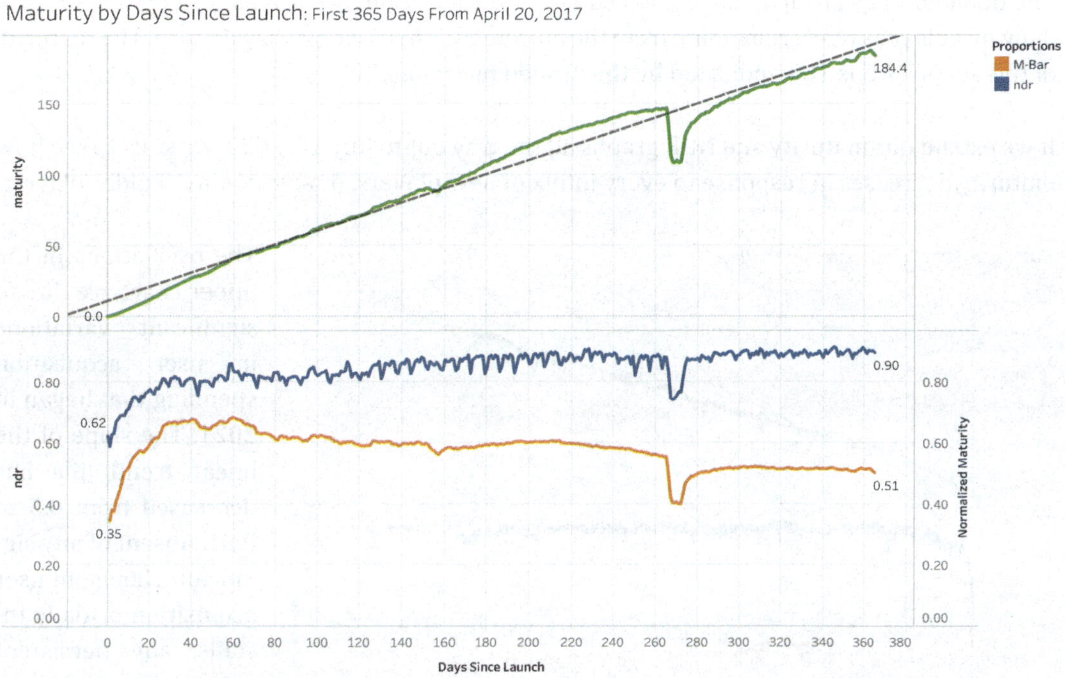

$\bar{M}_n$ measures where on the fingerprint's x-axis the average age (maturity) lies relative to the endpoint n. The denominator is the age of the game, i.e., the orange line is the green line divided by days since launch. In a perfectly balanced fingerprint, the value is 0.5. If $\bar{M}_n$ is < 0.5, the average age is less than $n/2$, indicating that a majority of the DAU are newish players. *TPB* ended its first 365 days with an almost perfect score of 0.51. The fingerprint for April 20, 2018, must bear this out. Let's go back in time and see.

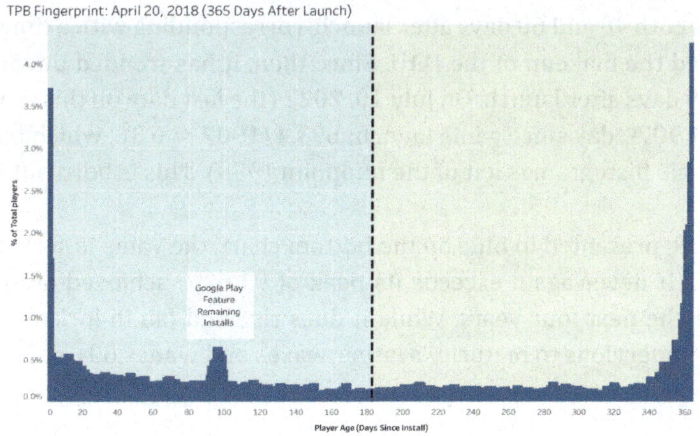

The dominant age group is the golden cohort, but their influence is balanced by the influx of daily installs plus those remaining from the aforementioned Google Play feature. The maturity of this set of DAU is 184, indicated by the dashed black line.

If we extend our maturity and NDR graphs all the way out to July 10, 2022, we start to see how maturity decreases in response to every influx of new players, or any exodus of older players.

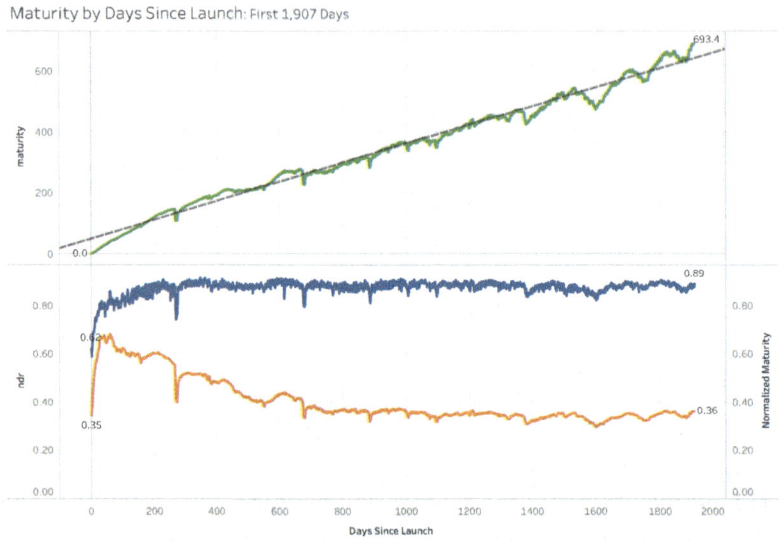

The oscillations in the upper chart are due to significant variations in user acquisition spending that began in 2021. The slope of the linear trend line has decreased from 0.5 to 0.31. Absent of any significant change in user acquisition or daily installs, any persistent non-linear relationship between a game's age and its maturity indicates a possible imbalance in the priorities of LiveOps. If the trend line bends downwards, the game is shedding too many elderly players, perhaps owing to a lack of new content. If it bends upwards, it is possible that LiveOps is catering too much to the elders at the expense of new installs.

The normalized maturity for *TPB* hasn't fluctuated a great deal since mid-2019. Its peak value of 0.68 occurred both 40 and 60 days after launch, corresponding with a time when the golden cohort dominated the makeup of the DAU. Since then, it has trended downwards, but stabilized around 800 days after launch. On July 10, 2022 (the last date on this graph), the maturity is 693.4 on the 1,907th day since game launch; $693.4/1907 = 0.36$, which indicates that most of the weight of the histogram is left of the midpoint (953). This is born out in Figure 10.1.

Likewise, for NDR, presented in blue on the bottom chart, the value is surprisingly consistent starting in 2019. It never again exceeds its peak of 91.62% achieved on n=345, but hovers around 88% for the next four years. While it does rise and fall in lockstep with maturity, it appears mostly impervious to maturity's larger waxes and wanes 60+ days post launch.

Correlating NDR

We saw that *TPB*'s NDR metric started out low but steadily increased with each passing day, reaching a peak of 91% nearly one year after world-wide launch. Intuition suggests that a game's maturity and its NDR are related. Newer games with a low average player age and a larger portion of their DAU comprised of new installs – or games with a large user acquisition budget – will exhibit lower NDR. We saw this happen to *TPB* when a sudden influx of organic installs about nine months after launch resulted in a sharp dip in NDR.

However, despite these occasional dips, NDR recovers and has remained remarkably stable. The charts above contradict any persistent relationship between maturity and NDR: maturity steadily climbs even after NDR has plateaued. Likewise, NDR remains stable while $\overline{M}_n$ begins a steady fall 60 days after world-wide launch. But what if we look at only the first 40 days after launch?

Correlating NDR to M-Bar: The First 40 Days

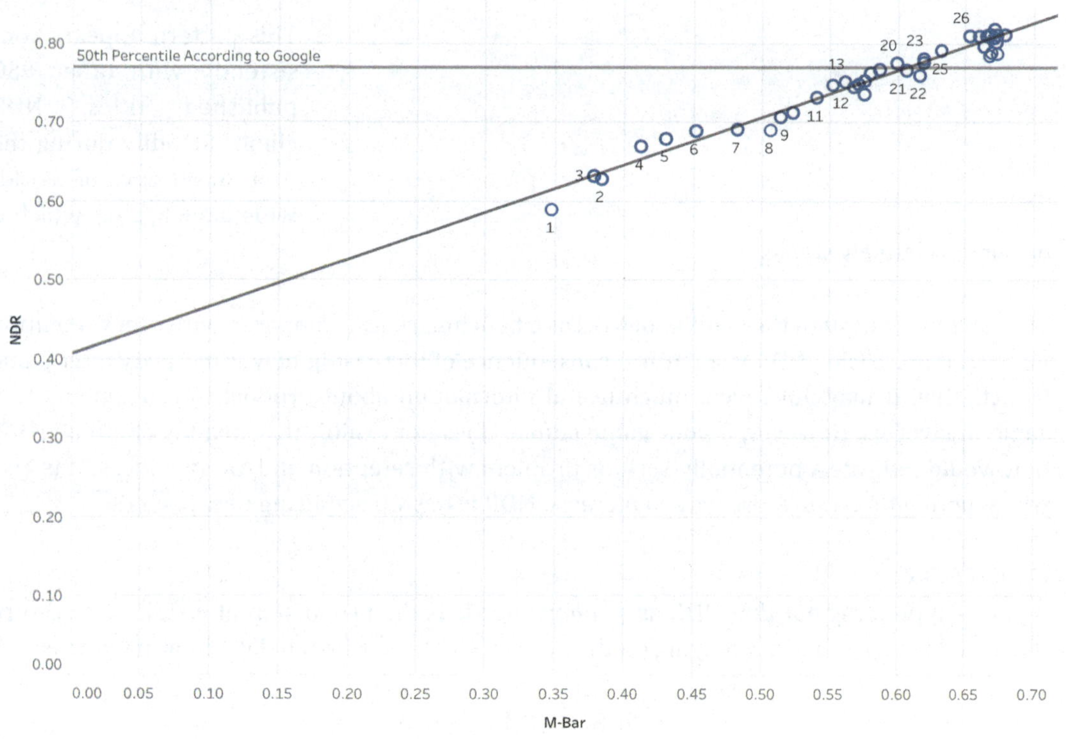

The scatterplot above reveals a very strong correlation between NDR and the maturity of the player base. The R-squared coefficient is 0.96. The labels on the points indicate the specific day since launch. Correlation isn't necessarily causation, and this graph is not meant to imply that NDR is caused by maturity. Correlation simply means the two variables move together: as $\bar{M}$ increases, so does NDR. The linear regression (the formula of the trend line that is a best fit to the data) is more specific, suggesting that NDR $= 0.6\bar{M} + 0.4$. But if we look at the first 120 days, the correlation between the two metrics begins to fall apart, with an R-squared of only 0.78. The scatter plot breaks into two distinct clusters:

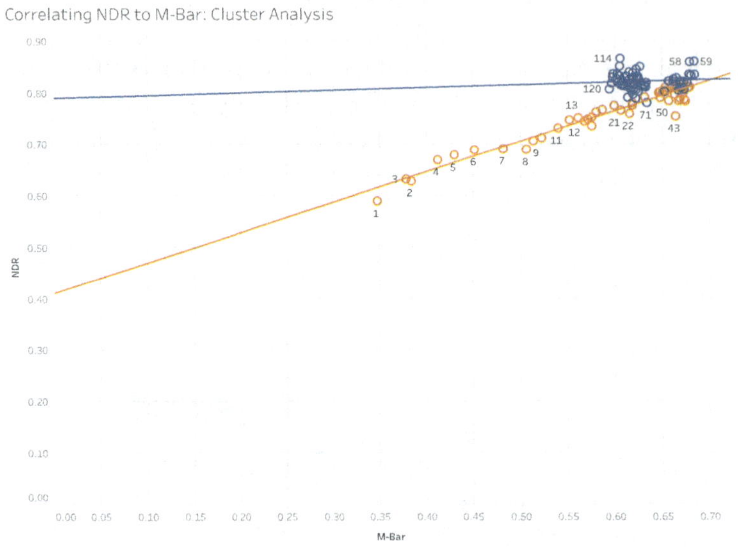

The orange cluster is comprised of the first 50 days after install, where we see both variables climbing together. Beyond that, the correlation disappears, largely due to NDR becoming relatively constant.

This pattern appears consistently with other ESG published titles: NDR climbs steadily during the first 30-60 days of worldwide launch, after which it becomes relatively stable.

This calls into question the validity of NDR as a benchmark KPI compared with other retention metrics. If increasing NDR is a natural consequence of increasing player maturity after game launch, then it may not reveal much useful information about product improvements to a game in LiveOps. However, if your game launch does not exhibit this steadily climbing NDR, that would indicate a potentially serious problem with retention and/or stickiness. It is also worth noting that a sure-fire way to increase NDR is to stop acquiring new players.

Cohort NDR

It is worth pointing out that NDR as a *cohort* metric is the proportion of installs who return the next day given they are playing on the *n*th day since their install date. In other words:

$$\mathrm{NDR}_n \cong P(\mathrm{D}_{n+1} \mid \mathrm{D}_n)$$

By definition, NDR_0 is just D1R, and NDR_1 is the proportion of players who play on D2 given they played on D1, etc. In Chapter 7, we built a Markov model of churn to calculate that specific conditional probability, but we did not chart its behaviour. Here it is now as a Tableau graph of cohort NDR for the first 90 days of game play for those trusty *TPB* installs from July 1-9 of 2022. A logarithmic trend line overlays the raw data.

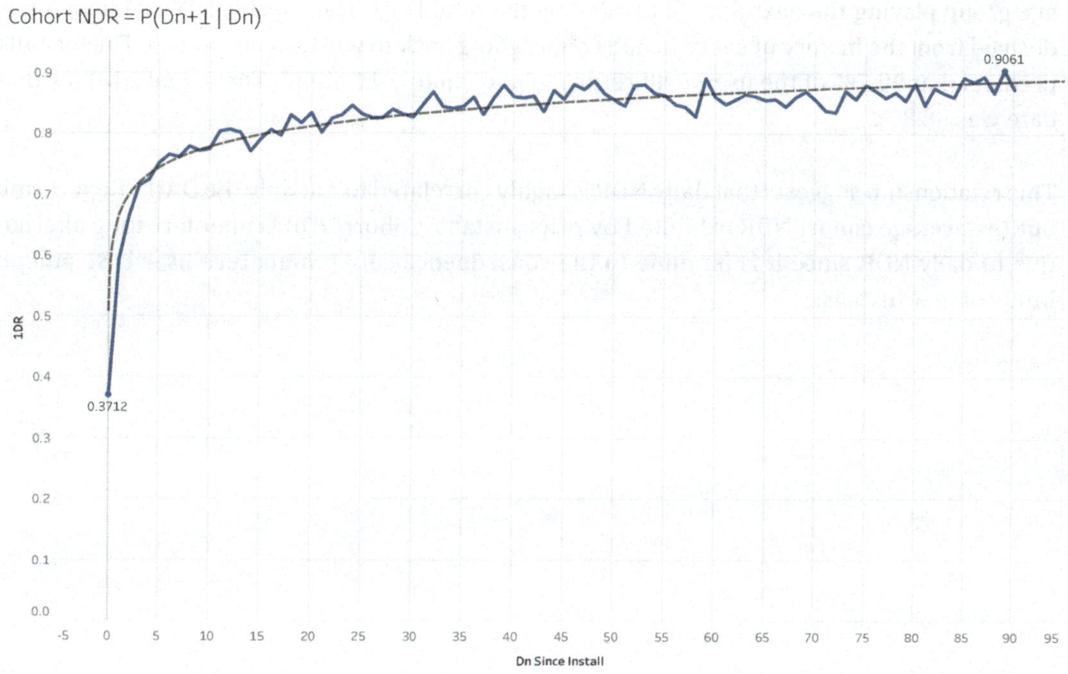

The first value, for $n = 0$, is our familiar D1R for this cohort: 37.12%. The propensity to return the next day grows with n, cresting 90% by D89. The curve fit to the data is defined by the function $\text{NDR}(n) = 0.05 * \ln(n) + 0.66$, though note that the function is neither defined for $n = 0$ nor a particularly great fit over the first few days.

Nevertheless, given a function $\text{NDR}(n)$ fit to historical cohort NDR data coupled with the fingerprint for a game's DAU on date d, a prediction for NDR_d is:

$$\widehat{\text{NDR}_d} = \frac{\sum_n (\text{NDR}(n) * \text{DAU}_{d,n})}{\text{DAU}_d}$$

For example, when applied to the DAU of d = July 10, 2022, the predicted number of users who will return the next day is given by:

$$\widehat{\text{NDR}}_d = \frac{\sum_{n=0}^{1,907}[(.017 \ln(n) + 0.82) * \text{DAU}_{d,n}]}{52{,}376}$$

i.e., the sum of the fingerprint presented in Figure 10.1 multiplied by the probability of each age group playing the next day, all divided by the total DAU. The specific NDR(n) function is derived from the history of every install cohort going back to world-wide launch. The formula predicts that 90.7% of the users will return to play on July 11, 2022. The actual NDR for that date was 88.8%.

This relationship suggests that daily NDR is highly correlated to not only the DAU's fingerprint, but the average cohort NDR exhibited by prior installs. Cohort NDR is an interesting alternative to daily NDR since it is immune to the consequences of an immature user base and an influx of new installs.

Optimized Pricing:
LEVEL 11

How do we increase our IAP revenue? In this chapter, we introduce two techniques that use diagnostic analytics to uncover potential opportunities for increasing IAP LTV. But first, let's check back in with our favourite café and see if there is anything we can glean from the marketing techniques of bricks and mortar stores.

Now that customer retention is improving, the focus at Café d'Arpdau shifts to maximizing the revenue from each customer visit. Our Yelp reviews indicate that patrons think our croissants are "heavenly," so someone on the team suggests that instead of offering a free coffee for signing up to our loyalty club we instead entice them with a free croissant. The hypothesis is that the excellent quality of the baked good is likely to create more return visits – and more croissant purchases! A different staff member counters that since the croissants are quite expensive, new customers should receive a free coffee and the option to buy a croissant at a 25% discount. François, the eternal skeptic, said we should do that and test whether customers who bought a croissant on their first visit exhibit a higher LTV compared to those who only took the free coffee. If they do not, he muses, then try something else like a sale price on croissants during the slowest weekday.

With that test underway, it's time to start thinking bigger. World-domination big. A Café d'Arpdau on every corner of every major city across the globe, starting with Manila. We lease a space on a busy pedestrian corner, replicate our café's vibe, and convert our prices from dollars to Philippine pesos. A 12oz coffee is ₱150.00, and a double espresso works out to about ₱250.00. Excitement builds and our grand opening is met with much fanfare and plenty of social media hype by the agency we hired to help with our branding.

However, sales in our first week of operation at the Manila location are abysmal. While plenty of potential customers walk through the door, most leave without making a purchase. Eventually, one of our team members (who, by the way, we are paying only ₱700 per day) points out that across the street at McDonald's, a coffee is ₱50.00, an entire Big Mac meal only costs ₱186.00, and you can even get a McSpaghetti meal with fries for only ₱100.00! No wonder our sales are slow (and can you believe McDonald's sells spaghetti in the Philippines?). We failed to incorporate the economics of the local market in our pricing.

It looks like there is a lot we can learn from the café team. In this chapter, we discuss two techniques motivated by the successes and failures at Café d'Arpdau. First, we consider a player's initial purchase and its effect on their LTV and retention. This analysis addresses the questions "What is the probability of a second purchase if the user's first purchase was this SKU?" and "What is the LTV of users whose first purchase is this SKU?" In general, IAPs that lead to follow-on purchases are likely to increase LTV, but not always. We introduce a Cartesian-style visualization for comparing SKUs to identify strengths and opportunities for improvement.

Next, we introduce a methodology for increasing conversion and LTV globally by adjusting country-specific prices based on the Big Mac Index. A Cartesian system for comparing monetization by country is useful in detecting geos that are underperforming in terms of IAP. Often this is due to pricing decisions that rely solely on currency exchange rates, and don't adequately address relative consumer purchasing power in these countries.

Correlating First Purchase Item to LTV

If a player makes an IAP, you want them to be happy they did so they make a bunch more. Conversely, if a player has a bad experience with their first purchase, odds are they are not going to make another. They may even churn out of frustration.

A simple way to ensure that your catalogue of SKUs is well-balanced with respect to perceived customer value is to determine the probability a customer makes any additional purchase given the item they first purchased. The **repeat purchase rate** (RPR) for a SKU *s* is the percentage of spenders who go on to make another purchase (of any item) given that *s* was their first purchase. The `first_purchase_item` column in the `user_ltv` view facilitates this analysis; it records the SKU of the item first purchased by monetizing players. The following query calculates the RPR by SKU. We are also interested in the effect each first-purchased SKU has on LTV, so our query includes LTV7 and LTV30.

```
SELECT first_purchase_item,
       AVG(ltv_7) AS ltv7,
       AVG(ltv_30) AS ltv30,
       SUM(CASE WHEN num_purchases > 1 THEN 1 END) / COUNT(*)::FLOAT
AS rpr
FROM  user_ltv
WHERE ltv > 0
AND   install_date BETWEEN CURRENT_DATE- 180 AND current_date-31
GROUP BY first_purchase_item
```

first_purchase_item	ltv7	ltv30	rpr
ep_4.99usd_b6_1	7.59	27.22	0.5
egp_4.99usd_b16_2	13.13	72.70	0.5455
promo.starterpackpromo	51.90	143.35	0.5581
hashcoins.extrasmall	9.08	24.57	0.5614
egp_4.99usd_b8_3	8.54	26.20	0.5714
sub_4.99usd	23.19	78.93	0.5773
egp_2.99usd_b19_1	4.43	16.52	0.6154
promo.firsttimebuyer	35.54	85.48	0.6348
...	...	...	...

The RPR for SKUs may vary significantly, but ideally, they should all be high and relatively similar. Keep in mind that while repeat purchases are great, LTV trumps conversion. The result set above indicates the FTBP (the last row) has a 63.48% repeat purchase rate (`rpr`), but its LTV30 is significantly lower than the starter pack promo's $143.35. The starter pack includes a character card and premium currency, whereas the FTBP only contains soft currency. The starter pack promo costs significantly more, which likely contributes to its higher LTV.

If your FTBP is doing its job, both the probability of a repeat purchase and the LTV30 of players who chose it as their first purchase should be high. If one or the other is low, consider changing its contents and/or experimenting with the price.

Another variable to consider is the impact each first-purchased SKU has on retention. Adding D7 and D30 retention to our analysis is a simple modification to the query:

```
SELECT first_purchase_item,
       AVG(ltv_7) AS ltv7,
       AVG(ltv_30) AS ltv30,
       SUM(CASE WHEN num_purchases > 1 THEN 1 END) / COUNT(*)::FLOAT
AS rpr,
       AVG(d7::FLOAT) AS d7r,
       AVG(d30::FLOAT) AS d30r
FROM  user_ltv l LEFT JOIN user_retention r USING(user_id)
WHERE ltv > 0
AND   l.install_date BETWEEN CURRENT_DATE- 180 AND current_date-31
GROUP BY first_purchase_item ORDER BY d30r LIMIT 8
```

first_purchase_item	ltv7	ltv30	rpr	d7r	d30r
promo.starterpackpromo	51.90	143.35	0.5581	0.4419	0.3256
promo.firsttimebuyer	35.54	85.48	0.6348	0.6011	0.3387
hashcoins.extrasmall	9.08	24.57	0.5614	0.6723	0.4289
hashcoins.medium	37.29	84.16	0.7748	0.7117	0.4595
hashcoins.small	15.52	41.52	0.7052	0.7112	0.4833
hashcoins.large	77.49	158.07	0.8704	0.6944	0.5093
promo.minieventfirsttimebuyer	26.94	87.62	0.7612	0.8209	0.5224
promo.eventfirsttimebuyer	26.45	89.19	0.7391	0.8116	0.6522

A sample of rows sorted by D30R is given above. The purpose of this analysis is to identify SKUs that lead to "one and done" behaviour: a low repeat purchase rate and higher churn rate. For example, the extra small hashcoins SKU (highlighted) exhibits poor D30 retention coupled with the lowest LTV. Should it be eliminated? That is something to A/B test.

Scatter plots of `first_purchase_item` (the *x*-axis) with LTV and RPR are a useful tool to unearth outliers and negative correlations with particular SKUs. Here is an example from Tableau:

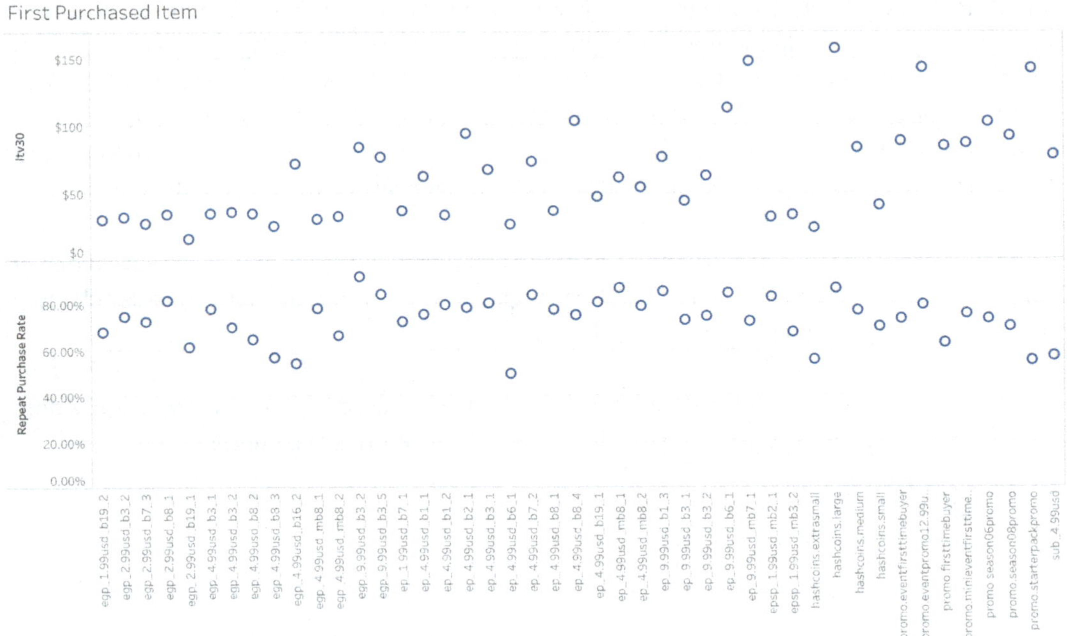

However, determining particular SKUs that exhibit bad performance in both metrics simultaneously is difficult to determine from this chart. Therefore, a better visualization is a scatter plot of LTV30 as a function of RPR (see Figure 11.1). Each `SKU` is added as a *Label* to the plot.

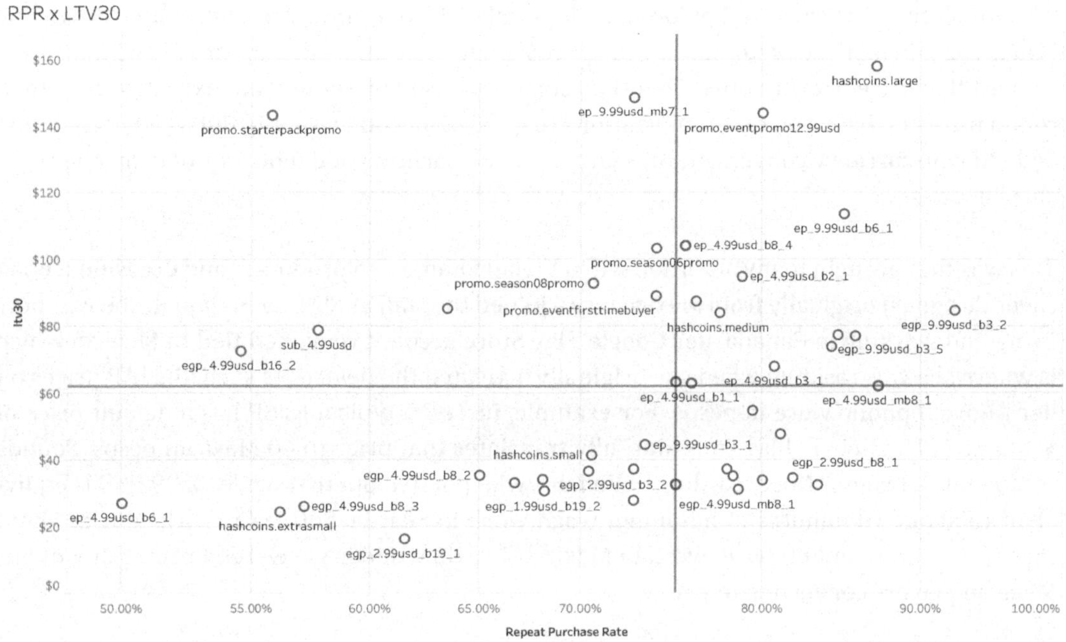

Figure 11.1 A scatter plot of repeat purchase rate and LTV30, with overlaid reference lines, creates a Cartesian coordinate view of SKU performance.

Using the *Analytics* tab to overlay a *Reference Line* defined as the median value of both dimensions produces a Cartesian coordinate system. The origin, where the two reference lines meet, defines a baseline of performance for first-time purchased SKUs. The bottom-left quadrant contains those SKUs that need improvement, whereas the top-right hosts the SKUs to be emulated. The purpose of this visualization is to spur discussion and formulate hypotheses to test. What is it about those SKUs in the top-right quadrant? Is it their content, price-point, or is it when and where they are made available to the player?

Geographical Pricing

Many game studios go to the trouble and expense of translating their games into other languages to broaden their appeal and expand opportunities in global markets. This activity is known as **localization**. Other studios simply make their game available for download everywhere without making any changes to adhere to local customs or languages. Regardless, if you make a game available for download in a foreign country, consider **geographical pricing** as a potentially powerful localization. Geographical pricing in this context is when a game publisher changes their IAP prices based on the location of the buyer.

Wait, don't the platforms do that for you? Not really. The platforms are lazy about IAP pricing. When you add a SKU to your store, you specify a currency and a default price. The platforms convert that price to every other country's currency based on the current exchange rate, then round prices up based on retail conventions (e.g., $3.82 becomes $3.99). But as any economist will tell you, currency conversion rates are not necessarily a good indicator of consumer purchasing power.

This was first brought to my attention when Viviana Ramos – a producer (and occasional book cover designer) originally from Mexico City – joined the staff at ESG. Even though she was now living and working in Canada, her Google Play Store account remained tied to Mexico, which is where she was residing when she originally activated the device. As such, the IAP prices on her Android phone were in pesos. For example, in *TPB* a typical FTBP has a default price of $2.99 USD. The Google Play store dutifully translates that price to 60 Mexican pesos. Sounds reasonable... I guess? Not according to Viviana, who pointed out that while $2.99 USD is equivalent to about 10 minutes of minimum wage work in Seattle, $60 MXN works out to about three *hours* of minimum wage work in Mexico City. No wonder we weren't seeing any of our Mexican players converting to paid.

This observation led to an obvious conclusion: IAP prices should reflect the same ratio of a typical worker's average hourly wages regardless of where they live. If it takes a Starbucks barista in Seattle 10 minutes to earn enough money to buy the $2.99 FTBP, then that same SKU should be priced so that it takes a Guadalajara Starbucks barista 10 minutes to earn enough pesos to also make that purchase. Ditto in Bangkok, Sydney, Cape Town, and Oslo. If all you do is set your default price in the App/Play Store in US$ and let the platforms decide on the price everywhere else, the result will be a lower conversion rate in countries with overvalued currency relative to wages; i.e., everywhere except the USA, Switzerland, and Norway.

"You Deserve a Break Today"

Fortunately, McDonald's restaurants have done most of this work for us already. Relative consumer purchasing power and the Big Mac Index (BMI) is a topic covered in most courses on international business and marketing. The concept is extremely important to freemium game publishers where IAPs make up the bulk of their revenue. Set the price right and you increase the likelihood of converting a non-payer into a spender. Get it wrong (like we were doing with promos in Mexico and pretty much every other country in the world) and you risk leaving money on the table.

> Apple iPhone owners are less price sensitive, especially outside of North America where the share of iOS players is typically much smaller. Focus on Android for better results and leave the prices as-is on iOS. This will mean that players on an iPhone will pay more for the same

SKU than players in the same country on Android. But we've never heard a single complaint from any of our iOS players.

The BMI is an adjustment to currency conversion rates based on the average retail price for a Big Mac in countries around the world. If currency conversion rates reflected consumer purchasing power, the price for a Big Mac would simply be the US$ price converted to the local currency. But it's not. McDonald's has priced the Big Mac according to prevailing local demand for fast-food *and* consumer purchasing power. For example, according to hellosafe.ca, the average price of a Big Mac in the USA in 2022 was $5.78 USD. That works out to about $115 MXN or $7.50 CAD if we simply convert currencies using prevailing exchange rates in 2022. If we walk into a McDonald's in Guadalajara and Vancouver, those should be the prices, right? However, the average price of a Big Mac in Mexico and Canada in 2022 was only US$3.32 (MXN$66) and US$5.30 (C$6.70), respectively. What gives?

Retail prices are what gives. Multinationals charge what each market will bear, and market prices are largely driven by the consumer. One need only compare the cost of mobile phone data plans in Canada versus Nigeria to recognize that profit margins are dictated not by cost of delivery, but by "how much can we get away with charging the consumer?" and its corollary "what price point maximizes our profit?"

Free-to-play IAPs have no cost of delivery: SKU pricing is not constrained by input costs such as raw goods and distribution. Apart from the 30% platform fee and any VAT/GST[1] mandated by law be included in the price, it's all profit. If I learned anything from that second-year elective in economics, it's the law of supply-and-demand: *consumer demand falls as prices rise*. In most of the world, the default Google Play pricing is too high to create demand from all but the bougiest of players.

As a supplier of virtual goods with no cost of delivery, the quantity a freemium game publisher chooses to produce is unlimited and unaffected by price. Any sale is one worth making, but what price point maximizes profit? This optimization problem is manifest in the following hypothetical demand curve for an IAP at various price points from $1.00 to $5.00.

[1] There are about 45 countries in total where a value-added tax is included in the list price, ranging from a low of 5% in Taiwan up to 27% in Hungary. Conversely, some jurisdictions like the USA and Canada do not have taxes included in the retail price, but instead add them during checkout.

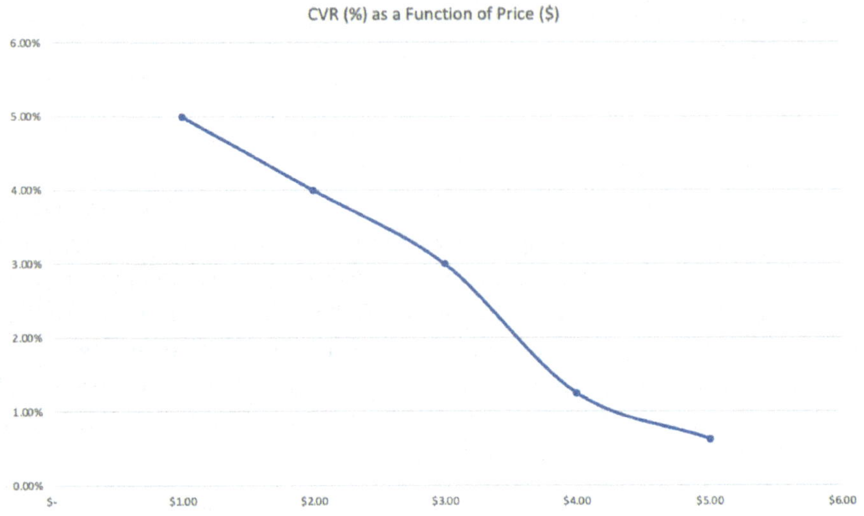

As dictated by micro-economic theory, demand (expressed as the daily conversion rate) is highest at the lowest price point. But that doesn't necessarily maximize revenue. For sake of illustration, assume we have 1,000 players. Then $daily\ revenue = 1{,}000 * CVR * price$, resulting in a non-linear curve (see next graph). Although conversion is 5% if we price the SKU at only $1.00, that generates only $50 in revenue. The optimal price is the inflection point at approximately $2.88 for this SKU, which becomes apparent if we plot *daily revenue* as a function of the SKU's *price*:

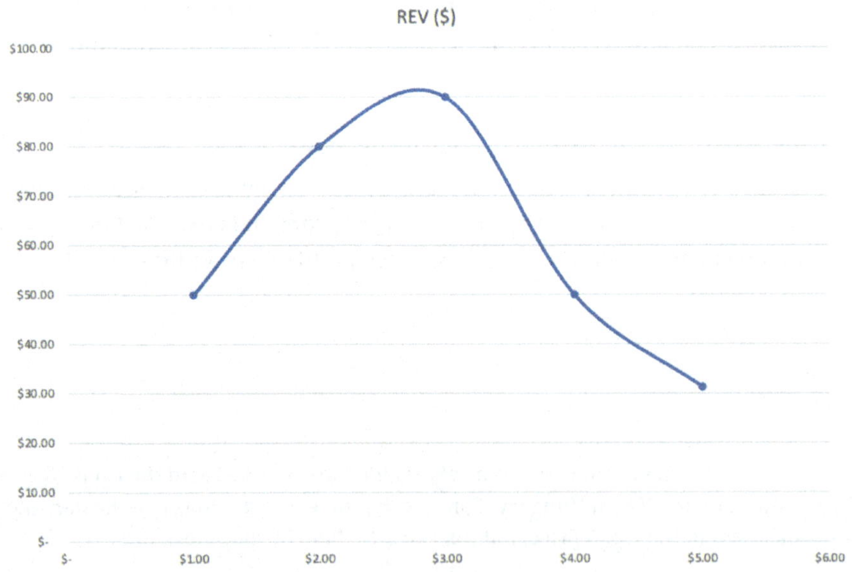

If we trust McDonald's – and honestly, I think they know what they are doing – we can expect our revenue to be maximized in each country if we adjust SKU prices by the BMI.

> Couched in this hypothesis are two big assumptions: (1) IAPs are elastic goods – demand decreases as prices rise; and (2) demand for non-essential goods like McDonald's fast food is a reasonable substitute for luxury goods like IAPs in a freemium mobile game.

For example, the BMI for Mexico is \$3.32/\$5.78 = 0.57. If we set the price for a small *hashcoin* bundle in *TPB* to US\$2.99 for players in the US, what should the price be in pesos for players in Mexico? The BMI-adjusted price for the same SKU in Mexico is US\$2.99 * 0.57 = US\$1.70. When converted to MXN, this works out to about 34 pesos. For players in Canada, the BMI is \$5.30/\$5.78 = 0.92. The price for that same SKU should be US\$2.74, which is approximately C\$3.49. The following table summarizes the adjustments, with the last column indicating the prescribed price to use.

Country	Default Price if up to Google	Big Mac Index (BMI)	BMI Adjusted Price (USD)	Local Price
USA	$2.99	1.00	$2.99	$2.99 USD
Mexico	$60.00 (MXN)	0.57	$1.70	$34.00 MXN
Canada	$3.89 (CAD)	0.92	$2.72	$3.49 CAD

Monetization with Default Pricing Only

The hypothesis is that we can improve conversion and LTV for Android users in other countries by adjusting prices to be more compatible with consumer purchasing power. But before we start changing any prices, let's look at a new game ESG recently launched without any pricing optimization; i.e., all we did was specify default prices for each SKU and let Google Play determine global prices. The following query gathers some monetization data for the top-10 geos by installs on Android:

```
WITH cohort AS
(
  SELECT user_id,
         country,
         ltv_7,
         ltv_30,
         converted
  FROM user_source s
    LEFT JOIN user_ltv USING (user_id)
  WHERE s.install_date >= CURRENT_DATE- 365
    AND s.platform = 'android'
)
SELECT country,
       COUNT(*) AS installs,
```

```
        AVG(converted::FLOAT) AS cvr,
        AVG(ltv_7) AS ltv7,
        AVG(ltv_30) AS ltv30
FROM cohort
GROUP BY country
ORDER BY installs DESC LIMIT 10
```

country	installs	cvr	ltv7	ltv30
CA	8830	0.0122	0.35	0.79
AU	5532	0.0183	0.32	0.50
US	4747	0.0362	2.15	1.90
BR	1469	0.002	0.03	0.05
DE	1285	0.014	0.49	0.78
IN	1059	0.0009	0.17	0.36
GB	956	0.0565	2.23	3.11
FR	896	0.0134	0.36	0.82
ID	726	0.0041	0.17	0.53
MX	650	0.0031	0.02	0.02

Note the conversion rate (`cvr`) ranges from a high of 5.65% in Great Britain to close to 0% in India and Brazil. Mexico is also lagging at only 0.31% conversion to paid. LTV7 in the US is decent at $2.15, indicating the game has potential to be a success. But other than GB, it appears that Google Play has not done a good job at price localizations. We can do better.

Adjusting Prices on Google Play

How does a game publisher go about managing prices in the Google Play Console? Every registered SKU for an Android app is found by navigating to the *One-time products* sub-section under *Monetize with Play - Products*. Android now refers to SKUs as *one-time products*, each identified by a unique `Product ID`:

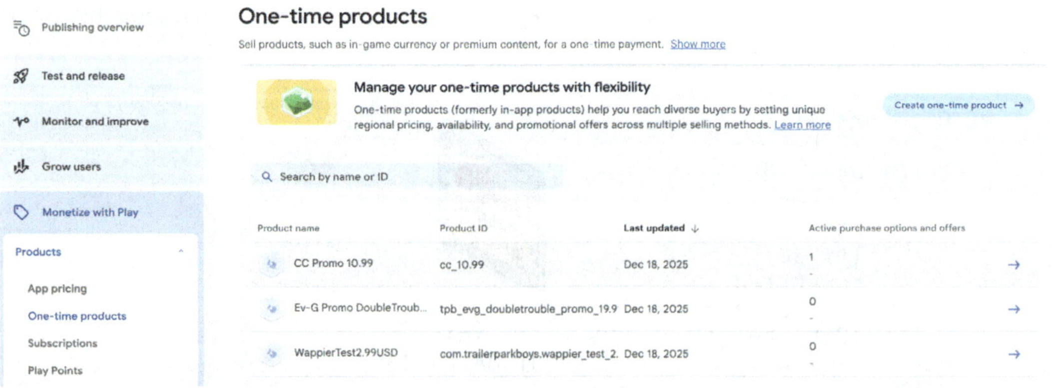

Country-specific prices live in the one-or-more purchase options defined for each SKU. To define a localized prize in any country where your app is available, you drill-down into a specific purchase option. There you can either set the prices one country at a time, or bulk edit by specifying a default price and currency:

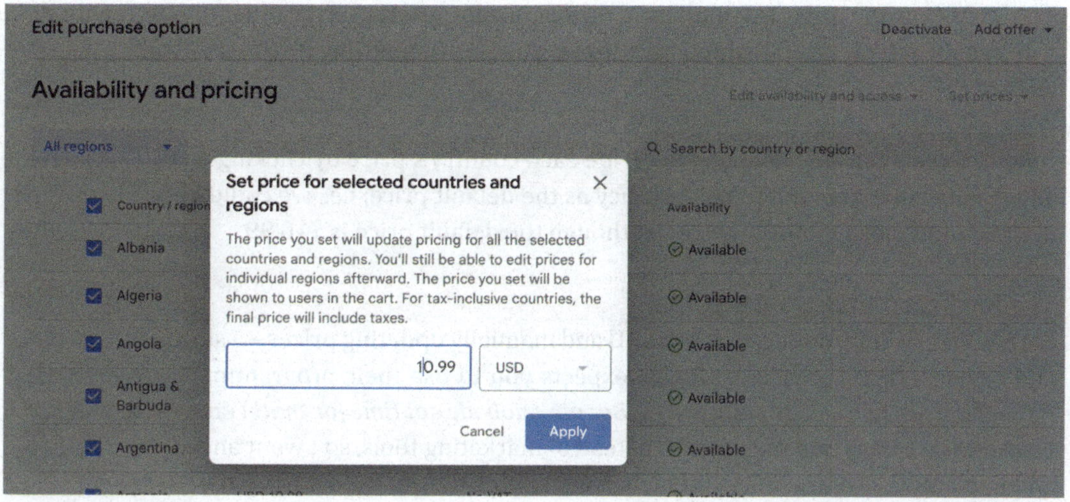

For the case shown above, a default price of $10.99 USD is specified. Google uses this default price to generate local prices using today's exchange rate and country-specific pricing patterns. After clicking *Apply*, we see that this SKU is now set to cost AUD $17.99 in Australia:

Edit purchase option

Aruba	USD 10.99	No VAT	Available
Australia	AUD 17.99	10%	Available
Austria	EUR 10.99	20%	Available
Azerbaijan	USD 10.99	No VAT	Available
Bahamas	USD 10.99	No VAT	Available
Bahrain	USD 11.99	10%	Available
Bangladesh	BDT 1,500.00	15%	Available

Note the Tax column, which indicates the presence of any value-added tax that is *included* in the price. For instance, while players in Australia pay $17.99 AUD for this SKU, that includes a 10% tax collected by Google and remitted to the Australian government. That leaves only $16.35 AUD as the gross IAP amount. The formula for gross IAP revenue for a SKU with price p in a country with an embedded tax rate r is $p/(1+r)$; multiply by 0.7 to calculate net revenue.

On this screen you can manually override each country's price by clicking on it. This includes any country that uses the same currency as the default price; i.e., we could override the price in Aruba and make it only $6.99 even though the default price is $10.99.

The Professor Arpdau Pricing Tool

Rather than drilling down into each SKU and manually updating prices – a slow and rather tedious process – Google expects you to use their programmatic Publishing API to manage your prices. *But ain't nobody got time for that!* I know your devs are busy building games instead of marketing tools, so I went ahead and implemented a price-management tool for you.

> In a previous version of this book, bulk editing of prices via CSV file import/export was described. However, Google deprecated that feature and it was removed in May of 2025. Likewise, other previous versions of this book referenced the now deprecated In-App Product API, which was replaced by the new One-Time Product model in November of 2025.

In particular, Professor Arpdau can read and write your Google Play Console data and adjust prices in the countries you choose. This enables quick and accurate bulk changes to all of your Android in-app products, saving you time and helping you make more money. The *Geographical Pricing* tool supports automatic price adjustments based on the BMI and purchasing power of local consumers, or refreshing prices based on current exchange rates.

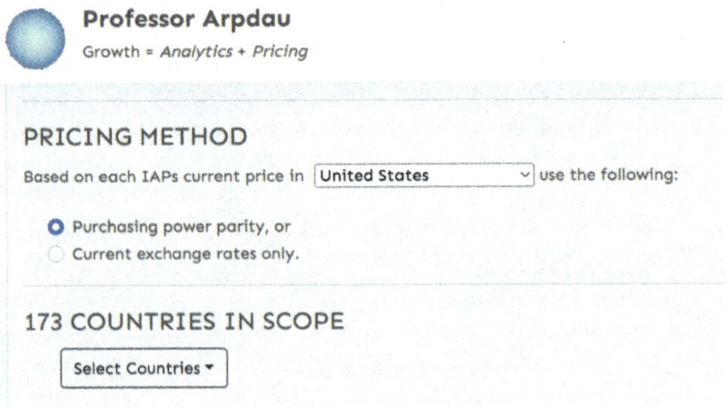

For those new to optimized pricing, a recommended course of action is to visit arpdau.com and use the *Geographical Pricing* tool to update all of your prices based on purchasing power parity (see above). This is particularly relevant if you have a lot of international users who don't ever make an IAP. Prices throughout most of the world will be reduced to better reflect what consumers in those countries can afford:

US$ 4.99 ▼

Country (Code)	Existing Price	Recommended Price	Change
Australia (AU)	A$ 7.99	A$ 6.49	-18.77%
Brazil (BR)	R$ 27.99	R$ 10.99	-60.74%
Canada (CA)	$ 6.99	$ 5.49	-21.46%
Costa Rica (CR)	CRC 2,500.00	CRC 1,100.00	-56.00%
Czech Republic (CZ)	CZK 119.99	CZK 74.99	-37.50%
France (FR)	€ 4.99	€ 3.69	-26.05%
Germany (DE)	€ 4.99	€ 3.89	-22.04%
India (IN)	₹ 520.00	₹ 110.00	-78.85%
New Zealand (NZ)	NZ$ 9.99	NZ$ 7.49	-25.03%
Norway (NO)	NOK 65.00	NOK 59.00	-9.23%
Switzerland (CH)	CHF 3.90	CHF 4.20	7.69%
Turkiye (TR)	TRY 254.99	TRY 96.99	-61.96%
United Kingdom (GB)	£ 4.39	£ 3.39	-22.78%

Testing the Results

While conducting geo-based pricing optimization, the following scatter plot of each country's LTV7 vs. D7 conversion rate is useful in determining where your monetization strategy is working and where it is underperforming. This Cartesian system is similar to the visualization we introduced for first-time buyer SKUs, but here we have used an *Average* for the *Reference Lines*. Average D7 conversion across these 47 countries with more than 50 installs each is only 1.39% while average LTV7 is $0.51. For this game, Germany (DE) sits right on the origin.

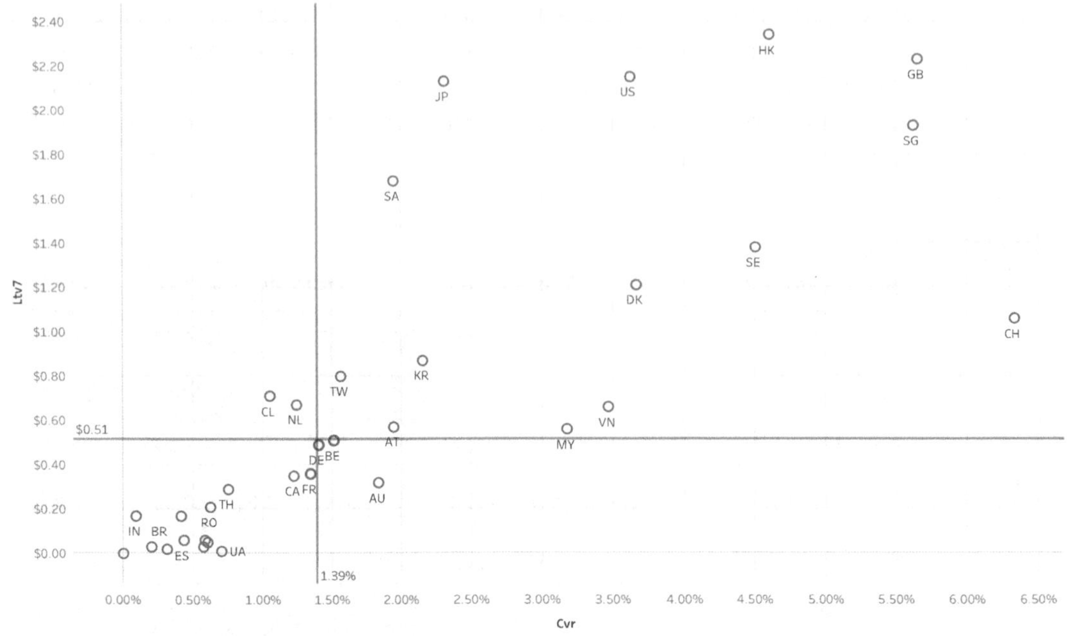

The interpretation of this plot is straightforward. Monetization is strong in the countries that appear in the top-right quadrant, and weak in the bottom-left. The prescribed action is to lower prices for countries in the bottom-left quadrant. Any country where the conversion rate is 0% is an obvious place to start since there is no risk that IAP revenue will drop: you have nothing to lose and only ARPDAU to gain.

Opportunities to increase prices are indicated by countries in the bottom-right quadrant (e.g., AU), though one should proceed with caution. In addition, this plot indicates that CH (that's Switzerland, not China) is underperforming in LTV relative to its nearly 6.5% conversion rate, and that prices should be increased for users in that geo. But again, the analytics should suggest A/B tests rather than blanket advice; follow the evidence but evaluate the results.

Finally, for the countries in the top-left quadrant (CL and NL), LTV is artificially buoyed by the presence of some big-spenders. A price decrease could actually reduce revenue while having no effect on conversion.

A successful pricing strategy will move the origin of this plot up and to the right.

In an equitable world, the conversion rate would be the same in every country. But achieving that level of parity may result in a decrease in LTV in certain countries; i.e., lowering the IAP prices may increase conversion but decrease overall revenue. In certain cases, it is better to have fewer purchasers that are willing to spend significantly more than it is to be benevolent. However, in the long run, increasing conversion is a good strategy since it makes your monetization less reliant on whales and leads to a coincident uptick in retention – payers are invested and tend to stick around longer.

The Cartesian plot identifies areas of opportunity and is good for a static before-and-after look at how *new* installs are affected by your applied price adjustments. But how do we know if our price adjustments have increased daily revenue? You could run an A/B test that compares the ARPU of a treatment cohort exposed to the new prices with that of a control group, but the best way to know if the new prices are working is to look at a time-series graph of ARPDAU by country. The purchasing behaviour of existing players has likely changed in the geos where price changes have been applied. In that case an immediate impact is apparent when you look at ARPDAU for dates after any price adjustments.

Return on Ad Spend:
LEVEL 12

Performance marketers[1] who work to build effective ad campaigns for mobile games are known as user acquisition (UA) managers. **UA managers** not only create new campaigns, but they also manage the budget allocation between campaigns. To do this, they rely heavily on the support of data analysts to provide the queries and dashboards they need to make informed, data-driven decisions about ongoing campaign performance. Which campaigns are predicted to lose money and should have their budgets reduced? Which campaigns are likely to generate profit, and when? In this chapter, we introduce the concepts that data analysts need to know to effectively work as part of a growth team.

The topic of digital advertising on mobile could fill an entire book or two on its own, so I have intentionally glossed over some of the finer details and focused on the aspects germane to analytics and to the responsibilities of the data analyst on a growth team. As I work towards completing this book, the mobile marketing industry continues to evolve. Regardless of how long the details within this chapter remain relevant, the underlying concepts of paid installs, CPI, ROAS, and predicting LTV should serve the reader well as a foundation to whatever shall come next. But first, let's grab a coffee.

[1] I'm not a marketer, but I used to play one at work. Very early on in my tenure as a senior data analyst at ESG, I was tasked by co-founder Josh Nilson to start the new "growth team." Josh paired me with Nancy Huang, a quiet yet cheerful graduate of UBC's business school. I had no idea what a growth team was or what it did, but Nancy quickly got me up to speed, and with the support of colleagues Kay Chan and William Hong, we soon learned the subtleties of attribution and the mobile advertising ecosystem. For most of that first year, the growth team was just Nancy and me. Together we built the methodology for predicting ROAS, defined ESG's best practices for profitable user acquisition, met a bunch of cool people, and learned to spend millions of dollars without losing sleep. Nancy would later become Head of UA Strategy at ESG, and lead a team of 12.

Profitable Customer Acquisition at Café d'Arpdau

Coffee bean prices have jumped substantially since Café d'Arpdau first opened its doors for business. Supply chain difficulties, climate change, a global pandemic, and now tariffs (!) have conspired to spike the input costs of each cup of coffee sold. This is not good news: we give away a lot of free coffee as a marketing incentive. How much is that costing us, and is it a good investment? First, we need to quantify the cost of each cup of coffee given away to entice customers to enter the café and signup for the loyalty club. Since we don't know how many first-time customers would have come in even without the "free coffee" promo advertised on our storefront, we assume that the sunk cost was $2.80 per customer – our retail price of a coffee. The total cost of each day's new loyalty club cohort is thus $280. But then a further 40 free coffees are given away on this cohort's next visit to entice the loyalty club members to agree to receive text messages. Total customer acquisition cost is $392, or $3.92 per customer. In games, we call this the cost per install (CPI).

But wait.... What if some of those acquired customers enjoyed their experience so much that they told a friend or two to give our café a try? Or maybe they wrote a great Yelp review that helped convince some locals to pop in and buy a croissant? Businesses grow by word of mouth and positive referrals; if every 100 new customers generate an additional 10 customers through referrals and testimonials, our effective cost of customer acquisition is actually $392/(100+10) = $3.56. In games, the *effective* cost per install (eCPI) attempts to factor in the extra organic installs that arise for free due to referrals from paid users.

The free coffee promo is not without risk. We know that as many as half of our customers take the coffee and run, and never return to our fine establishment. What is the ROI on that marketing spend? When we last calculated the LTV for these loyalty club customers back in Chapter 5, it was $7.97. Our effective cost to acquire each of those customers was only $3.56, leaving us with a tidy profit of $4.41 per customer. Put another way, our return on ad spend (ROAS) is 7.97/3.56 = 224%. "C'est bon!"

How long does it take us to earn that $3.56 back? The days to break even is the day *n* when LTV*n* first becomes greater than or equal to $3.56. When we last calculated our average LTV by day, we noted that LTV0 was $2.01 and LTV1 was $5.07. We conclude that it only takes us one day for our ad spend (the lost revenue from giving away 140 coffees) to back out and become profitable! Every customer visit beyond then is gravy. We decide to seriously consider spending more on customer acquisition: if we can keep acquiring customers for less than $5.07 each, we can expect to recoup that cost in one day.[2]

It seems pretty easy to buy café patrons and it looks to be money well spent. But how do game publishers profitably acquire new users? Quantifying the performance of paid user acquisition for free-to-play games is the topic of this chapter. Spending money to advertise a product you give away for free is a risky proposition. Even if the ads are performance-based (where the advertiser is charged only for actual installs and not just for ad impressions or clicks), these new players must monetize. We want our ads to find users whose predicted LTV exceeds their CPI.

Our goal this chapter is to learn how to measure and predict campaign ROAS and how to apply the monetization curve to the important tasks of defining ROAS targets for ad campaigns and predicting their days to break even as quickly as possible. We also present a simple means of incorporating organic lift into your ROAS calculations. Finally, we consider the problem of predicting ROAS without a monetization curve, a situation that arises when a game is first launched.

Where's My SKAN LTV Solution At?

If you were hoping for a turnkey solution to measuring and predicting LTV for iOS users acquired through SKAdNetwork (SKAN) campaigns, you are out of luck. Though if you squint hard enough and keep reading carefully, you might find inspiration as to how to solve the problem yourself. Or wait for the second edition of this book. Fore!

ROAS=LTV/CPI

UA managers live and die by their ad campaign's ROAS, defined by the ratio of LTV to CPI:

$$\text{ROAS} = \text{LTV}/\text{CPI}$$

ROAS is measured on a cohort basis and rarely at the individual user level. If every install is accurately attributed by the MMP, we call this **row-level** or **user-level** attribution.[3] With row-

[2] And so long as our cost of customer acquisition remains less than $7.97, the ad spend will back out. But our profit on those customers is now zero. Maximizing profit is not the same as maximizing revenue.

[3] This is only possible if every new user was not limiting ad tracking on their device and had agreed to share their mobile advertising ID.

level attribution, a cohort is defined at the ad campaign (or even ad creative) level and consists of all users attributed to the same ad campaign within a specific time window (day, week, month, etc.).

Rather than looking at lifetime total revenue for a cohort, ROAS is ordinarily defined by the cohort's revenue *n* days after install. For instance, **D7ROAS** is the ratio of the total revenue by D7 from acquired players divided by the total ad spend to acquire those players. In general:

$$\text{D}n\text{ROAS} = \frac{\text{revenue by D}n}{\text{ad spend}} = \text{LTV}_n/\text{CPI}$$

With regards to ROAS, data analysts on a growth team are expected to contribute three things:

1. accurate measures of cohort LTV*n* in order to properly measure D*n*ROAS at the campaign level;
2. D*n*ROAS targets for UA managers to employ when running app-event optimized (AEO) campaigns; and,
3. accurate predictions of LTV that model the expected days to break even for a campaign based on current observed D*n*ROAS.

This all seemed remarkably simple at Café d'Arpdau, but it's not that easy when you are advertising a free-to-play game where only 5% of your customers will ever make a purchase. Let's look at each of these tasks in more detail.

Campaign LTV and DnROAS

To measure ROAS, we need the LTV of the users acquired by each campaign. Campaigns are uniquely identified by the ad networks with a `campaign_id`. With an eye towards calculating D7ROAS, let's start by measuring LTV7 by `campaign_id`:

```
WITH users AS
(
  SELECT user_id,
         s.install_date AS date,
         s.platform,
         type AS ad_network,
         source AS campaign_id,
         ltv_7
  FROM user_source s LEFT JOIN user_ltv USING (user_id)
),
installs AS
(
  SELECT date,
         ad_network,
```

```
            platform,
            campaign_id,
            COUNT(*) AS users,
            AVG(ltv_7) AS ltv7
    FROM users
    GROUP BY date,
             ad_network,
             platform,
             campaign_id
)
```

Sample data from the `installs` CTE (excluding the `date` field) is as follows:

ad_network	platform	campaign_id	users	ltv7
Apple Search Ads	ios	191934920	23	1.55
Google	ios	12087924903	7	20.79
Google	android	1757244663	177	6.13
Google	android	8100630612	108	2.11
Unity	android	5fcad1c046100f26507963d4	19	0.00

We now have the cohort LTV7 for each of these five active campaigns. Our ROAS calculation involves joining this data with campaign `spend` on that date, stored in the `adspend` table. The details of that query are omitted for brevity, but here is an example result set for those five campaigns after the join:

ad_network	campaign_id	spend	users	cpi	ltv7	d7roas
Apple Search Ads	191934920	19.05	23	0.83	1.55	1.87
Google	12087924903	532.47	7	76.07	20.79	0.27
Google	1757244663	2545.44	177	14.38	6.13	0.43
Google	8100630612	951.23	108	8.81	2.11	0.24
Unity	5fcad1c046100f26507963d4	4.79	19	0.25	0.00	0

Other than the Unity campaign, which did not generate any D7ROAS, everything appears to be on track. Note that despite a $76.07 CPI, the Google iOS campaign still managed a 27% D7ROAS, which suggests it is likely to break even by D90 (see below for why we think so). But how did this campaign actually perform in the long run? Let's see how they all fared:

ad_network	campaign_id	cpi	ltv7	ltv90	ltv
Apple Search Ads	191934920	0.83	1.55	6.26	6.26
Google	12087924903	76.07	20.79	66.13	66.13
Google	1757244663	14.38	6.13	37.24	73.27
Google	8100630612	8.81	2.11	6.88	7.75
Unity	5fcad1c046100f26507963d4	0.25	0.00	0.00	0.00

In hindsight, it appears it never did break even, tapping out at $66.13 in IAP LTV90, and nothing since. Neither did the Google Android campaign `8100630612`, at least not yet. (It probably did if we include ad mon.) But look how well the remaining Google campaign performed to date, with its 177 installs averaging $73.27 in LTV compared with a $14.38 CPI! Such is the randomness of daily ad campaign ROAS.

> Daily fluctuations in campaign ROAS are mainly due to small sample sizes and are mitigated by aggregating campaign spend and revenue figures into weekly snapshots. Predicted D90ROAS and days to break even are likewise more accurate when comprised of a weekly cohort.

ROAS Targets

App-event optimization (AEO) is the term used to describe ad campaigns that go beyond simply finding installs for the lowest CPI possible. With AEO, the goal is to find users that will pay back their CPI - regardless of its absolute value - by taking desirable post-install actions like making IAPs or watching ads.

Armed with *purchase* event data collected from users acquired by their campaign so far, ad networks can optimize campaign performance based on ROAS targets provided to them by the UA manager. Recall that a ROAS target is a proportion of LTVn/CPI, typically LTV7. For example, if a UA manager creates an ad campaign and specifies a D7ROAS target of 20%, the ad network will try to acquire cohorts whose LTV7 is at least 20% of their CPI, *regardless of the actual* CPI. This ensures that the budget is spent appropriately; if there is an opportunity to acquire users at an efficient CPI, the ad network will bid accordingly. This is realistic given the wealth of historical data at the hands of the ad network (especially Meta, Google, and Apple): they know which device (user) is about to watch an ad for your game, and from their accumulated player profile based on historical sharing and tracking of mobile ad identifiers, they can estimate the expected LTV should that user choose to install your game. At the same time, every other ad network involved in bidding on the impression will have its own player profile database and bid accordingly. For this reason, the coveted players cost more to acquire.

Specifying a ROAS target is a straightforward application of the monetization curve we learned to build in Chapter 5. With a historical monetization curve, $m_N(n)$, defined for a terminal day N, a D7ROAS target with expected days to break even of N days is simply $m_N(7)$. Refer to the following chart.

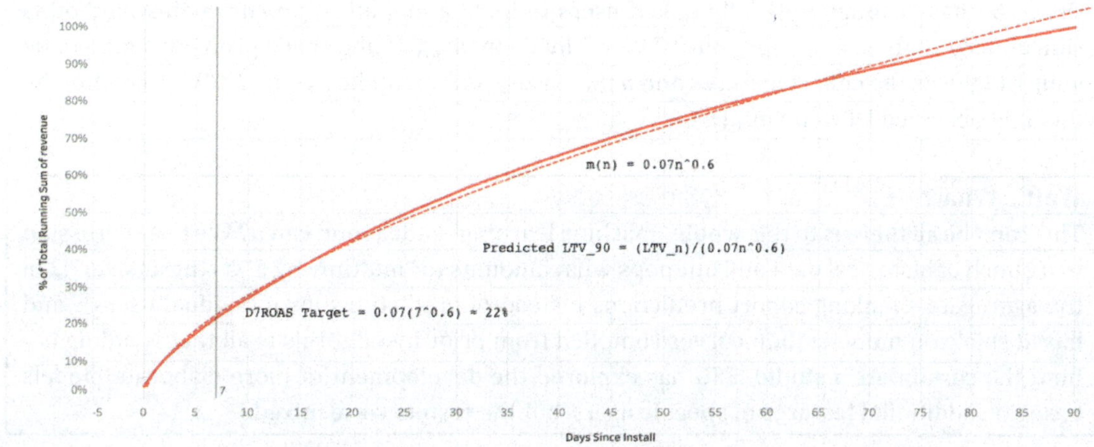

The solid red line indicates historical IAP behaviour of a set of 90D fully-baked installs. A curve fit to this data is the dashed line defined by the function $m_{90}(n) = 0.07n^{0.6}$. This curve defines the following D7ROAS target:

$$\text{D7ROAS Target} = 0.07(7^{0.6}) \approx 22\%$$

Ad campaigns where LTV7 is 22% of the CPI are expected to break even by D90. Why? Because on average we know that 22% of LTV90 is generated by D7. If the cohort stays the course, LTV90 will therefore equal the CPI.

If LTV7 is greater than 0.22*CPI, then the campaign is expected to back out in less than 90 days. For example, after one week of activity, an ad campaign has driven 100 installs at a cost of $1,000. CPI is $10.00, which seems high, but keep in mind that absolute CPI is irrelevant if a campaign is driving installs whose LTV is greater than their CPI. The total revenue generated by these 100 installs after seven days (R_7) is $240. The D7ROAS is 24%, which exceeds our target of 22%. Therefore, the campaign is expected to become profitable (i.e., generate > $1,000 in revenue) over the next 83 days.

How profitable? The predicted revenue by D90 for this same cohort of 100 installs is given by:

$$\widehat{R}_{90} = \frac{R_7}{m_{90}(7)} = \frac{\$240}{0.22} = \$1090$$

D90ROAS is expected to be $1090/$1000 = 109%. This is *expected*, based on historical average user purchase behaviour, but not guaranteed.

Once you have enough 90D fully-baked users to build a monetization curve, this method is ridiculously simple: whatever your LTV7 is, divide by $m_{90}(7)$ and that's probably going to be your LTV90. As the cohort matures and *n* increases, you can update your LTV90 prediction by dividing observed LTV*n* by $m_{90}(n)$.

Wait... What?
This can't be all there is to this whole "machine learning" endeavour, can it? We fit a regression to a bunch of historical data and out pops what amounts to "multiply by 5" as the answer?!? In the aggregate – making cohort predictions instead of predictions for individual users – and based solely on monetization curves compiled from prior installs, this is all that is hiding behind the curtain. As a studio, ESG has explored the development of more elaborate models based on additional features of specific users, but the results were mixed.

However, if you aren't concerned with ongoing predictions of LTV but only require a D7ROAS target based on historical users, this query suffices:

```
SELECT AVG(ltv_7)/AVG(ltv_90) AS d7roas_target
FROM user_ltv
WHERE install_date > current_date - 365
```

d7roas_target
0.2243

No monetization curve required.[4] The D7ROAS target is simply the average ratio of LTV7 to LTV90 (or LTV180, or whatever terminal day you decide you'd like to see a positive ROI). Breaking this down by platform and geo is probably a good idea as well since many UA managers like to create specific campaigns for tiers of countries; e.g., tier 1 = US, tier 2 = CA, GB, AU, etc. This breakdown is a straightforward modification of our previous query:

```
SELECT u.platform,
       country,
       AVG(ltv_7) / AVG(ltv_90) AS d7roas_target
FROM user_ltv u
  LEFT JOIN user_source s USING (user_id)
WHERE u.install_date > CURRENT_DATE- 365
GROUP BY u.platform,
         country
HAVING AVG(ltv_90) > 0 AND COUNT(*) > 1000
```

---

[4] If cohort ARPDAU by days since install is relatively constant, another heuristic is to take the ratio of PD_7/PD_{90}. Professor Arpdau, at arpdau.com, uses a similar approach when calculating D7ROAS targets as part of the *LTV Predictor* tool.

```
ORDER BY u.platform,
         COUNT(*) DESC,
         country
```

platform	country	d7roas_target
android	US	0.2017
android	CA	0.1996
android	GB	0.1909
android	PL	0.2822
android	BR	0.3157
android	PH	0.1724
android	IN	0.1833
android	AU	0.1924
android	DE	0.2952
android	FR	0.1346
android	ZA	0.2458
android	TR	0.4634
...	...	...
ios	US	0.2689
ios	CA	0.3078
ios	GB	0.2885
ios	AU	0.3640
ios	PL	0.2436
ios	DE	0.2729
ios	NZ	0.3614
...	...	...

The lower that target, the more users the ad networks are likely to find who meet that criterion. Note the wide range of values, particularly on Android. But also note that for Android installs in the US and Canada, the expected value of LTV90 for this game is approximately 5 * LTV7.

The Days to Break Even Formula

For an ad campaign, the *days to break even* is the first day after install when a cohort's revenue exceeds its acquisition cost: the day n where DnROAS $= 100\%$, or when LTVn = CPI. From that day on, every dollar earned from that cohort is profit. But often the growth team is asked to predict how long it will take for a particular ad campaign to break even. Predicting the day *i* where LTV_*i* = CPI is a matter of solving the following equation for *i*:

$$\widehat{\text{LTV}}_i = \text{CPI}$$

When a new ad campaign begins, we know the CPI. After n days, we observe LTVn for the cohort of installs attributed to that campaign. Given a monetization curve with a terminal day *N*, recall that our prediction for $\widehat{\text{LTV}}_i$ for any day $n < i < N$ is $m_N(i) * \text{LTV}_n / m_N(n)$. Substituting for the left-hand side of the equation, we have:

$$m_N(i) * \frac{\text{LTV}_n}{m_N(n)} = \text{CPI}$$

$$m_N(i) * \text{LTV}_n = \text{CPI} * m_N(n)$$

$$m_N(i) = \frac{\text{CPI} * m_N(n)}{\text{LTV}_n}$$

Let's pause there for a moment. Everything on the right side of that equation is known, while the left side is a function of the form ai^b with known values for a and b. We need to solve for i. For our example 100 installs with an LTV7 of \$2.40, a CPI of \$10.00, and a monetization curve $m_{90}(i) = 0.07i^{0.6}$, we have the following values:

$$0.07i^{0.6} = \frac{10 * 0.07 * 7^{0.6}}{2.40} = 0.92$$

$$i^{0.6} = \frac{0.92}{0.07} = 13.14$$

$$0.6\ln(i) = \ln(13.14) = 2.58$$

$$\ln(i) = \frac{2.58}{0.6} = 4.29$$

$$i = e^{4.29}$$

$$i = 73$$

73 days to break even. In general, the estimated days to break even given a monetization curve $m_N(n) = an^b$ and observed $\text{LTV}_n, n < N$, is:

$$e^{([\ln(\text{CPI} * an^b) - \ln(a * \text{LTV}_n)]/b)}$$

You might want to write that one down.

Predictions can begin immediately, but the more mature the campaign's installs are, the more accurate the estimate. However, we want a prediction as quickly as possible: paid UA is expensive, and we can easily light a pile of cash on fire if the ad network is selling us poor quality users. The sooner we know whether a campaign's predicted LTV is looking good relative to CPI, the better.

What happens if the days to break even is greater than the terminal day N in the monetization curve? This is predicted to happen any time the observed $\text{LTV}n/\text{CPI}$ is less than the DnROAS target for a particular terminal day *N*. For instance, what if LTV7 was only $2.00 for our 100 installs? D7ROAS is only 20%, which is below the target of 22%. In this case, the expected days to break even formula predicts 99 days. However, that prediction is based on a curve where 100% of the expected LTV90 is generated by D90. The behaviour of the curve outside of the training set is not necessarily reliable since the trajectory beyond D90 is not grounded in any actual data, as we see here:

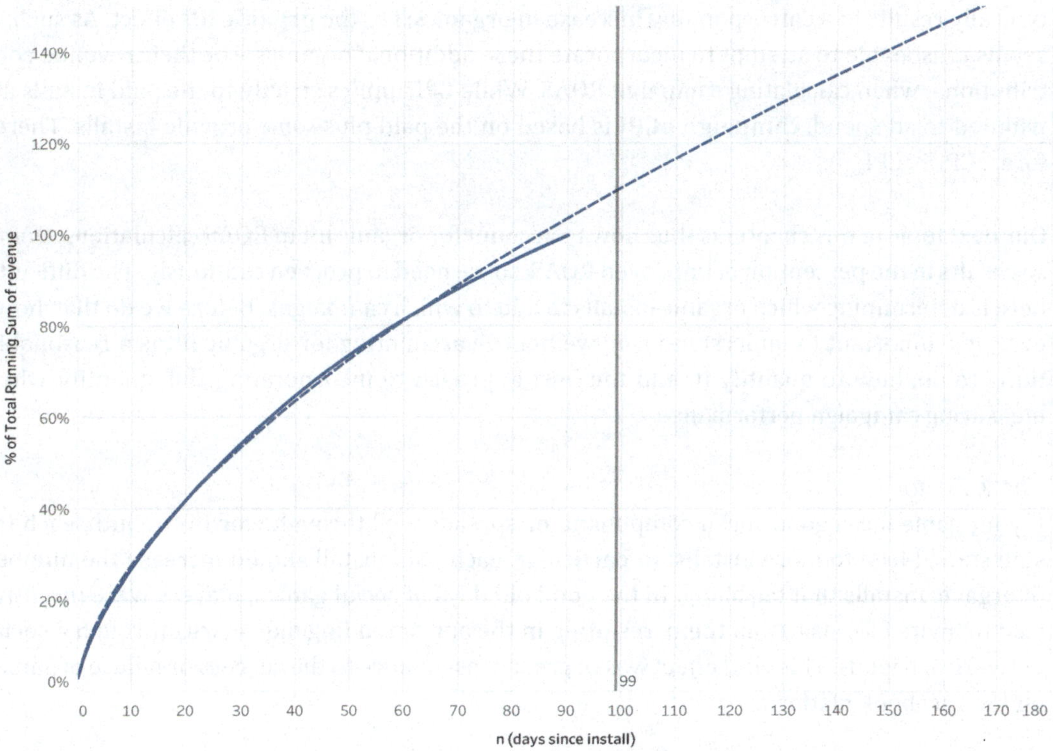

All we can safely say that is the day to break even is greater than 90.

If available, deploy a monetization curve with a greater terminal day *N* to predict days to break even when the early performance of a campaign doesn't appear to be backing out. If we instead use our *N*=180 monetization curve $m_{180}(n) = 0.059n^{0.56}$ trained from the same historical data set, the predicted days to break even with a $2.00 LTV7 on a $10 CPI is:

$$e^{\frac{\ln(10*0.059*7^{0.56})-\ln(0.059*2.00)}{0.56}} = e^{(0.56-(-2.14))/0.56} = 125$$

The difference between 125 and 99 days is significant when it comes to cash flow effects on a small business, and those numbers will diverge even more with increasingly poor early monetization.

Organic Lift

If a growth team is strict about measuring ROAS based on attributed installs only, our calculation of ROAS is complete. However, many UA managers recognize that running paid campaigns typically results in a corresponding increase in organics; i.e., the **organic lift** effect. As such, it seems reasonable to attempt to incorporate these additional organics – or their revenue contribution – when calculating campaign ROAS. While CPI applies strictly to the paid installs attributed to ad spend, **campaign eCPI** is based on the paid plus *some* organic installs. Therefore, eCPI $\leq$ CPI.

Our next topic in this chapter is thus how to account for organic lift in ROAS calculations. Doing so results in the perception of improved ROAS, so we need to proceed cautiously. The difficulty here is determining which organic installs to add to which campaigns. Before we do that, however, it's important to understand *why* we believe accounting for organic lift is a reasonable thing to do, how to quantify it, and the best approach to incorporating this quantity when measuring campaign performance.

The k*-Factor*

If your game has a good social component, or spreads well through word-of-mouth, each install should lead to more installs; in particular, each paid install should increase the number of organic installs that tag along. In the good old days of social games, players were incentivized to invite friends to join them, resulting in the app spreading like a virus through a social network of friends. This viral effect was of great consequence to the success or failure of games on the Facebook platform.

In mobile games, the ***k*-factor** is often used to describe and quantify the viral spread of app downloads. The *k*-factor is a concept borrowed from the basic reproduction number R_0 of epidemiology, where the R value of a virus indicates how many additional people are likely to become infected as a consequence of each new person infected. A $k > 1.0$ indicates exponential growth, whereas $k < 1.0$ indicates exponential decline.

The general marketing definition of k is based on actual customer-to-customer invites and conversions of invites to installs, but in the anti-social world of mobile games, direct invites are rare. Therefore, our concept of virality is defined as the lift in organic installs due to each paid install. For example, if a game has no ad spend, all installs are organic; in this case, the average number of organic installs per day is the **baseline**. If we start spending money on ads that drive installs, we expect the number of organics to also increase. Why? Well, imagine your best friend sees an ad for *Crime Boss Tycoon* and installs the game on their iPhone. Your friend loves how the characters drive the narrative of the idle game play, and they tell you all about it the next day at school. You decide to see what all the fuss is about by searching for the game in the Play store and installing it on your Android device. Our paid ad increased the organics by one. You were infected by your friend.

Another reason that organics increase with ad spend is that **discoverability** in the app stores improves as a result of ranking higher in various popularity categories, e.g., the lists of top games based on the number of downloads.

Quantifying organic lift can get complicated pretty quickly. Consider three scenarios. First, what if you were about to install the app anyway, and it just so happened to coincide with your friend raving about the game? Second, if the growth team is running multiple campaigns simultaneously, how does the data analyst attribute your organic install back to the specific ad campaign that convinced your friend to install the game in the first place? Third, what if your friend had *limit ad tracking* enabled on their iPhone, or selected "Ask App Not to Track" in response to the app tracking transparency (ATT) prompt when the game first launched on their device? In this case, the MMP is unable to attribute their install to any ad campaign. In the evolving era of consumer privacy, older approaches to quantifying ROAS like media mix modelling are suddenly back in vogue. For now, let us consider a straightforward way to quantify the lift in organics from paid installs by defining k as the number of additional organic installs we can expect to gain from each paid install.

The ripple effect of additional organic installs leading to even more organic installs is rolled up into this single value. For example, if k=0.4, this means that if we pay for 5 installs, we should see an additional $5(0.4) = 2$ organic installs. This does not mean that in addition to these 2 we should also see an additional $2(0.4) = 0.8$ organics, and so on, and so on. If k=0.4, the total number of extra organic installs due to a paid ad campaign is simply 0.4 ∗ *paid installs*.

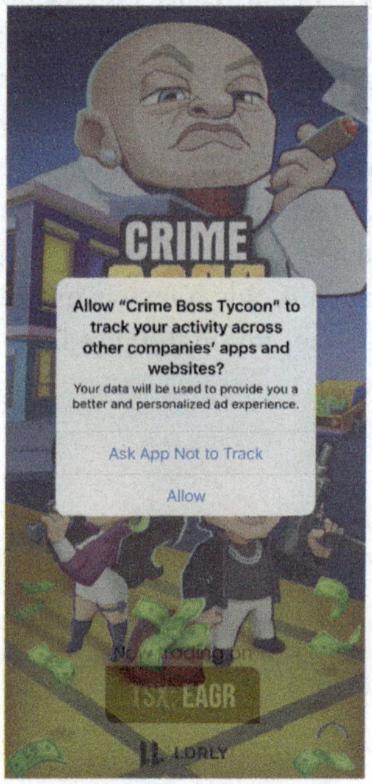

Caution: Heuristic Failure Alert
This does not necessarily mean that eCPI = $(ad\ spend)/(paid\ installs * (k+1))$, nor does it mean that eCPI = $\mathrm{CPI}/(k+1)$. More about this subtlety in a minute.

Calculating the k-Factor

One technique for deriving a game's *k*-factor is to correlate the historic organic installs as a function of paid installs with a linear regression. The resulting slope and *y*-intercept of the regression line are the *k*-factor and baseline (expected organics absent of spend), respectively. To build the regression, we need a relation of the following form:

install_date	paid	organic
2022-07-01	169	312
2022-07-02	176	357
2022-07-03	182	352
2022-07-04	236	328
2022-07-05	231	327
2022-07-06	219	478
2022-07-07	218	578
...	...	...

We don't segregate by platform. Virality is independent of device type; your friend may be on iOS while you prefer Android. However, with the deprecation of the iOS mobile device ID for advertisers (IDFA), many organics on that platform are actually unattributed paid installs. For this reason, one may consider this approach only viable with Android data. Conversely, virality is *not* independent of location: your friend can't infect you if they aren't close or connected to you somehow, like in the same country. Ad spend in France doesn't affect the top ranking apps in Belgium. You may choose to only count the paid and organic users within geos where a significant amount of money is spent on user acquisition. With that said, this query is useful for generating the data required to build the regression. Optional clauses are highlighted.

```
WITH users AS
(
  SELECT install_date,
         CASE WHEN TYPE = 'Organic' THEN 'Organic' ELSE 'Paid' END AS
           user_type,
         COUNT(*) AS users
  FROM user_source
  WHERE install_date BETWEEN CURRENT_DATE-90 AND CURRENT_DATE-1
    AND country = 'US' AND platform='android
  GROUP BY install_date,
           user_type
)
SELECT p.install_date,
       p.users AS paid,
       o.users AS raw_organic,
       AVG(o.users) OVER (ORDER BY o.install_date
          ROWS BETWEEN 1 FOLLOWING AND 2 FOLLOWING) AS organic
FROM users p
  INNER JOIN users o
```

```
    ON o.install_date = p.install_date
   AND o.user_type = 'Organic'
   AND p.user_type = 'Paid'
```

Note the moving average implemented as a window function as an alternative to only looking at the number of organics on the same day as the paid. We might choose to use this field instead of `raw_organic` because the world-of-mouth effect on organic installs is often delayed: as in our example, you didn't install *Crime Boss Tycoon* until the day *after* your friend's install was attributed to a paid ad campaign. You can also build the moving average in Tableau instead, where you are able to experiment with the parameters that work best for your particular game.

After plugging our query into Tableau, it's a simple step to create the linear regression. Be sure the *x*-axis (*Columns*) contains the `paid`.

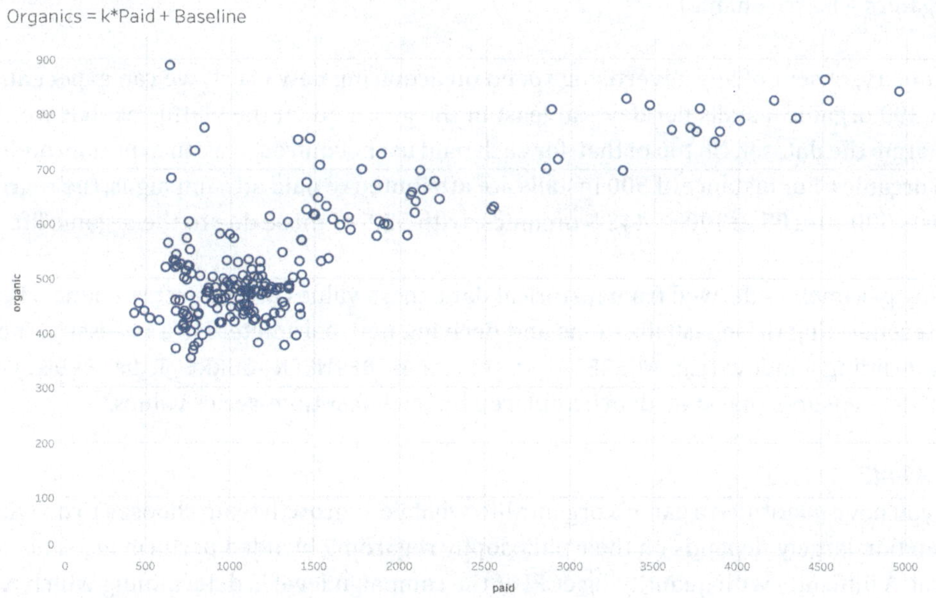

Each point in the graph represents a single day. The data looks random, but as the number of paid installs exceeds 2000/day, there definitely appears to be an organic lift. Let's see if fitting a line gives us a reasonably strong correlation coefficient. Using the *Analytics* tab, we add a linear *Trend Line* to the graph, which results in the following parameters:

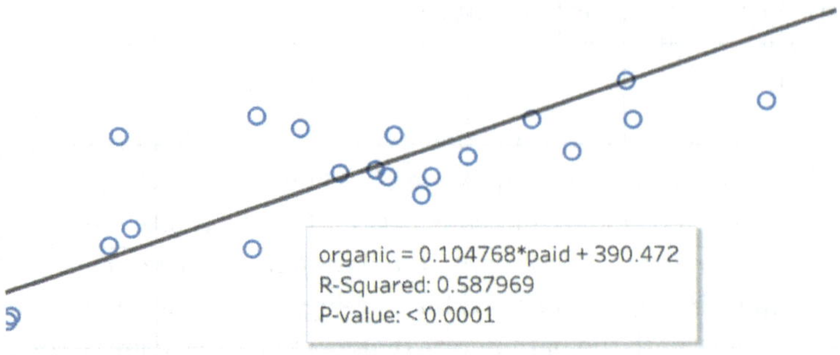

The number of organic installs = 0.105 * *paid installs* + 390. This is, of course, the familiar $y = mx + b$ formula for a straight line, where y is the number of organic installs as a function of paid installs (the x-axis). The baseline organic installs per day is the y-intercept ($b = 390$) while the k-factor is the slope ($m = 0.105$). The R-Squared of 0.59 is reasonable, but indicative of a fair number of outliers. However, the P-value suggests there is indeed a correlation (which may not be causation, but we are confident that our hypothesis – increased paid advertising will lift organics – is reasonable).

In summary, absent of any advertising spend on acquiring new users, we can expect an average of 390 organic installs per day – at least in the geos and on the platforms that were used to generate the dataset. On top of that, for each paid user acquired, we can expect an additional 0.105 organics. For instance, if 500 installs are attributed to paid ad campaigns, the regression suggests $500 * 0.105 + 390 = 442.5$ organics, with 52.5 of those due to the organic lift.

Like any parameters derived from historical data, these values are subject to change. Periodically regenerating these visualizations and deriving new parameters is a necessity. Incorporating a sliding window (e.g., `WHERE install_date BETWEEN CURRENT_DATE-90`...) of historical data ensures that stale data is replaced by the latest time-series values.

Now What?

Once you have quantified a game's organic lift, what your growth team chooses to do with that information largely depends on their philosophy regarding blended performance and eCPI in general. A difficulty with quantifying eCPI at the campaign level is determining which organic installs to add to which active campaigns: you can't simply add the same k-factor to every active campaign without running the risk of attributing more organics than were actually generated.

> Without a reliable mechanism to quantify the organic lift associated with each paid ad campaign, some studios might simply resort to comparing overall game LTV_N (predicted or actual) with *blended* CPI to assess the effectiveness of user acquisition and the viability of spending money to grow a game.

For example, if you calculate eCPI on paid users as CPI/(*k*+1) and then calculate ROAS as LTV/eCPI, you are assuming those anonymous organic lift installs monetize at the exact same rate as their paid counterparts in each campaign. Why? Because:

$$\text{ROAS} = \frac{\text{LTV}}{\text{CPI}/(k+1)} = \frac{\text{LTV}(k+1)}{\text{CPI}}$$

If you do that, you can paradoxically end up with the total hypothetical ROAS on paid installs coming out higher than the actual blended ROAS; revenue that doesn't necessarily exist has been created out of thin air. We need a better approach.

Organic Lift as Effective LTV

Rather than adjust the CPI downward, what if we increase campaign LTV by allocating each active campaign a proportion of the organic revenue? To illustrate, let's return to our sample ROAS data from earlier in this chapter, with summary rows added for the paid, organic, and blended installs:

ad_network	campaign_id	spend	users	cpi	ltv7	d7roas
Apple Search Ads	191934920	19.05	23	0.83	1.55	1.87
Google	12087924903	532.47	7	76.07	20.79	0.27
Google	1757244663	2545.44	177	14.38	6.13	0.43
Google	8100630612	951.23	108	8.81	2.11	0.24
Unity	5fcad1c046100f26507963d4	4.79	19	0.25	0.00	0
Paid		4052.98	334	12.13	4.47	0.37
Organic			686		0.73	
Blended		4052.98	1020	3.97	1.95	0.49

Rather than decrease `cpi`, the goal is to increase `ltv7` by allocating some of the revenue contributed by the organic lift, but without accidentally creating revenue that doesn't exist. Here is one approach:

1. Identify the pool of organic installs to associate with the paid installs. This may be all organics with the same install date as the paid installs, or the average over some specific number of days after. Continuing with our example, let's assume we identify a pool of 686 *organics* associated with the day when those five ad campaigns were active.
2. Measure the total *organics revenue* generated by these organic installs; e.g., 686 organics generated \$500 over the first seven days since install. Organic LTV7 is 500/686 = \$0.73.
3. Quantify the number of additional organic users above the daily *baseline* defined by the *y*-intercept in your regression; e.g., 686 − 390 = 296. If this number is negative, there is no organic lift: "do not pass Go, do not collect any additional LTV." Otherwise, proceed.

4. Measure the *extra revenue* due to the additional organic users as their proportion of the total *organics revenue*:[5]

$$\text{extra revenue}_n = \text{organics revenue}_n * \frac{\text{organics} - \text{baseline}}{\text{organics}}$$

   For our example, we have:

$$\begin{aligned}\text{extra revenue}_7 &= \$500 * (296/686)\\ &= \$215.74\end{aligned}$$

   That *extra revenue* belongs to the ad campaigns. Steps 5 and 6 allocate that revenue based on each campaign's share of the paid installs.

5. Divide that pie of *extra revenue* into *paid installs* equal pieces:

$$\text{extra LTV}_n = \text{extra revenue}_n/\text{paid installs}$$

   That \$215.74 of revenue was a result of 334 paid installs acquired. Therefore, we have \$215.74/334 = \$0.65.

6. Add that *extra* LTV_n to every active campaign's LTV_n. The organic lift results in an *effective* LTV (eLTV):

$$\text{eLTV}_n = \text{LTV}_n + \text{extra LTV}_n$$

   CPI remains unchanged. D*n*ROAS is now the ratio of eLTV*n* to CPI.

If we apply this logic to our result set by replacing `ltv7` with `ltv7+0.65` for the paid campaigns, we have the following:

ad_network	campaign_id	spend	users	cpi	eLTV7	d7roas
Apple Search Ads	191934920	19.05	23	0.83	2.20	2.65
Google	12087924903	532.47	7	76.07	21.44	0.28
Google	1757244663	2545.44	177	14.38	6.78	0.47
Google	8100630612	951.23	108	8.81	2.76	0.31

[5] Or equivalently, the organic LTV*n* * the additional organics; e.g., \$0.73 * 296.

ad_network	campaign_id	spend	users	cpi	eLTV7	d7roas
Unity	5fcad1c046100 f26507963d4	4.79	19	0.25	0.65	2.60
Paid		4052.98	334	12.13	5.12	0.42
Organic			686		0.73	
Blended		4052.98	1020	3.97	1.95	0.49

While the overall paid D7ROAS has increased from 0.37 to 0.42, it remains below the blended D7ROAS.

One downside to this particular heuristic is that every campaign benefits equally, regardless of their campaign type, platform, or geo. Every campaign is expected to monetize at the rate of at least the $eLTV_n$. Therefore, if you are running a campaign generating inexpensive Android installs from South Asia, that cohort's LTV is lifted the same amount as an AEO campaign targeting US players on iOS.

In our example data, the lift is added to the Unity campaign that generated 19 installs at a CPI of only $0.25, but without a single monetizing user. An eLTV7 of $0.65 makes that campaign look obscenely profitable. Allocating the *extra revenue* based on each campaign's share of the total revenue from paid users would solve for that.

This approach is by no means foolproof, but heuristics such as these become more relevant as the industry retreats from row-level attribution and seeks ways to quantify iOS SKAN campaign performance.

Predicting ROAS from Early Signals

A key objective of a growth team data analyst is to generate an accurate prediction of when a paid user acquisition campaign is likely to break even based on only a few days of cohort data. At ESG, our preferred approach is to build a historical monetization curve, $m_N(n)$, and apply that to each ad campaign's early and on-going revenue metrics to estimate total revenue by day *N*. But what do we do with a new game launch that doesn't have any fully-baked installs to build a historical monetization curve to predict LTV_N and/or define ROAS targets that are likely to back out within *N* days? In this case, data analysts fit a curve to the first few days of cohort retention and monetization behaviour, then extrapolate those curves to predict future LTV. In other words, we predict LTV using only **early signals** of monetization and retention. By "early" we mean everything we observe about a campaign cohort by D7.

Things are more like they are now than they've ever been before.
Dwight D. Eisenhower

On the surface, this approach makes a lot of sense. We've seen when analyzing daily cohort monetization with the Bondy curve that there is significant variance in how individual groups monetize over their first *N* days. Historical performance is not necessarily a good predictor of future monetization, so it seems reasonable to look at the specific cohort behaviour and extrapolate from there. But how reasonable? Let's find out.

What Do We Know at D7?

After seven days, what do we know about the cohort of installs we acquired a week ago? The following observations are present:

- Daily active users DAU_n for $n \in \{0, 1, .., 7\}$ where 0 is the day of install and DAU_0 is the size of the cohort; and,
- The cohort's daily IAP[6] monetization, $revenue_n$ for $n \in \{0, 1, .., 7\}$.

Other attributes are derivable from this raw data for $n \in \{0, 1, .., 7\}$, including:

- $\text{D}n\text{R} = \text{DAU}_n/\text{DAU}_0$;
- running sum of retention, $\text{PD}_n = \sum_{i=0}^{n} \text{D}i\text{R}$;
- $\text{LTV}_n = \sum_{i=0}^{n} \text{revenue}_i \,/\, \text{DAU}_0$;
- Cohort $\text{ARPDAU}_n = \text{revenue}_n/\text{DAU}_n$; and, in the case of a paid cohort of installs,
- $\text{D}n\text{ROAS} = \text{LTV}_n/\text{CPI}$.

The predictions we wish to make from this data are LTV90 and LTV180.

To facilitate collection of the raw data, we return to our Swiss-army-knife query first defined back in Chapter 6. Recall that the CTE `cohort` defines a relation of the following structure:

```
<user_id, install_date, days_since_install, revenue>
```

which includes a row for each day *played* by a member of the cohort defined by the shared install date, regardless of whether they monetized. A query to derive the early signals from each daily install cohort is:

```
SELECT install_date,
       days_since_install AS n,
       COUNT(*) AS dau,
       SUM(revenue) AS rev
```

---

[6] Without loss of generality, LTV consists of IAP revenue only.

```
FROM cohort
WHERE n BETWEEN 0 AND 7
GROUP BY install_date, n ORDER BY install_date, n
```

Dropping this query into Tableau, we see the early evolution of the raw data broken down by the installs from July 1 to 9, 2022:

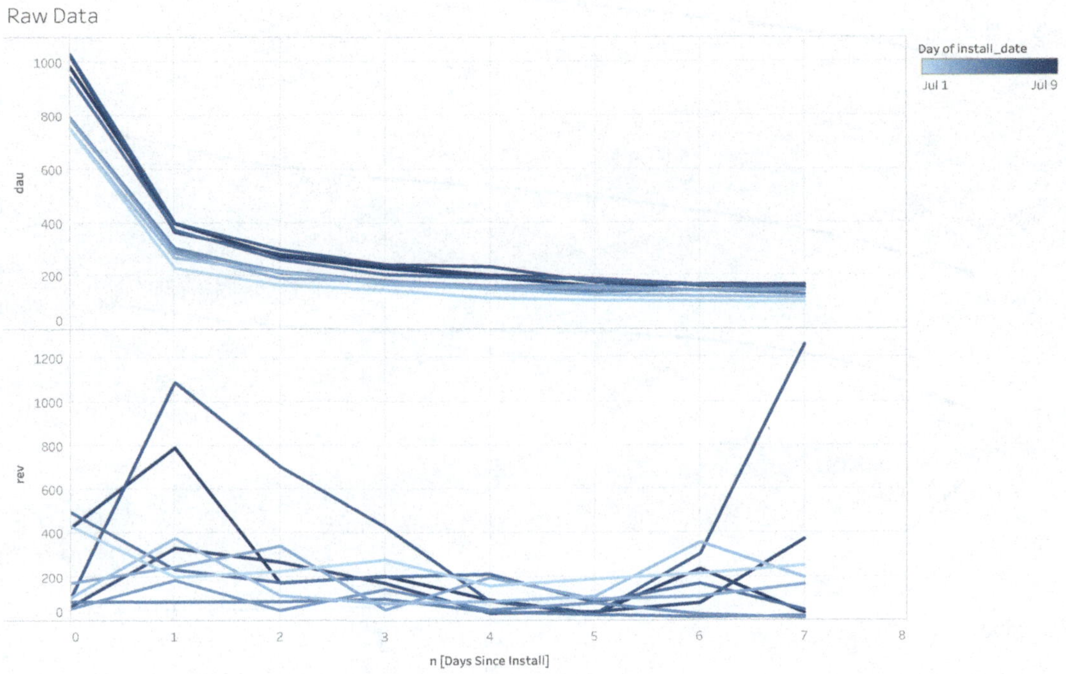

A number of *Calculated Fields* are defined to derive retention and monetization metrics from this raw data. These are:

Calculated Field	Formula	Description
installs	WINDOW_MAX(SUM([dau]))	The maximum DAU for any cohort is its size
DnR	SUM([dau])/[installs]	Dn retention
LTVn	RUNNING_SUM(SUM([rev]))/[installs]	LTV by Dn
PDn	RUNNING_SUM([DnR])	Player days is the summation of retention
wARPDAUn	RUNNING_SUM(SUM([rev]))/RUNNING_SUM(SUM([dau]))	Weighted ARPDAU by Dn is the running sum of revenue divided by the running sum of DAU

Figure 12.1 contains graphs of some of these metrics for a cohort consisting of all installs in the first week of July 2022.

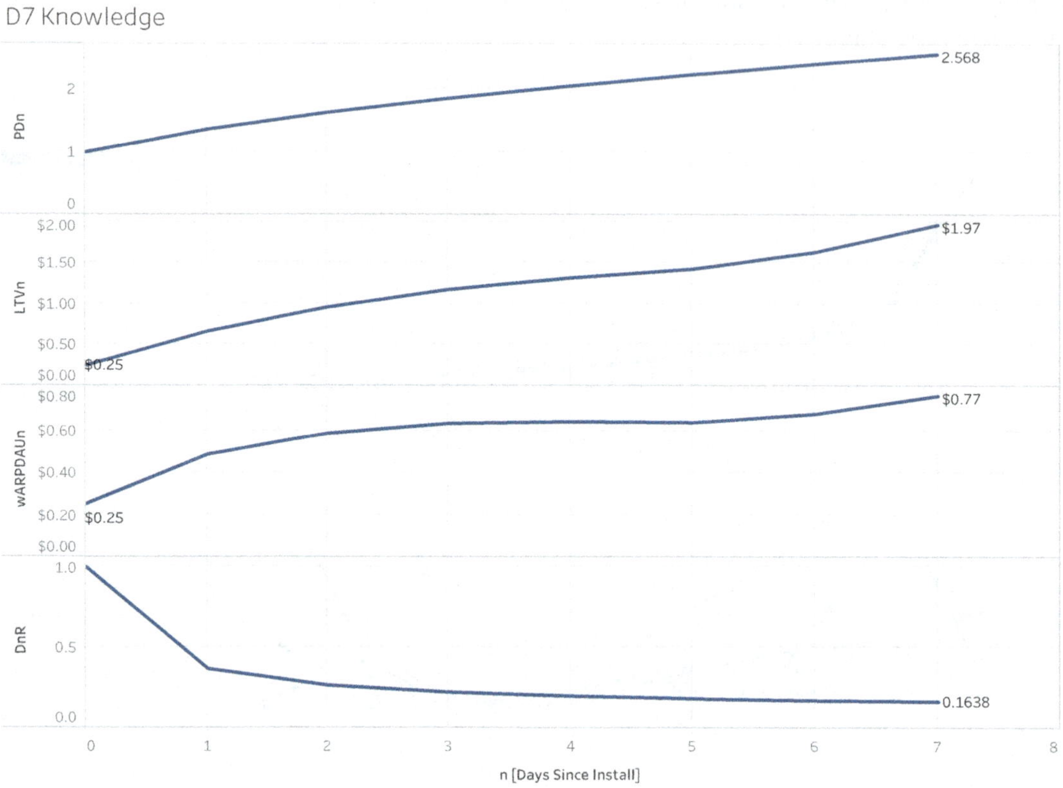

Figure 12.1. Some of the data available at D7 for a cohort of installs. Curves fit to these graphs enable our predictions beyond D7. Note that none of this data is normalized; the curves are built on absolute values.

Predictions Based on Extrapolations of Curves Fit to Early Signals

We can estimate a predictive function $\mathrm{LTV}(n)$ for any cohort by fitting a curve to the observations of LTV collected by D7. Then, for any day $n > 7$, we have $\widehat{\mathrm{LTV}}_n = \mathrm{LTV}(n)$. For example, the following graph includes both a power function (the dashed line in blue) and a logarithmic function (the dashed line in orange) fit to the same eight LTV*n* data points collected by D7 that make up the LTVn graph in Figure 12.1.

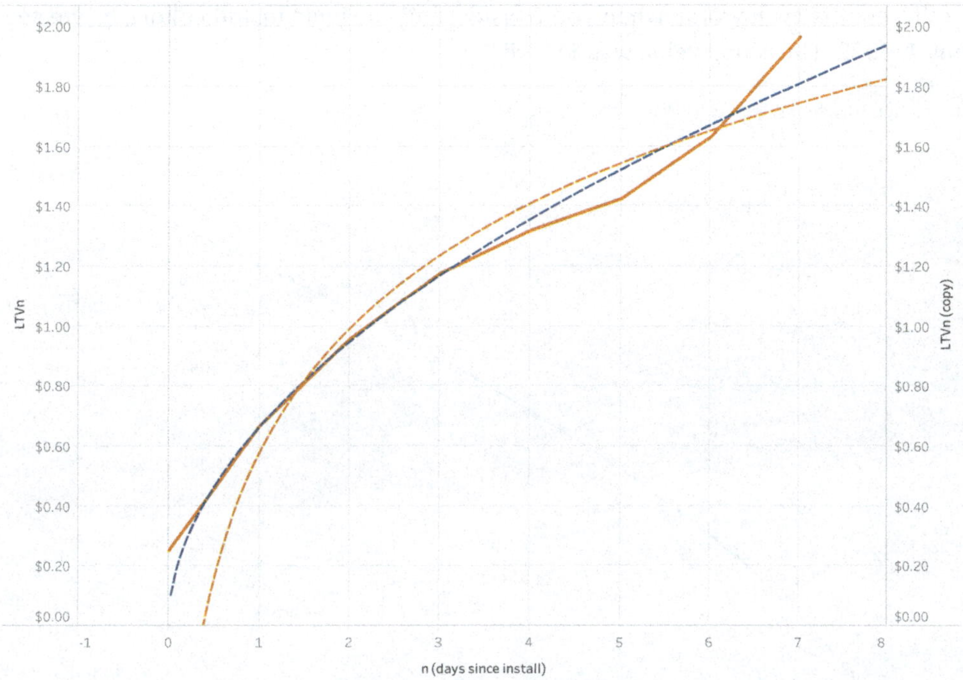

On the surface, these two curves seem like reasonable estimates. However, the two trend lines appear to be on very different trajectories. What happens if we extend that same graph out to D90? See below.

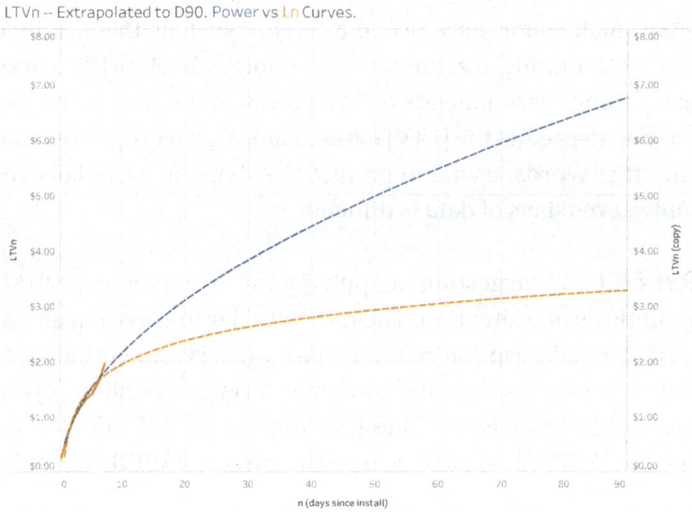

The danger of making predictions from only D7 signals is manifest in how divergent the two functions are as they expand out to D90. The power function predicts more than twice the LTV90 compared with the logarithmic curve.

Which was more correct? The actual LTV90 landed at $7.18, so while both underestimated to true value, the power function ended up being a much better prediction.

This difference is even worse when you consider only a single install cohort, as we see here for July 1, 2022. The actual value was $12.18.

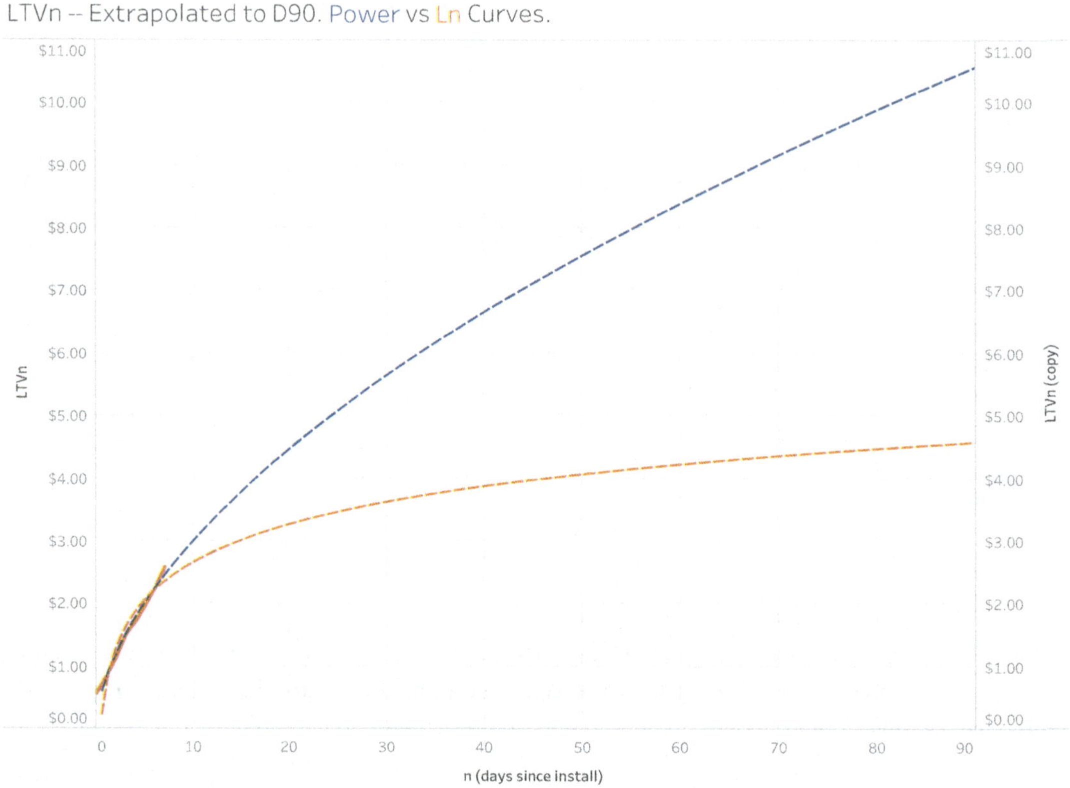

Extrapolations of the LTV curve for small cohorts are prone to errors such as these. Runge (2014) investigated the complexity of attempting to estimate each cohort's absolute LTV curve (which he called the "golden" curve). Runge recommends to "wait for 30 days of data and use a three-parameter logarithmic function to predict the [LTV] curve. Things aren't super reliable unless the cohort size is 200+." In other words, trying to predict the shape of each daily cohort's absolute LTV curve using only seven days of data is difficult.

Maybe our salvation lies in Seufert's (2014) suggestion of applying the *retention* × ARPDAU approach to LTV prediction when in this same situation. The difficulty lies in choosing an appropriate estimate of ARPDAU at D7. For subscription-based services, this is straightforward: so long as a customer is retained, we can expect the same amount of revenue per billing cycle. With freemium games, the variance in IAP behaviour makes this much more difficult. Our solution back in Chapter 6 was to develop ARPDAU as a cohort metric and use *w*ARPDAU*n* in the formula. In this case, LTV(n) is identical whether we fit a curve to LTVn data points, or to wARPDAUn * PDn. This is expected based on the equivalency of the models.

Moreover, the "problem" with weighted ARPDAU is it can take a long time to stabilize at its peak value, as we see here:

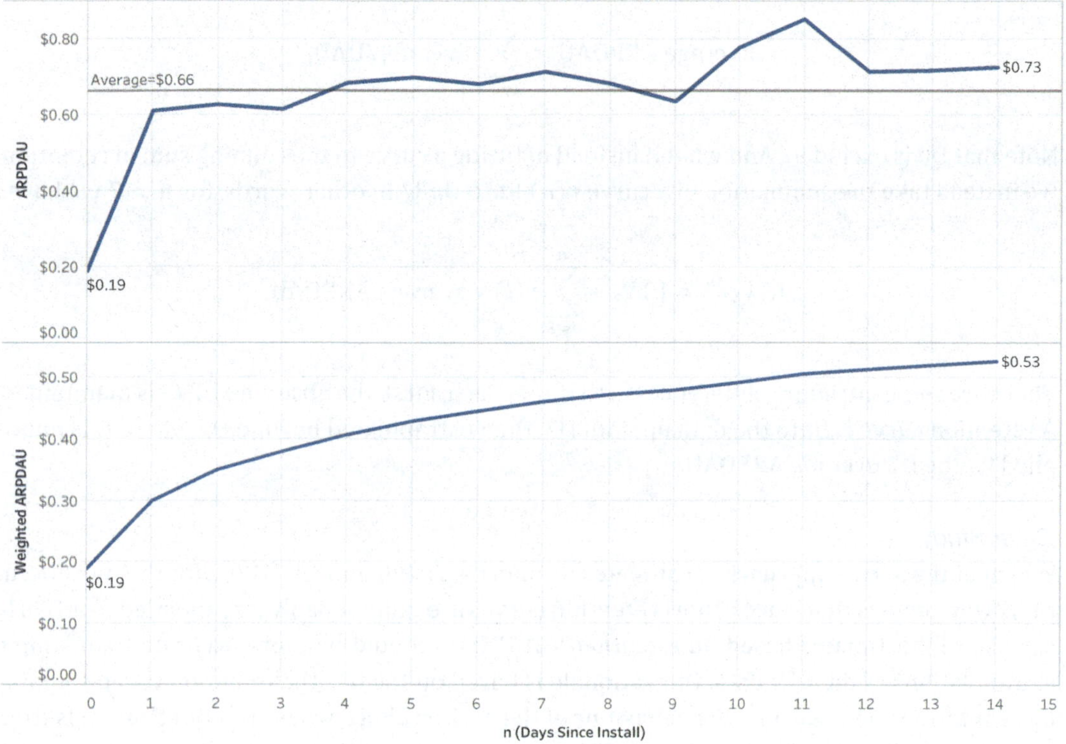

The chart above compares the first 14 days since install for a large cohort. The average ARPDAU (top) is $0.66, but the weighted ARPDAU (bottom) is only $0.53, and still climbing. At D7, the delta is even greater. Predictions of LTV using $w\text{ARPDAU}_7$ typically underestimate the true value, which can lead to lost growth opportunities.

One solution is to fit a curve to the weighted ARPDAU observations, WA(n), collected by D7, then use WA(n) to predict future $w\text{ARPDAU}_n$. Predicted LTVn for $n > 7$ is thus:

$$\widehat{\text{LTV}_n} = \text{WA}(n) * \text{PD}(n)$$

However, given the equivalence of the two models, the predictions are not expected to diverge significantly from those based on regression functions fit to the LTV observations.

But what if we use a slightly different estimate of ARPDAU? The weighted ARPDAU is significantly impacted early on by the drag from D0. Instead, let D7 *average* ARPDAU be:

$$\text{average ARPDAU} = \sum_{i=1}^{7} \text{revenue}_i / \text{DAU}_i$$

Note that D0 is excluded. And what if instead of fitting a curve to the running sum of retention, we instead take the summation of a curve $r(n)$ fit to DnR? In other words, for $n > 7$ we have:

$$\text{LTV}(n) = \text{LTV}_7 + \sum_{i=8}^{n} r(i) * \text{average ARPDAU}$$

There are some intriguing differences in this approach. First, the observed LTV7 is maintained. A retention curve is fit to the data up until D7, then extrapolated beyond D7 where it is multiplied by the D7 *average* ARPDAU.

Case Study

Which of these two approaches estimates a cohort's LTV90 and LTV180 with the most accuracy? Our guess is that since cohort retention curves are quite reliably extrapolated from early signals, LTV estimates based on *retention* × ARPDAU should be more accurate than simple extrapolations of the LTV data. Our rationale is based on the fact the retention curve contains more information regarding the behaviour of the entire cohort, whereas monetization is from a small sample of the cohort's players. This is especially true if you are only considering IAP; all it takes is one whale to churn early and your curve goes flat. Therefore, our hypothesis is that LTV predictions from early retention and ARPDAU observations are a more reliable predictor of LTV90+.

As a case study, we tested these two models on *BFIT* for each calendar date in 2021. If we had predicted LTV90 and LTV180 using only early signals, how accurate would the predictions be compared with the actual values that arose? The dataset is of the following form:

install_date	n	dau	pdau	rev	sum_rev	retention	ltv
2021-01-01	0	2676	68	1347.97	1347.97	1	0.5037
2021-01-01	1	1244	56	2123.65	3471.62	0.4649	1.2973
2021-01-01	2	897	41	931.97	4403.59	0.3352	1.6456
2021-01-01	3	679	29	507.65	4911.24	0.2537	1.8353

install_date	n	dau	pdau	rev	sum_rev	retention	ltv
2021-01-01	4	582	40	639.65	5550.89	0.2175	2.0743
2021-01-01	5	499	22	612.97	6163.86	0.1865	2.3034
2021-01-01	6	476	22	589.50	6753.36	0.1779	2.5237
2021-01-01	7	438	21	465.92	7219.28	0.1637	2.6978
2021-01-01	90	99	11	341.59	36357.22	0.037	13.5864
2021-01-01	180	57	5	195.58	47095.80	0.0213	17.5993
2021-01-02	0	2778	88	1643.59	1643.59	1	0.5916
2021-01-02	1	1236	69	1468.33	3111.92	0.4449	1.1202
2021-01-02	2	830	48	890.09	4002.01	0.2988	1.4406
2021-01-02	3	670	44	499.06	4501.07	0.2412	1.6203
2021-01-02	4	570	41	1119.29	5620.36	0.2052	2.0232
2021-01-02	5	542	27	499.08	6119.44	0.1951	2.2028
2021-01-02	6	510	39	1087.18	7206.62	0.1836	2.5942
2021-01-02	7	491	29	915.61	8122.23	0.1767	2.9238
2021-01-02	90	125	12	181.97	26400.99	0.045	9.5036
2021-01-02	180	71	4	202.08	37979.41	0.0256	13.6715
...	...	...	...	...	...	...	...

Presented above is the data for the first two install cohorts. The last three columns are derivable from the remaining columns but included for convenience. Cohort PDAU (pdau) is also included, opening an avenue to explore average revenue per PDAU as an alternative predictor of LTV (left as an exercise to the reader). The actual LTV90 and LTV180 are in the highlighted rows. The problem is to predict those values accurately using only the data available in the rows where $n <= 7$. Summary statistics for the actual LTV90 and LTV180 values for the 365 cohorts are as follows.

	LTV90	LTV180
MIN	$ 1.90	$ 2.27
MAX	$ 15.73	$ 21.35
AVG	$ 6.37	$ 8.49
Standard Deviation (SD)	$ 2.87	$ 3.89

The two approaches are now illustrated using the data from the January 1st install cohort, and visualized within Tableau. Keep in mind the regression function parameters are specific to this date only.

Method 1. The Runge Method: Extrapolate the LTV curve. Fit a power curve to the first eight LTVn data points. See the following chart. The regression function is $1.27n^{0.37}$, which predicts LTV90 of \$6.79 and LTV180 of \$8.82.

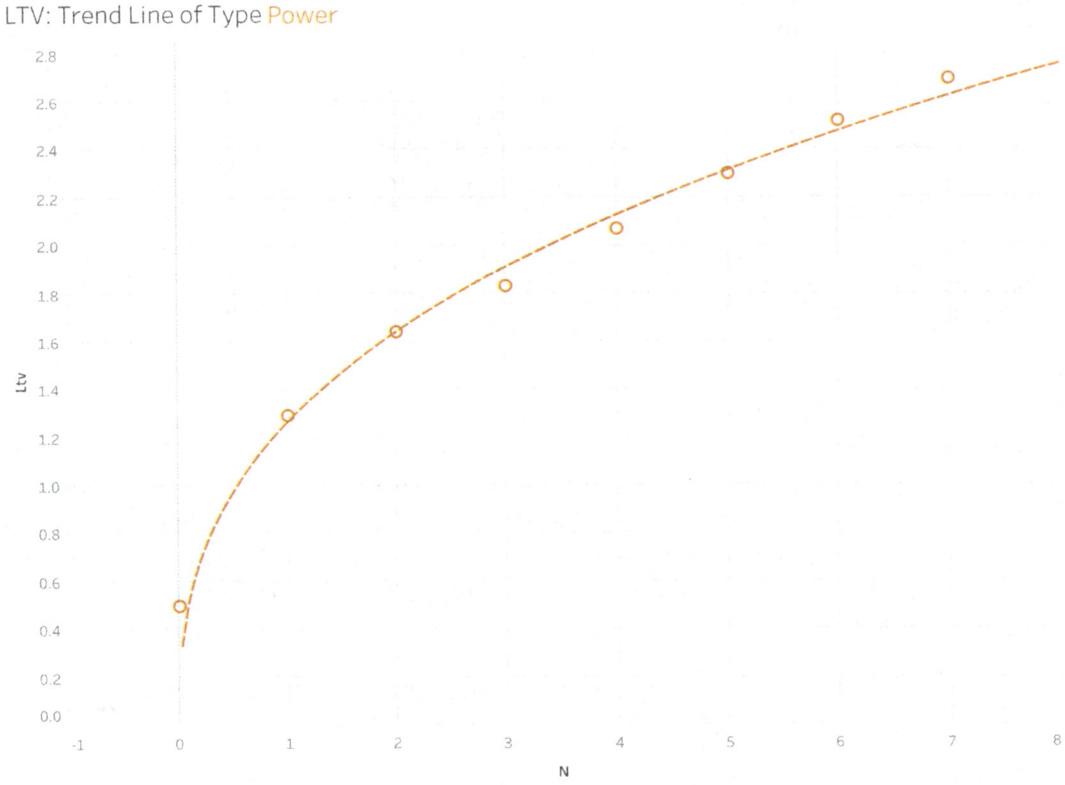

Method 2. The Seufert Method: LTV is *retention* × ARPDAU. Excluding D0, calculate the arithmetic average ARPDAU over D1 to D7. Derive a retention curve by fitting a power function to the seven observed DnR values from D1R to D7R. From Tableau, the values are:

$$\text{average ARPDAU} = 1.16$$
$$r(n) = 0.47n^{-0.55}$$

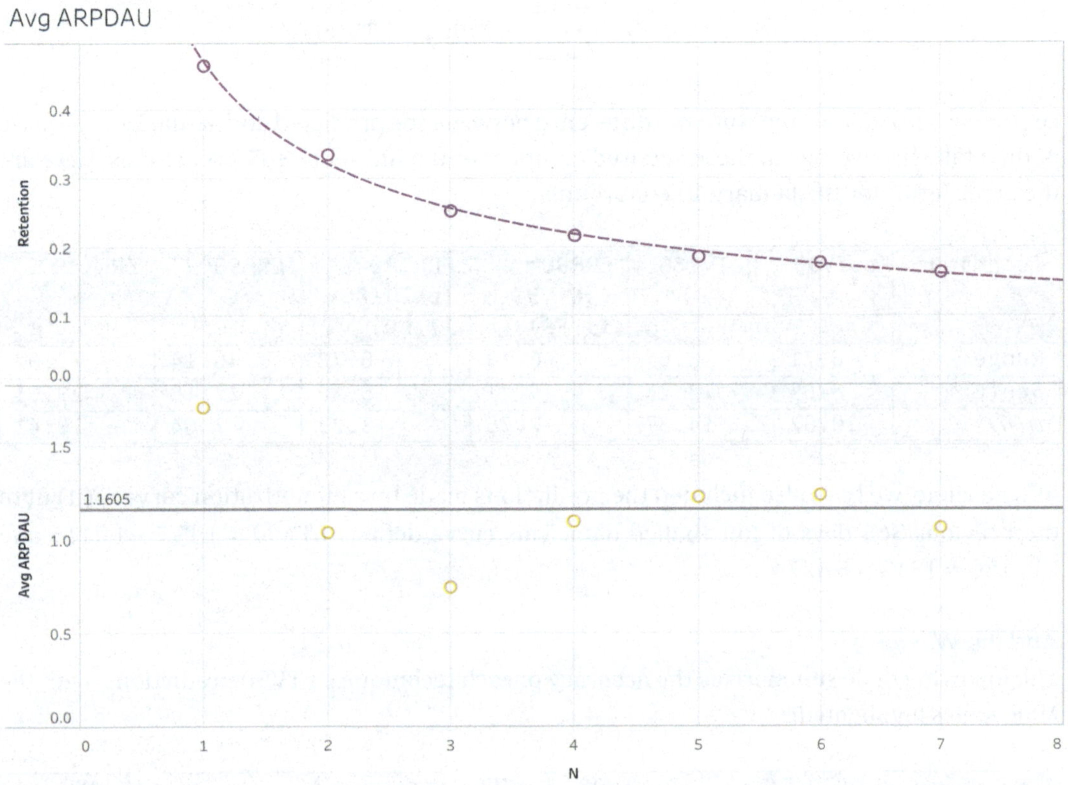

Then multiply the summation of the retention curve beyond D7 by the average ARPDAU and add that to the observed LTV7 (which was $2.70):

$$\text{LTV}(n) = 2.70 + \sum_{i=8}^{n} 0.47 i^{-0.55} * 1.16$$

For $n = 90$, the summation works out to 5.35, and predicted LTV90 is $8.89. For LTV180, the prediction is $12.25.

The actual LTV90 and LTV180 for the January 1st install cohort was $13.59 and $17.60, respectively. Both methods significantly underestimate the actual LTV90 and LTV180 values. We're not off to a great start, but how do these models fare over the entirety of the 365 cohorts? Before we jump into the results, we need a suitable error term to judge performance. The traditional approach is to use the **mean squared error** (MSE) calculation, which in the case of LTV90 is:

$$\text{MSE}_{90} = 1/365 \sum_{d=1}^{365} (\widehat{\text{LTV90}}_d - \text{LTV90}_d)^2$$

i.e., for each prediction, measure the difference between the predicted and actual LTVn, square it, then take the average of these squared errors over the full set of 365 predictions. Here are the error terms for the January 1st cohort only:

Technique	pLTV90	pLTV180	ERR90= (pLTV90- 13.59)	ERR180= (pLTV180- 17.60)	ERR90^2	ERR180^2
Runge	6.71	8.67	-6.79	-8.78	46.14	77.02
Seufert	8.89	12.25	-4.71	-5.39	22.18	29.06
m(n)	10.82	14.37	-2.76	-3.23	7.64	10.41

As a baseline, we have also included the predictions made by a monetization curve $m(n)$ fit to the previous 365 days of fully-baked data. This curve defines $\widehat{\text{LTV90}} = \text{LTV7} * 4.0116$ and $\widehat{\text{LTV180}} = \text{LTV7} * 5.3274$.

And the Winner Is!

The following table summarizes the accuracy of each technique's LTV90 predictions, with the MSE values highlighted:

	AVG LTV90	SD LTV90	MSE	MAE	MAX AE
Runge	5.69	2.85	5.07	1.68	10.15
Seufert	5.25	2.72	3.28	1.41	5.87
m(n)	5.95	2.58	2.14	1.09	4.77
ACTUAL	6.37	2.87			

The `MAE` column is mean *absolute* error, where the absolute value of the difference between predicted and actual is averaged over all 365 cohorts. The `MAX AE` column indicates the maximum absolute error; i.e., how badly did the technique misjudge any one particular cohort? While all three techniques tend to underestimate the actual LTV90, the *retention* × ARPDAU approach (Seufert) is more accurate than extrapolating the LTV curve (Runge). Neither approach performs as well as the monetization curve.

For LTV180, the results are similar:

	AVG LTV180	SD LTV180	MSE	MAE	MAX AE
Runge	8.33	4.51	13.80	2.66	21.88
Seufert	7.31	4.01	6.69	1.99	10.19
$m(n)$	7.90	3.43	5.07	1.65	9.63
ACTUAL	8.49	3.89			

The monetization curve once again takes the blue ribbon, which suggests that as soon as possible, build one and start using it! Not only is it simple, but it also works quite well. Until you have enough fully-baked data, extrapolating the retention curve appears to be a more reliable and conservative mechanism for predicting LTV.

Summary

In a mobile game studio, analysts are often segregated according to whether they work on game or marketing data. This chapter introduced the latter role, and some of the specific tasks a marketing data analyst might be called upon to complete as part of a larger growth team. First and foremost, measuring ROAS at the campaign level, and predicting each ad campaign's days to break even. We presented a formula for the latter based on a monetization curve.

We also looked at the advanced topic of how to quantify organic lift in ROAS calculations. Rather than try to derive an effective CPI, we looked at adding extra LTV to each active ad campaign based on a share of the extra organic revenue attributable to the ad spend.

Finally, we looked at the gnarly problem of predicting LTV for a newly-launched game using only the first seven days of data. Our approach was to build distinct curves from aggregate cohort D7 data via non-linear regression analysis. However, the back testing of each daily cohort in isolation was largely an intellectual exercise driven by my own curiosity. In practice, one could build an evolving estimation of the LTV and retention curves based on combining the weighted contribution of new cohorts with the prior installs; i.e., rather than make unique predictions based on daily install cohorts, a single predictive model is refined as each new install cohort becomes fully baked. As the cohorts mature, we can expand the time window used to build our model, resulting in more accurate predictions of D90R and LTV90+. Eventually, the game becomes mature enough to model a normalized monetization curve $m_{90}(n)$.

Moreover, nothing stated here precludes experimenting with more finely-grained machine learning libraries available in R and Python. As indicated in the Preface, where you go from here is entirely up to you.

Bibliography

This is not an exhaustive list, but rather the sources I either referenced in the text or I found particularly helpful throughout the writing process.

Bari, Anasse, Mohamed Chaouchi, and Tommy Jung. *Predictive Analytics for Dummies, 2nd Edition* (John Wiley & Sons, 2017).

Bruce, Peter, and Andrew Bruce. *Practical Statistics for Data Scientists* (O'Reilly, 2017).

Burelli, Paolo. "Predicting Customer Lifetime Value in Free-to-Play Games." In Wallner, Günter (editor). *Data Analytics Applications in Gaming and Entertainment* (CRC Press, 2019), pp. 79–107.

Carpenter, Adam. *Why Focusing on Tomorrow Brings Back Players in the Long Run* (2018). Retrieved from https://medium.com/googleplaydev/why-focusing-on-tomorrow-brings-back-players-in-the-long-run-e57c51bd3481

Davies, Tilman M. *The Book of R* (No Starch Press, 2016).

Fields, Timothy Victor. "Game Industry Metrics Terminology and Game Analytics Case Study." In El-Nasr, Magy Seif *et al* (editors). *Game Analytics: Maximizing the Value of Player Data* (Springer-Verlag, 2013), pp. 53-71.

Foreman, John W. *Data Smart: Using Data Science to Transform Information into Insight* (John Wiley & Sons, 2014).

Kurt, Will. *Bayesian Statistics the Fun Way* (No Starch Press, 2019).

Luton, Will. *Free2play: Making Money from Games You Give Away* (New Riders, 2013).

Runge, Julian. *The Golden Curve: Determining Player Value in Freemium Apps* (2014). Retrieved from https://thenextweb.com/news/golden-curve-determining-player-value-freemium-apps

Seufert, Eric Benjamin. *Freemium Economics: Leveraging Analytics and User Segmentation to Drive Revenue* (Morgan Kaufman, 2014).

Wonnacott, Thomas H., and Ronald J. Wonnacott. *Introductory Statistics, Third Edition* (John Wiley & Sons, 1977).

Index of Key Terms